SHORTCAKE CAKE

STORY AND ART BY

suu Morishita

Characters

SHORTCAKE CAKE

NEKOCHIYA HIGH SCHOOL

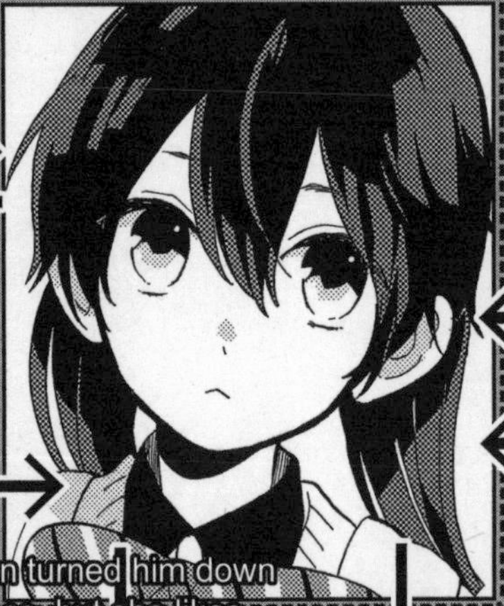

TEN

First-year. She moved into the boardinghouse about a month after the new school year started. She has pluck.

Invites Ten to move into the boardinghouse.

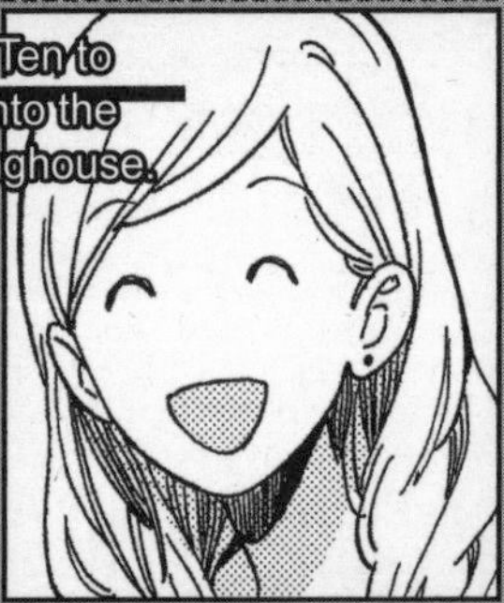

AGEHA

First-year. She attended the same junior high school as Ten.

Ten turned him down once, but she likes him now.

Ten thinks Chiaki likes another girl.

Chiaki likes Ten even though he knows she likes Riku.

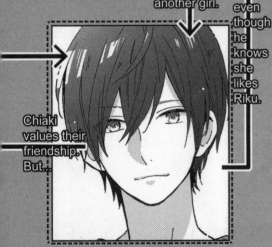

Chiaki values their friendship. But...

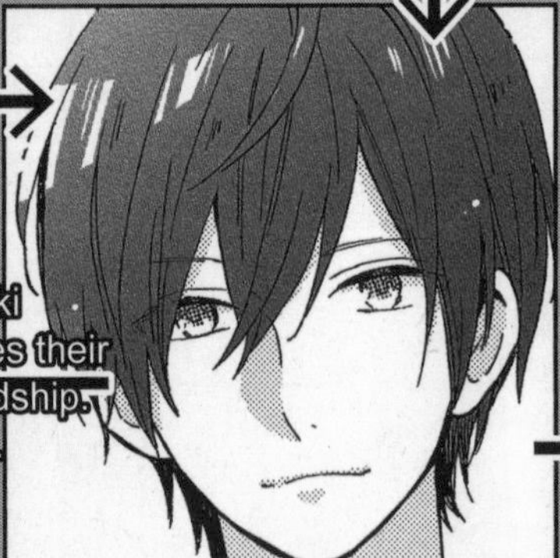

CHIAKI

First-year. A gorgeous guy who loves reading books.

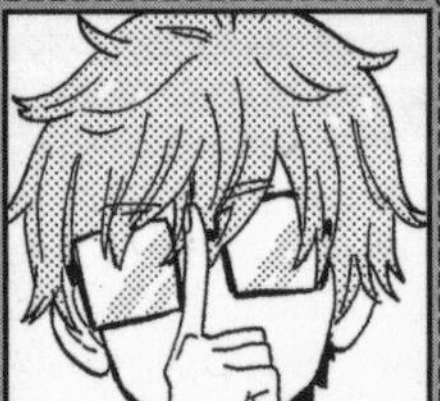

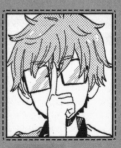

YUTO

Second-year. He tutors Ten and the other first-years.

REI

Age 16. The son of the owner of Hoshino Boardinghouse.

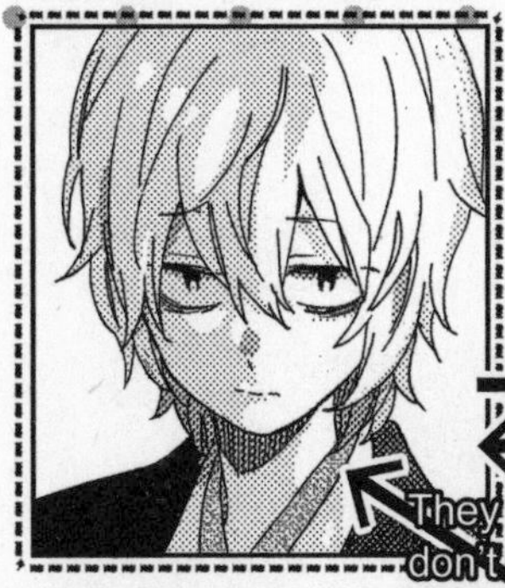

SHIRAOKA

Rei's driver. What's his connection to Ran?

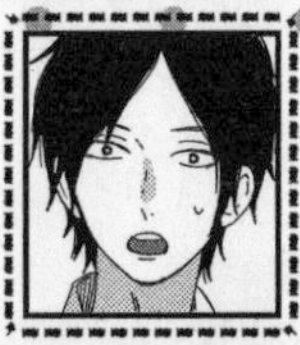

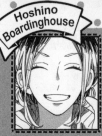

Hoshino Boardinghouse

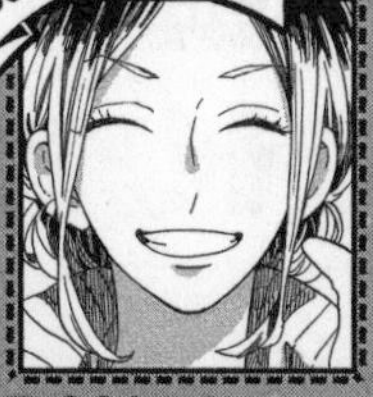

RAN

House mom. She likes cooking and cars.

"Be my girlfriend."

She thinks he's weird.

They don't get along.

NEKOCHIYA SHOGYO HIGH SCHOOL

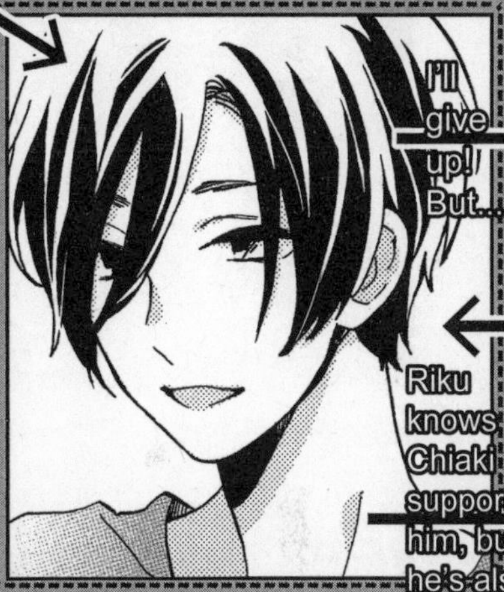

I'll give up! But...

Riku knows Chiaki supports him, but he's also a rival...

RIKU

First-year. Lives in the boardinghouse though he grew up nearby. Very friendly with girls.

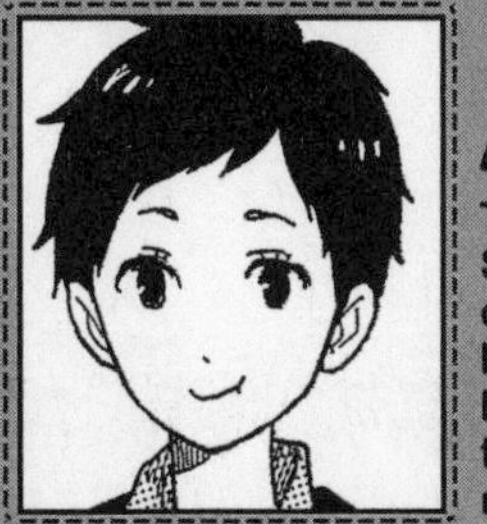

AOI

Third-year. She's the oldest in the boardinghouse. Likes talking about relationships.

Story Thus Far

Ten is a first-year in high school who lives in a boardinghouse with boys.

Lightning strikes and knocks out the power at the boardinghouse. In the darkness, Riku unexpectedly kisses Ten on the cheek. She doesn't know why he did it and is left spinning in confusion.

Meanwhile Chiaki had been pretending to be Ten's boyfriend to stop Rei's pursuit of her. Chiaki soon realizes that he truly likes Ten, and he reveals this to Riku.

During summer vacation, Ten, Riku and Chiaki head to the beach. Ten finds herself looking at Riku differently. She returns home for a few days but rushes back to the house sooner than planned. On the bus ride home, she realizes she has a crush on Riku.

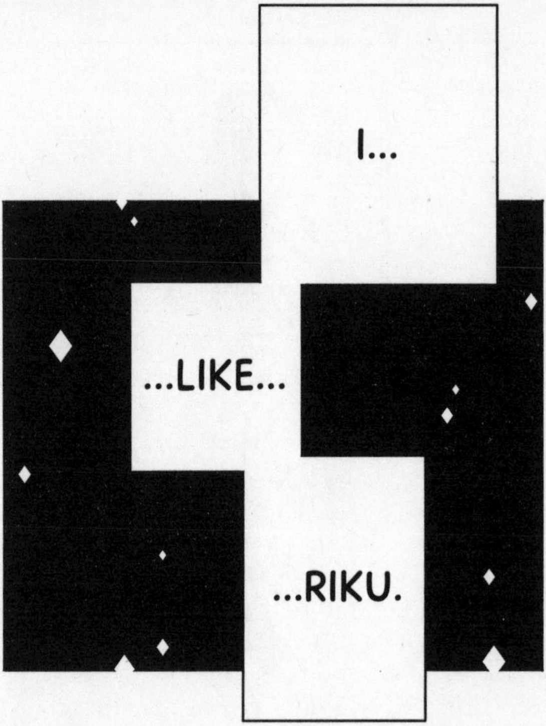
I...
...LIKE...
...RIKU.

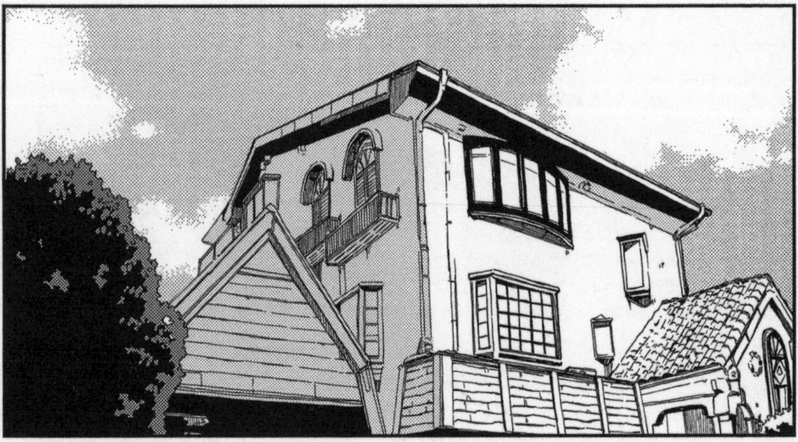

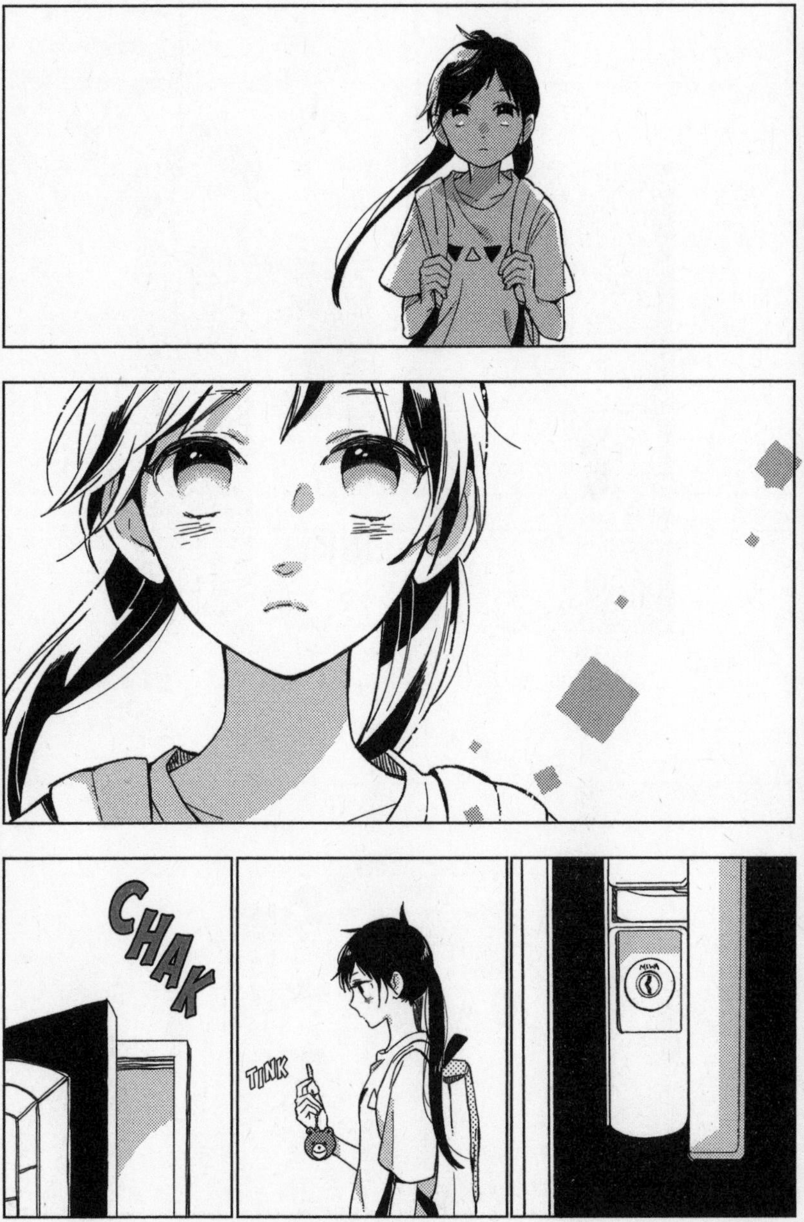
TINK
CHAK

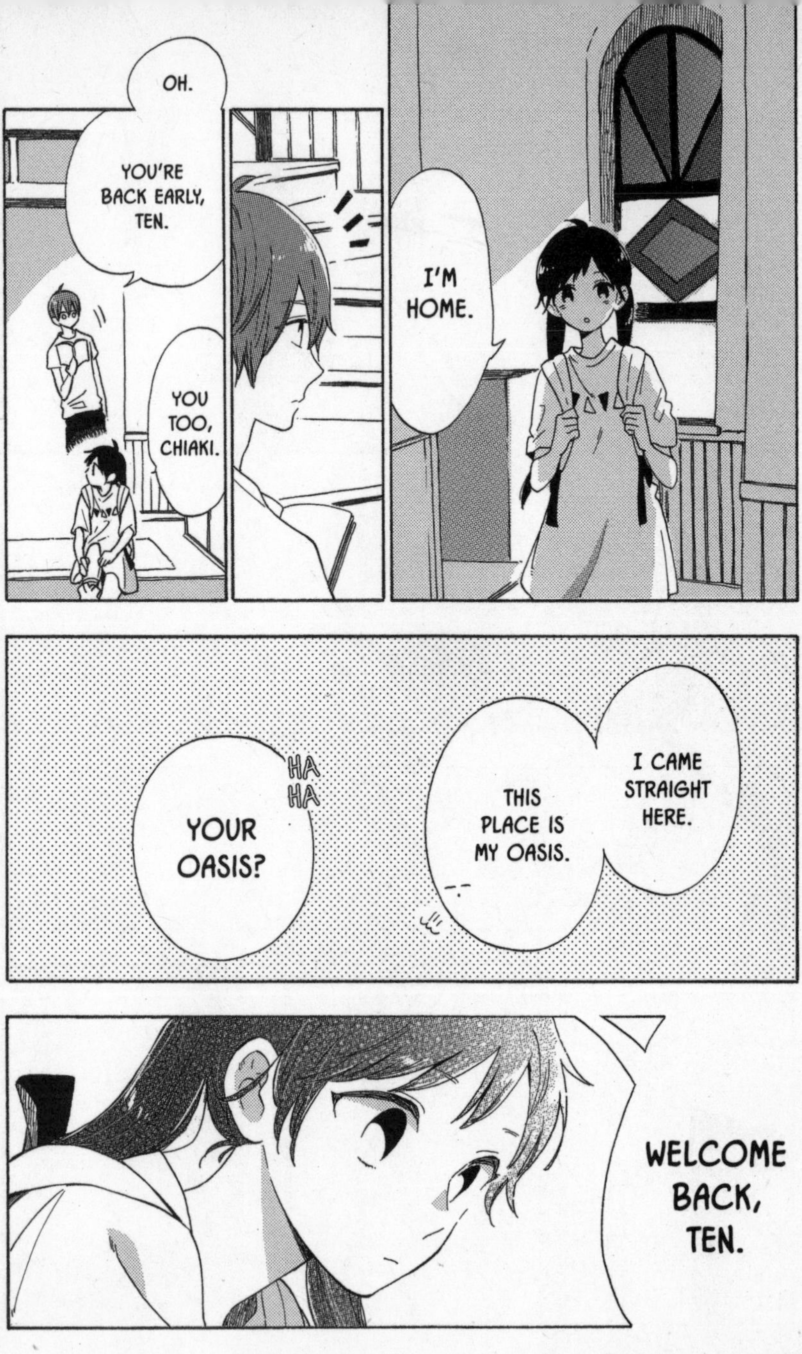
I'M HOME.
OH.
YOU'RE BACK EARLY, TEN.
YOU TOO, CHIAKI.
I CAME STRAIGHT HERE.
THIS PLACE IS MY OASIS.
HA HA
YOUR OASIS?
WELCOME BACK, TEN.

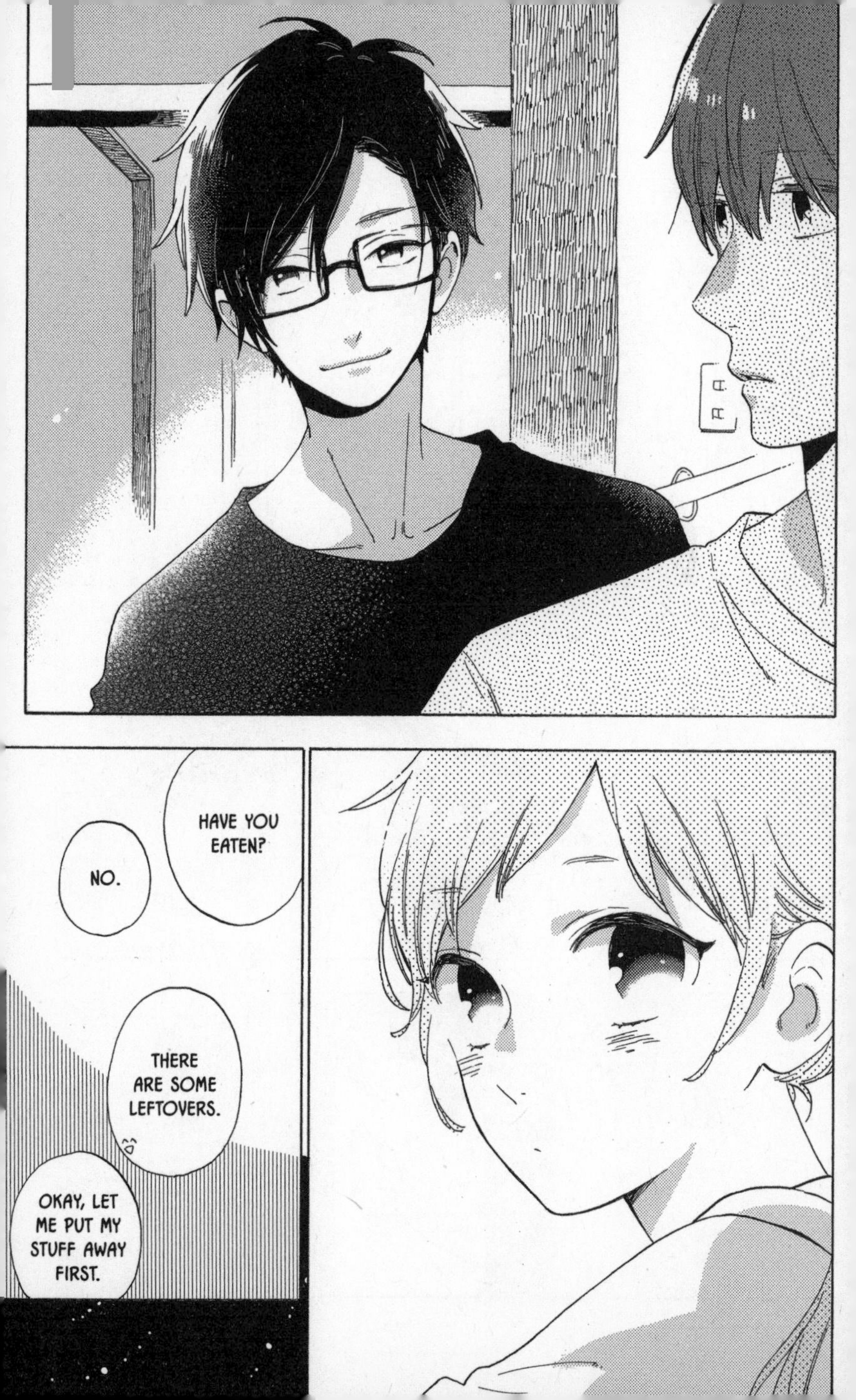
HAVE YOU EATEN?
NO.
THERE ARE SOME LEFTOVERS.
OKAY, LET ME PUT MY STUFF AWAY FIRST.

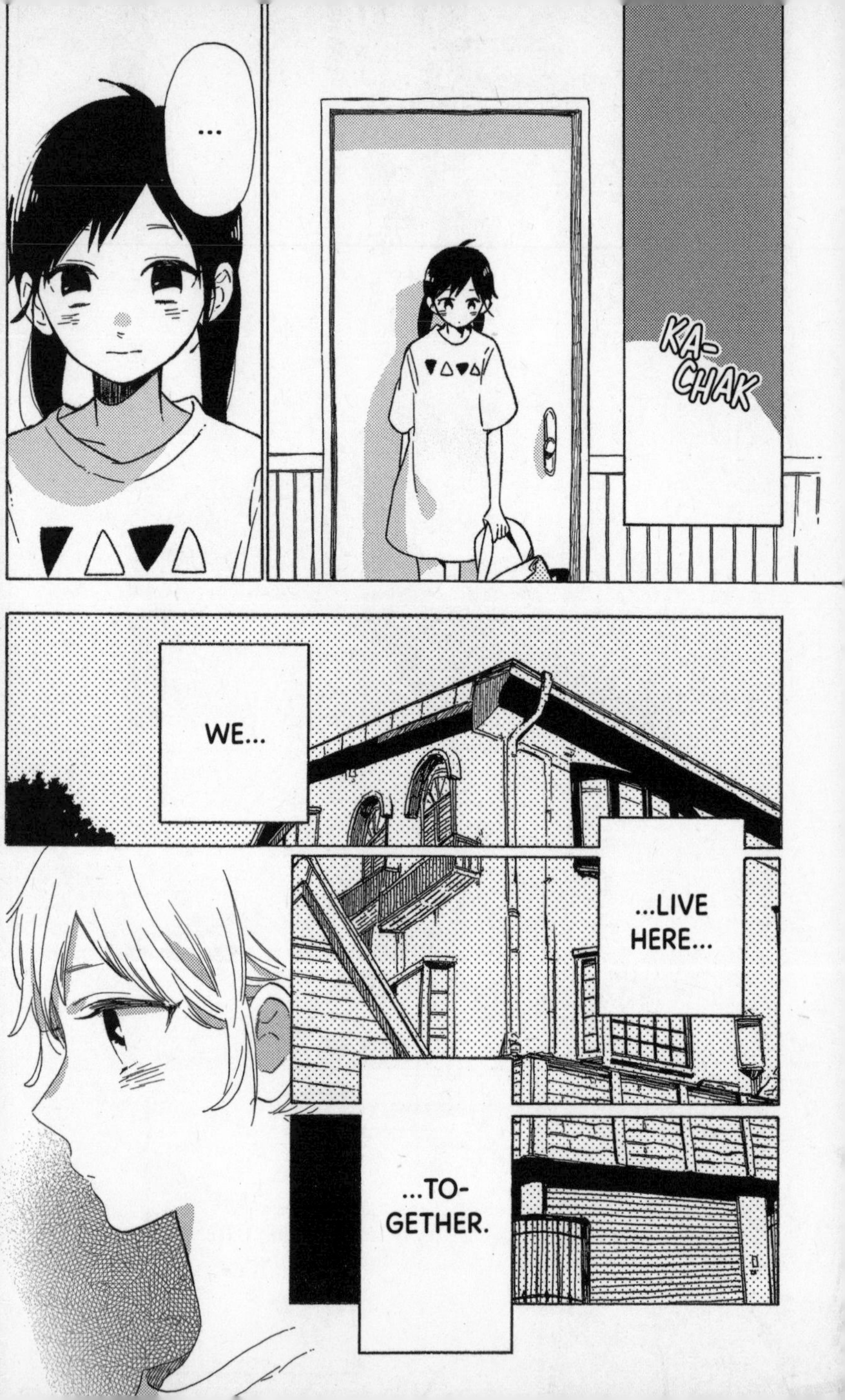
KA-CHAK
...
WE...
...LIVE HERE...
...TO-GETHER.

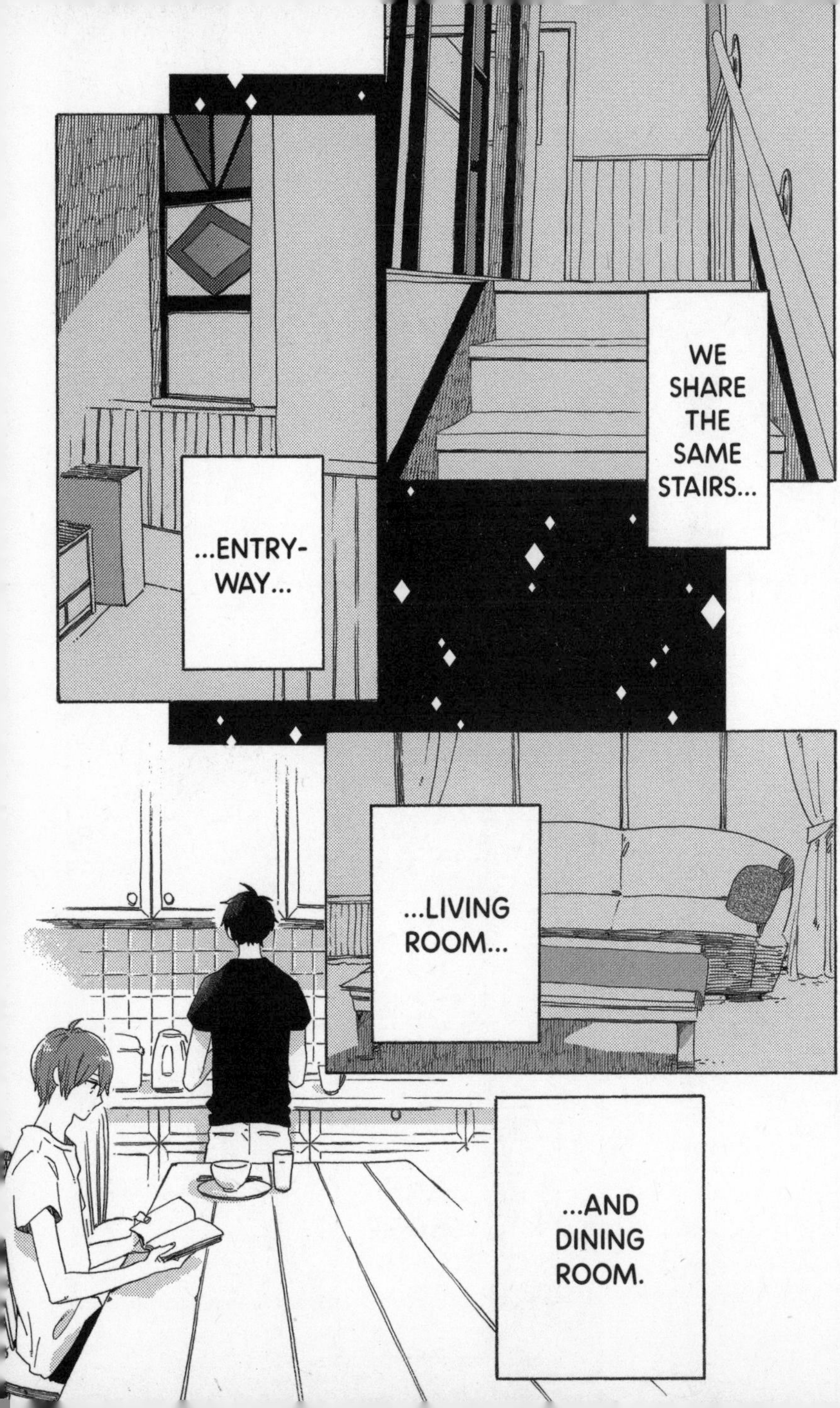
WE SHARE THE SAME STAIRS...
...ENTRY-WAY...
...LIVING ROOM...
...AND DINING ROOM.

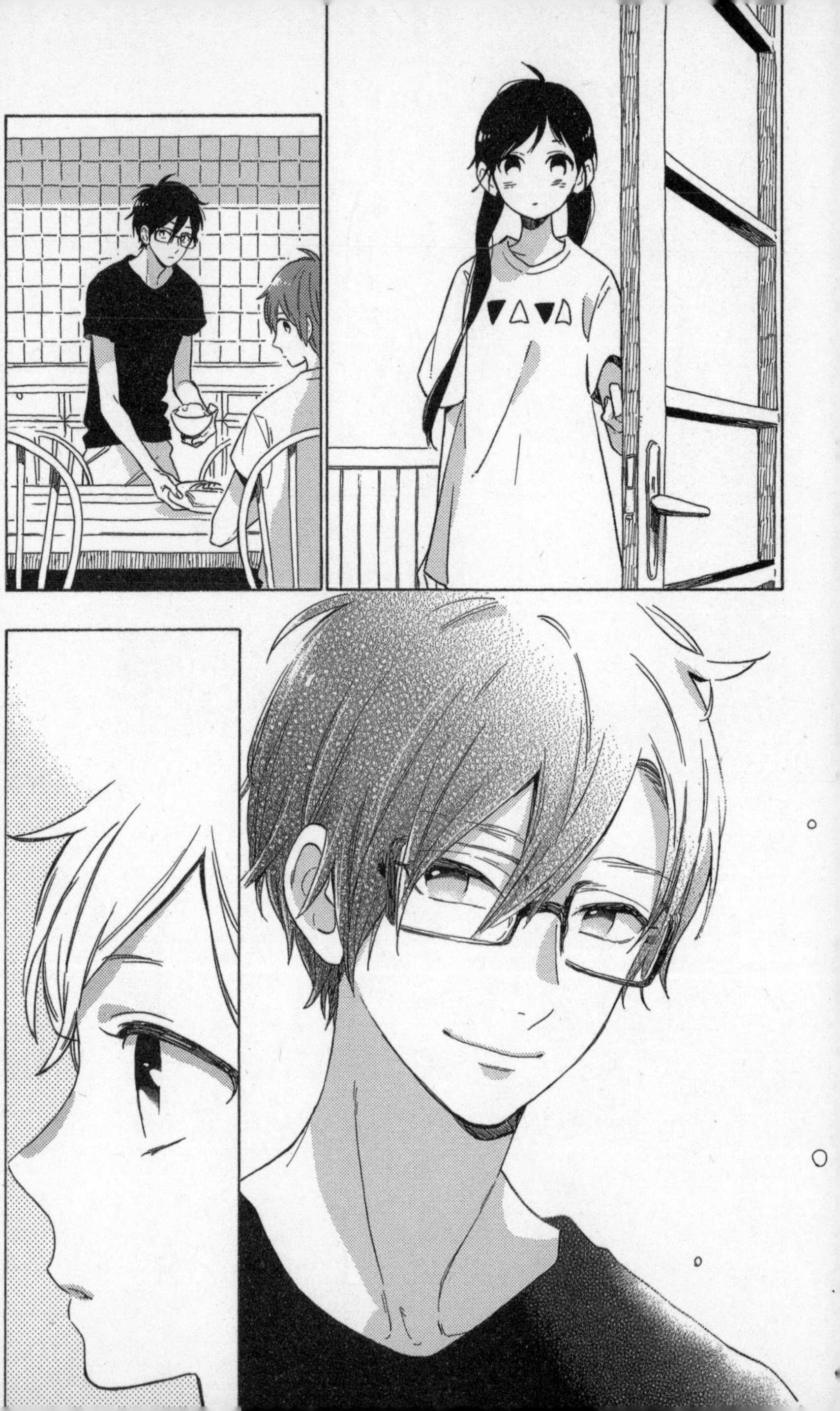

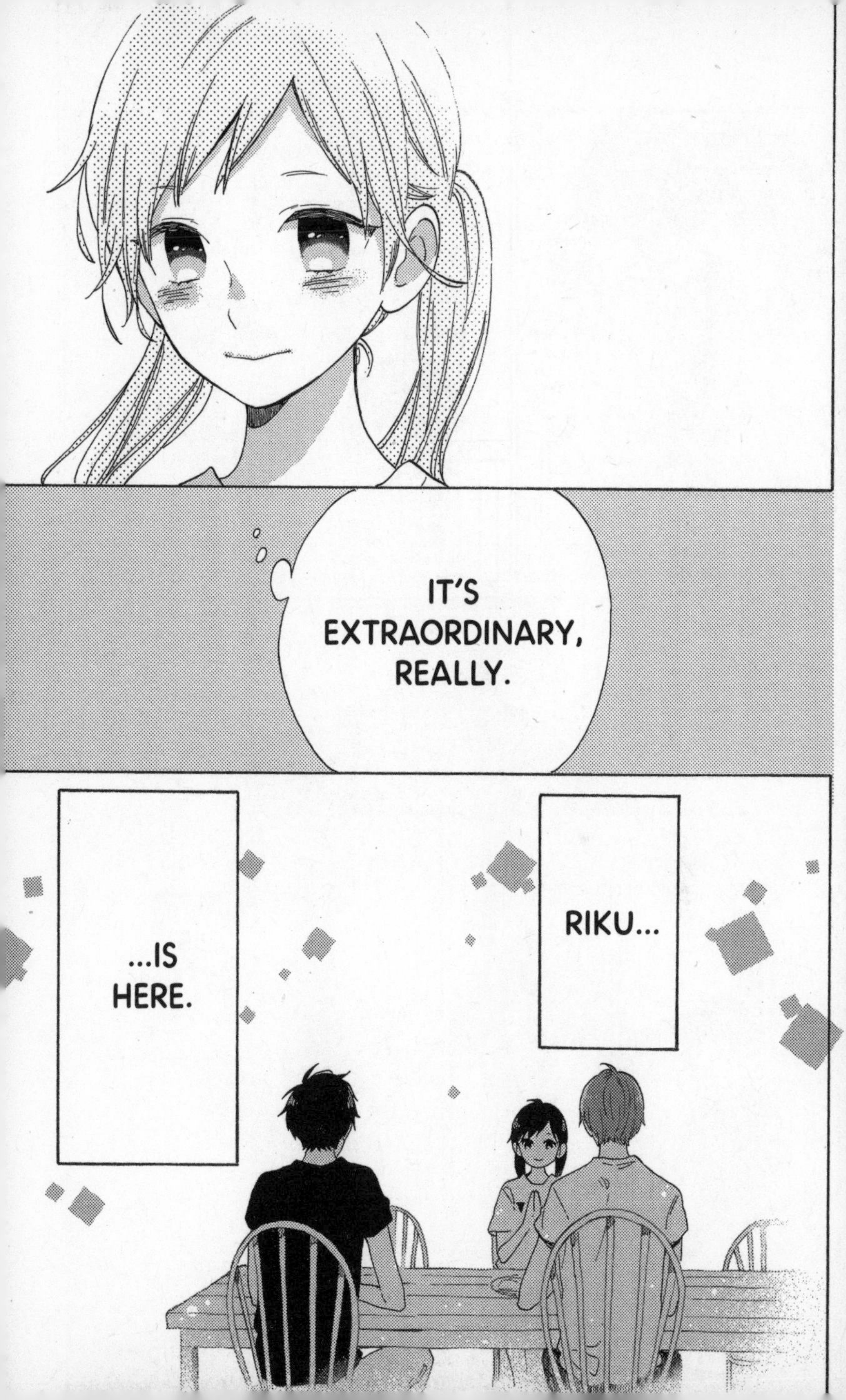
IT'S EXTRAORDINARY, REALLY.
RIKU...
...IS HERE.

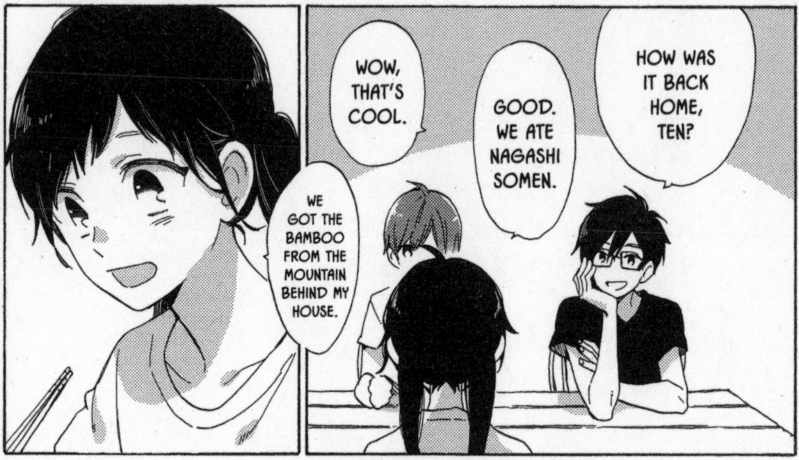
HOW WAS IT BACK HOME, TEN?
GOOD. WE ATE NAGASHI SOMEN.
WOW, THAT'S COOL.
WE GOT THE BAMBOO FROM THE MOUNTAIN BEHIND MY HOUSE.

**Nagashi somen* are cold noodles delivered by running water down a bamboo stalk.

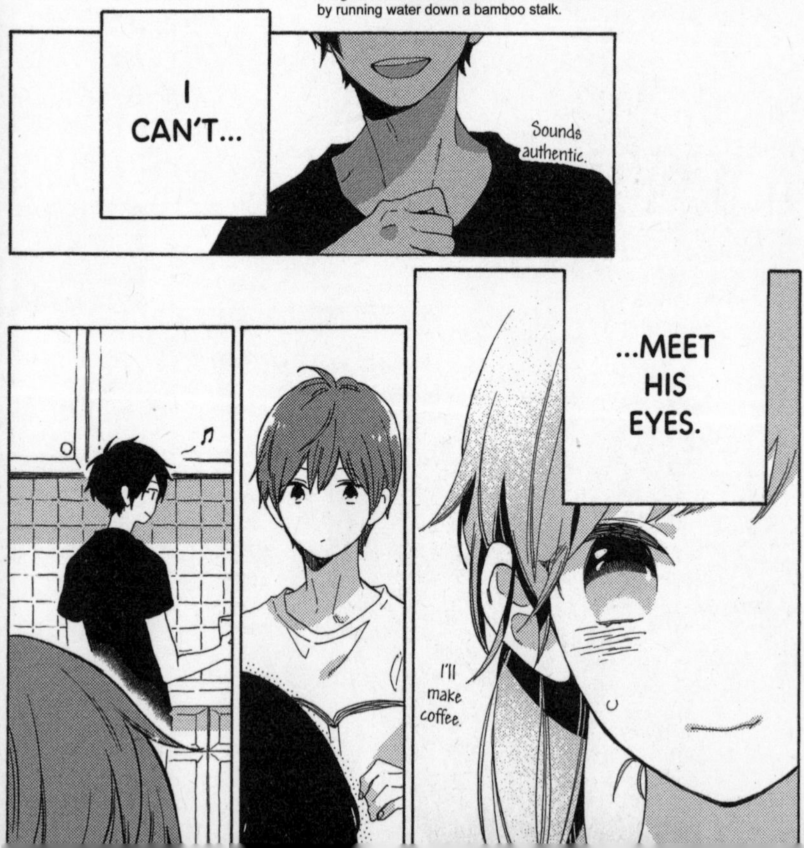
Sounds authentic.
I CAN'T...
...MEET HIS EYES.
I'll make coffee.

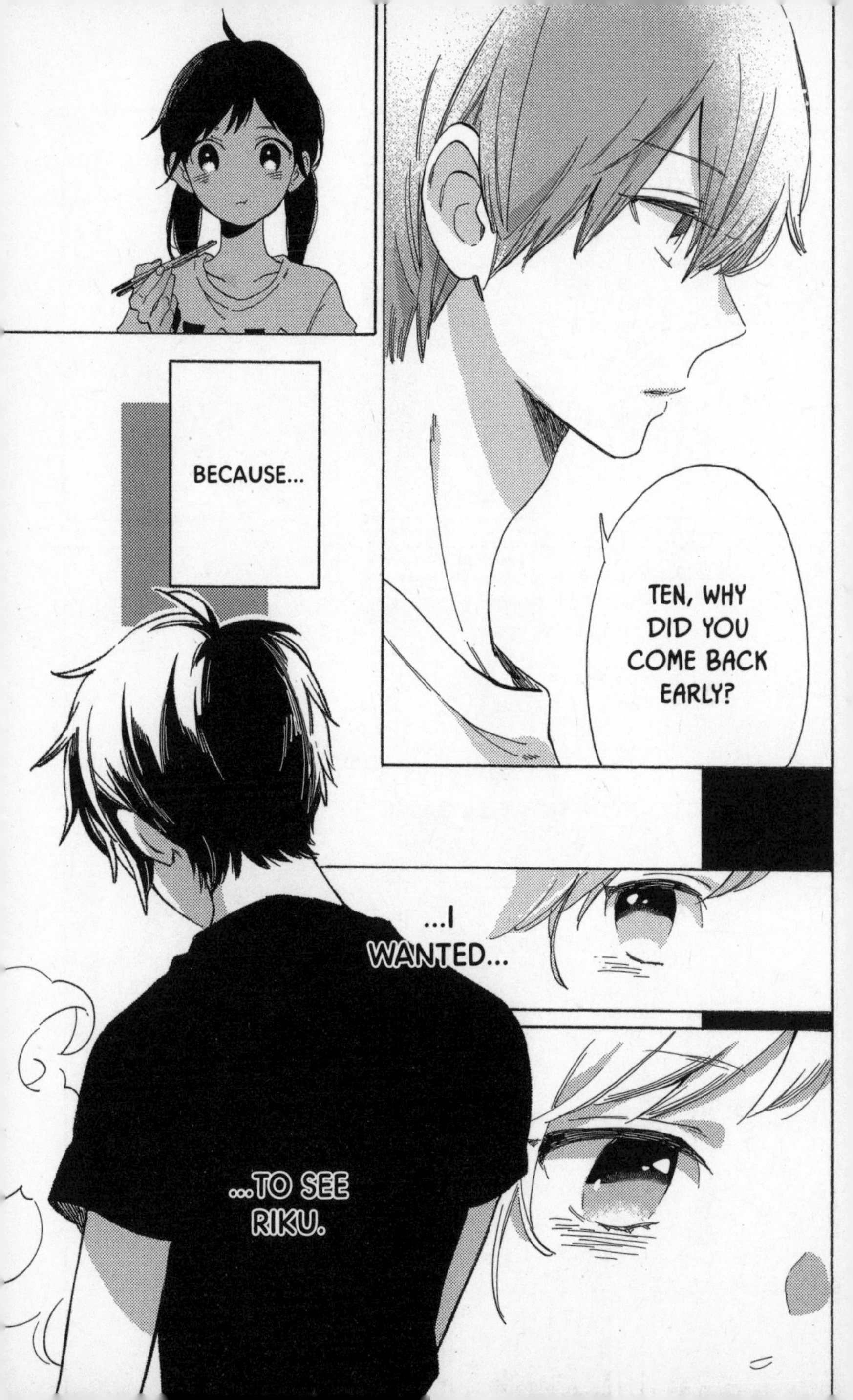
TEN, WHY DID YOU COME BACK EARLY?
BECAUSE...
...I WANTED...
...TO SEE RIKU.

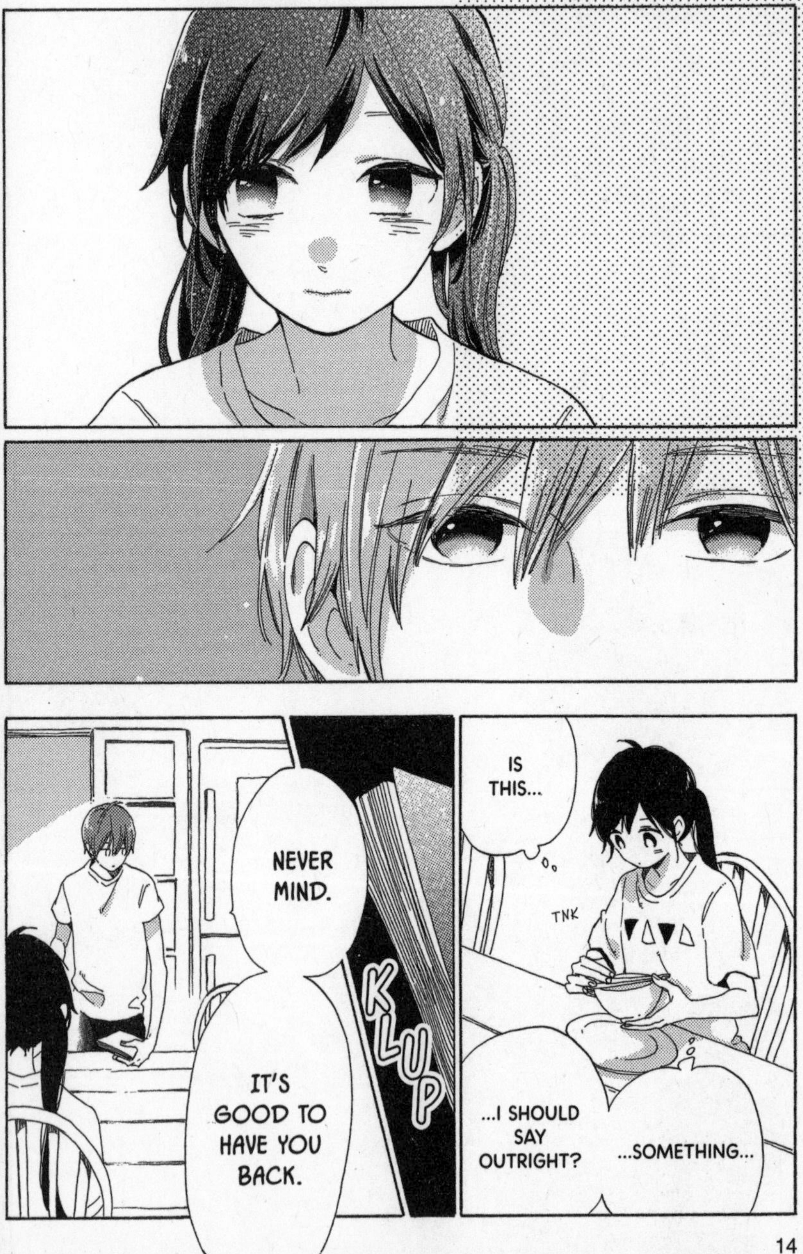
IS THIS...
TNK
...SOMETHING...
...I SHOULD SAY OUTRIGHT?
NEVER MIND.
KLUP
IT'S GOOD TO HAVE YOU BACK.

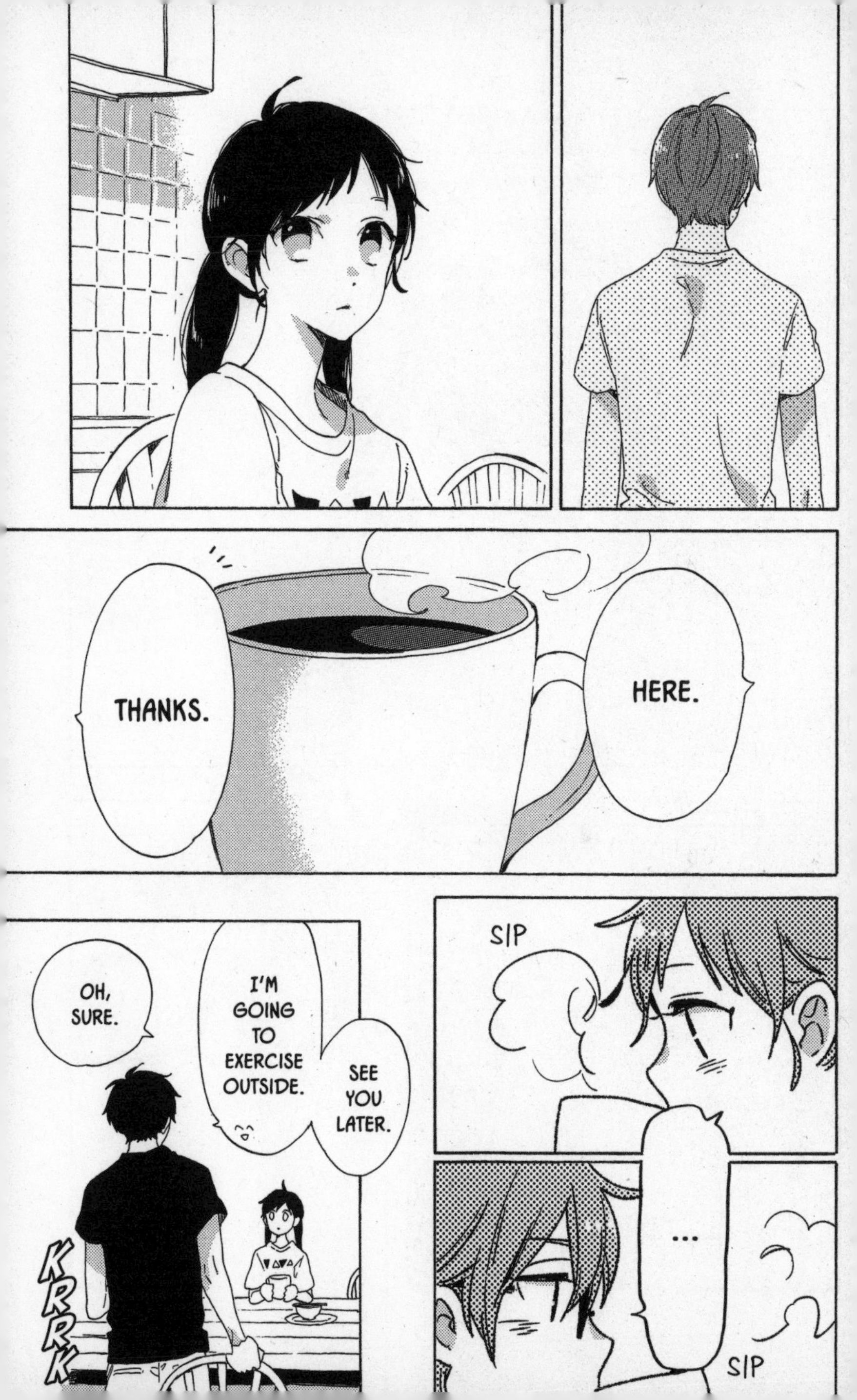
HERE.
THANKS.
SIP
...
SIP
I'M GOING TO EXERCISE OUTSIDE.
SEE YOU LATER.
OH, SURE.
KRRK

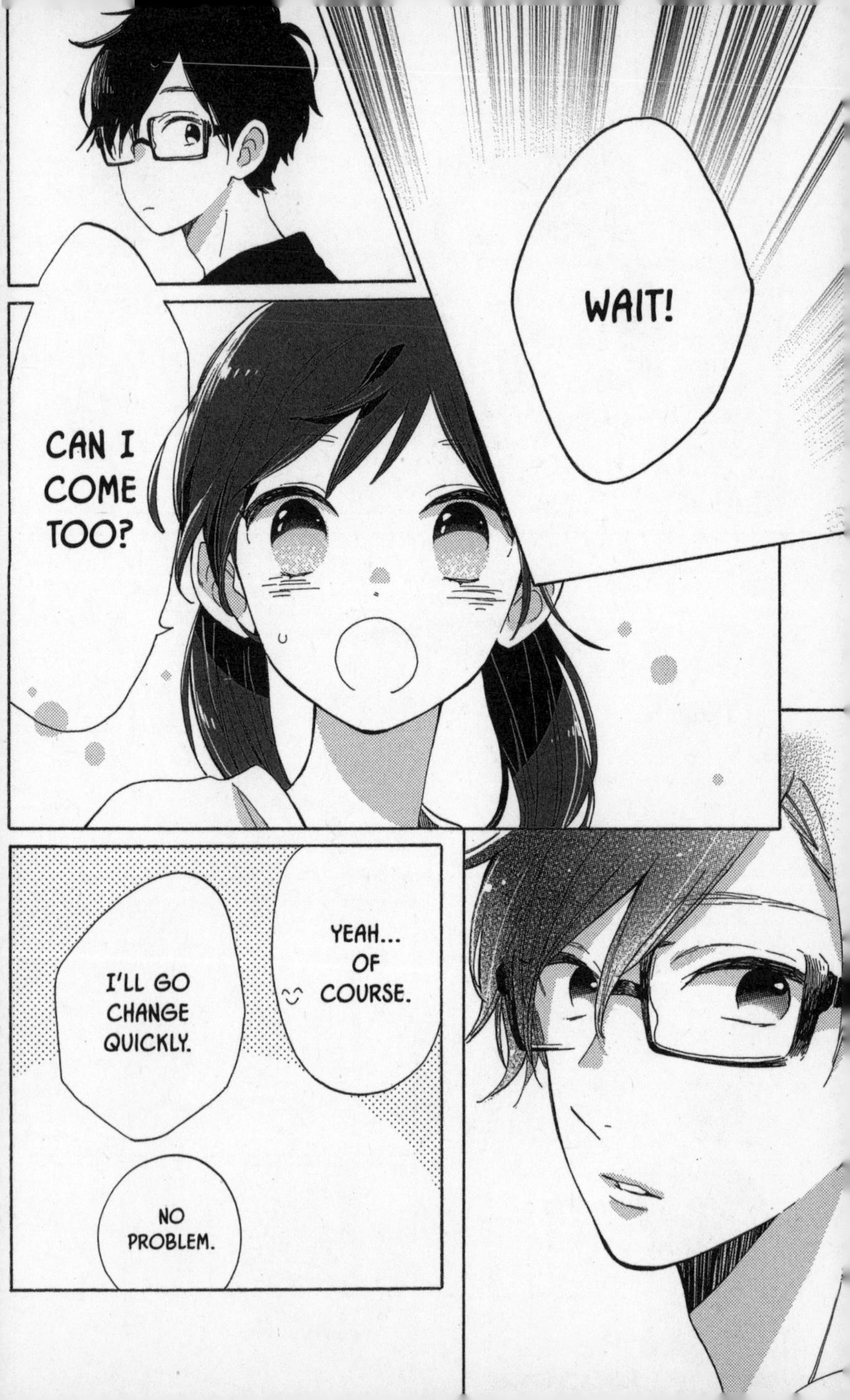
WAIT!
CAN I COME TOO?
YEAH... OF COURSE.
I'LL GO CHANGE QUICKLY.
NO PROBLEM.

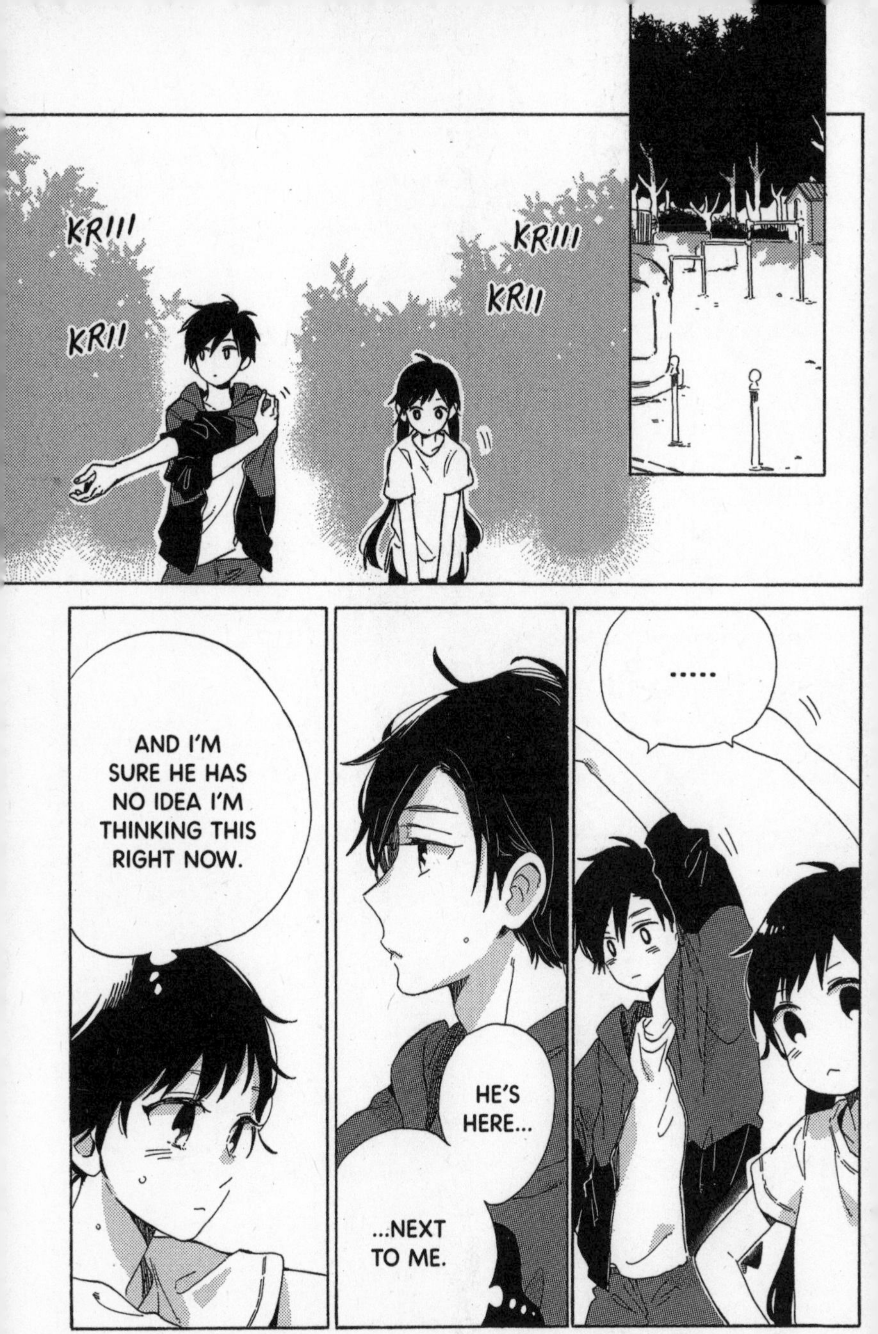
KRIII
KRII
KRIII
KRII
.....
HE'S HERE...
...NEXT TO ME.
AND I'M SURE HE HAS NO IDEA I'M THINKING THIS RIGHT NOW.

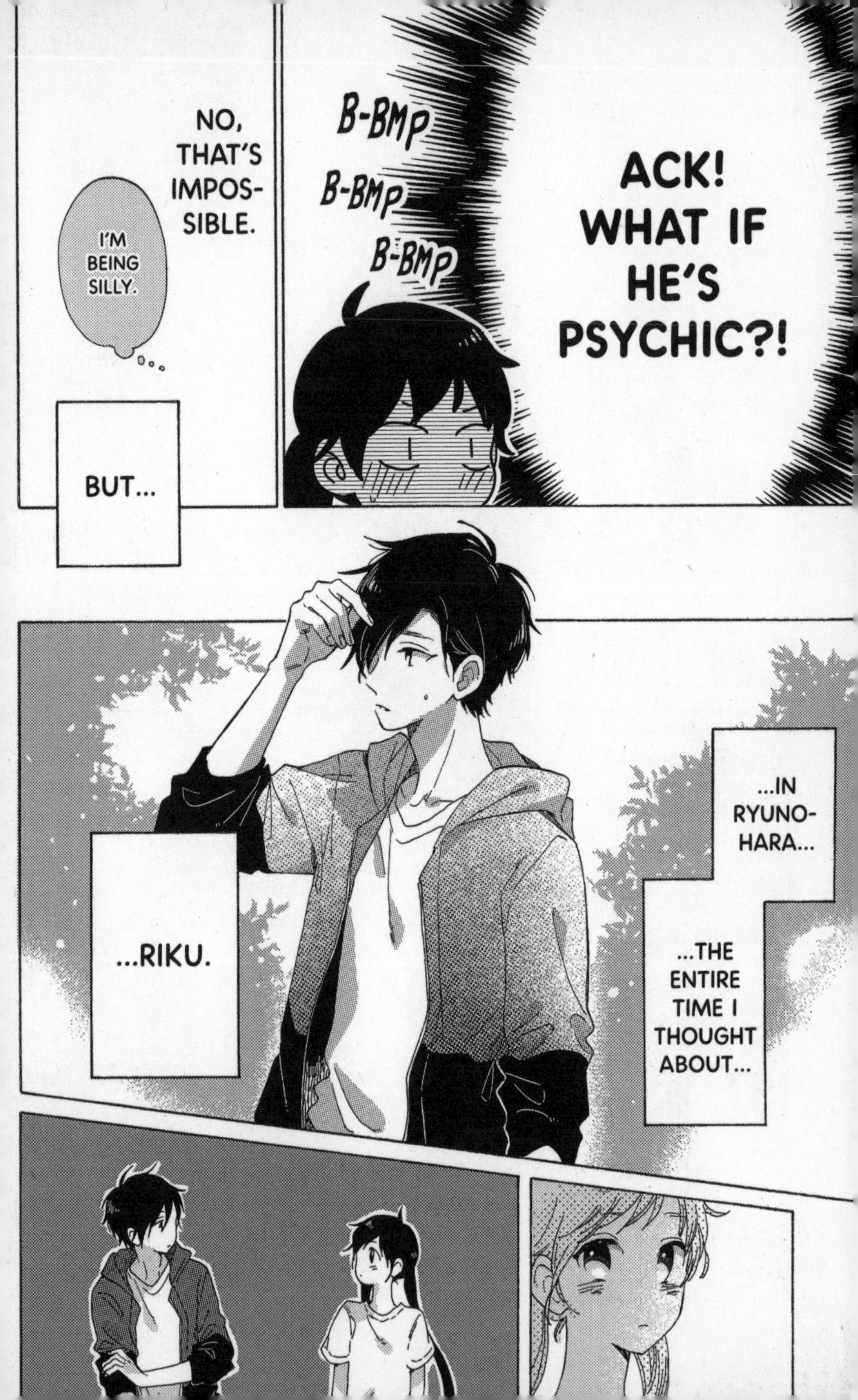
ACK! WHAT IF HE'S PSYCHIC?!
B-BMP
B-BMP
B-BMP
NO, THAT'S IMPOS-SIBLE.
I'M BEING SILLY.
BUT...
...IN RYUNO-HARA...
...THE ENTIRE TIME I THOUGHT ABOUT...
...RIKU.

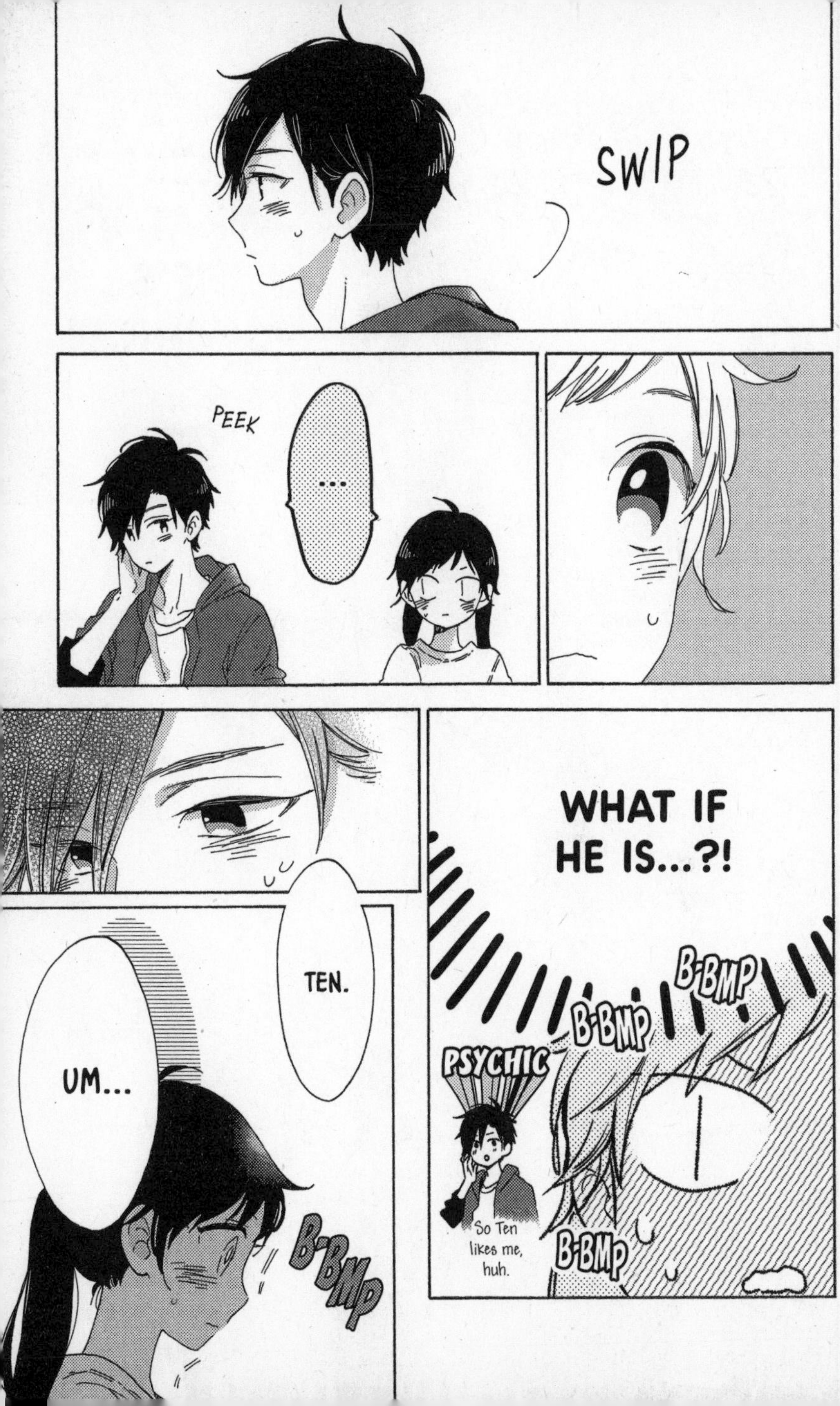
SWIP
PEEK
...
WHAT IF HE IS...?!
B-BMP
B-BMP
PSYCHIC
So Ten likes me, huh.
B-BMP
TEN.
UM...
B-BMP

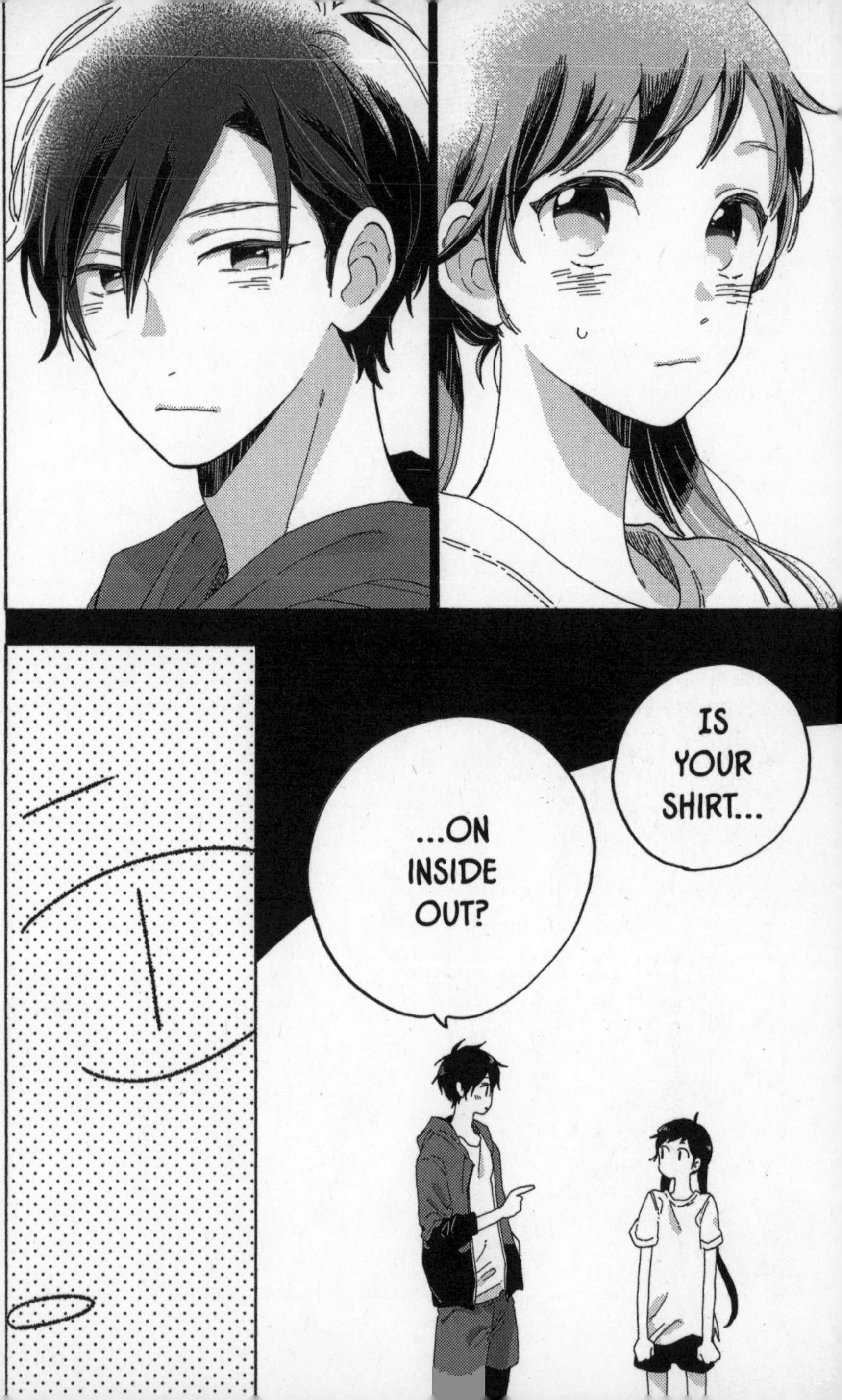
IS YOUR SHIRT...
...ON INSIDE OUT?

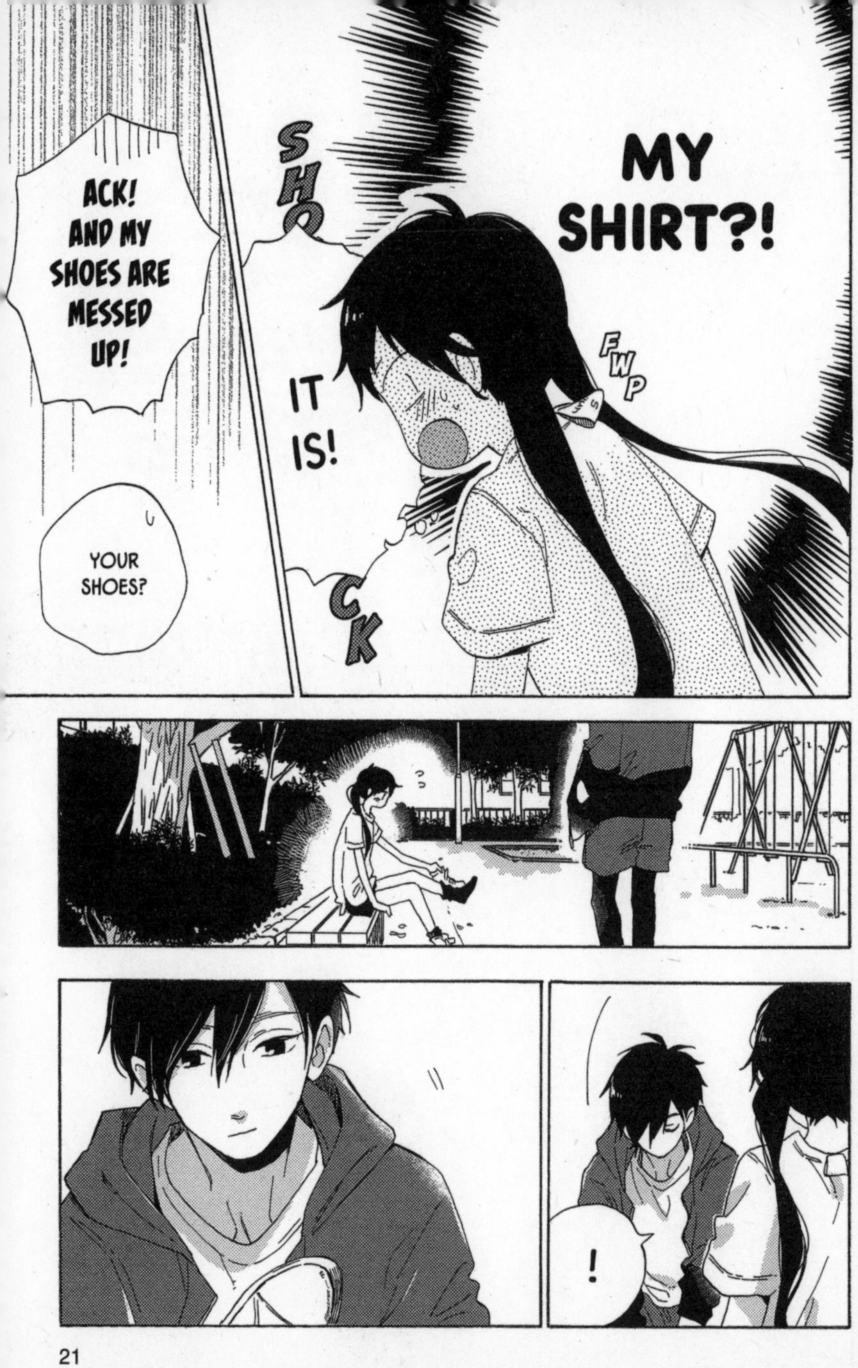

MY SHIRT?!
SHOCK
FWP
IT IS!
ACK! AND MY SHOES ARE MESSED UP!
YOUR SHOES?
!

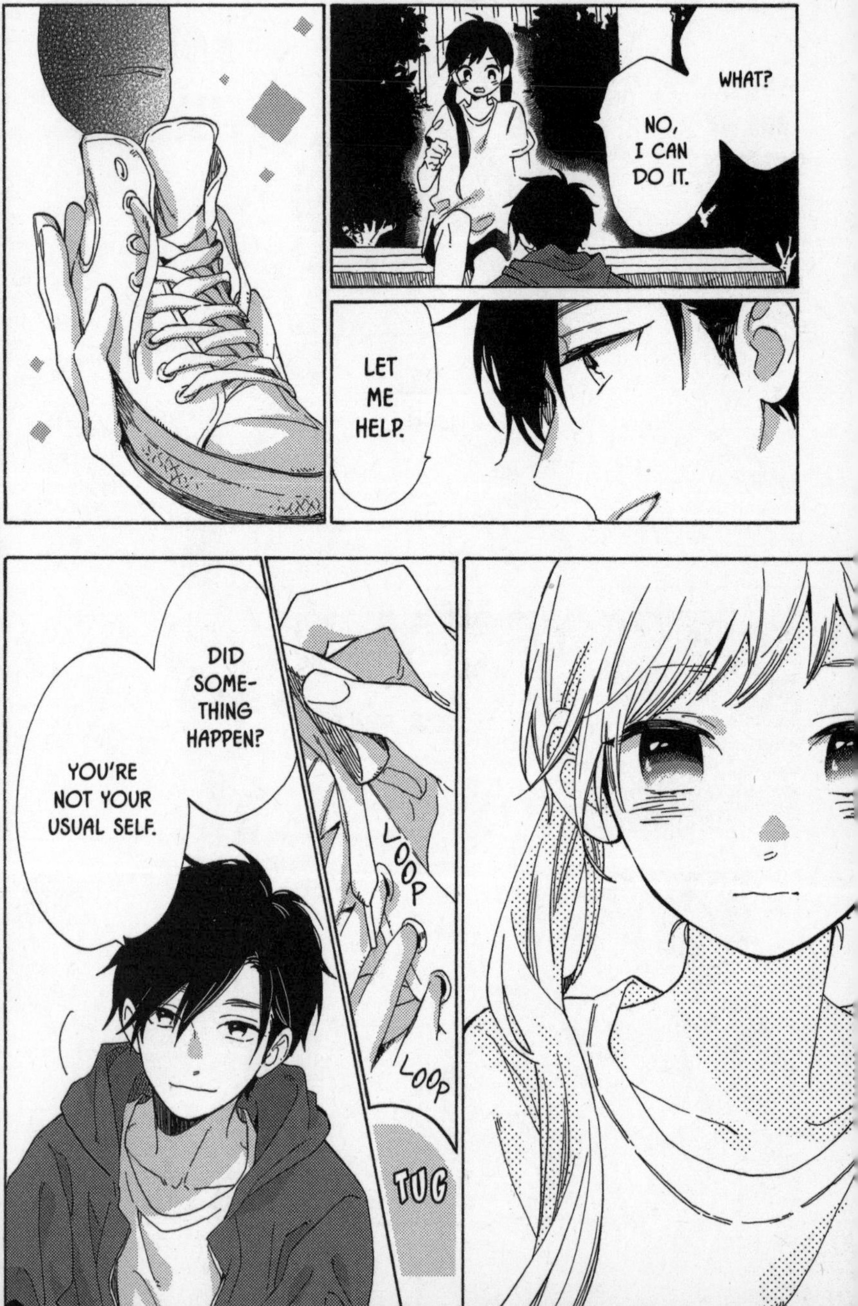
WHAT?
NO, I CAN DO IT.
LET ME HELP.
LOOP
LOOP
TUG
DID SOMETHING HAPPEN?
YOU'RE NOT YOUR USUAL SELF.

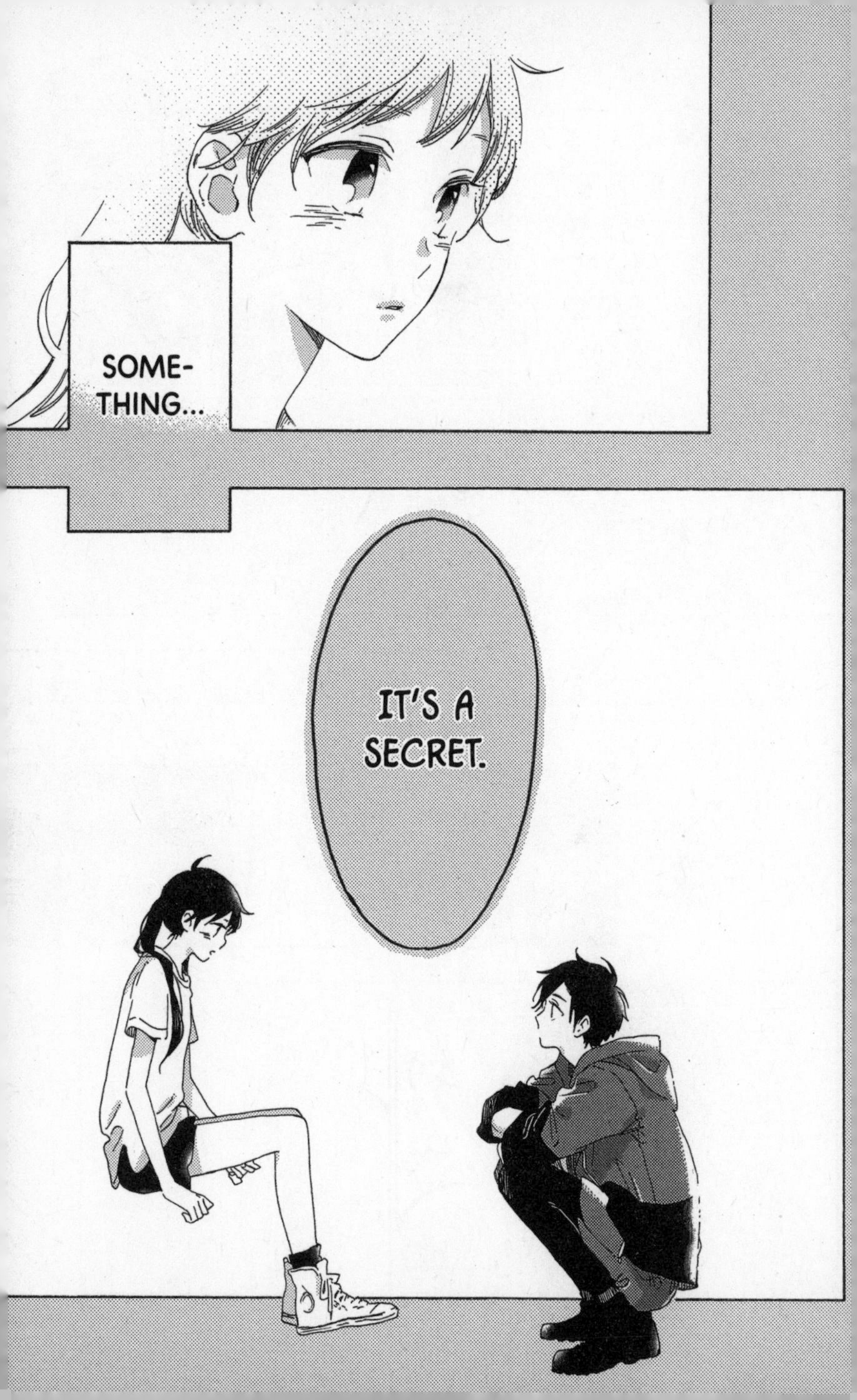
SOME-THING...
IT'S A SECRET.

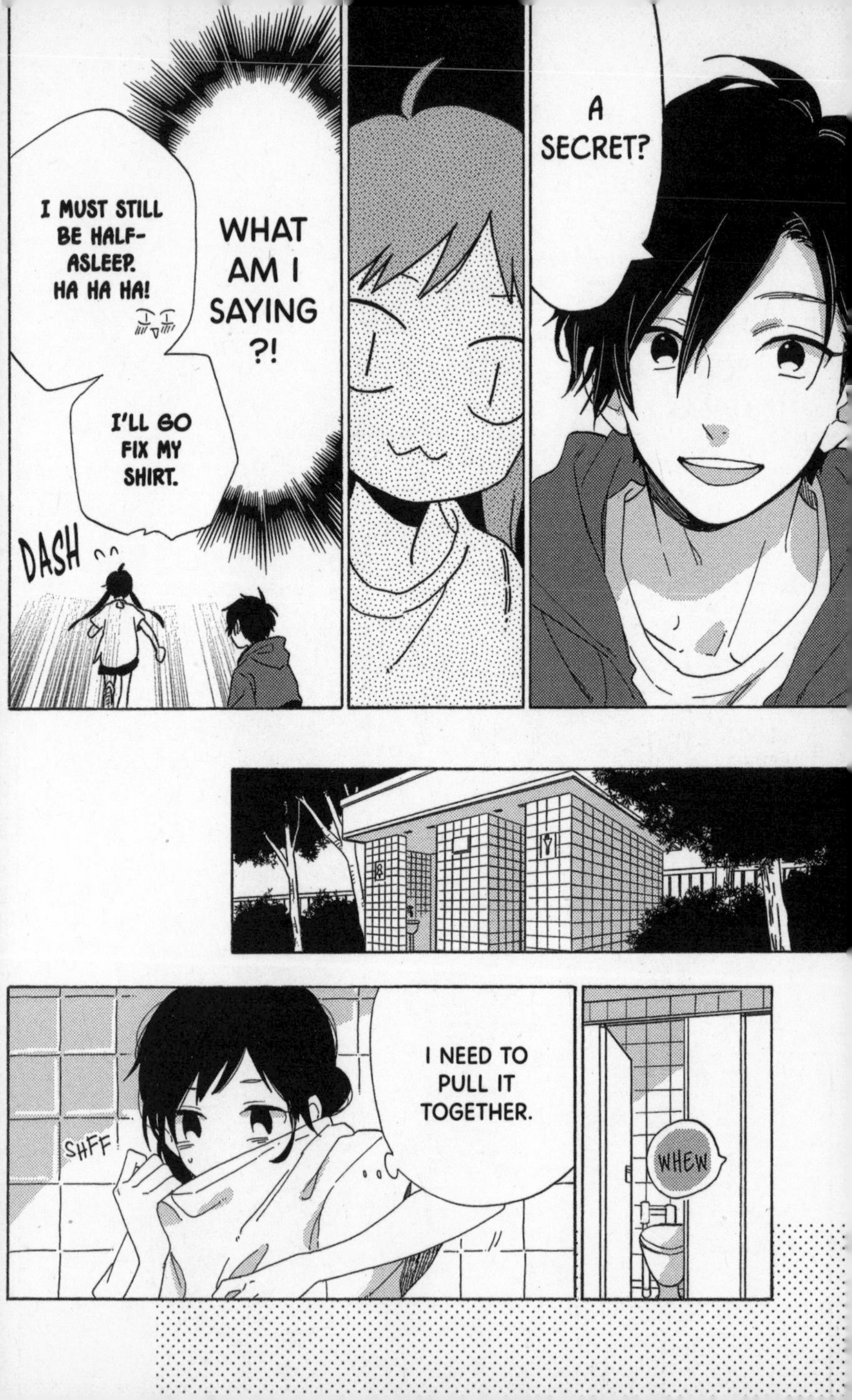
A SECRET?
WHAT AM I SAYING?!
I MUST STILL BE HALF-ASLEEP. HA HA HA!
I'LL GO FIX MY SHIRT.
DASH
WHEW
I NEED TO PULL IT TOGETHER.
SHFF

IF I DID, YOU'D BE NUMBER ONE.

AFTER THAT...

I'M SORRY, BUT I DON'T...

...RIKU ACTED AS USUAL...

WHAT WAS HE FEELING?

...TO SET ME AT EASE.

GOOD MORNING.

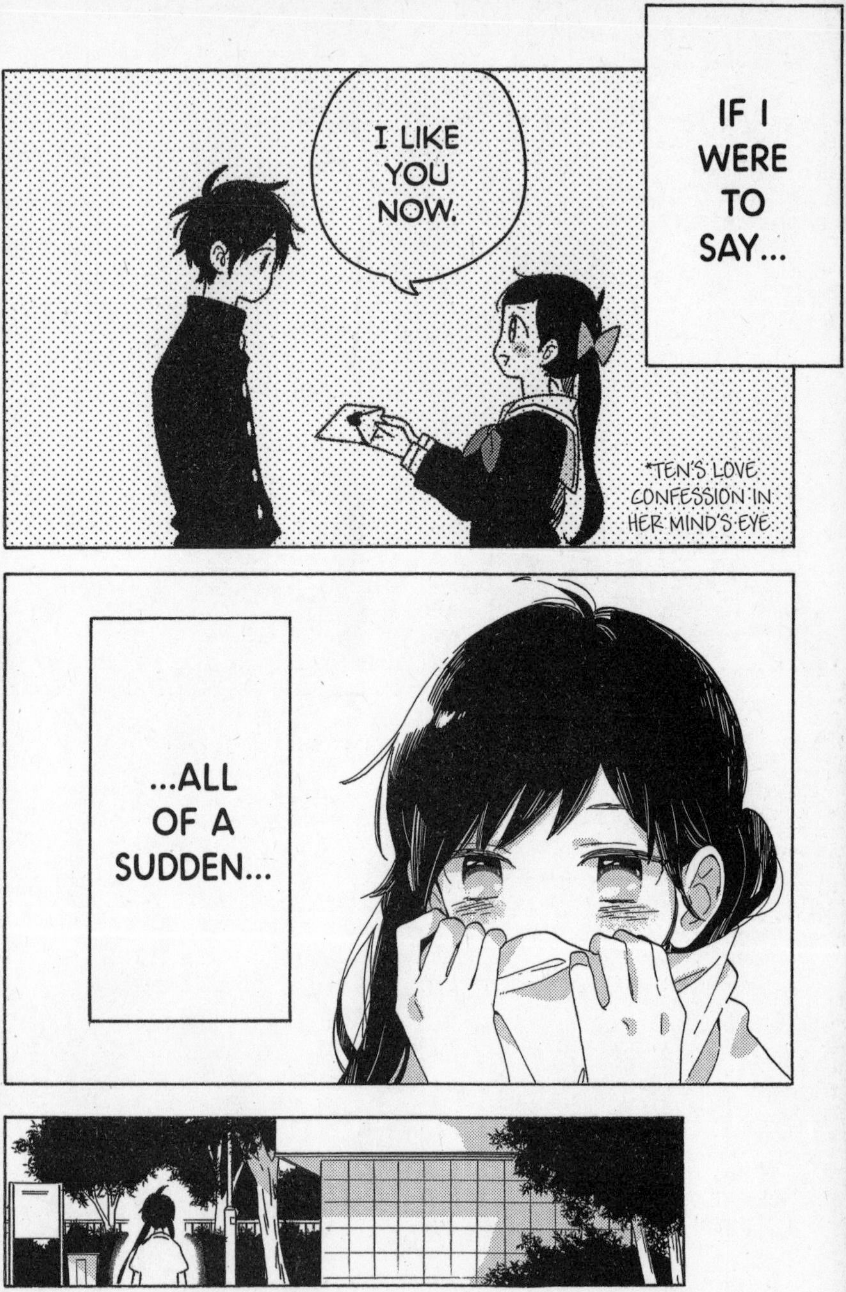
IF I WERE TO SAY...
I LIKE YOU NOW.
*TEN'S LOVE CONFESSION IN HER MIND'S EYE
...ALL OF A SUDDEN...

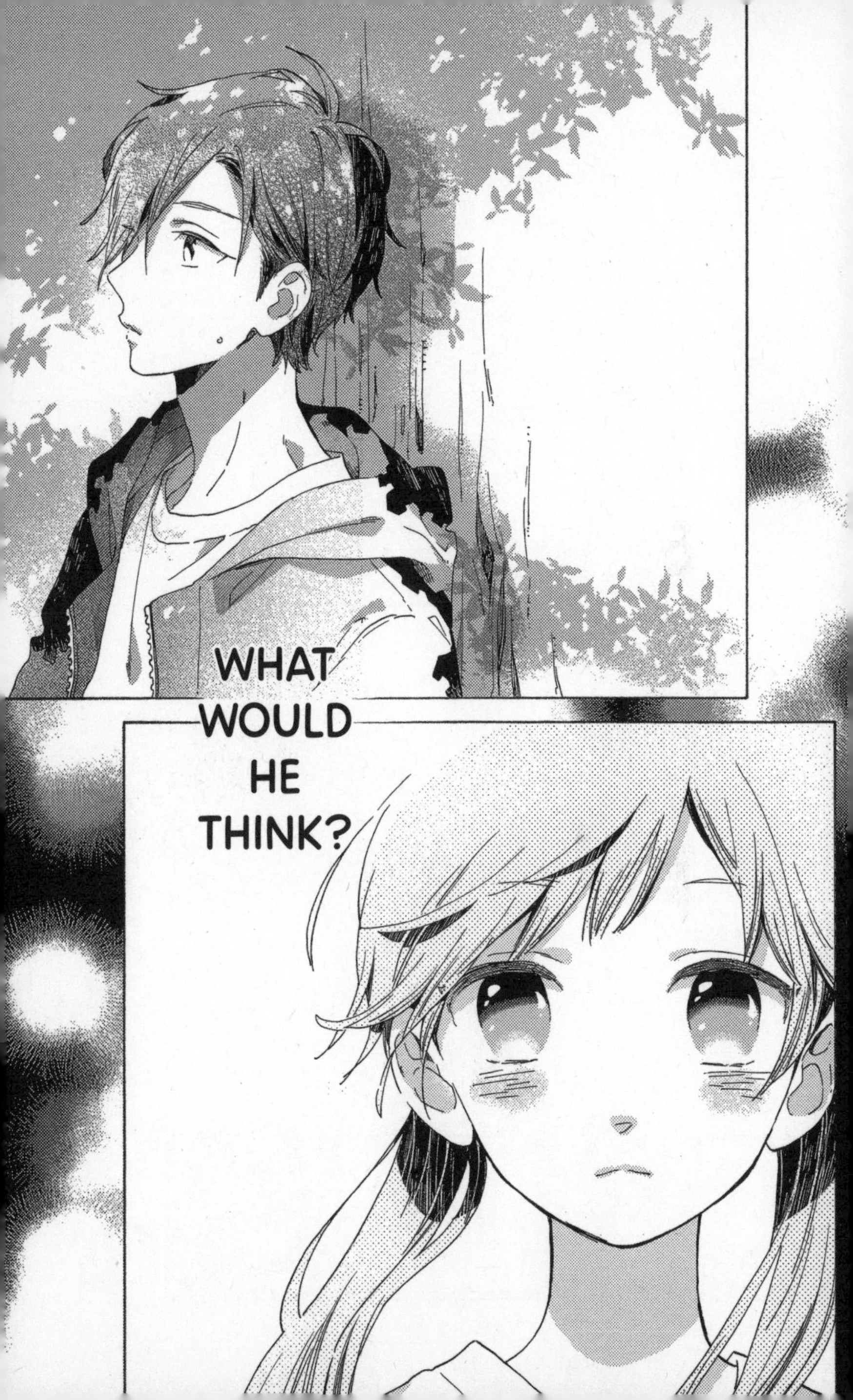
WHAT WOULD HE THINK?

SHORTCAKE
CAKE

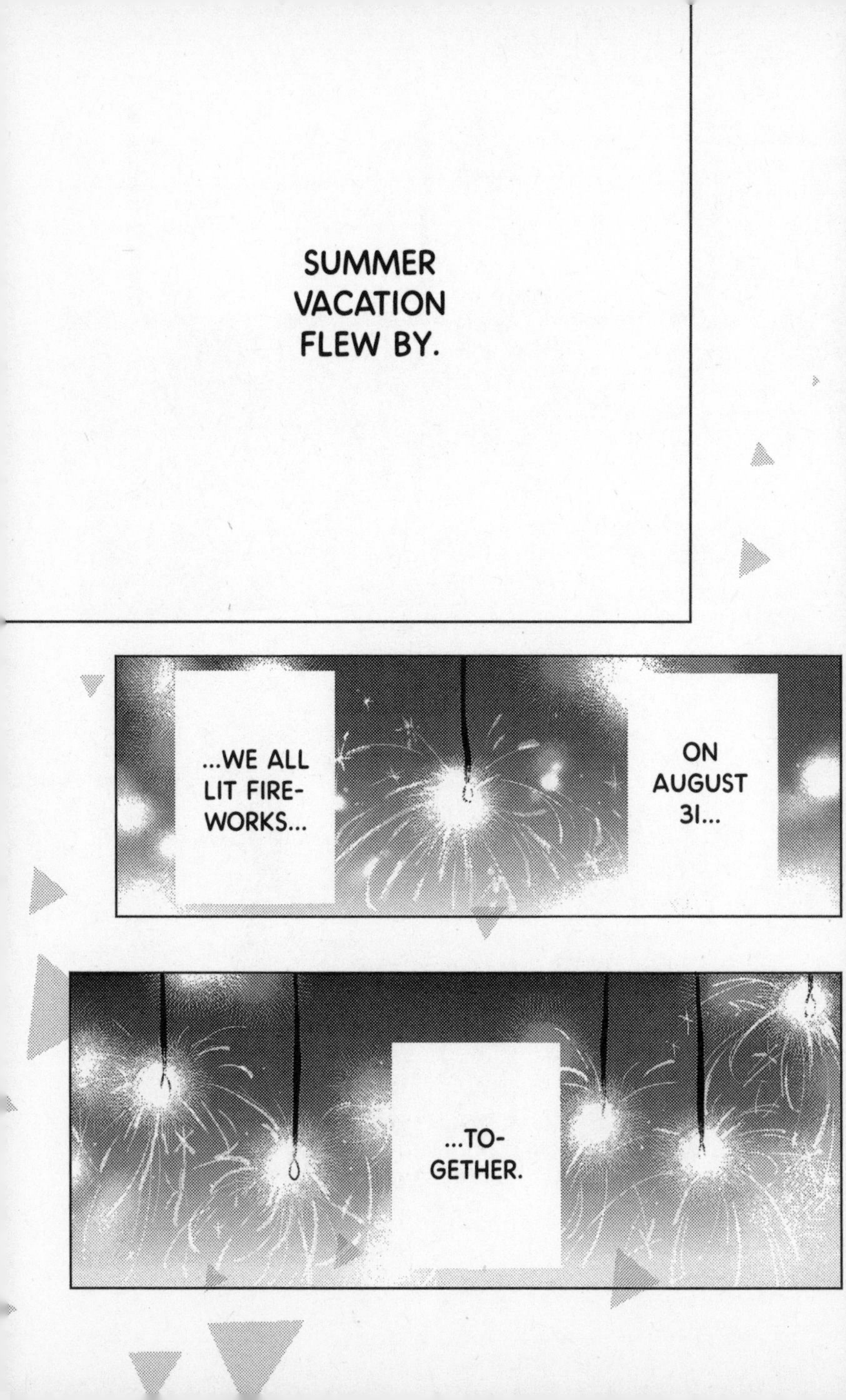
SUMMER VACATION FLEW BY.
ON AUGUST 31...
...WE ALL LIT FIRE-WORKS...
...TO-GETHER.

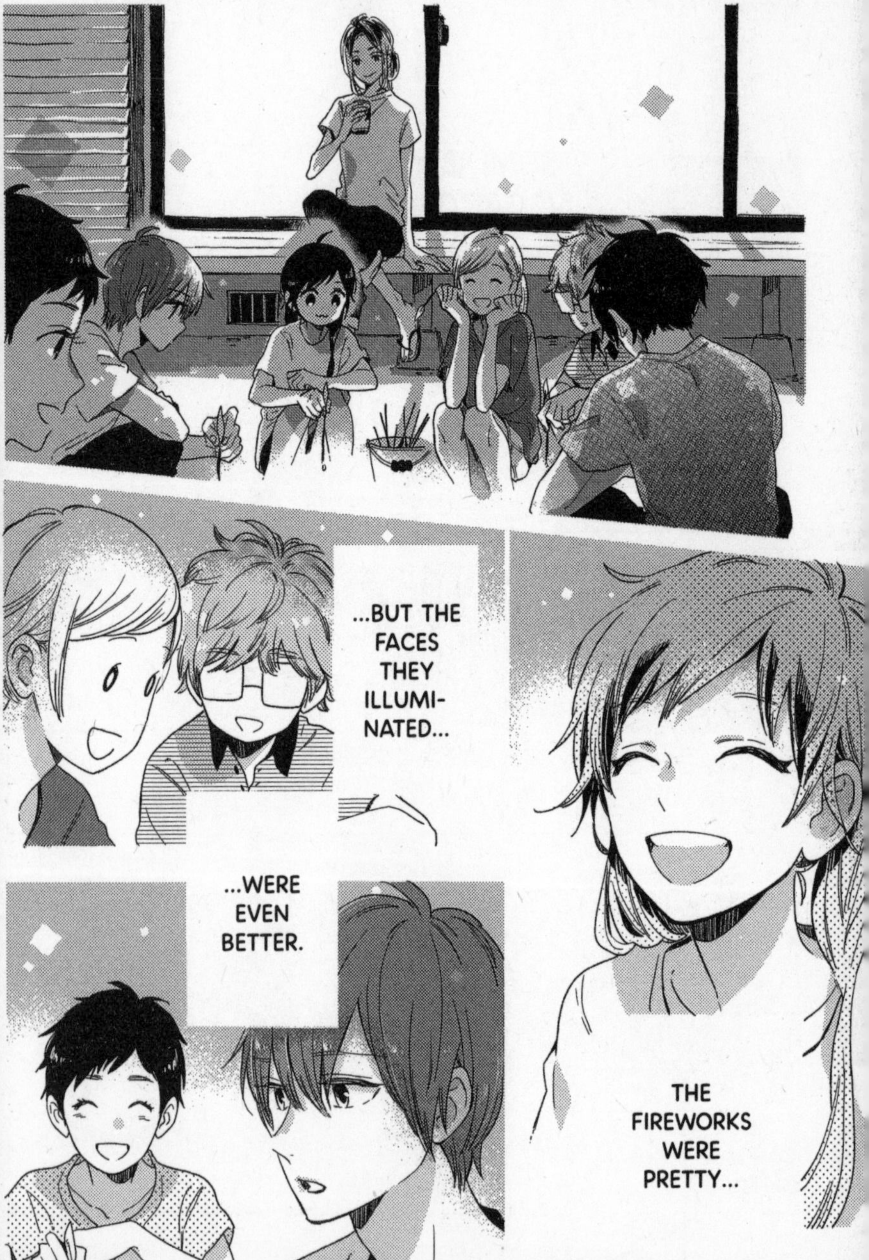
THE FIREWORKS WERE PRETTY...
...BUT THE FACES THEY ILLUMINATED...
...WERE EVEN BETTER.

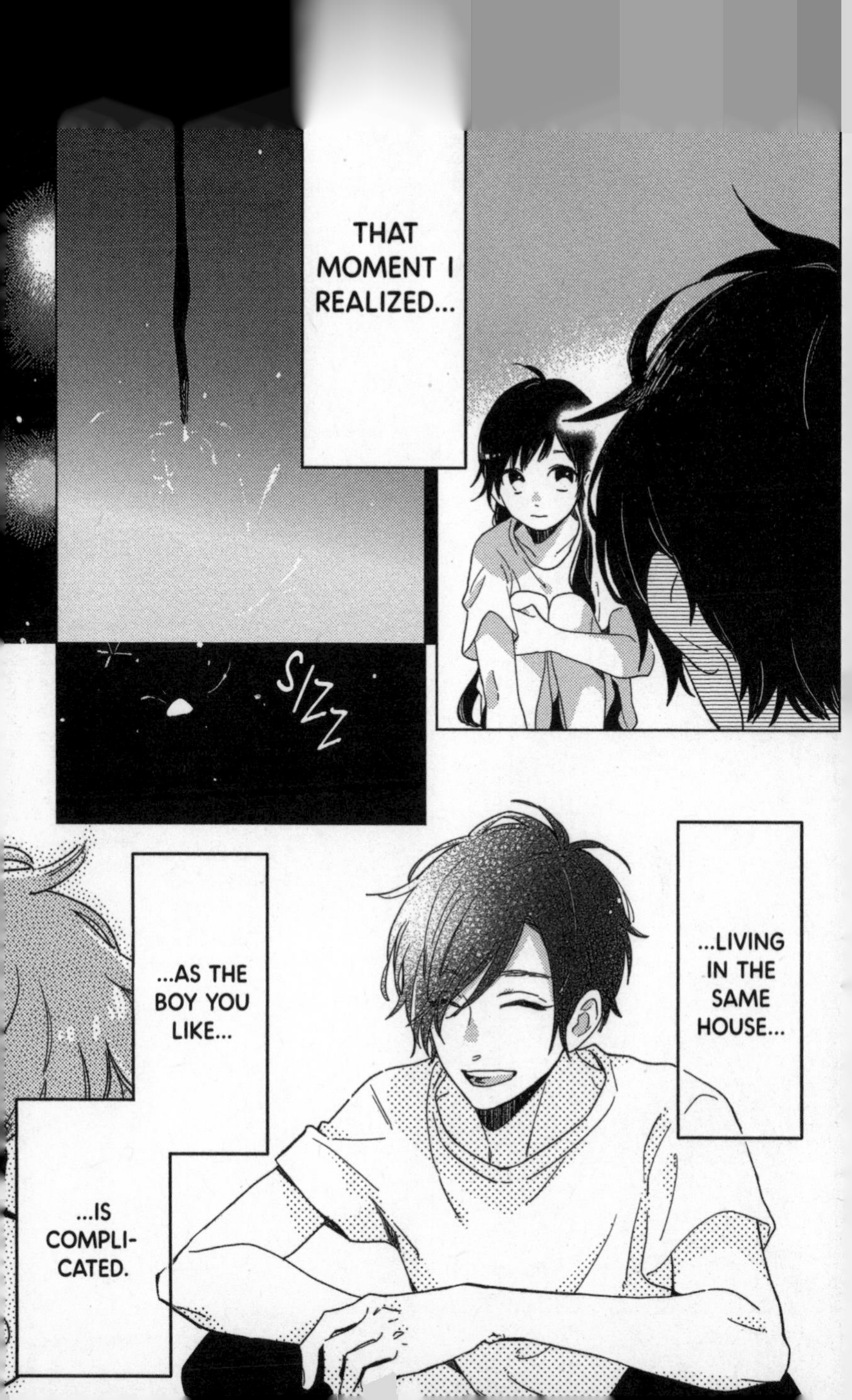
THAT MOMENT I REALIZED...
SIZZ
...LIVING IN THE SAME HOUSE...
...AS THE BOY YOU LIKE...
...IS COMPLI- CATED.

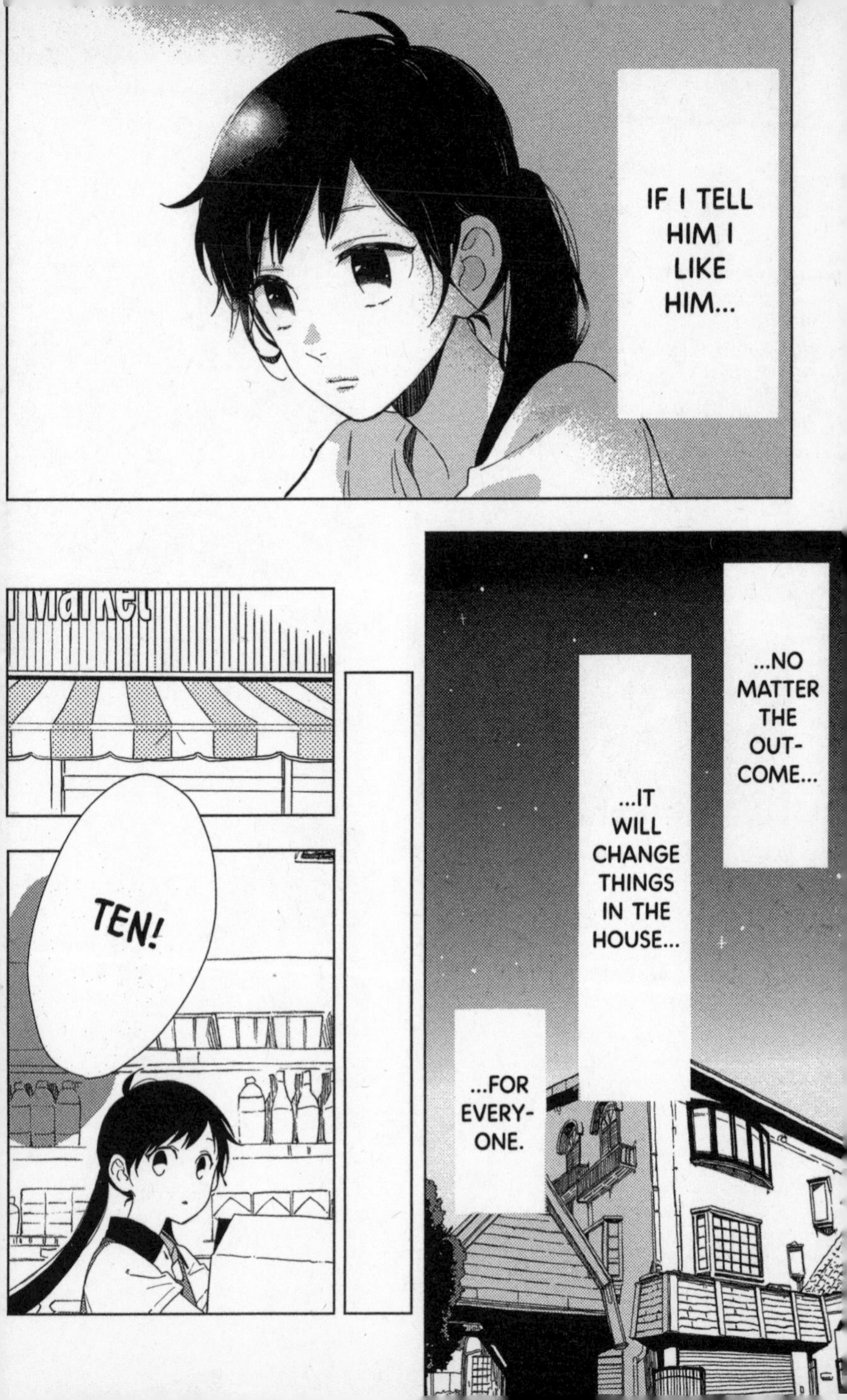
IF I TELL HIM I LIKE HIM...
...NO MATTER THE OUT-COME...
...IT WILL CHANGE THINGS IN THE HOUSE...
...FOR EVERY-ONE.
TEN!

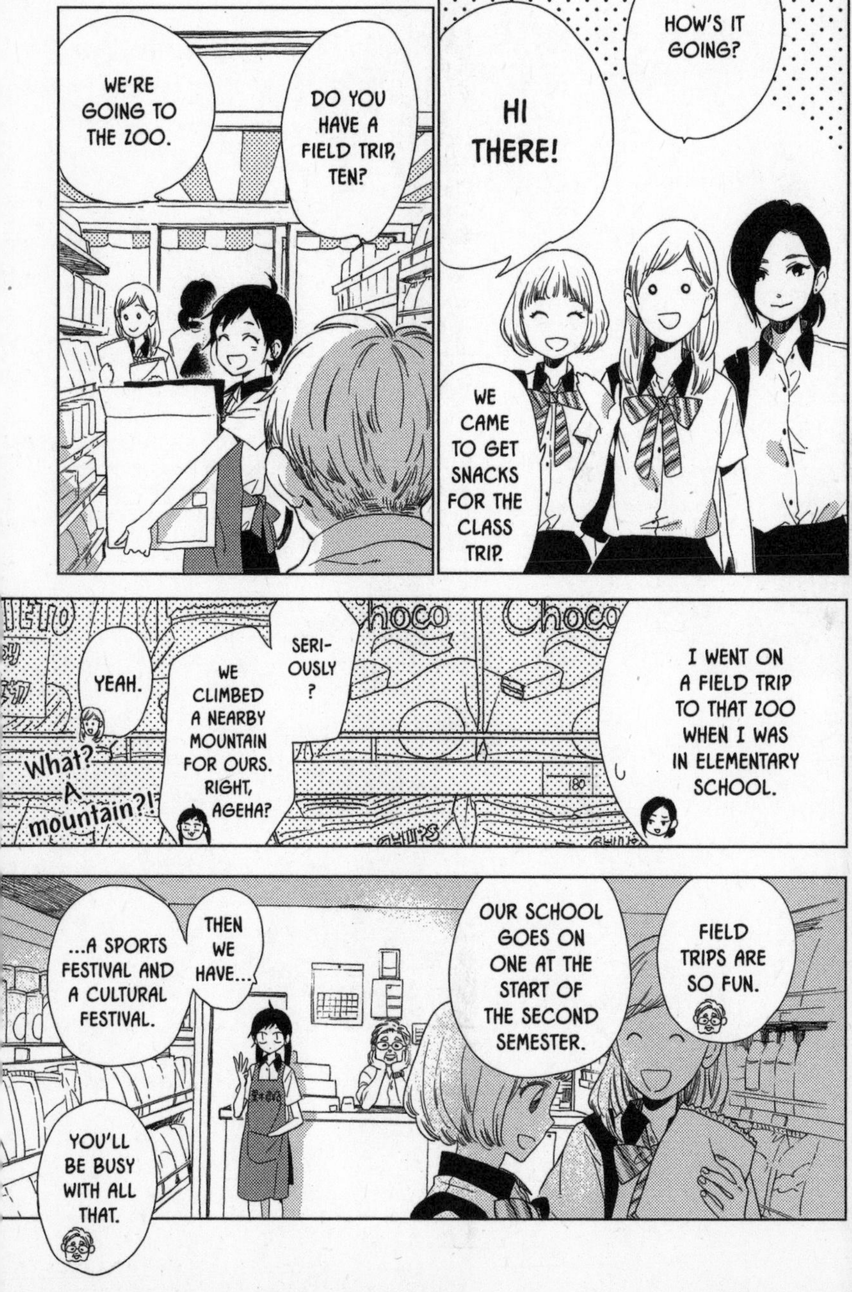
HOW'S IT GOING?
HI THERE!
WE CAME TO GET SNACKS FOR THE CLASS TRIP.
DO YOU HAVE A FIELD TRIP, TEN?
WE'RE GOING TO THE ZOO.
I WENT ON A FIELD TRIP TO THAT ZOO WHEN I WAS IN ELEMENTARY SCHOOL.
SERIOUSLY?
WE CLIMBED A NEARBY MOUNTAIN FOR OURS. RIGHT, AGEHA?
YEAH.
What? A mountain?!
FIELD TRIPS ARE SO FUN.
OUR SCHOOL GOES ON ONE AT THE START OF THE SECOND SEMESTER.
THEN WE HAVE...
...A SPORTS FESTIVAL AND A CULTURAL FESTIVAL.
YOU'LL BE BUSY WITH ALL THAT.

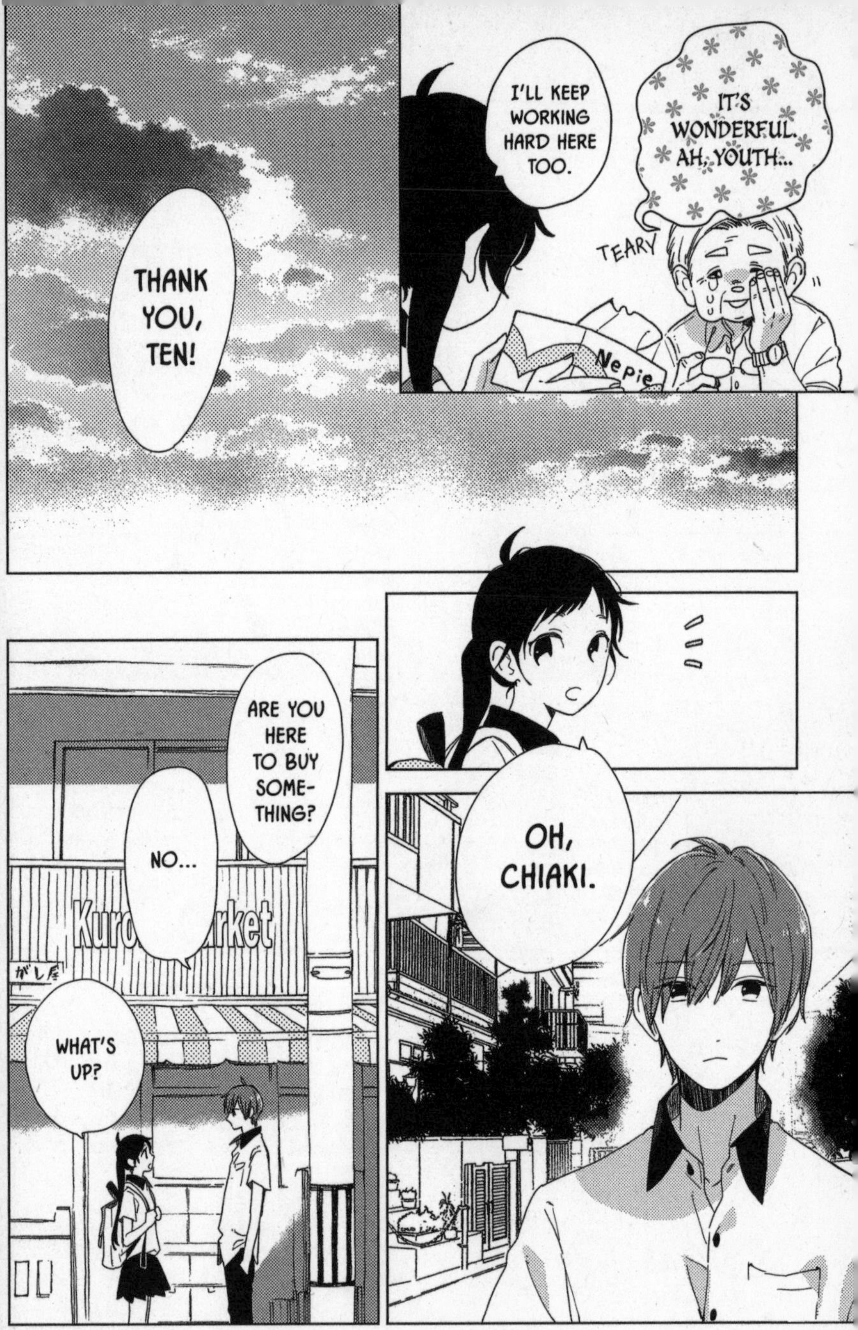
I'LL KEEP WORKING HARD HERE TOO.
IT'S WONDERFUL. AH, YOUTH...
TEARY
Nepie
THANK YOU, TEN!
OH, CHIAKI.
ARE YOU HERE TO BUY SOMETHING?
NO...
WHAT'S UP?

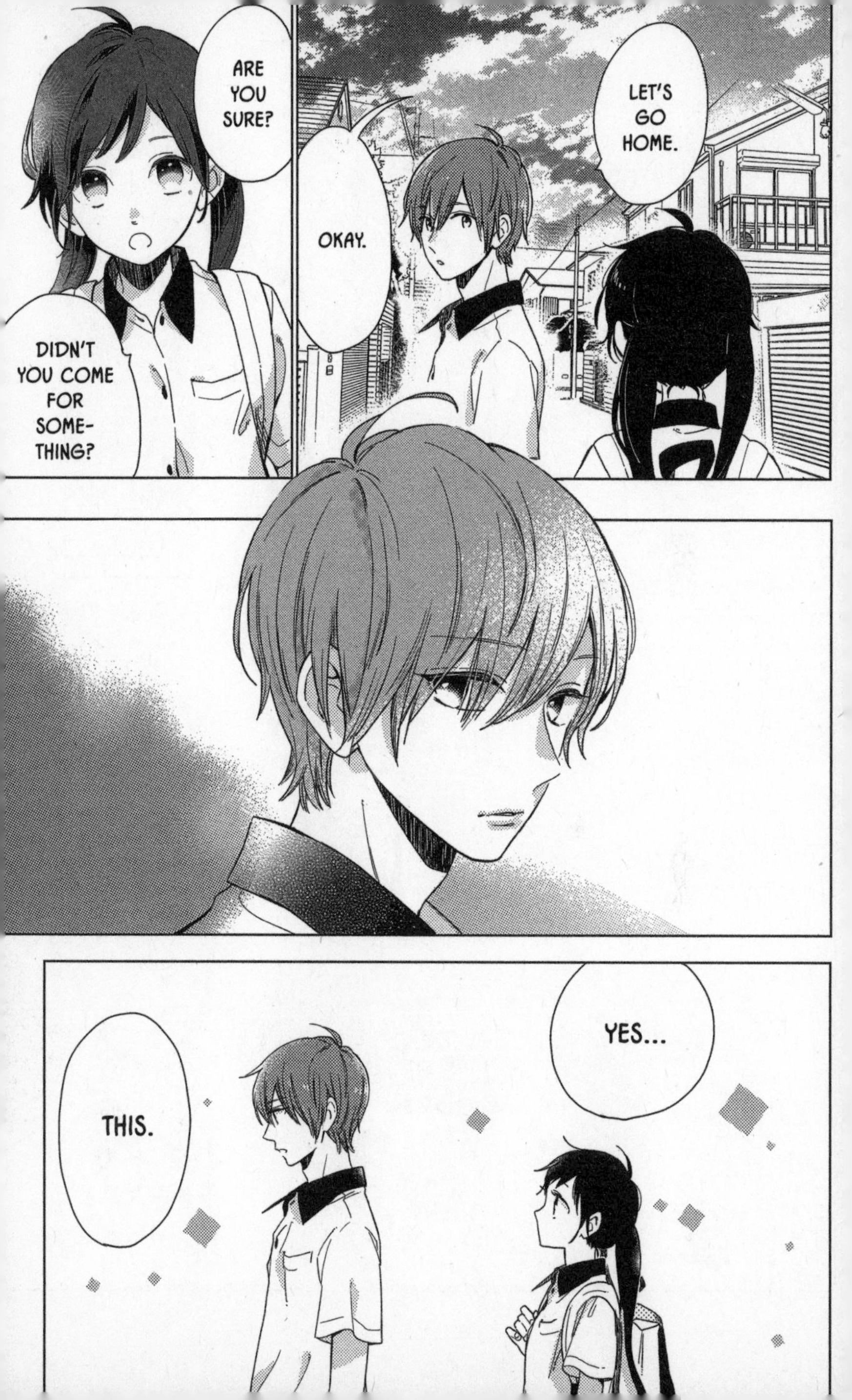
LET'S GO HOME.
OKAY.
ARE YOU SURE?
DIDN'T YOU COME FOR SOME-THING?
YES...
THIS.

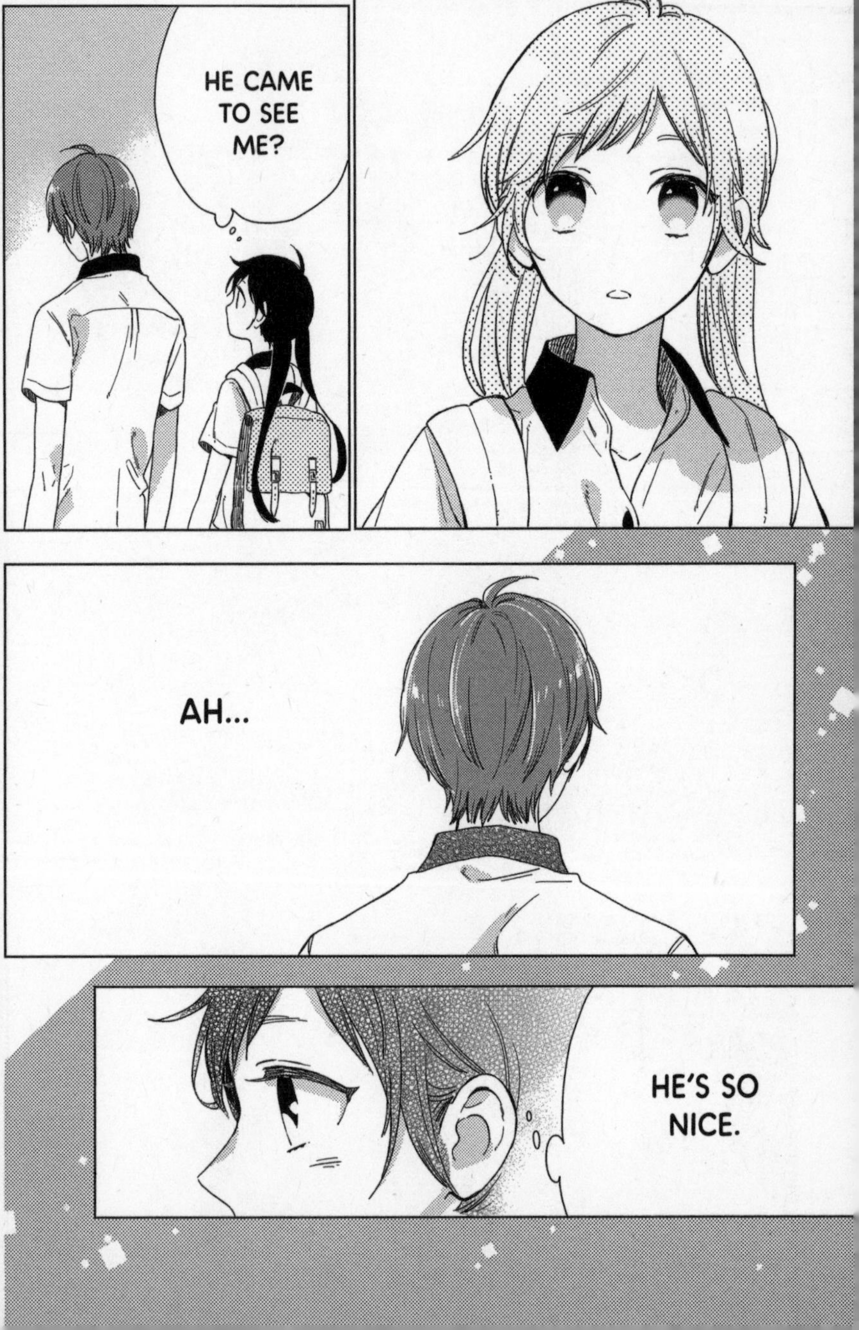
HE CAME TO SEE ME?
AH...
HE'S SO NICE.

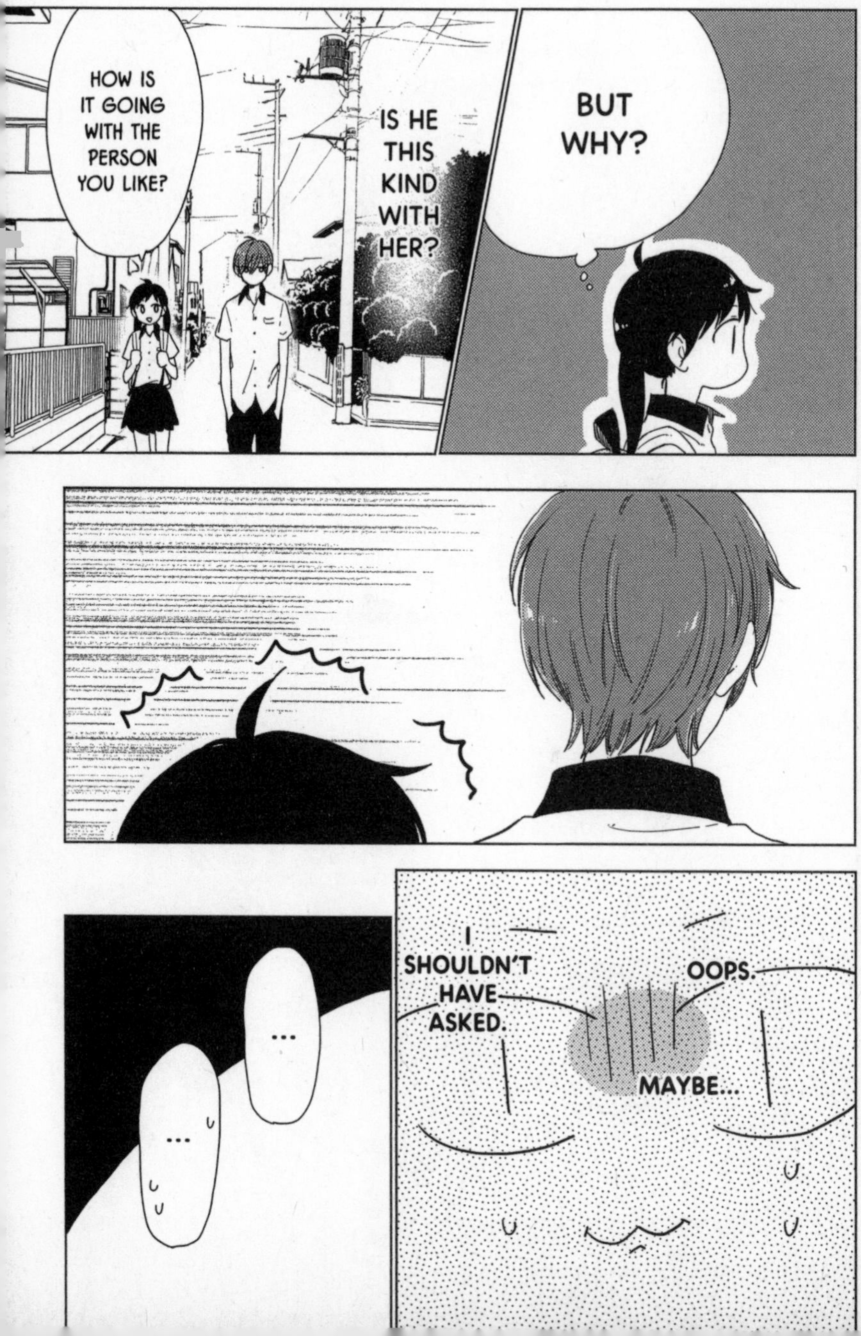
BUT WHY?
IS HE THIS KIND WITH HER?
HOW IS IT GOING WITH THE PERSON YOU LIKE?
OOPS.
I SHOULDN'T HAVE ASKED.
MAYBE...
...
...

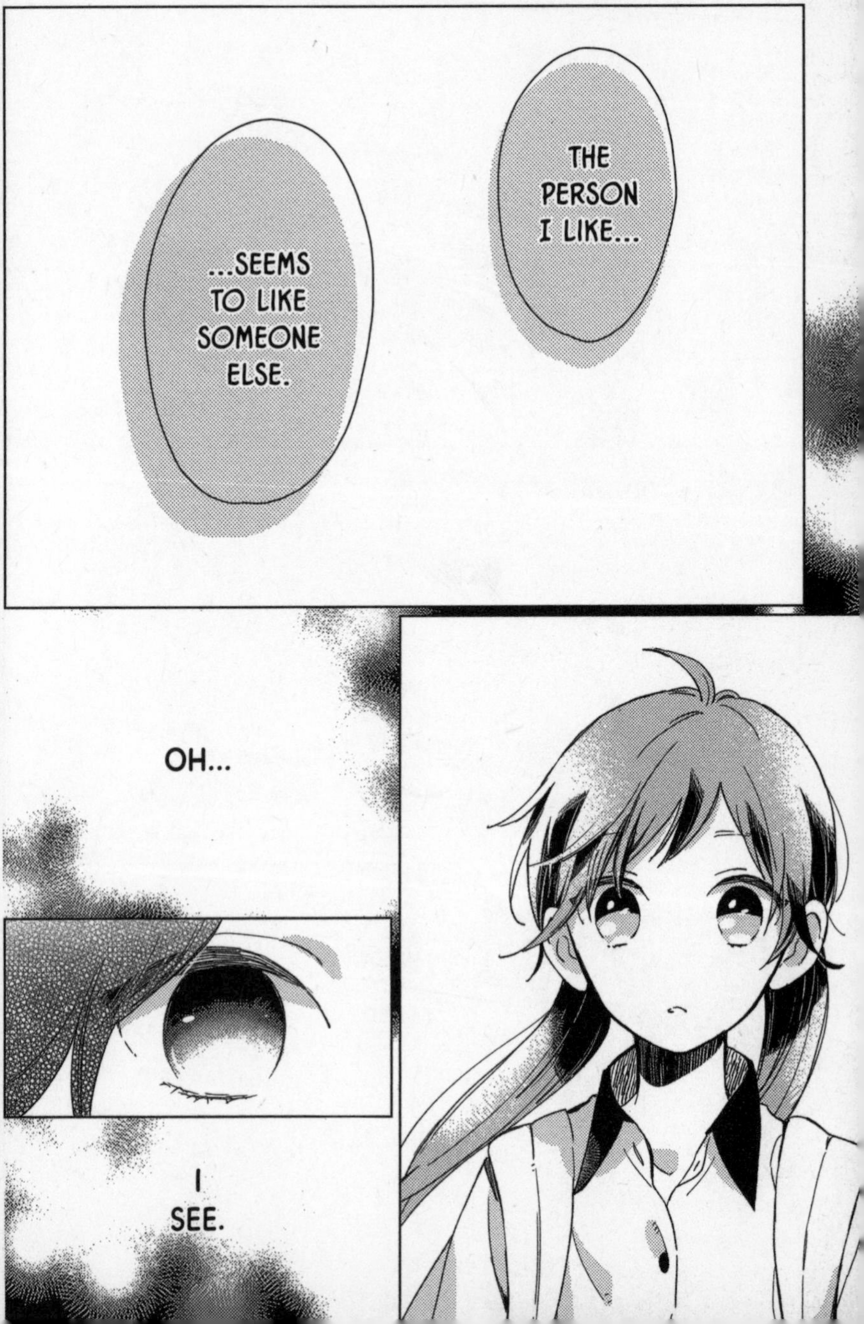
THE PERSON I LIKE...
...SEEMS TO LIKE SOMEONE ELSE.
OH...
I SEE.

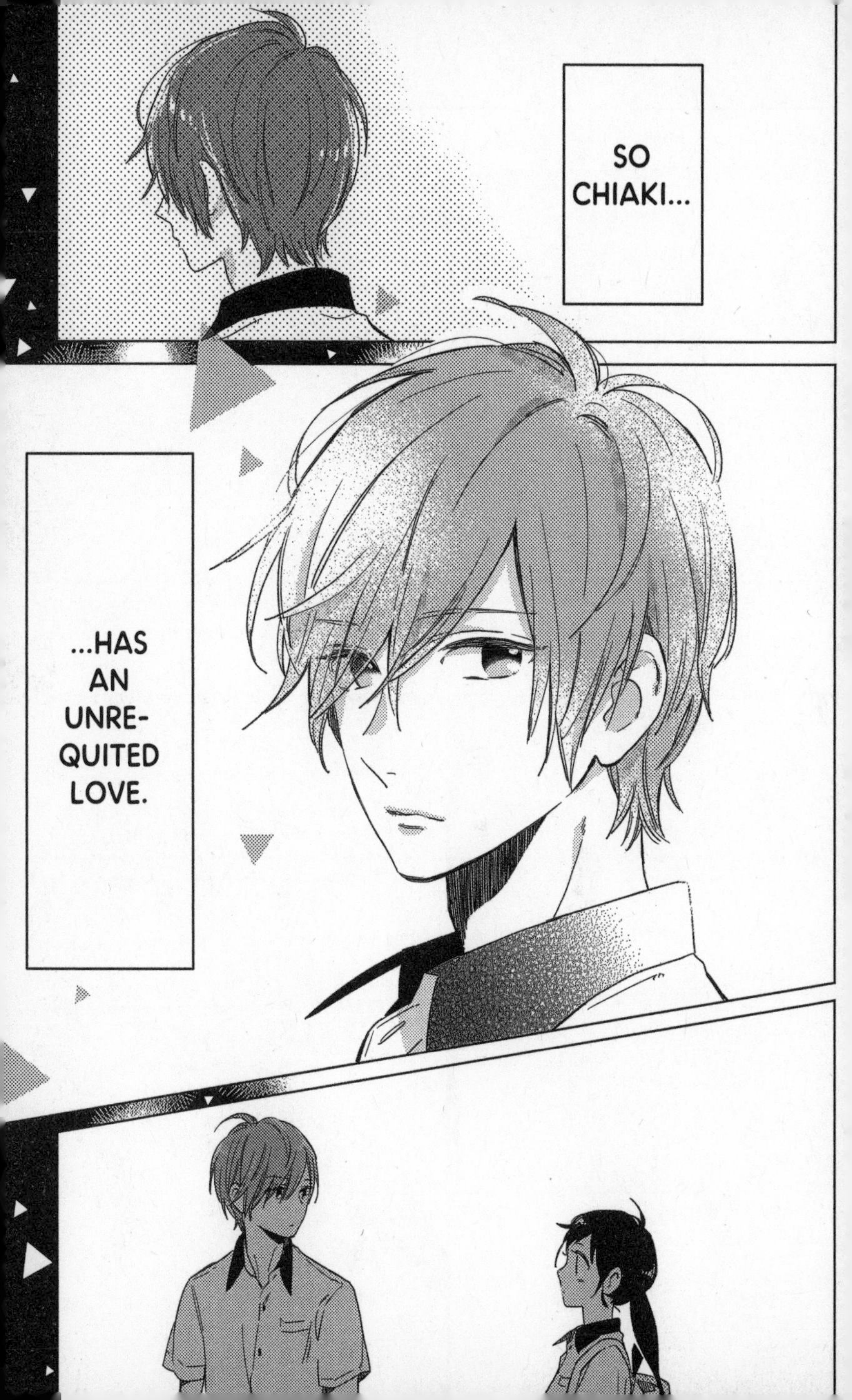
SO CHIAKI...
...HAS AN UNRE-QUITED LOVE.

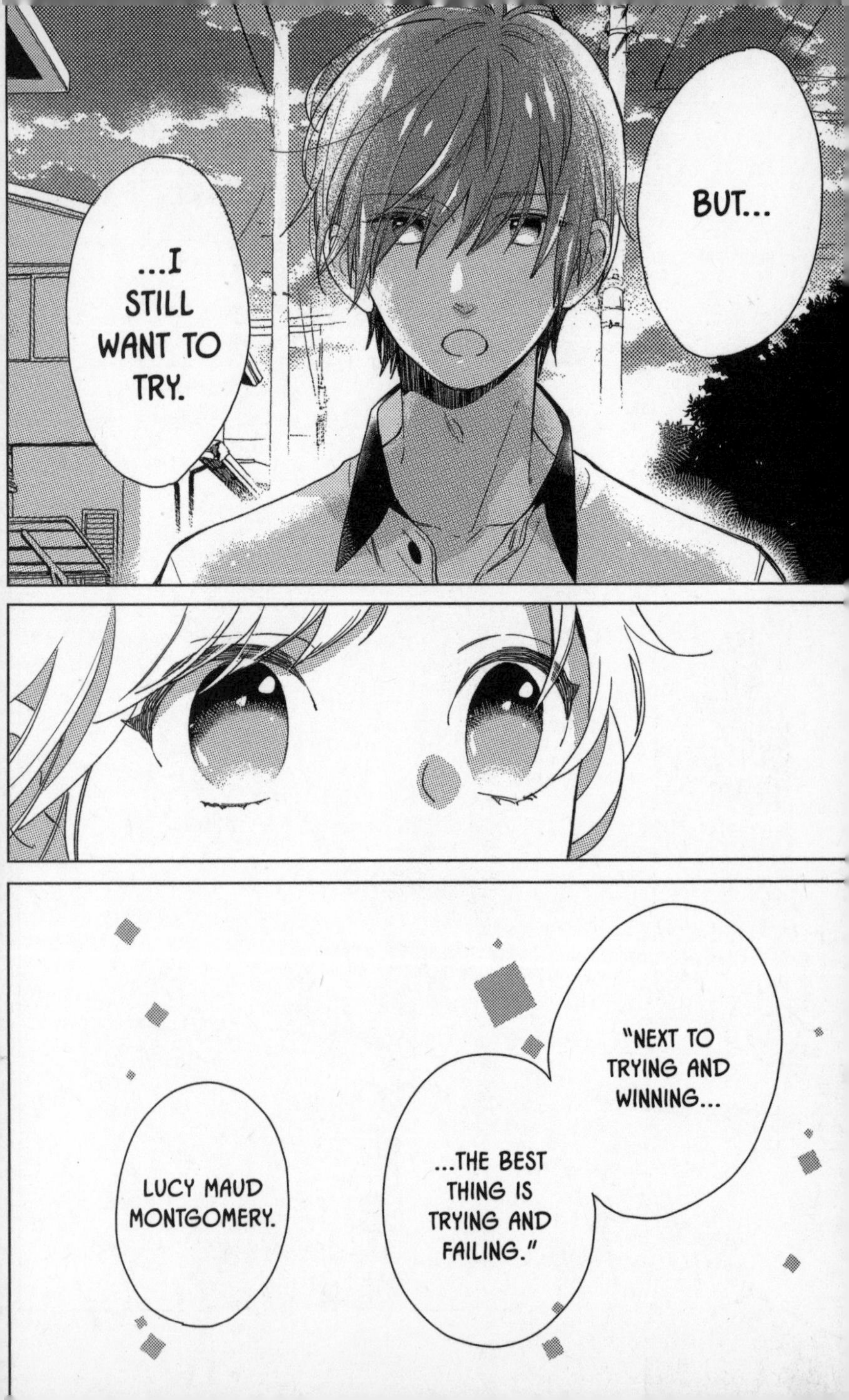
BUT...
...I STILL WANT TO TRY.
"NEXT TO TRYING AND WINNING...
...THE BEST THING IS TRYING AND FAILING."
LUCY MAUD MONTGOMERY.

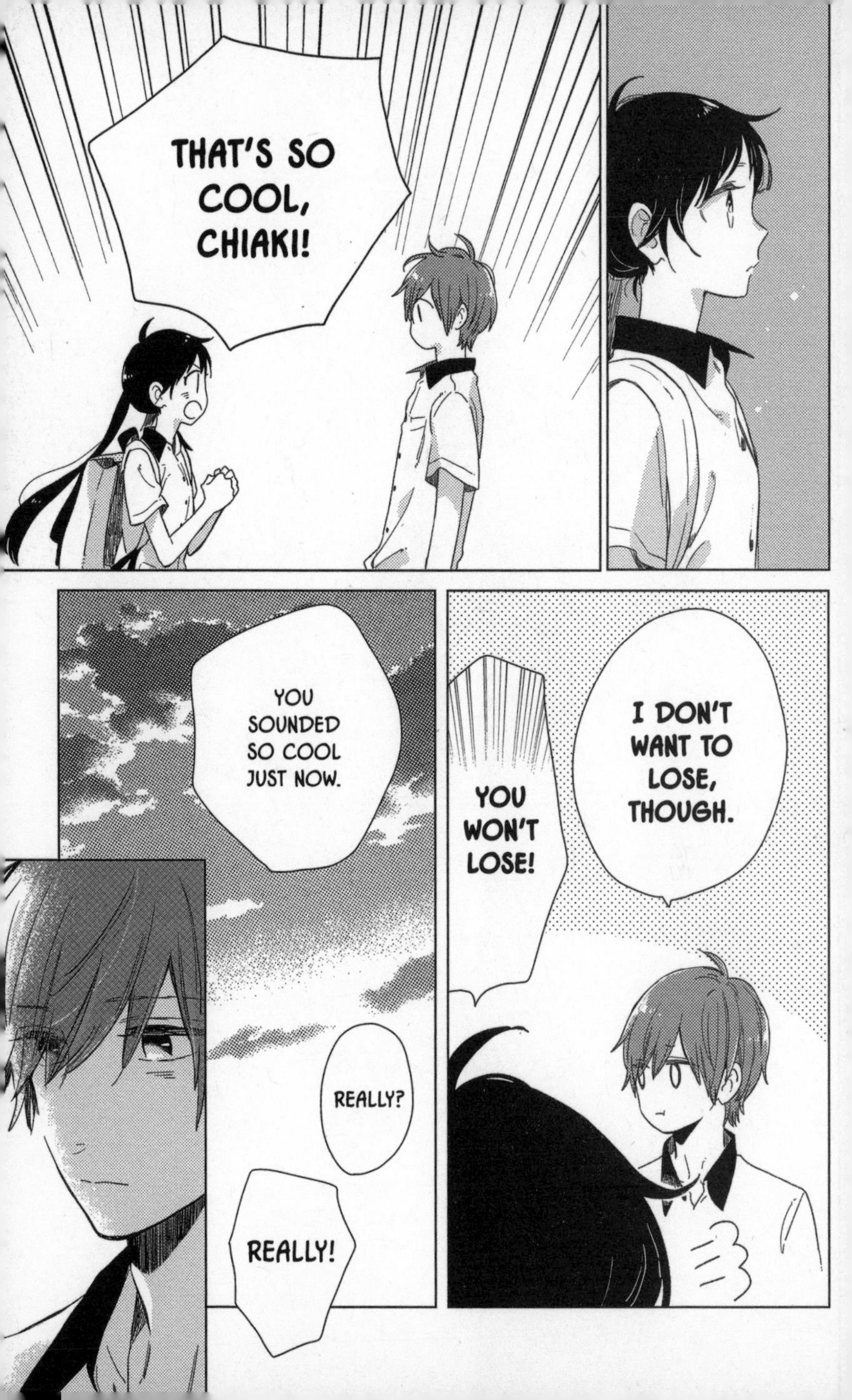
THAT'S SO COOL, CHIAKI!
I DON'T WANT TO LOSE, THOUGH.
YOU WON'T LOSE!
YOU SOUNDED SO COOL JUST NOW.
REALLY?
REALLY!

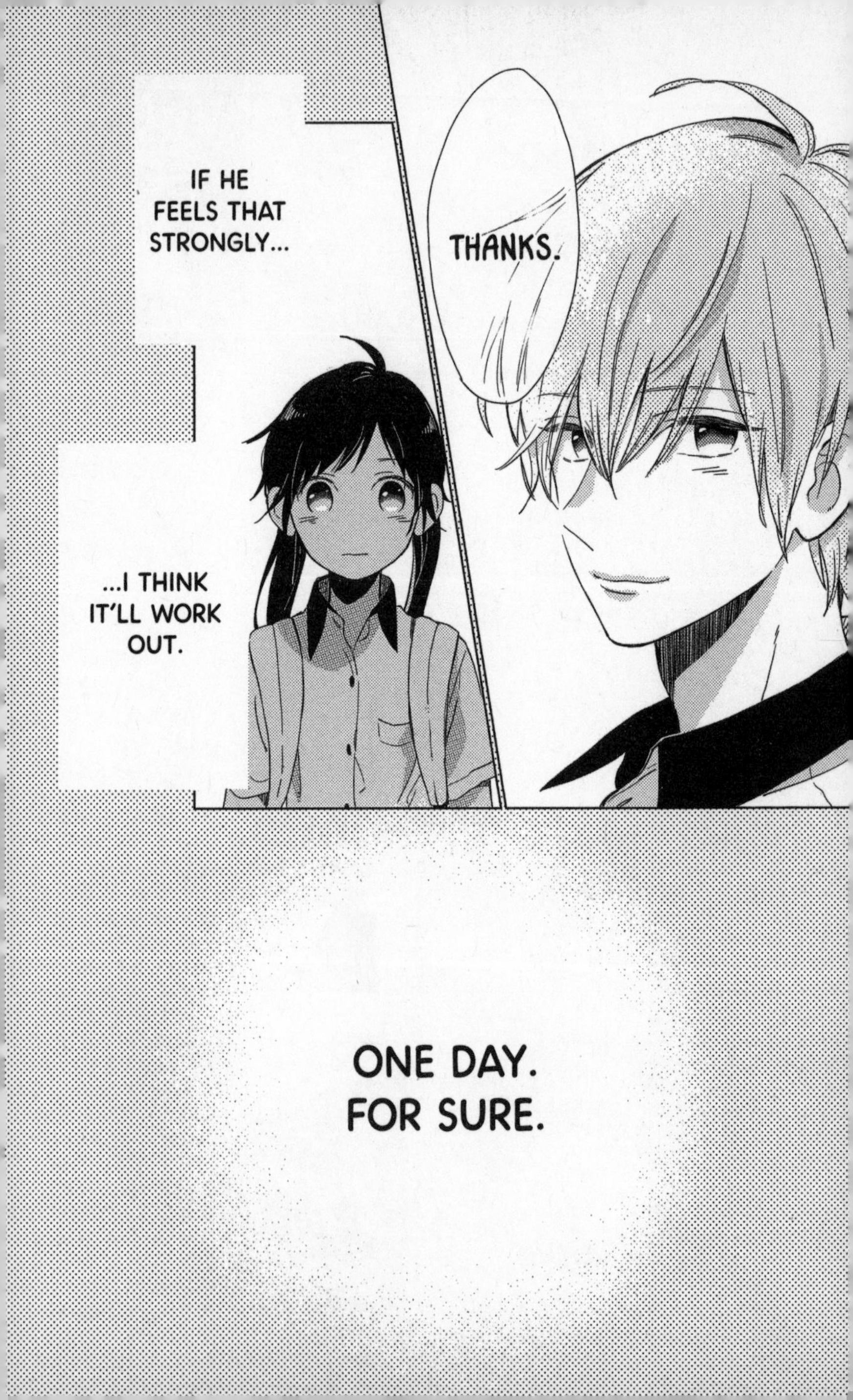
THANKS.
IF HE FEELS THAT STRONGLY...
...I THINK IT'LL WORK OUT.
ONE DAY. FOR SURE.

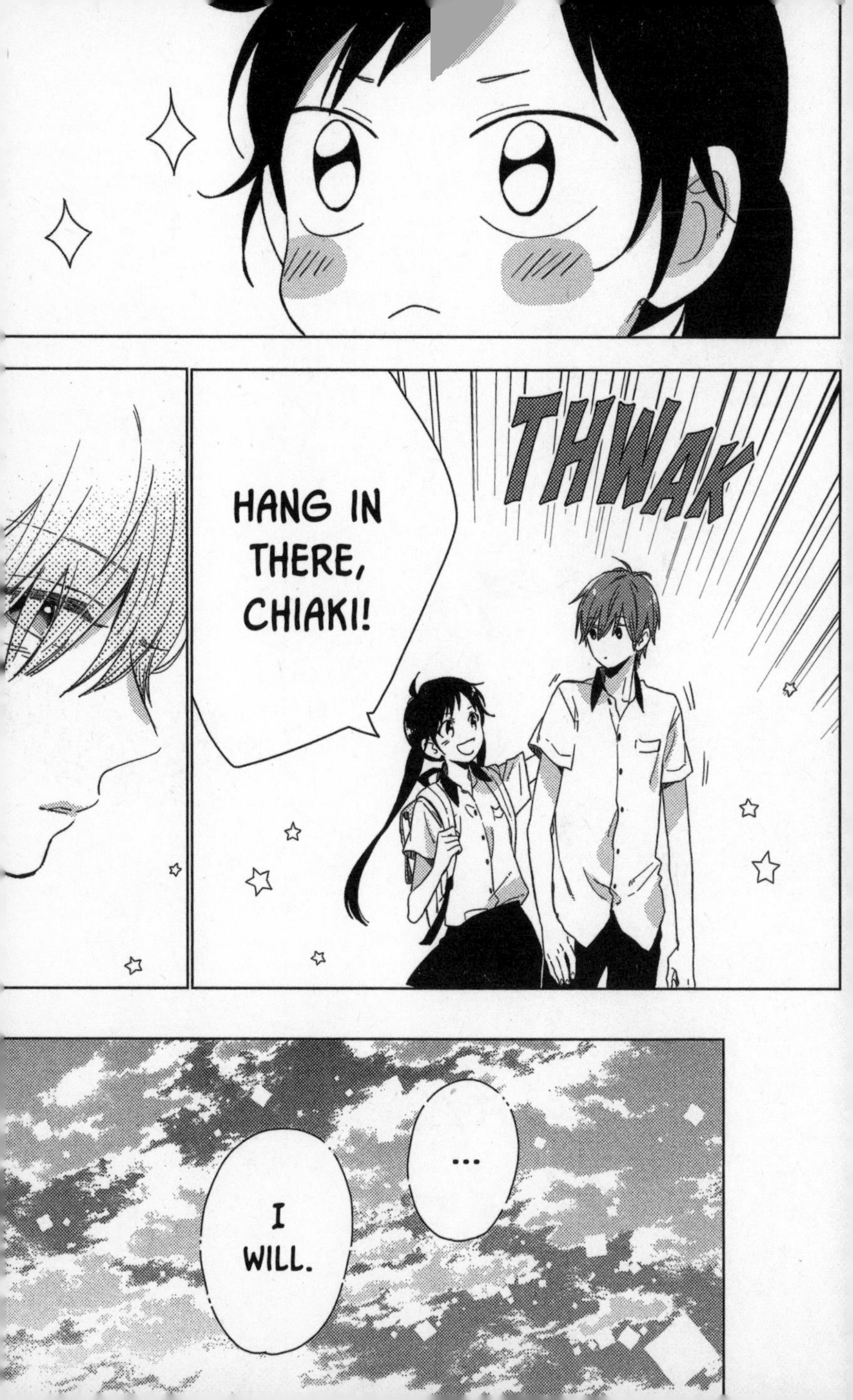
THWAK
HANG IN THERE, CHIAKI!
...
I WILL.

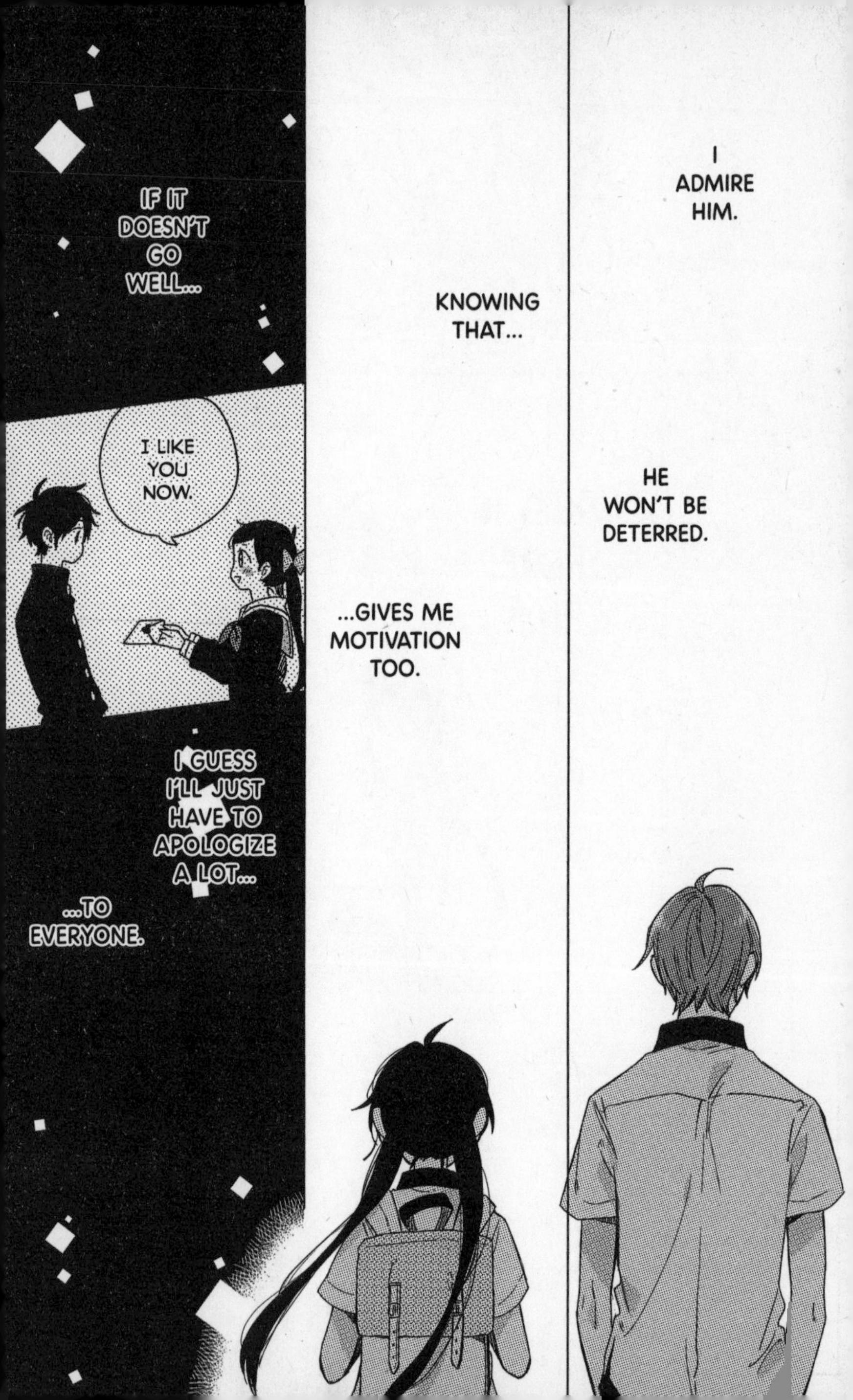
I ADMIRE HIM.
HE WON'T BE DETERRED.
KNOWING THAT...
...GIVES ME MOTIVATION TOO.
IF IT DOESN'T GO WELL...
I LIKE YOU NOW.
I GUESS I'LL JUST HAVE TO APOLOGIZE A LOT...
...TO EVERYONE.

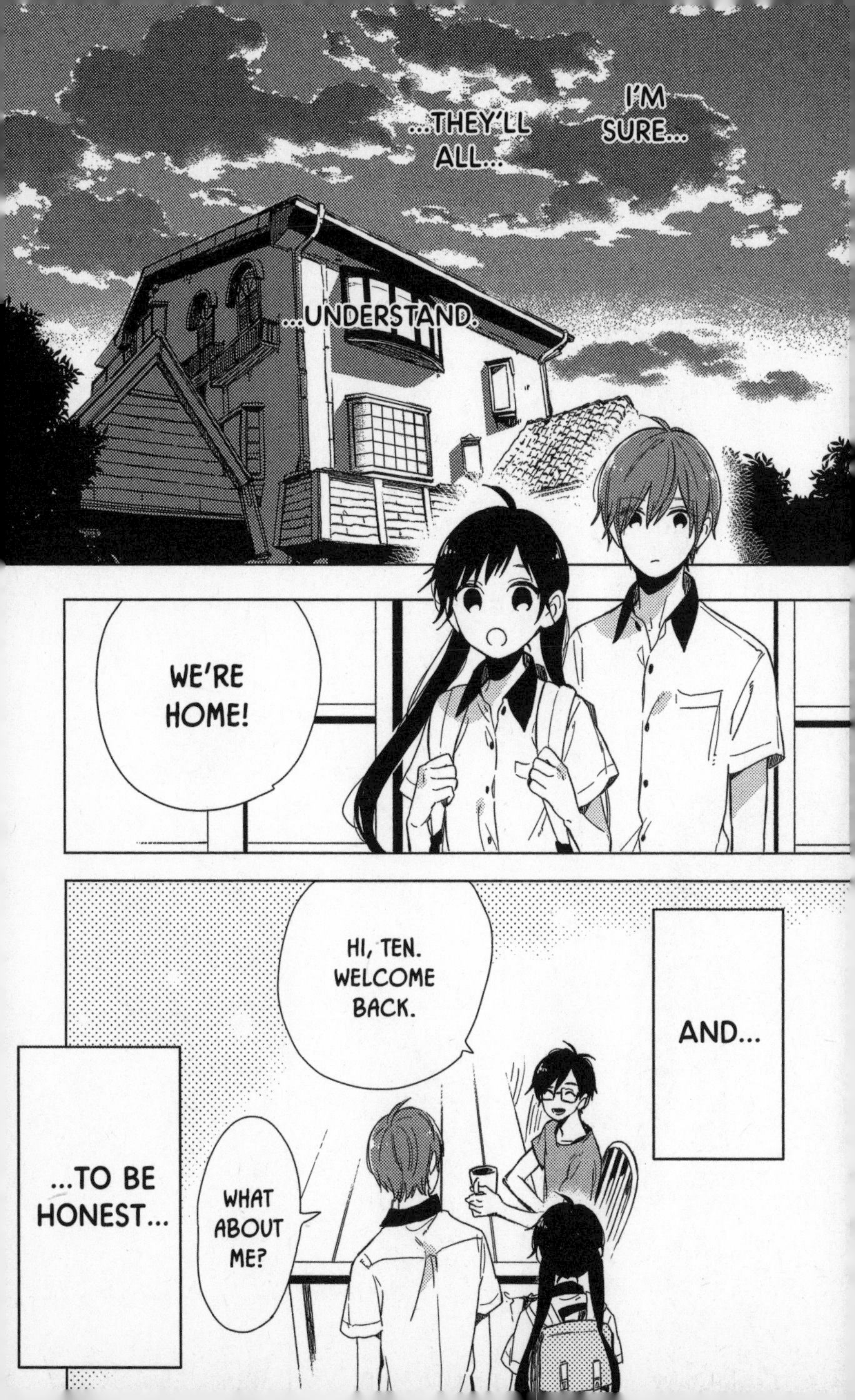
I'M SURE...
...THEY'LL ALL...
...UNDERSTAND.
WE'RE HOME!
AND...
HI, TEN. WELCOME BACK.
WHAT ABOUT ME?
...TO BE HONEST...

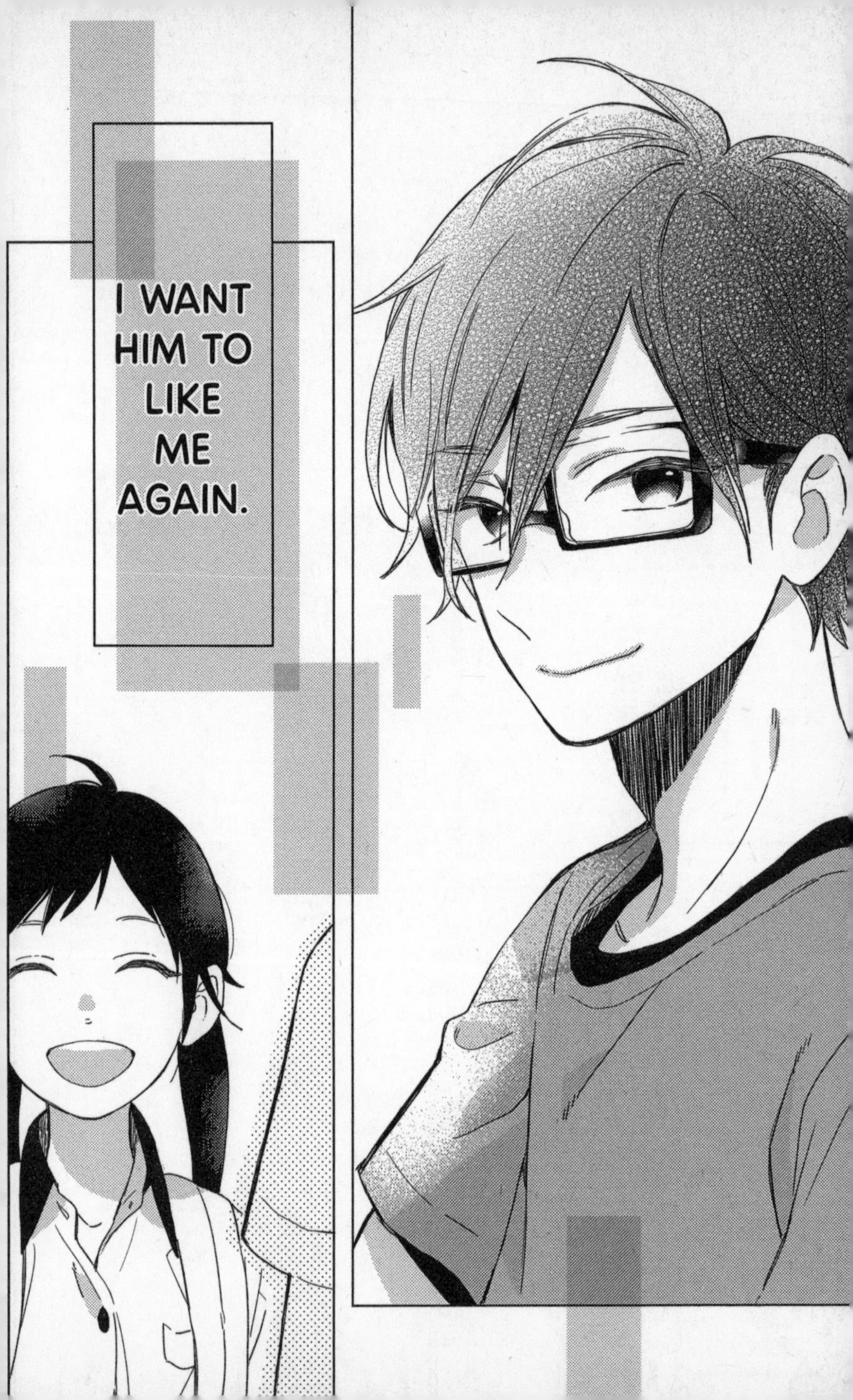
I WANT HIM TO LIKE ME AGAIN.

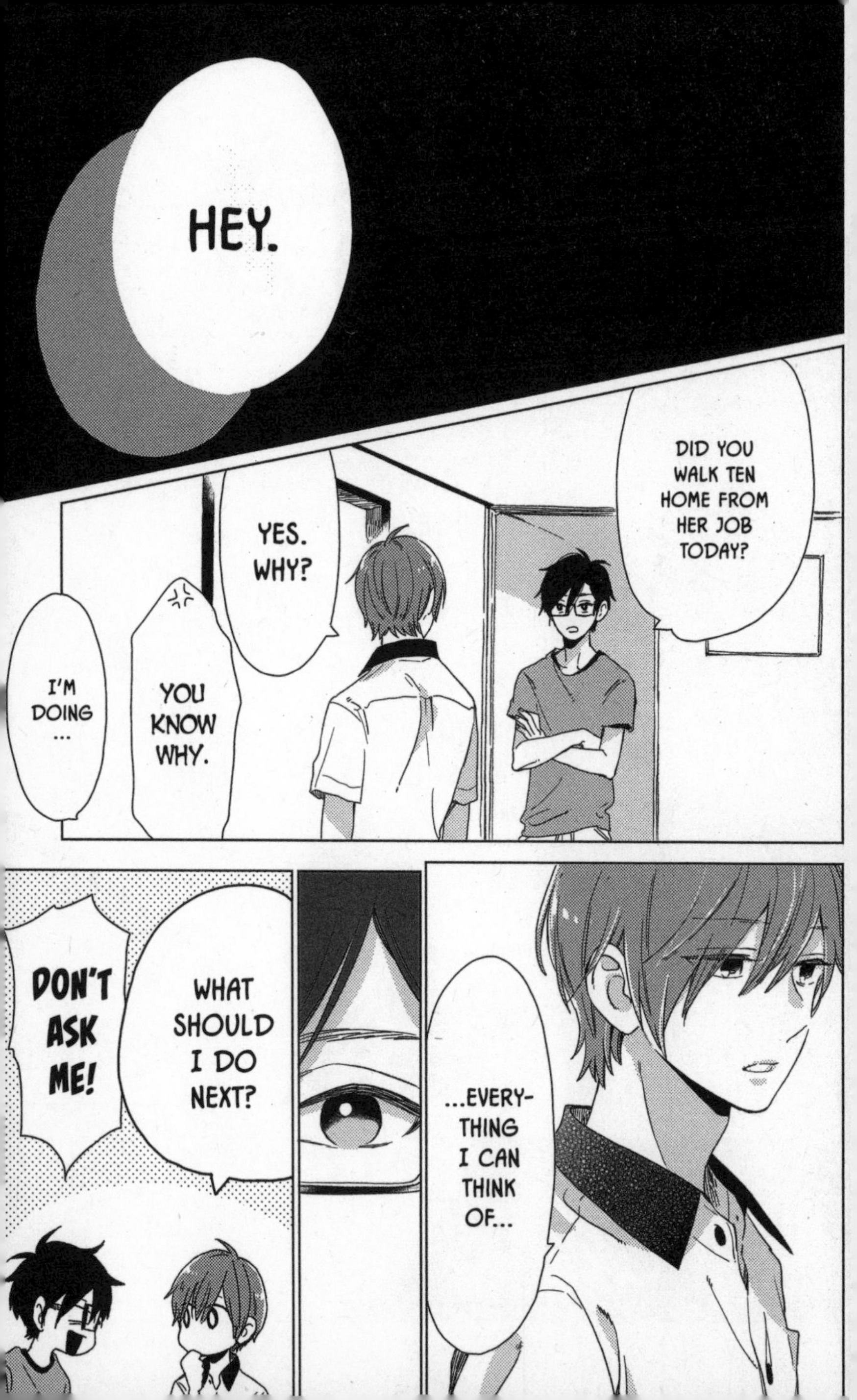
HEY.
DID YOU WALK TEN HOME FROM HER JOB TODAY?
YES. WHY?
YOU KNOW WHY.
I'M DOING ...
...EVERY-THING I CAN THINK OF...
WHAT SHOULD I DO NEXT?
DON'T ASK ME!

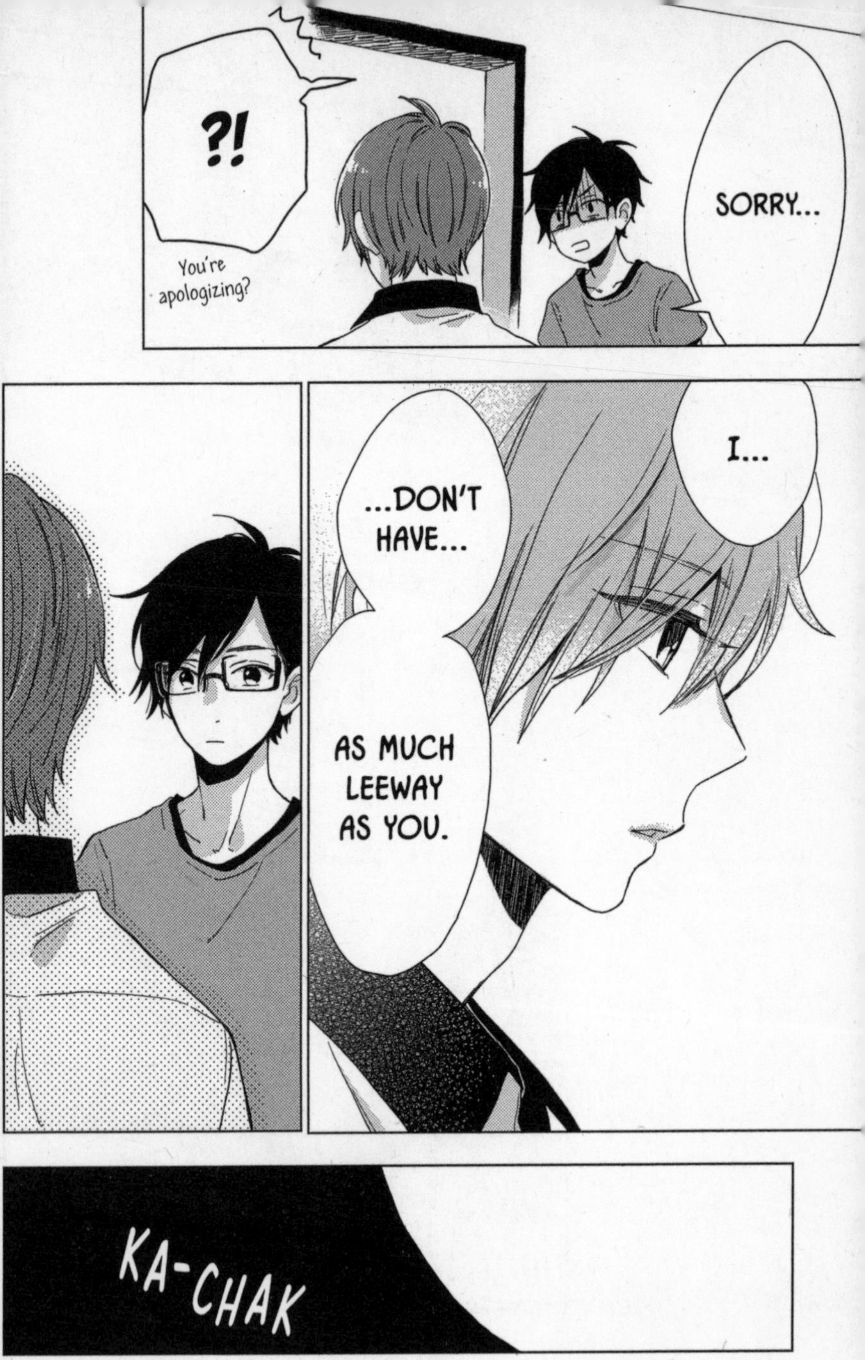
SORRY...
?!
You're apologizing?
I...
...DON'T HAVE...
AS MUCH LEEWAY AS YOU.
KA-CHAK

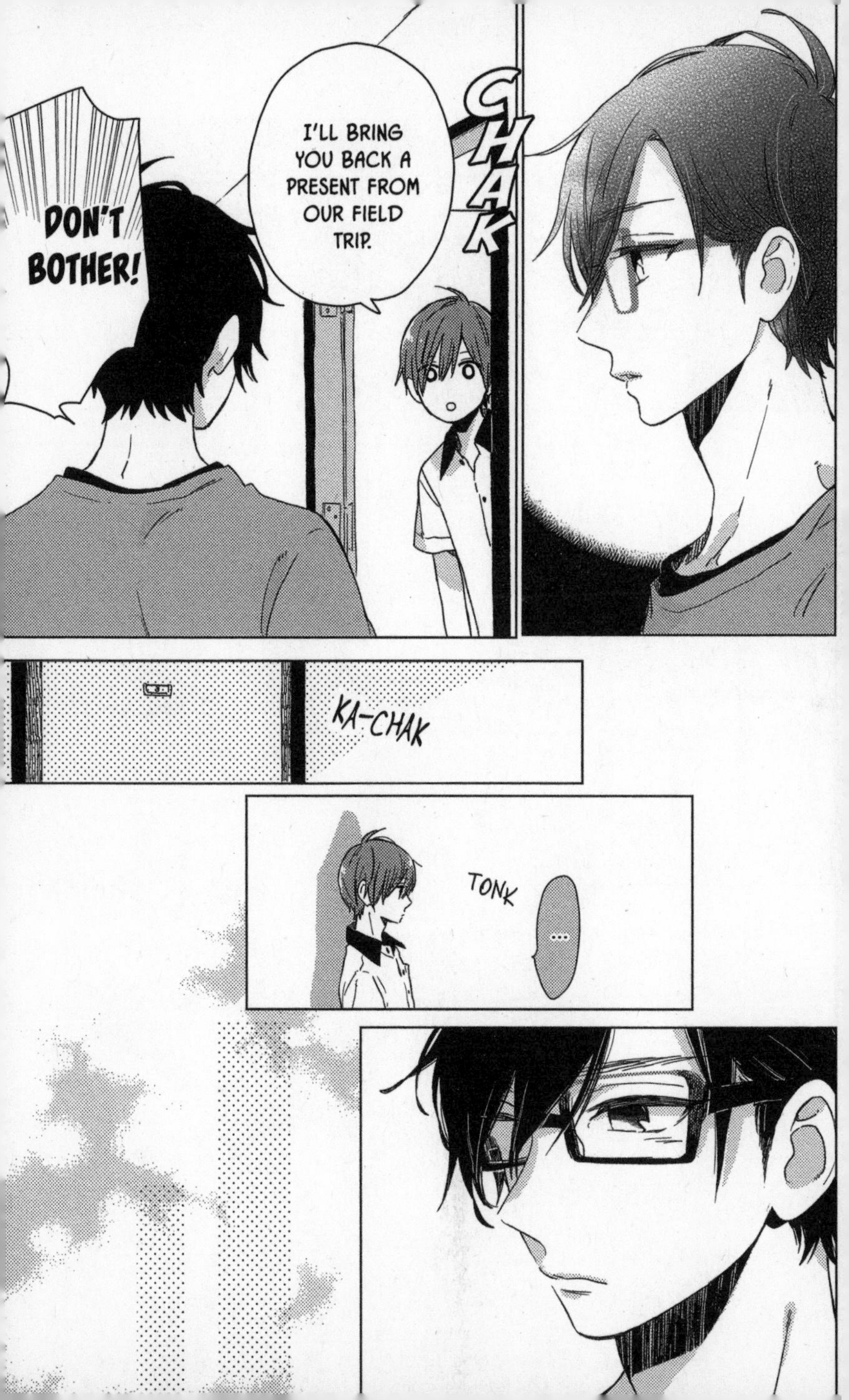
CHAK
I'LL BRING YOU BACK A PRESENT FROM OUR FIELD TRIP.
DON'T BOTHER!
KA-CHAK
TONK
...

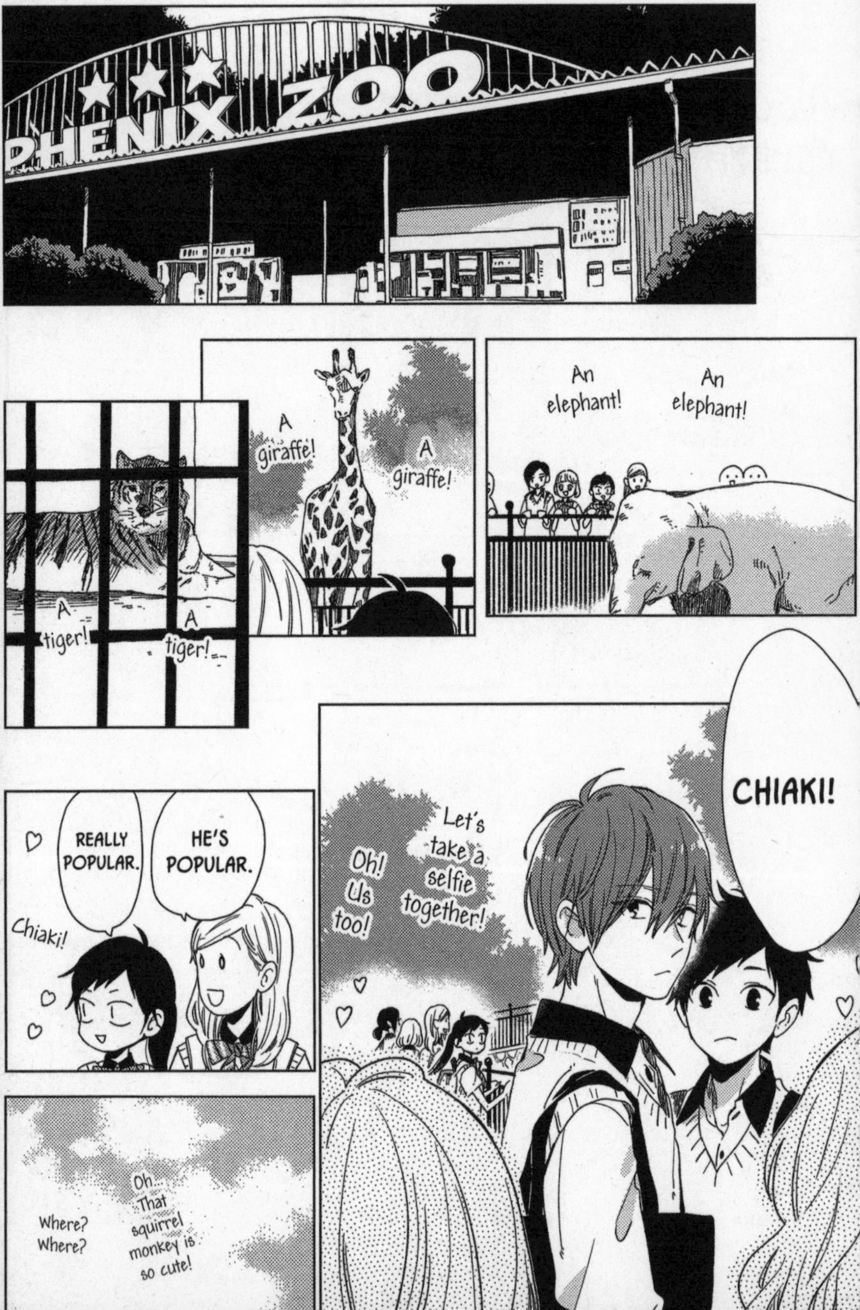
PHENIX ZOO
An elephant!
An elephant!
A giraffe!
A giraffe!
A tiger!
A tiger!
CHIAKI!
Let's take a selfie together!
Oh! Us too!
HE'S POPULAR.
REALLY POPULAR.
Chiaki!
Oh.. That squirrel monkey is so cute!
Where? Where?

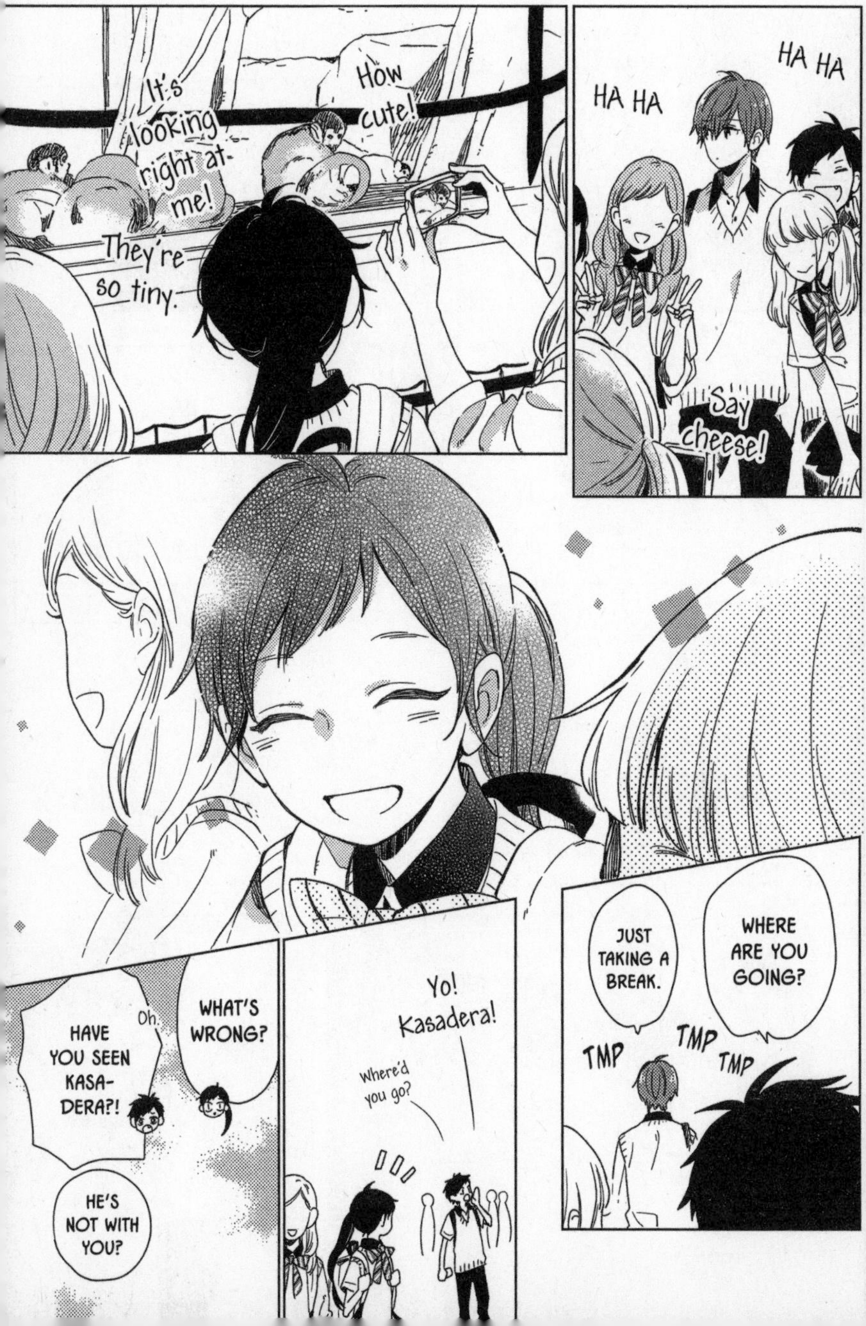
HA HA
HA HA
Say cheese!
How cute!
It's looking right at me!
They're so tiny.
WHERE ARE YOU GOING?
JUST TAKING A BREAK.
TMP
TMP
TMP
Yo! Kasadera!
Where'd you go?
WHAT'S WRONG?
Oh.
HAVE YOU SEEN KASA-DERA?!
HE'S NOT WITH YOU?

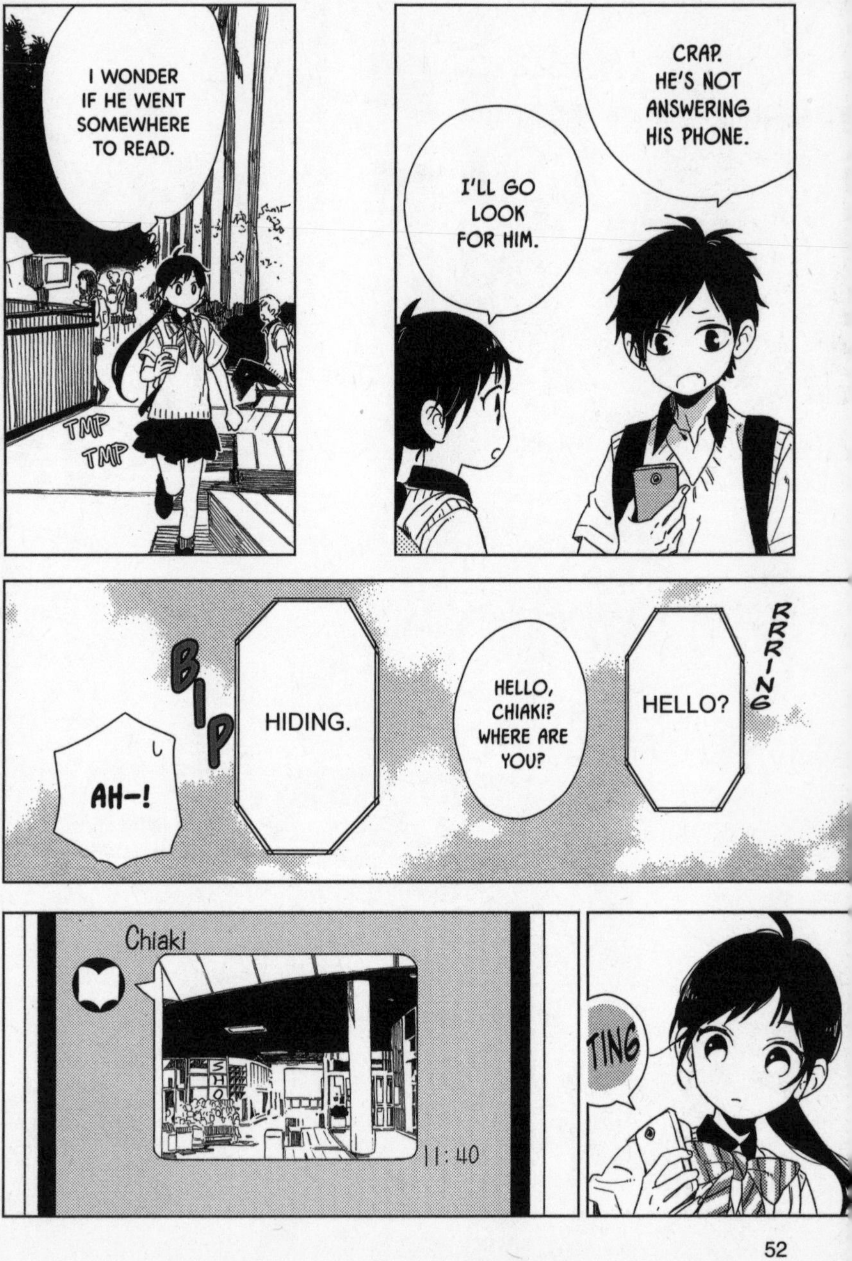
CRAP. HE'S NOT ANSWERING HIS PHONE.
I'LL GO LOOK FOR HIM.
I WONDER IF HE WENT SOMEWHERE TO READ.
TMP TMP
RRRING
HELLO?
HELLO, CHIAKI? WHERE ARE YOU?
HIDING.
BIP
AH-!
TING
Chiaki
11:40

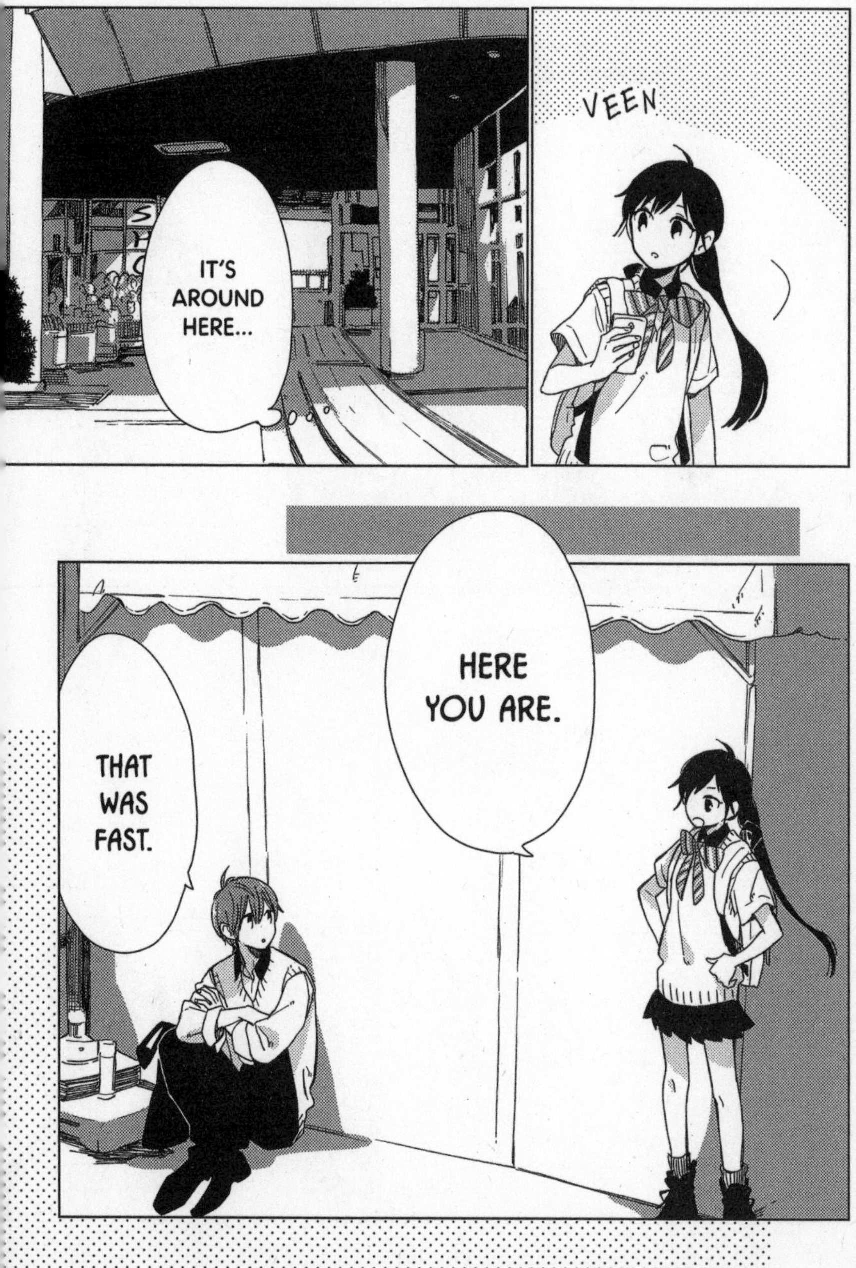
VEEN
IT'S AROUND HERE...
HERE YOU ARE.
THAT WAS FAST.

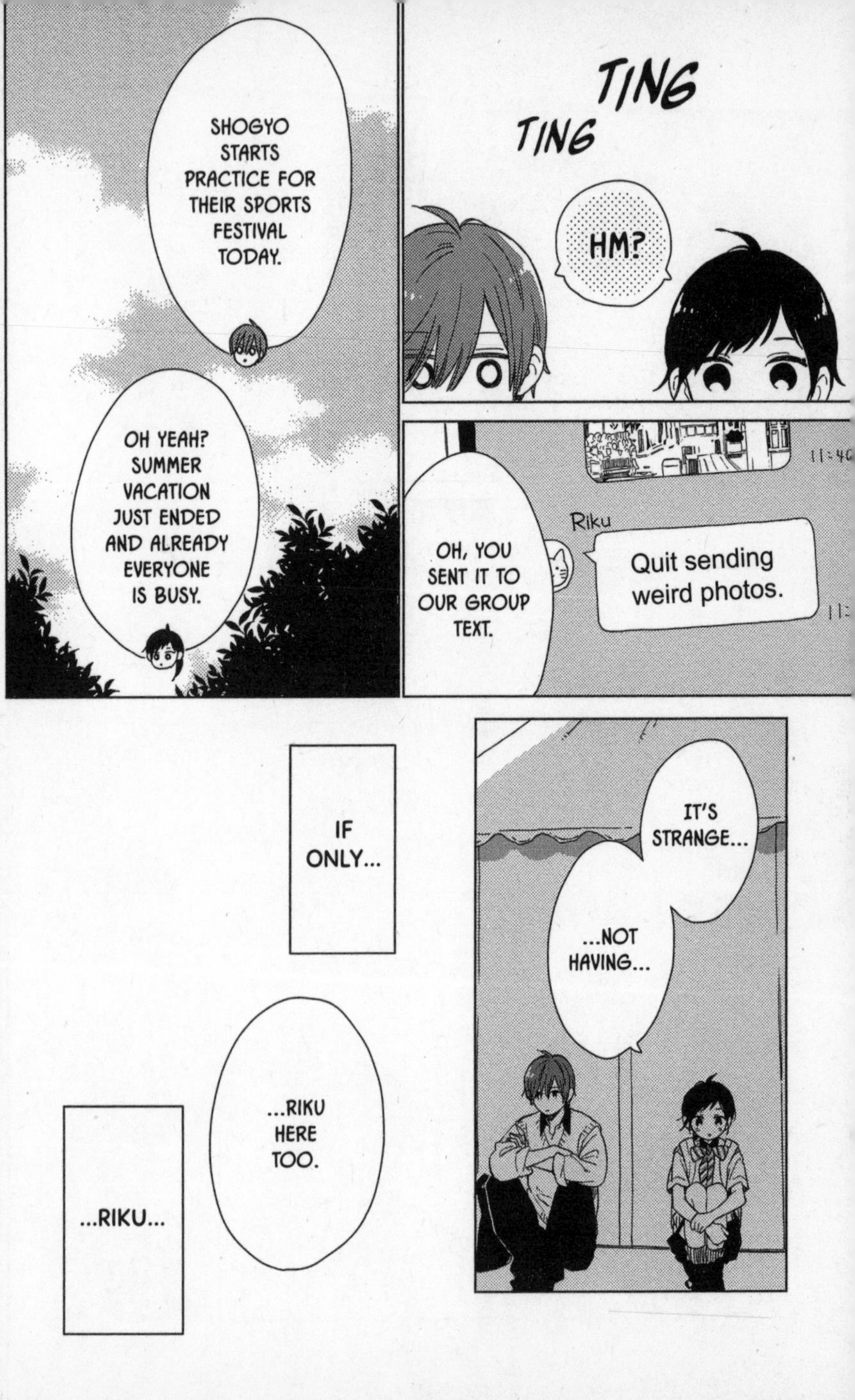
TING
TING
HM?
Riku
Quit sending weird photos.
OH, YOU SENT IT TO OUR GROUP TEXT.
SHOGYO STARTS PRACTICE FOR THEIR SPORTS FESTIVAL TODAY.
OH YEAH? SUMMER VACATION JUST ENDED AND ALREADY EVERYONE IS BUSY.
IT'S STRANGE...
...NOT HAVING...
IF ONLY...
...RIKU HERE TOO.
...RIKU...

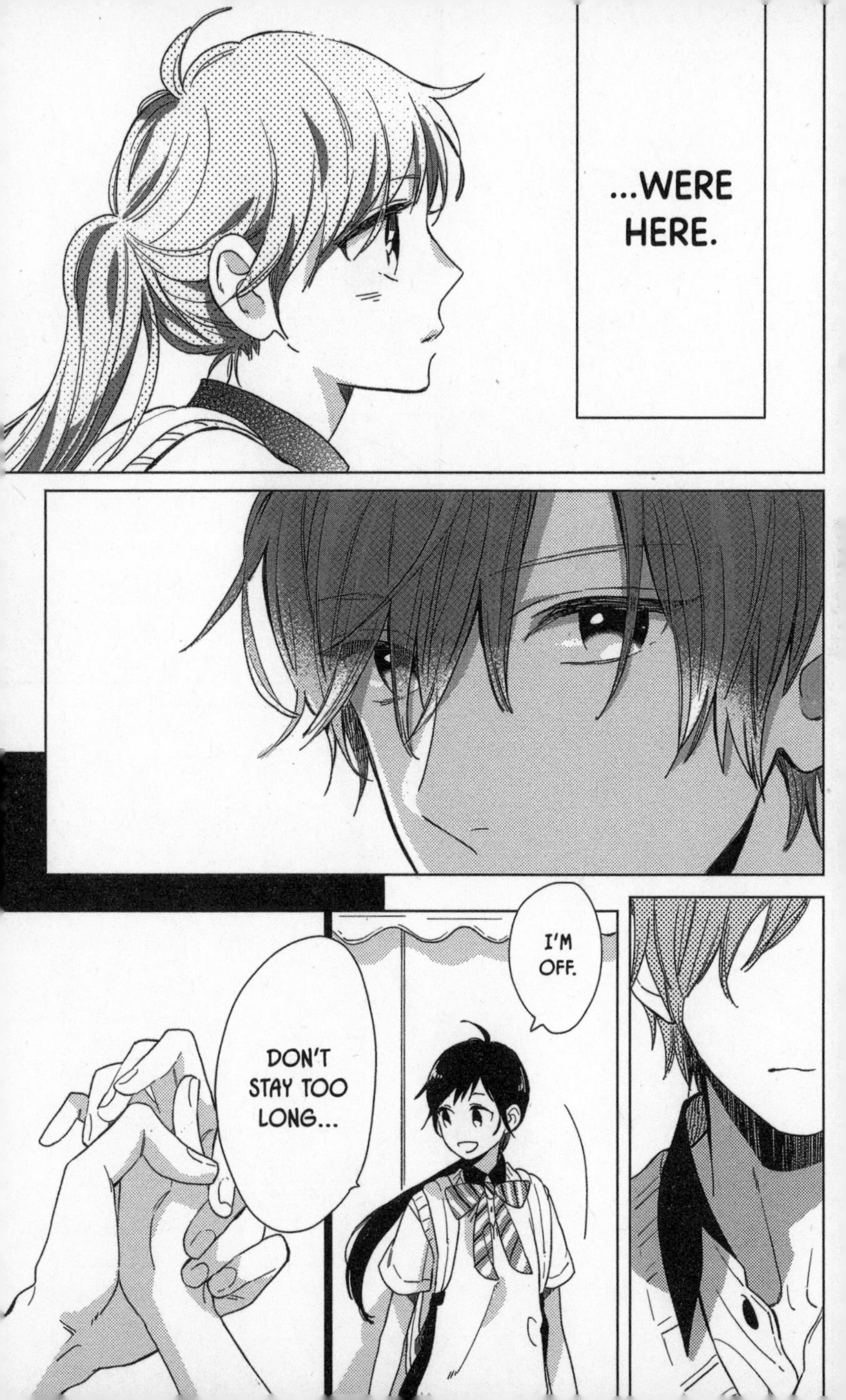
...WERE HERE.
I'M OFF.
DON'T STAY TOO LONG...

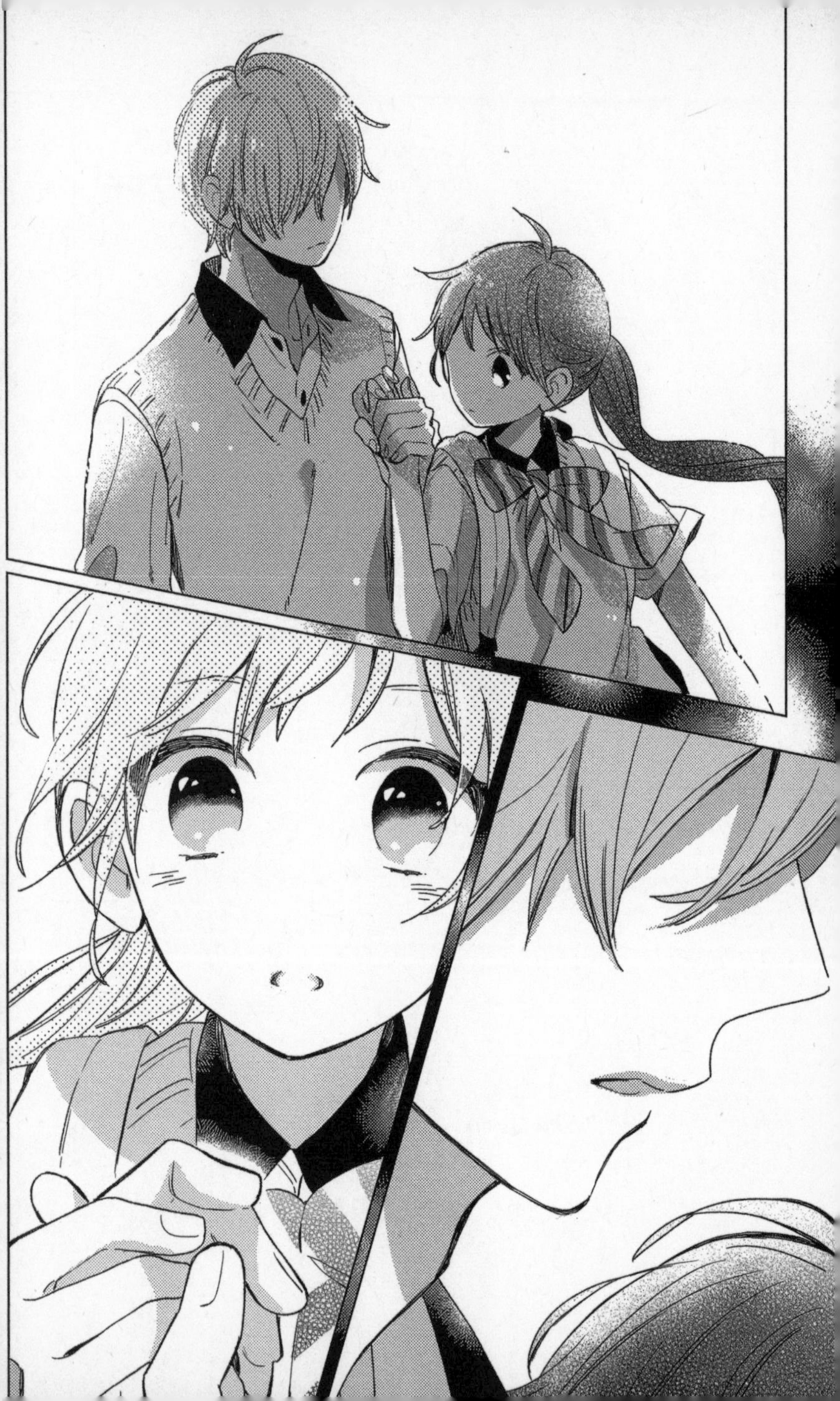

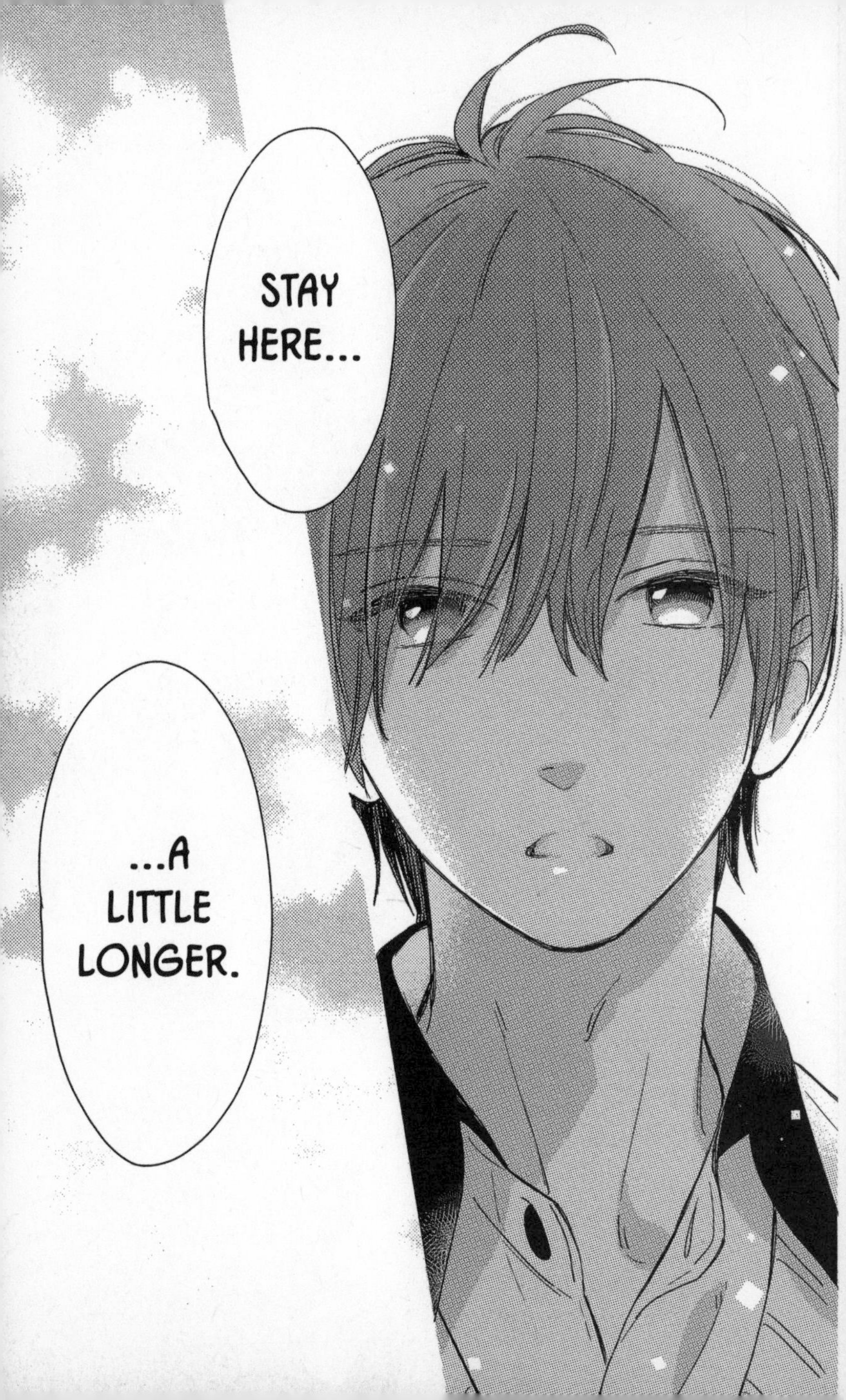
STAY HERE...
...A LITTLE LONGER.

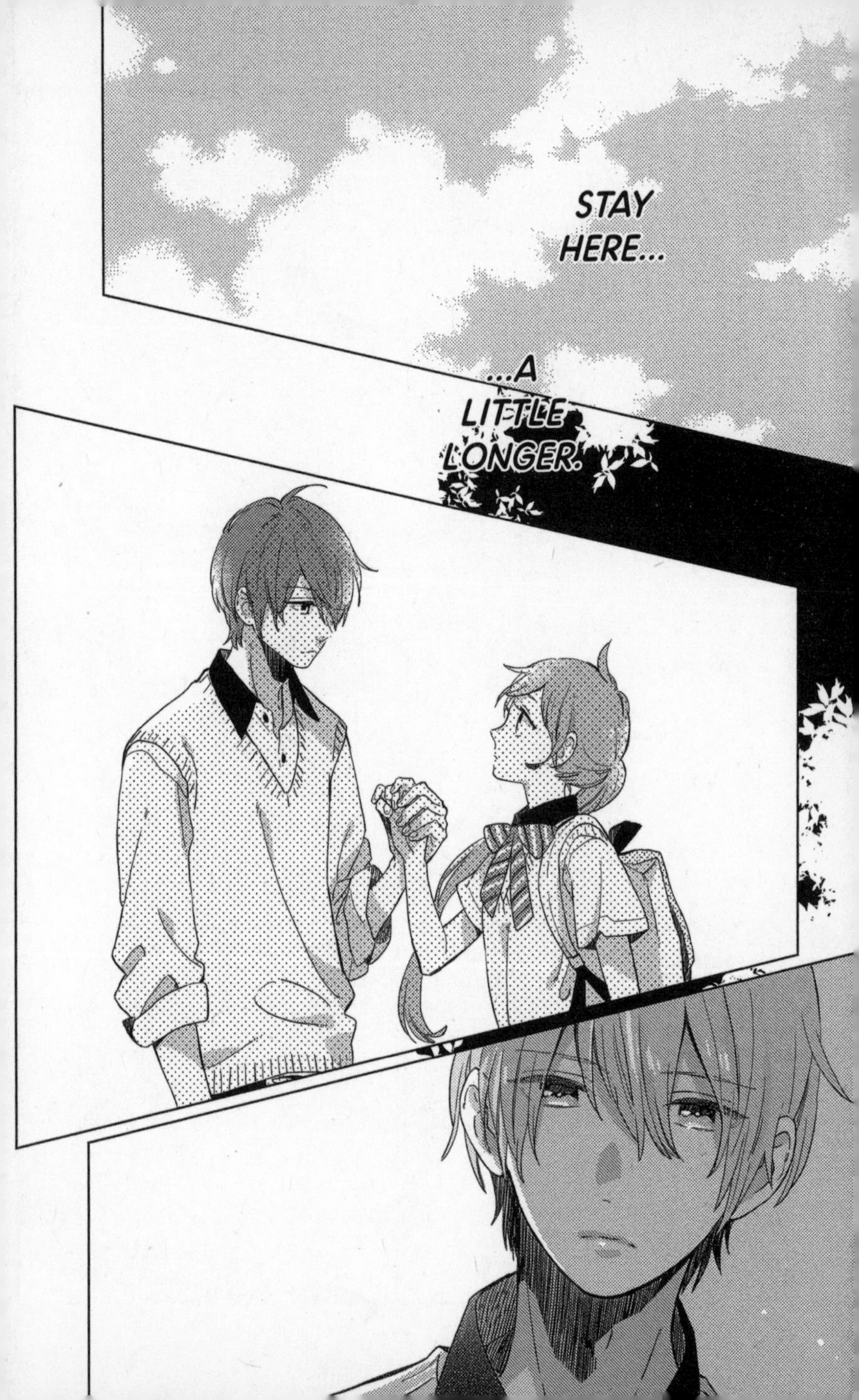
STAY HERE...
...A LITTLE LONGER.

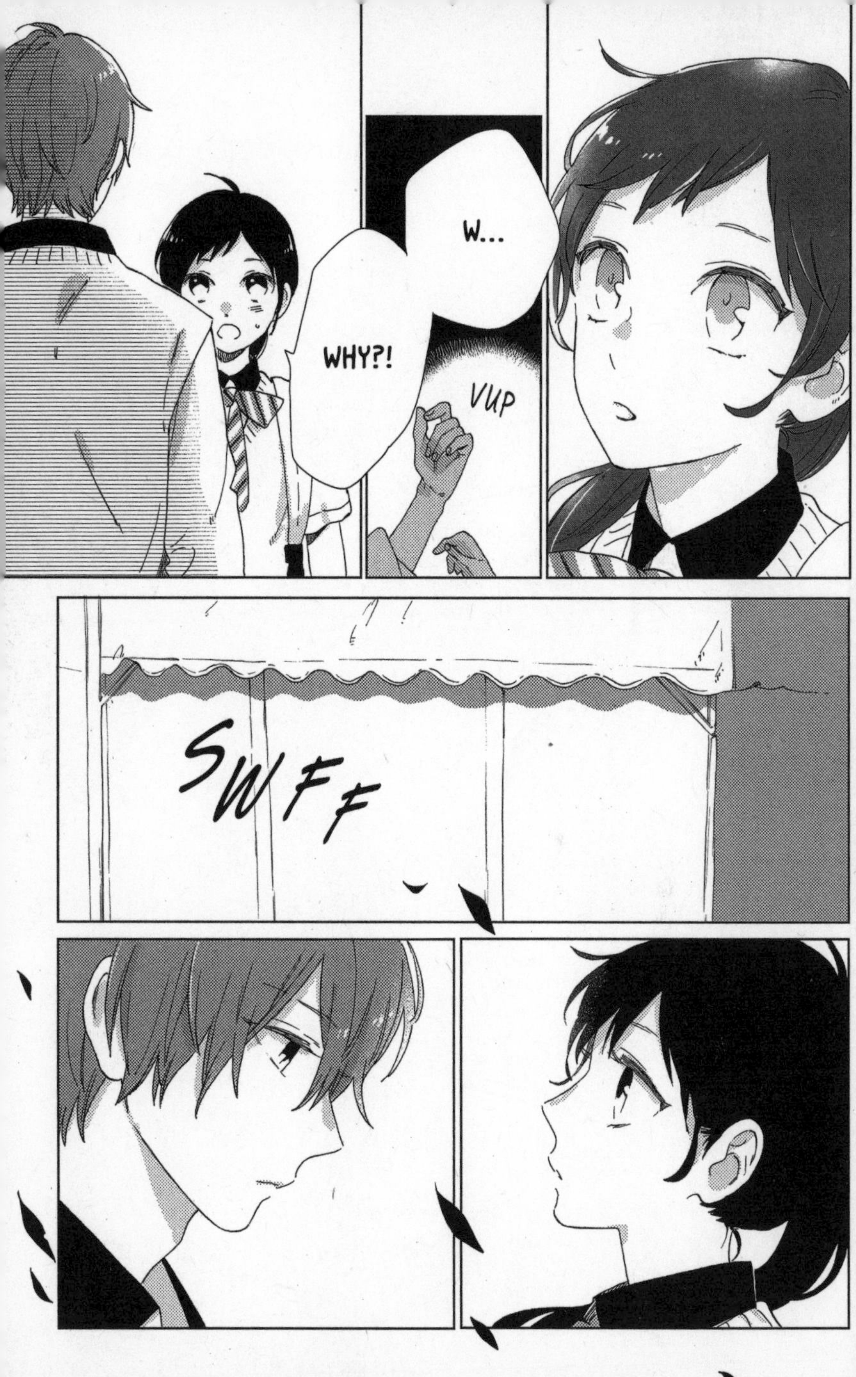
W...
VUP
WHY?!
SWFF

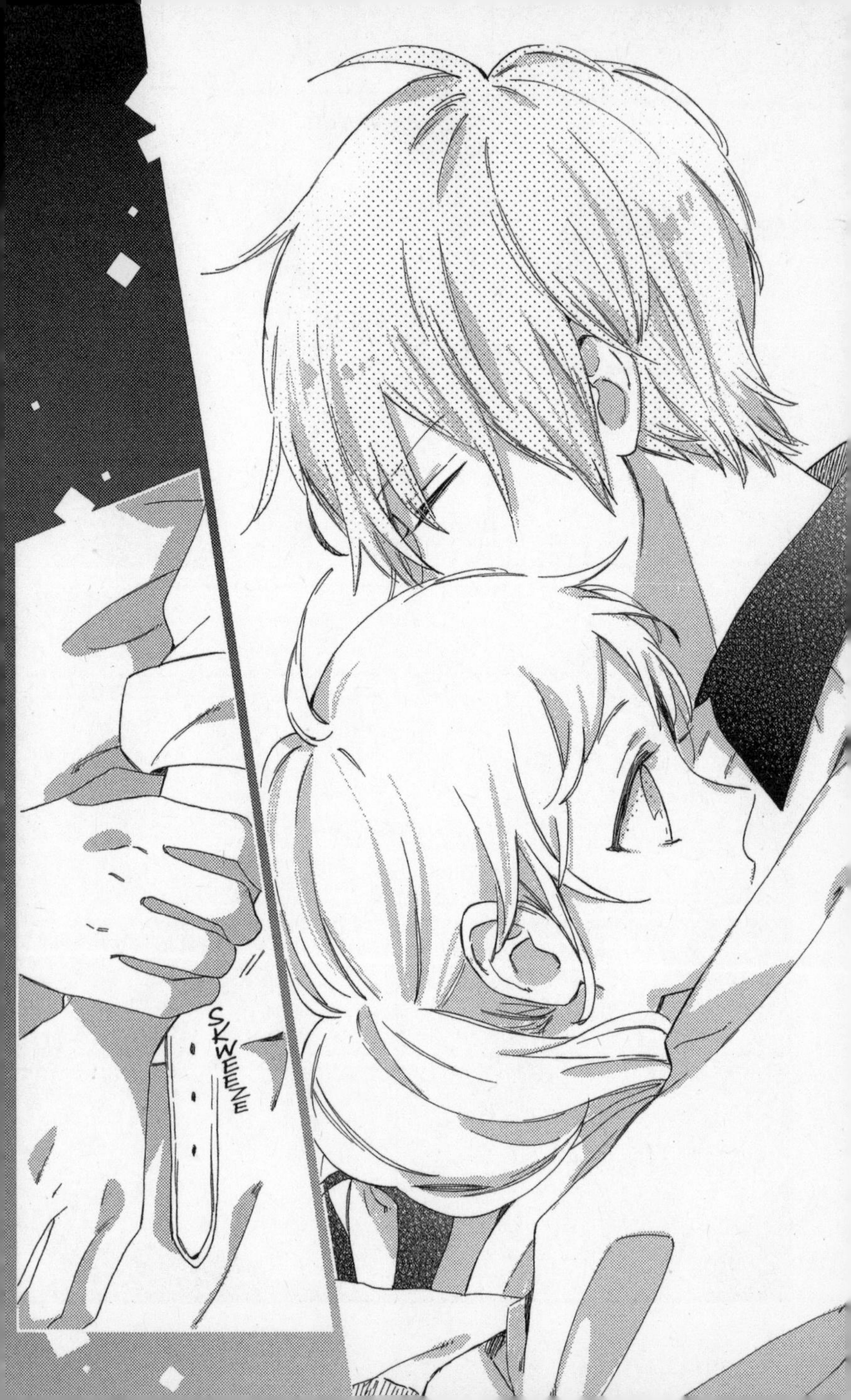
SKWEEZE

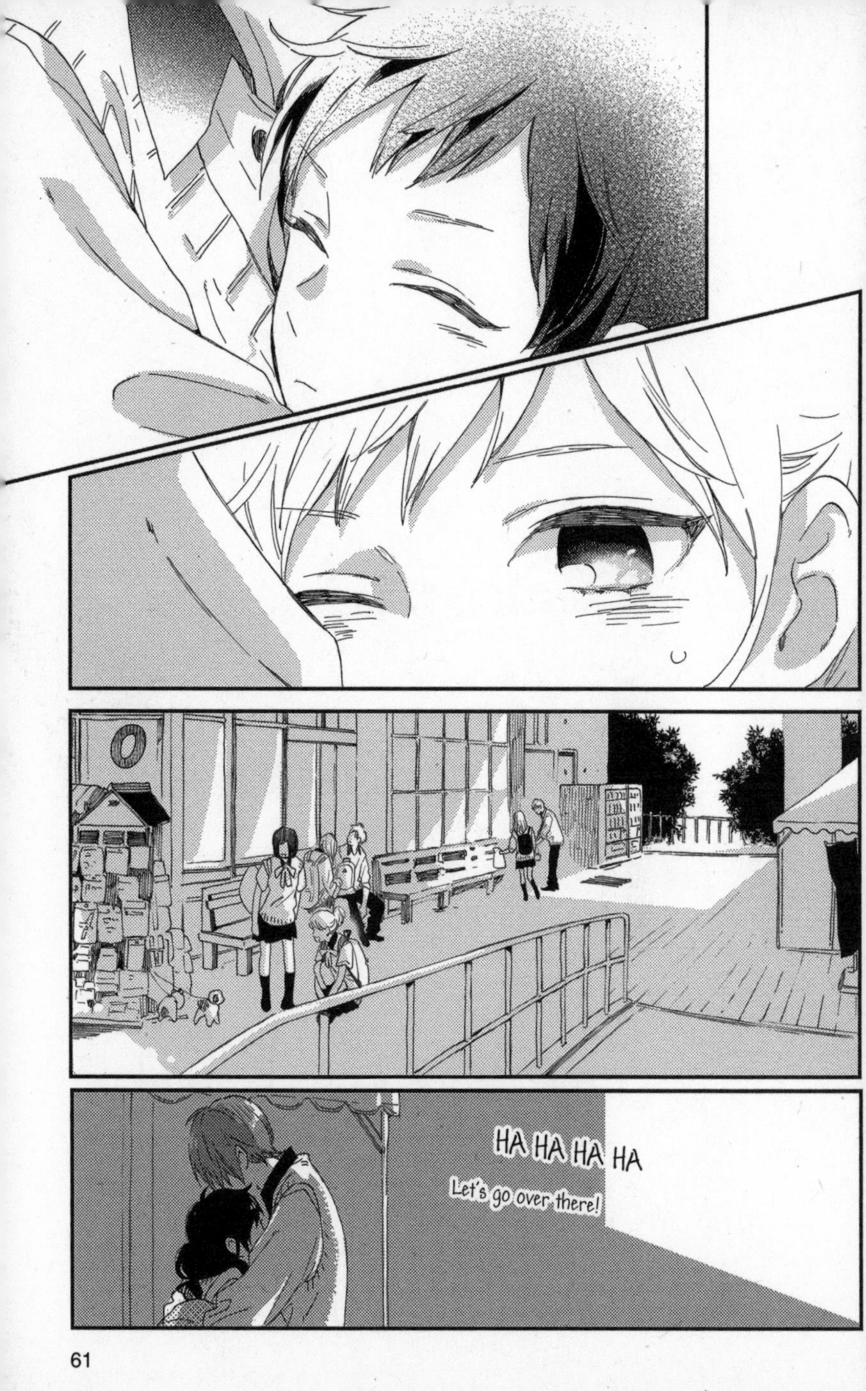
HA HA HA HA
Let's go over there!

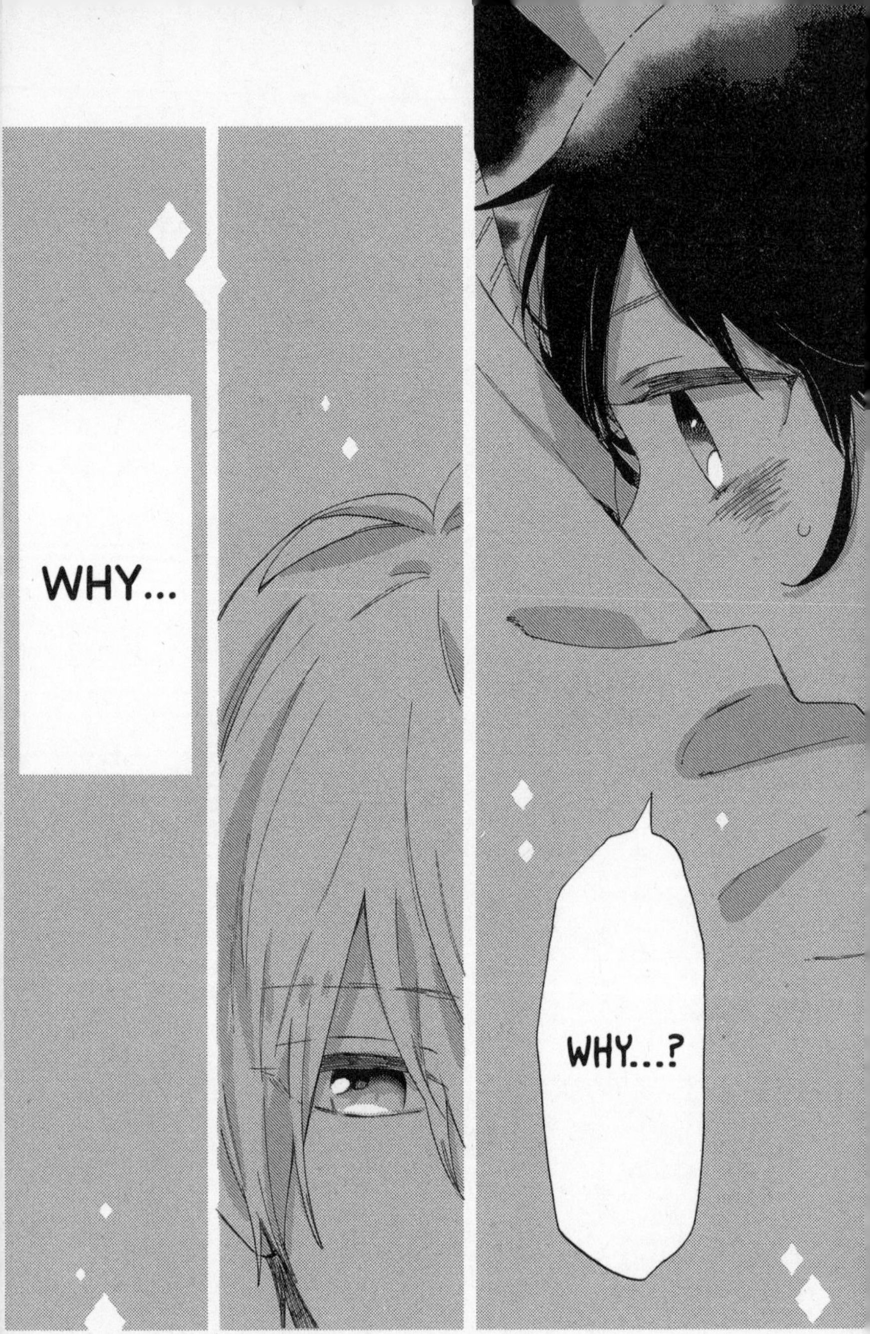
WHY...?
WHY...

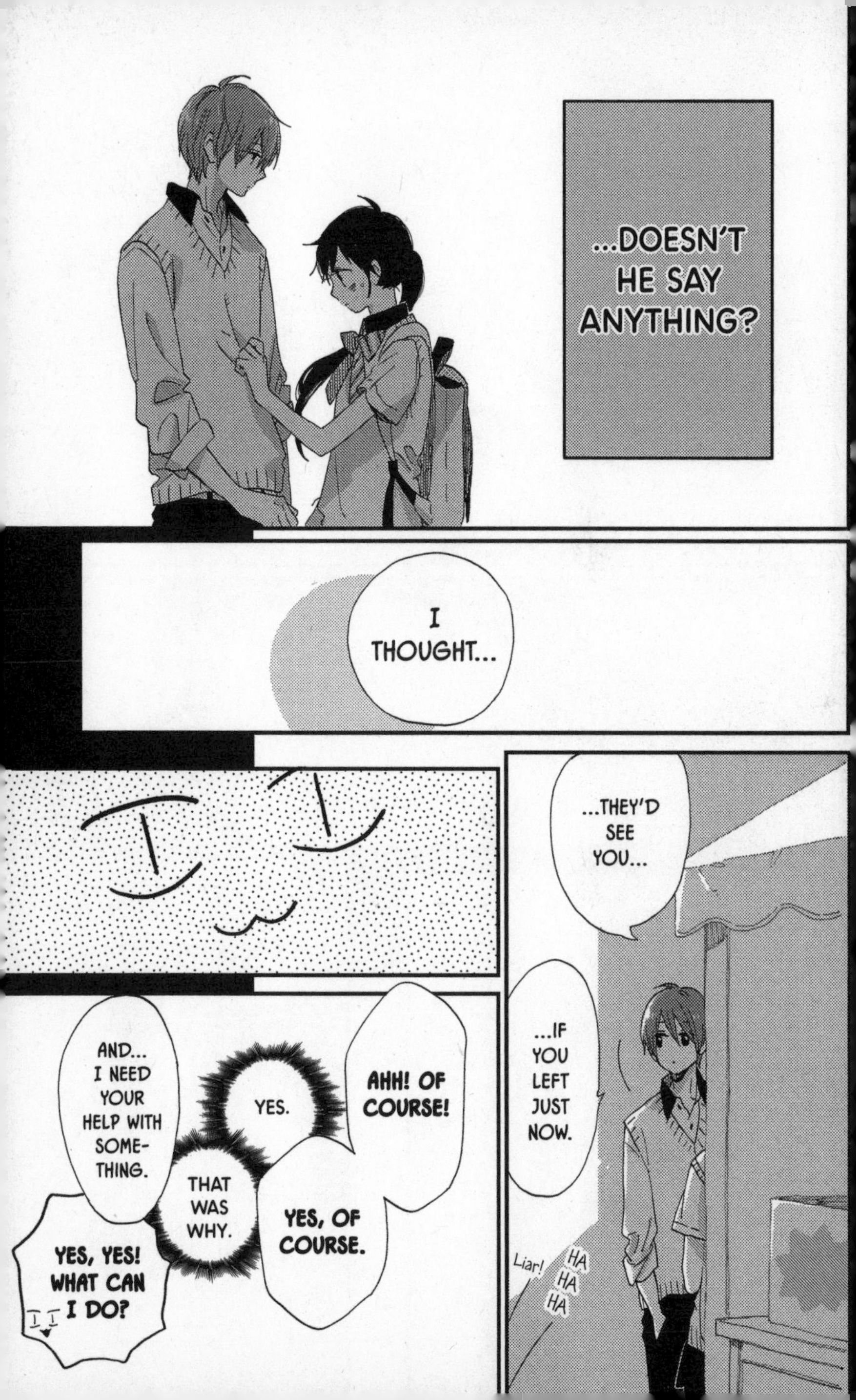
...DOESN'T HE SAY ANYTHING?
I THOUGHT...
...THEY'D SEE YOU...
...IF YOU LEFT JUST NOW.
Liar!
HA HA HA
AHH! OF COURSE!
YES.
AND... I NEED YOUR HELP WITH SOME-THING.
YES, OF COURSE.
THAT WAS WHY.
YES, YES! WHAT CAN I DO?

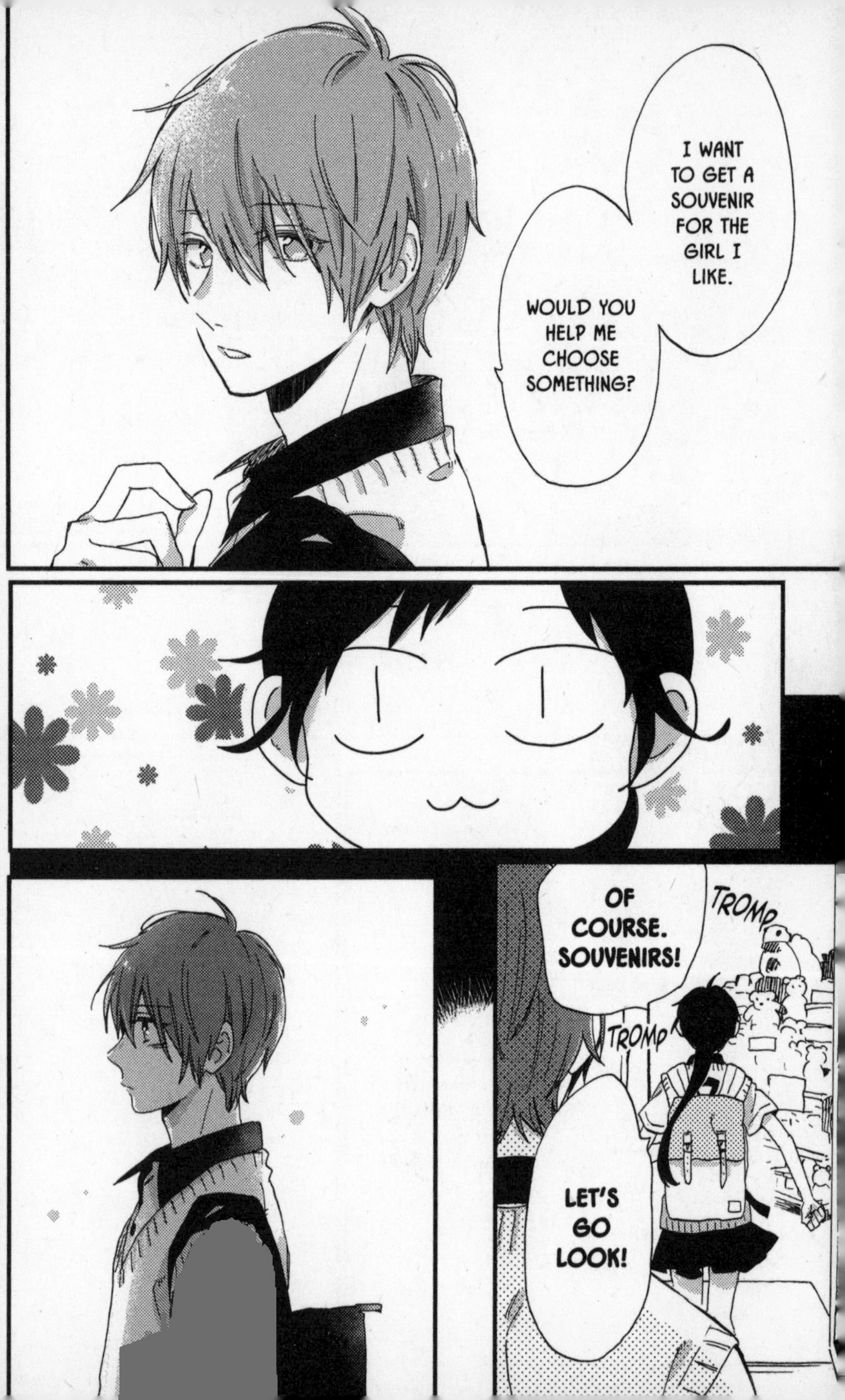
I WANT TO GET A SOUVENIR FOR THE GIRL I LIKE.
WOULD YOU HELP ME CHOOSE SOMETHING?
OF COURSE. SOUVENIRS!
TROMP
TROMP
LET'S GO LOOK!

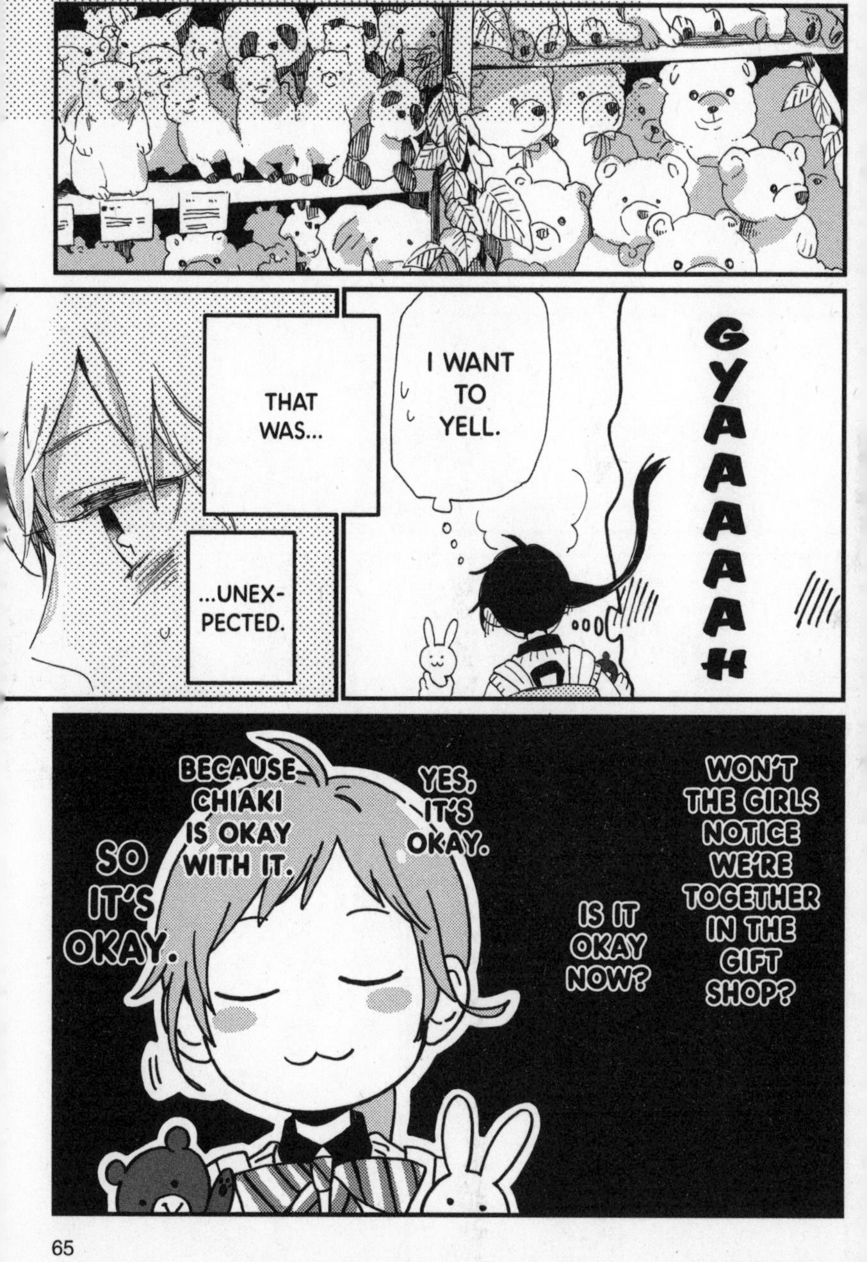
GYAAAAAAH
I WANT TO YELL.
THAT WAS...
...UNEXPECTED.
WON'T THE GIRLS NOTICE WE'RE TOGETHER IN THE GIFT SHOP?
IS IT OKAY NOW?
YES, IT'S OKAY.
BECAUSE CHIAKI IS OKAY WITH IT.
SO IT'S OKAY.

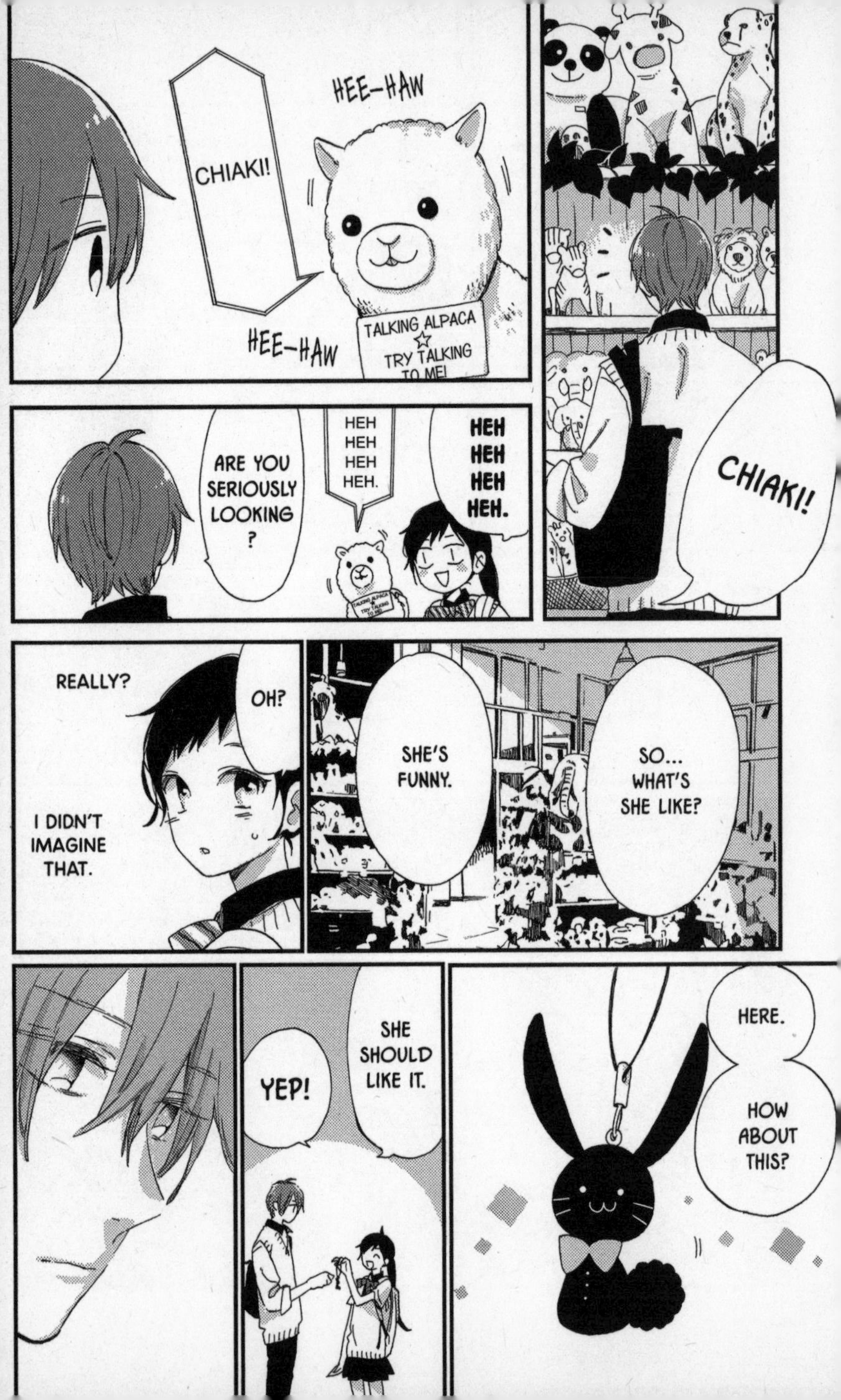
CHIAKI!
HEE-HAW
CHIAKI!
TALKING ALPACA ☆ TRY TALKING TO ME!
HEE-HAW
HEH HEH HEH HEH.
HEH HEH HEH HEH.
ARE YOU SERIOUSLY LOOKING?
SO... WHAT'S SHE LIKE?
SHE'S FUNNY.
OH?
REALLY?
I DIDN'T IMAGINE THAT.
HERE.
HOW ABOUT THIS?
SHE SHOULD LIKE IT.
YEP!

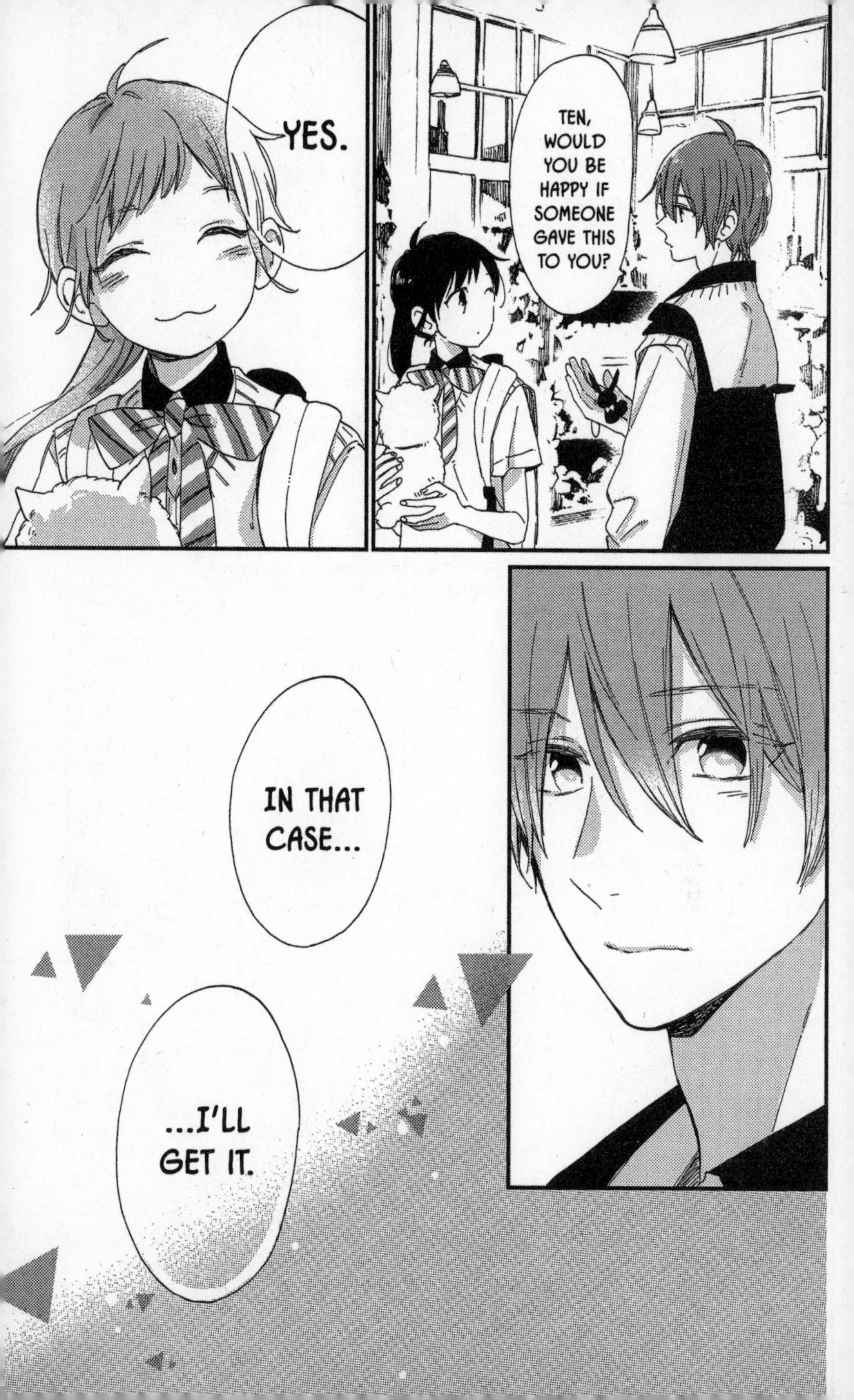
TEN, WOULD YOU BE HAPPY IF SOMEONE GAVE THIS TO YOU?
YES.
IN THAT CASE...
...I'LL GET IT.

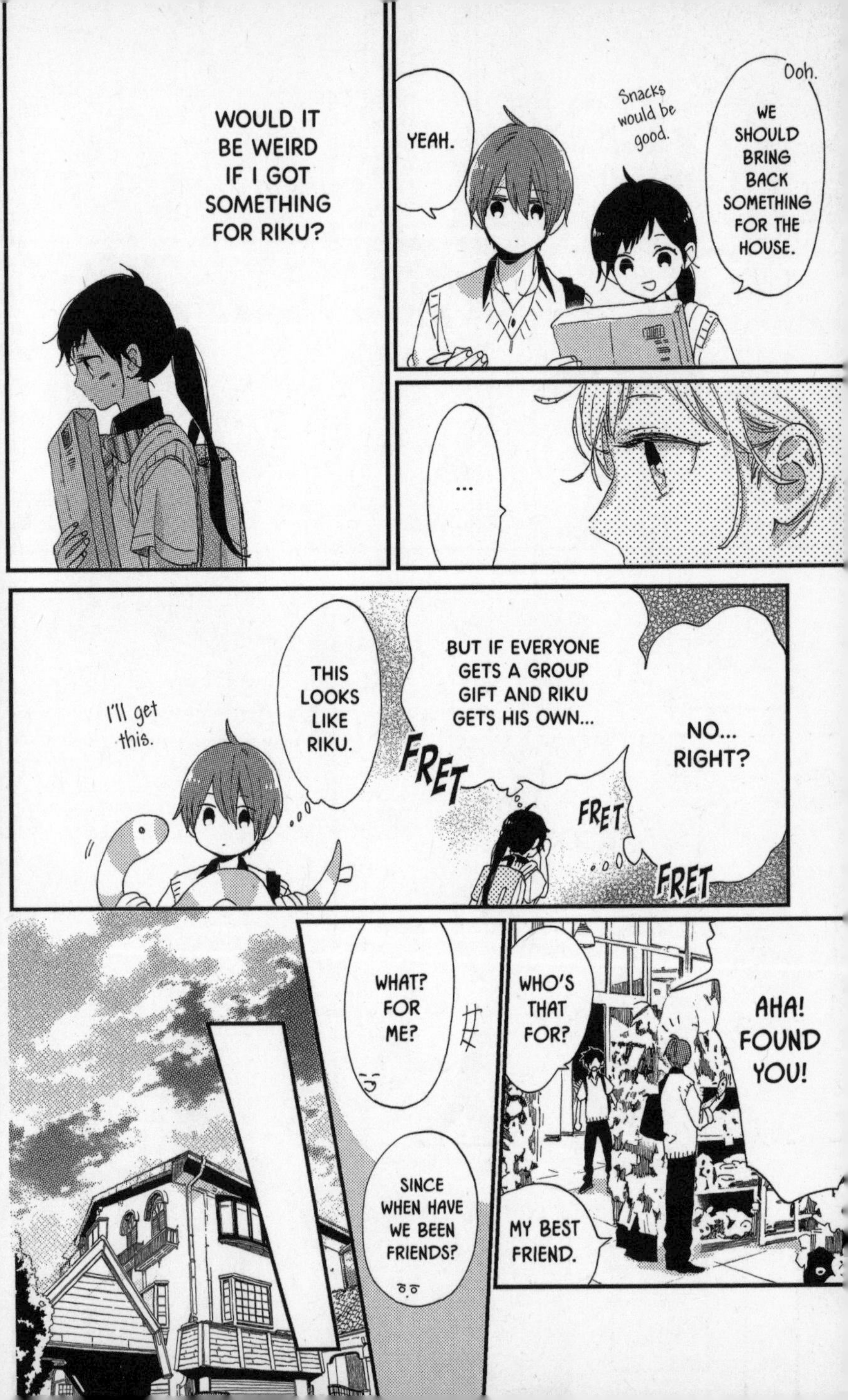
Ooh.
WE SHOULD BRING BACK SOMETHING FOR THE HOUSE.
Snacks would be good.
YEAH.
...
WOULD IT BE WEIRD IF I GOT SOMETHING FOR RIKU?
NO... RIGHT?
BUT IF EVERYONE GETS A GROUP GIFT AND RIKU GETS HIS OWN...
FRET
FRET
FRET
THIS LOOKS LIKE RIKU.
I'll get this.
AHA! FOUND YOU!
WHO'S THAT FOR?
MY BEST FRIEND.
WHAT? FOR ME?
SINCE WHEN HAVE WE BEEN FRIENDS?

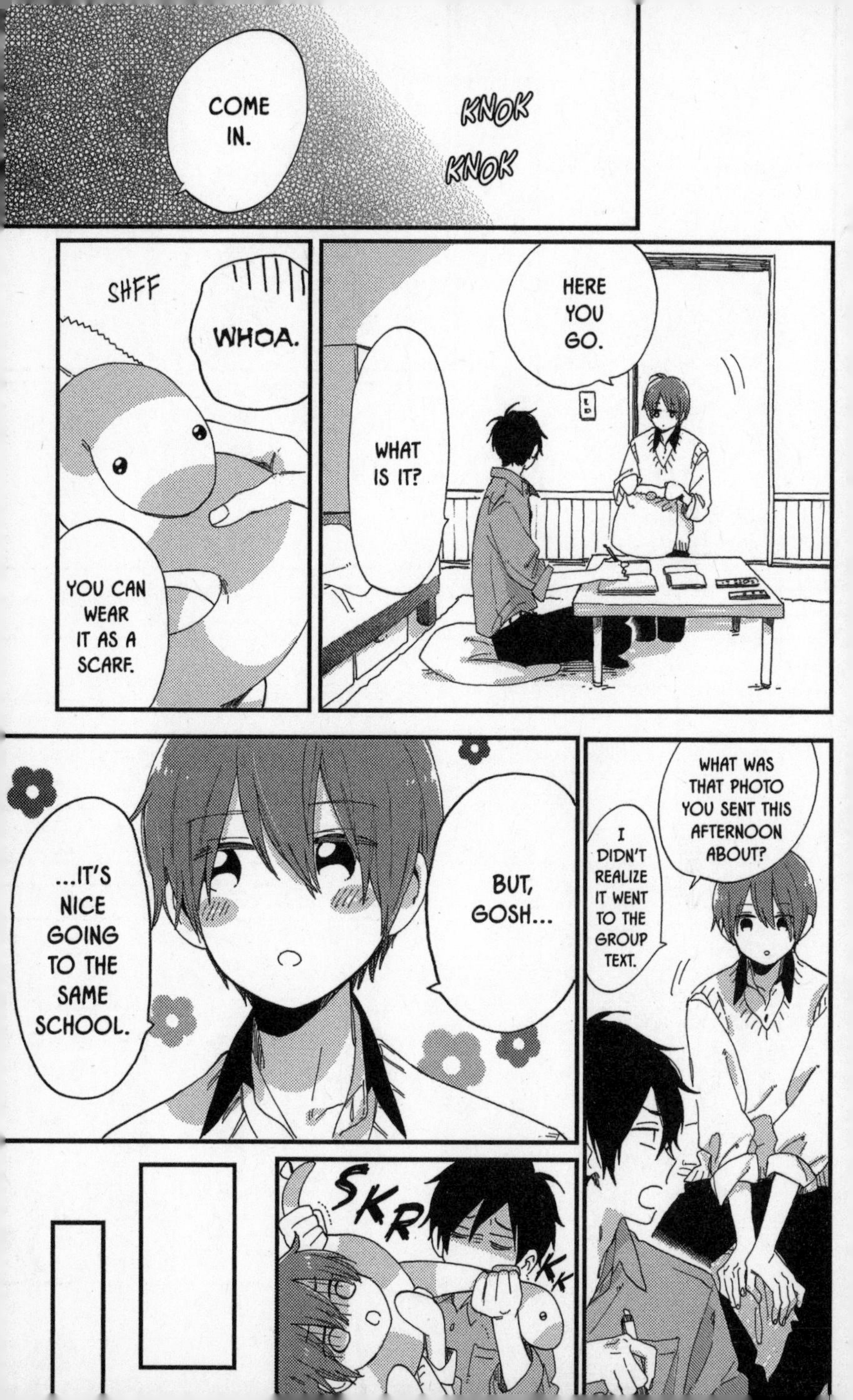
KNOK
KNOK
COME IN.
HERE YOU GO.
WHAT IS IT?
WHOA.
SHFF
YOU CAN WEAR IT AS A SCARF.
WHAT WAS THAT PHOTO YOU SENT THIS AFTERNOON ABOUT?
I DIDN'T REALIZE IT WENT TO THE GROUP TEXT.
BUT, GOSH...
...IT'S NICE GOING TO THE SAME SCHOOL.
SKR
KK

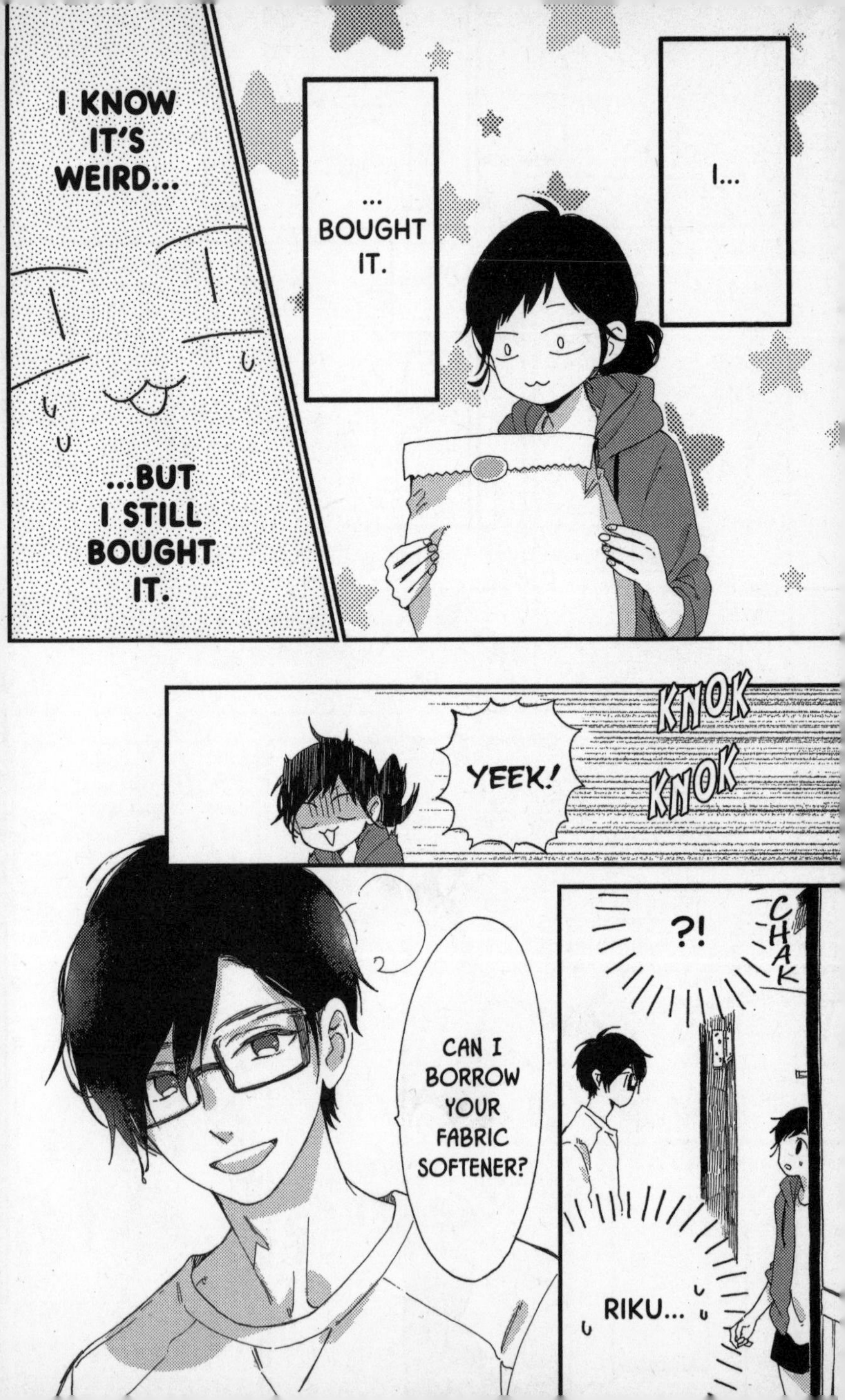
I...
...BOUGHT IT.
I KNOW IT'S WEIRD...
...BUT I STILL BOUGHT IT.
KNOK KNOK
YEEK!
CHAK
?!
RIKU...
CAN I BORROW YOUR FABRIC SOFTENER?

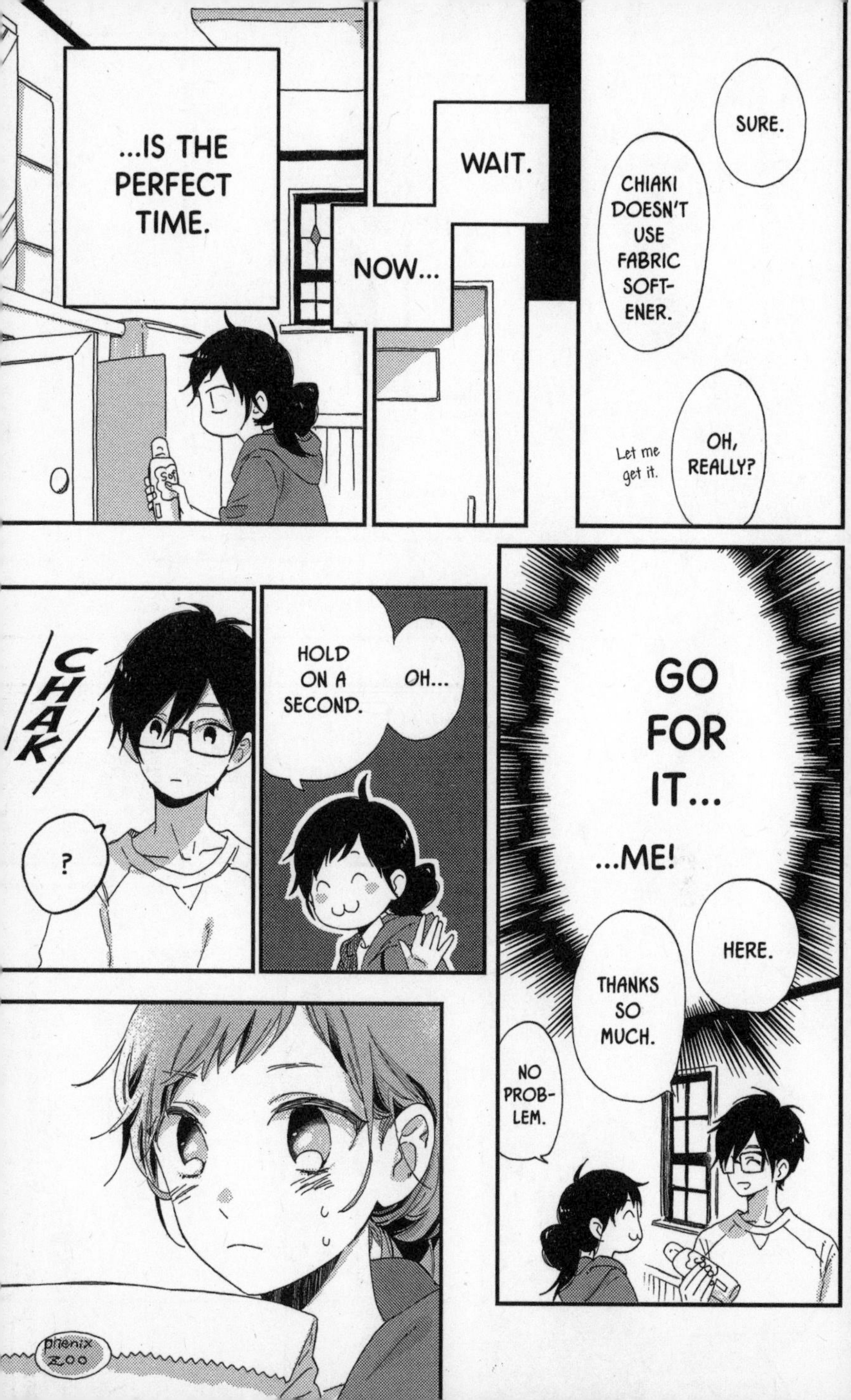
SURE.
CHIAKI DOESN'T USE FABRIC SOFT-ENER.
OH, REALLY?
Let me get it.
WAIT.
NOW...
...IS THE PERFECT TIME.
GO FOR IT...
...ME!
HERE.
THANKS SO MUCH.
NO PROB-LEM.
OH...
HOLD ON A SECOND.
CHAK
?
phenix zoo

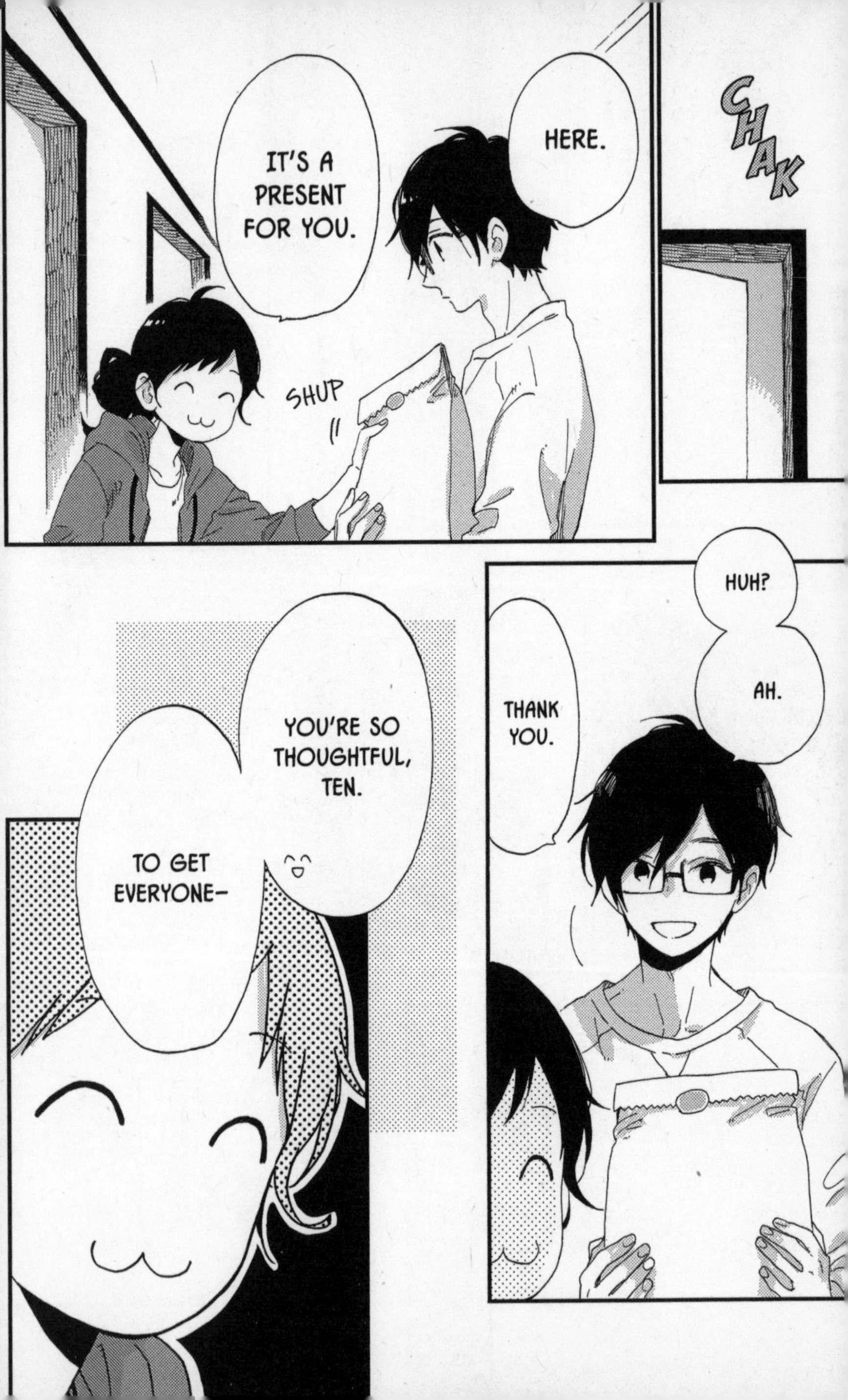
CHAK
HERE.
IT'S A PRESENT FOR YOU.
SHUP
HUH?
AH.
THANK YOU.
YOU'RE SO THOUGHTFUL, TEN.
TO GET EVERYONE-

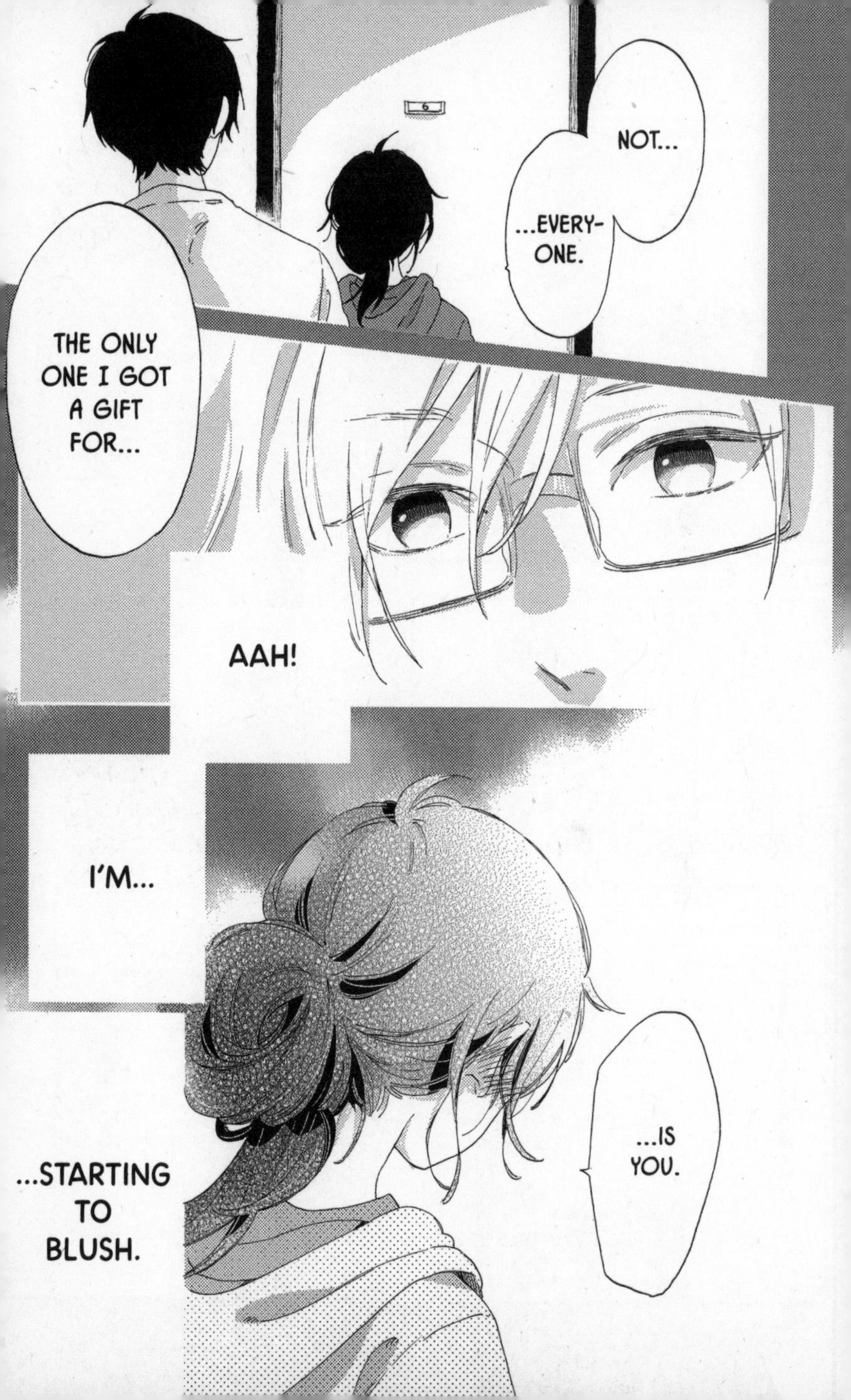
NOT...
...EVERY-ONE.
THE ONLY ONE I GOT A GIFT FOR...
AAH!
...IS YOU.
I'M...
...STARTING TO BLUSH.

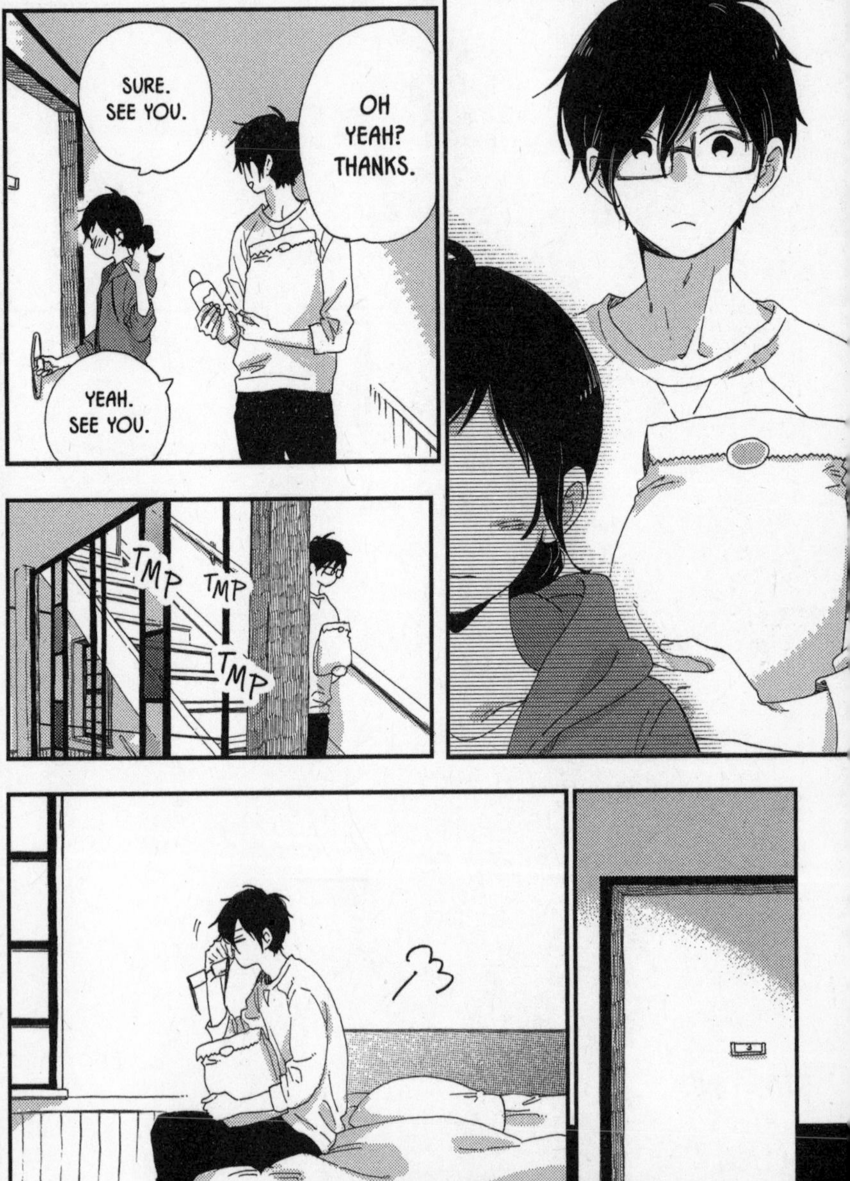
OH YEAH? THANKS.
SURE. SEE YOU.
YEAH. SEE YOU.
TMP
TMP
TMP

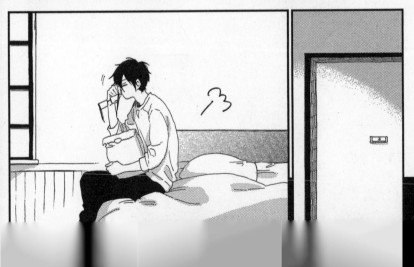

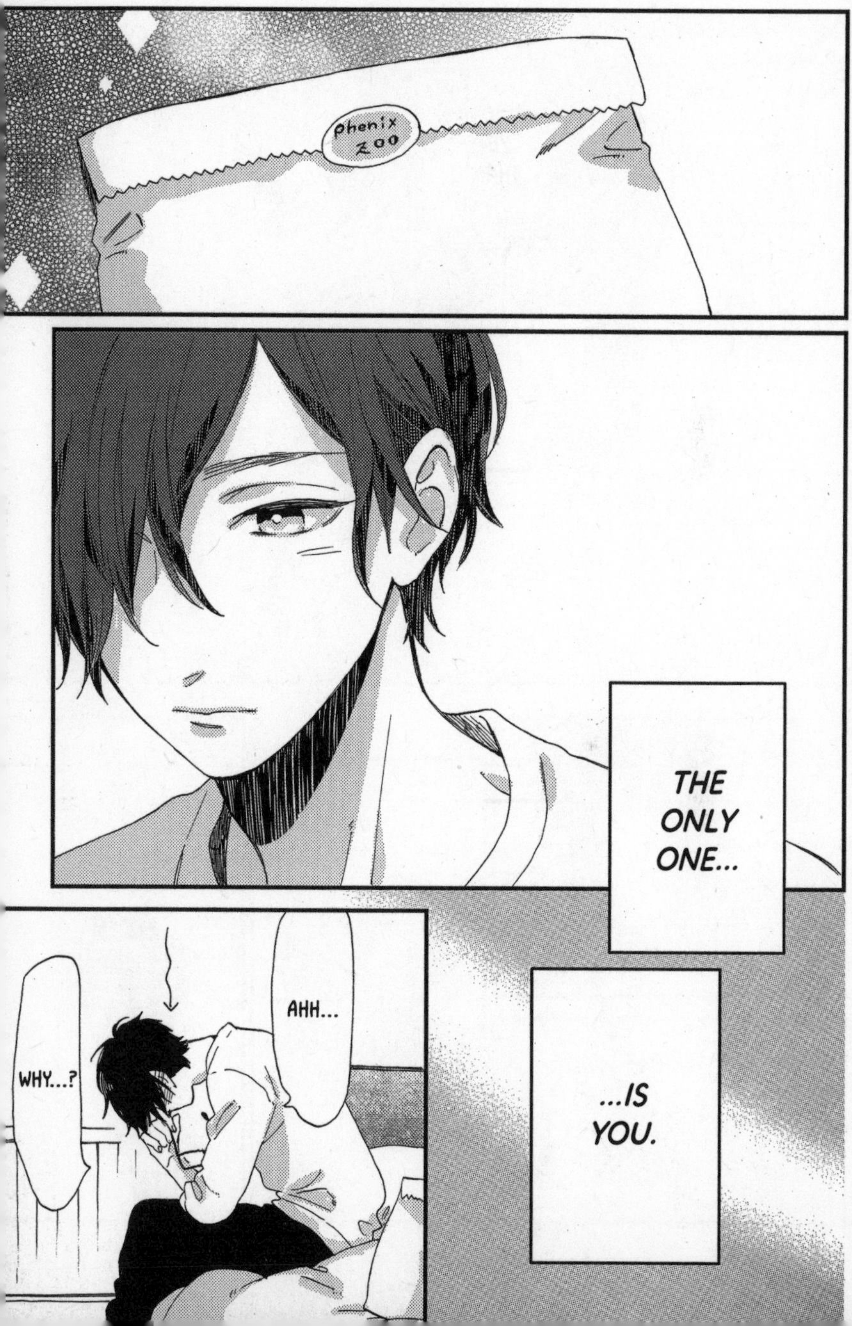
phenix zoo
THE ONLY ONE...
...IS YOU.
AHH...
WHY...?

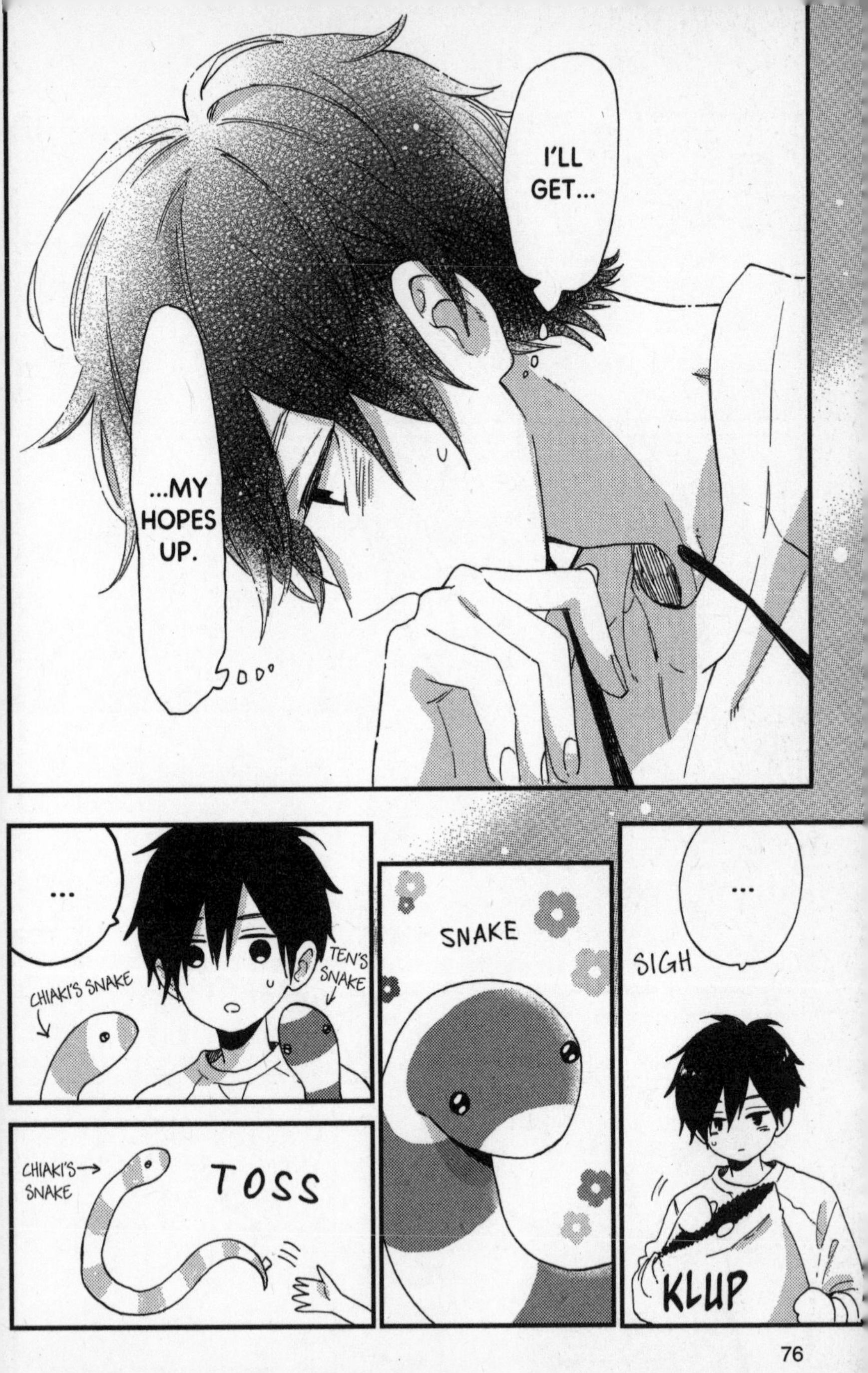

I'LL GET...
...MY HOPES UP.
...
SIGH
KLUP
SNAKE
...
TEN'S SNAKE
CHIAKI'S SNAKE
CHIAKI'S SNAKE
TOSS

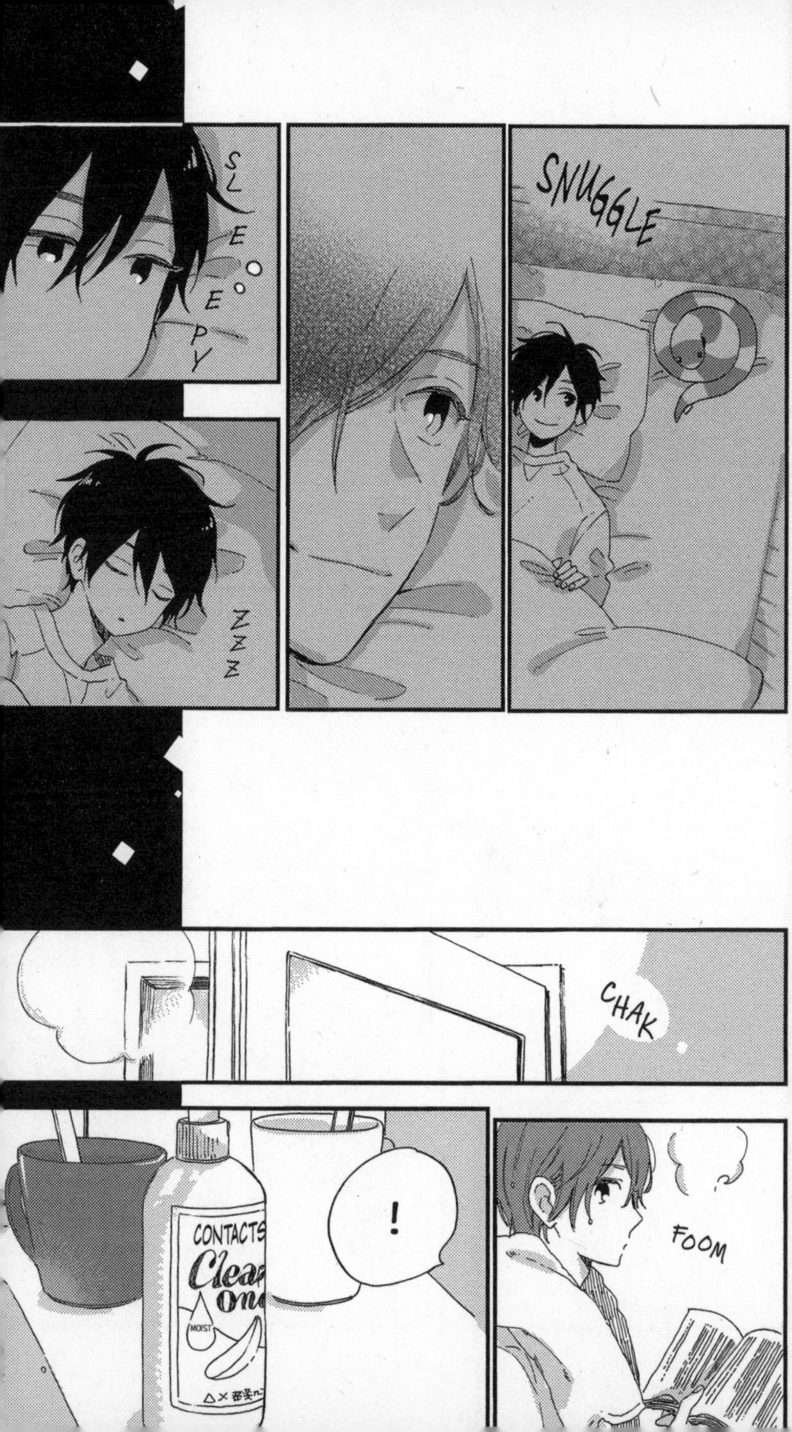
SNUGGLE
SLEEPY
ZZZ
CHAK
FOOM
!
CONTACTS
MOIST

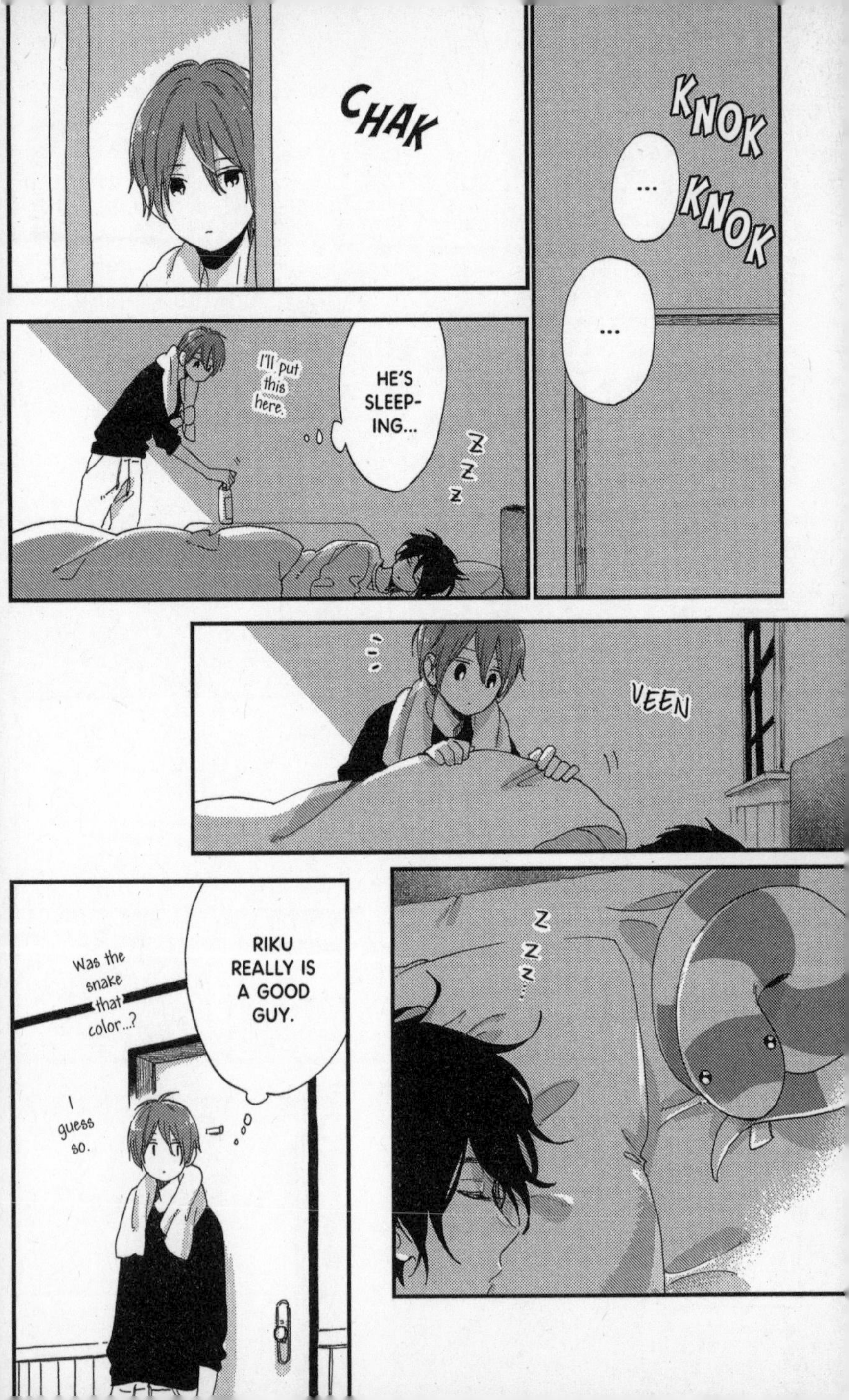
KNOK
KNOK
...
...
CHAK
HE'S SLEEPING...
I'll put this here.
Z Z Z
VEEN
Z Z Z...
RIKU REALLY IS A GOOD GUY.
Was the snake that color...?
I guess so.

I GAVE IT TO HIM.

BUT...

PHOO.

FOMP

...AND GIVE IT TO HIM.

...I CAN'T HELP BUT THINK...

...TO BUY IT...

IT WAS WEIRD...

...THAT...

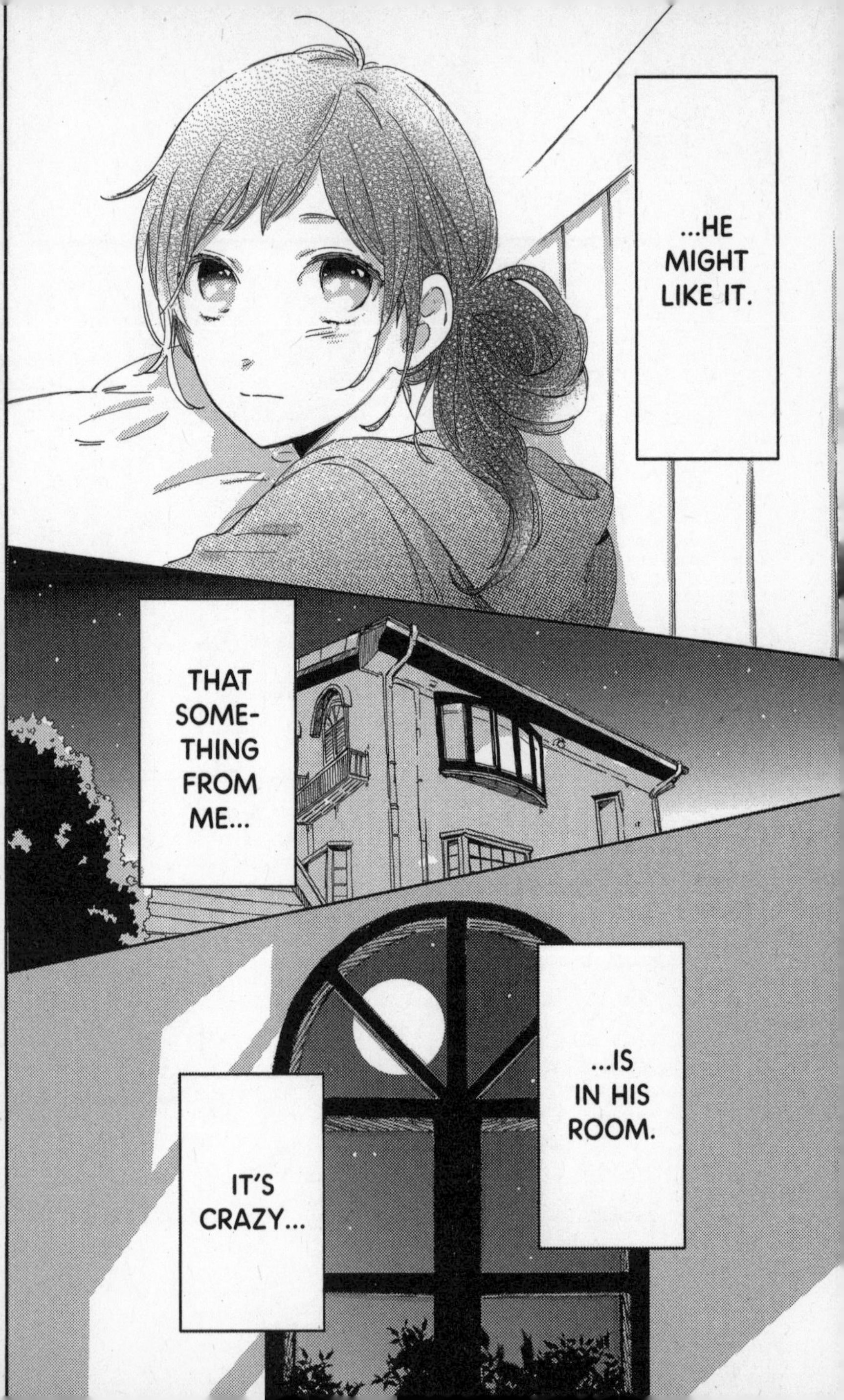
...HE MIGHT LIKE IT.
THAT SOME-THING FROM ME...
...IS IN HIS ROOM.
IT'S CRAZY...

THE
POWER
OF
LOVE.

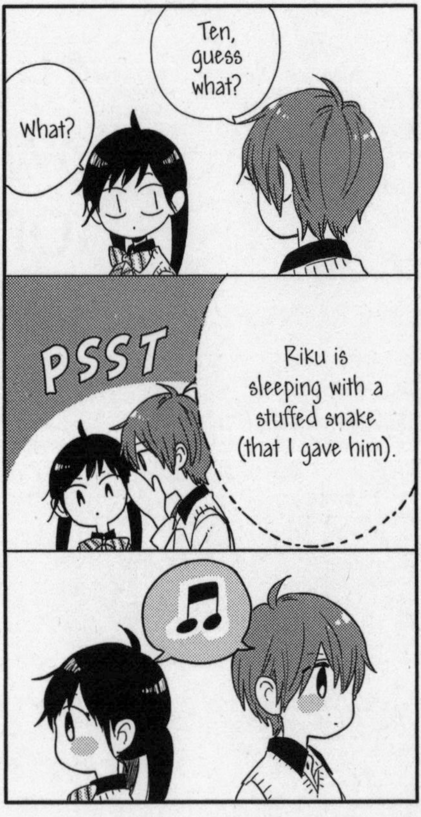
Ten, guess what?
What?
PSST
Riku is sleeping with a stuffed snake (that I gave him).

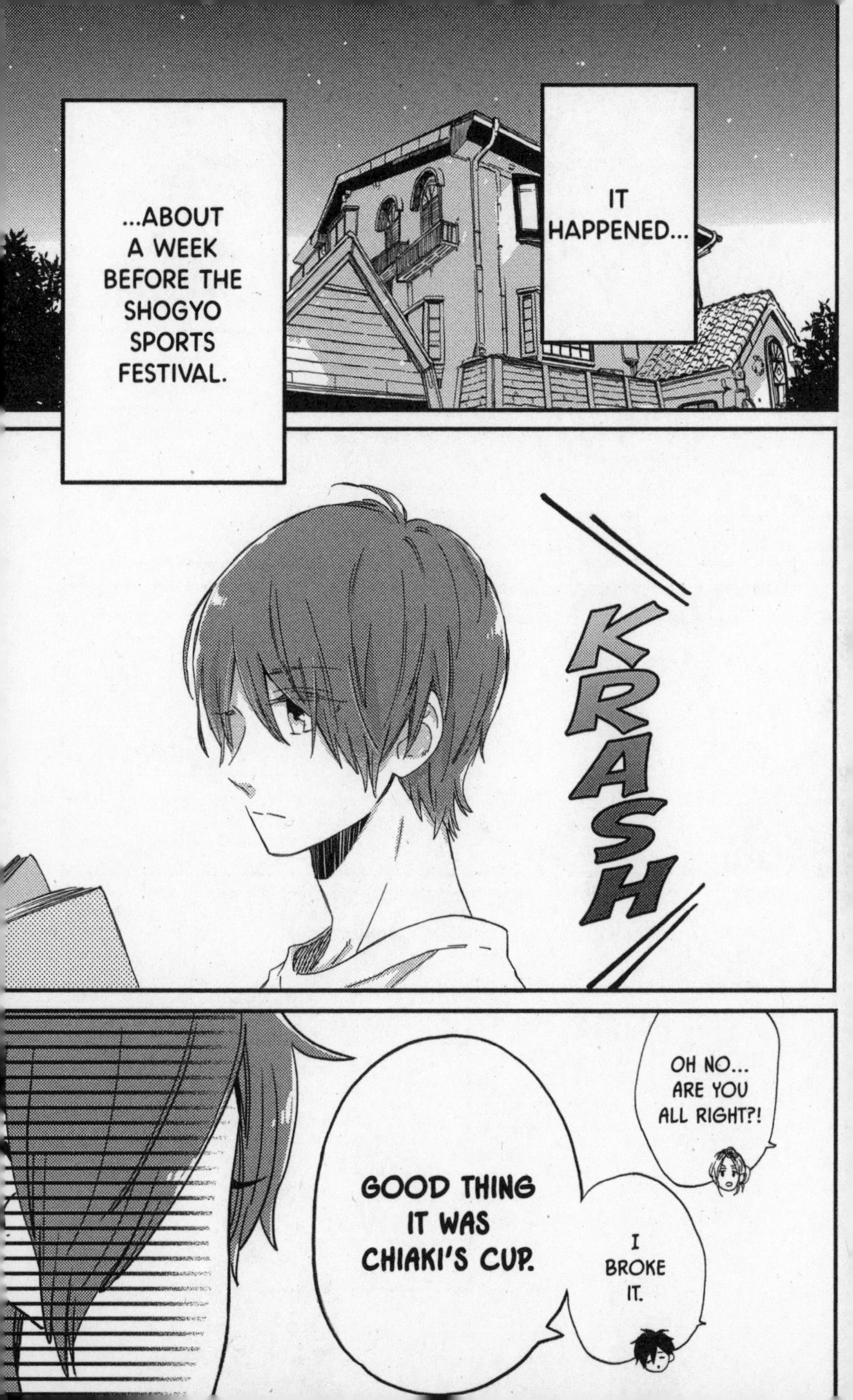
IT HAPPENED...
...ABOUT A WEEK BEFORE THE SHOGYO SPORTS FESTIVAL.
KRASH
OH NO... ARE YOU ALL RIGHT?!
I BROKE IT.
GOOD THING IT WAS CHIAKI'S CUP.

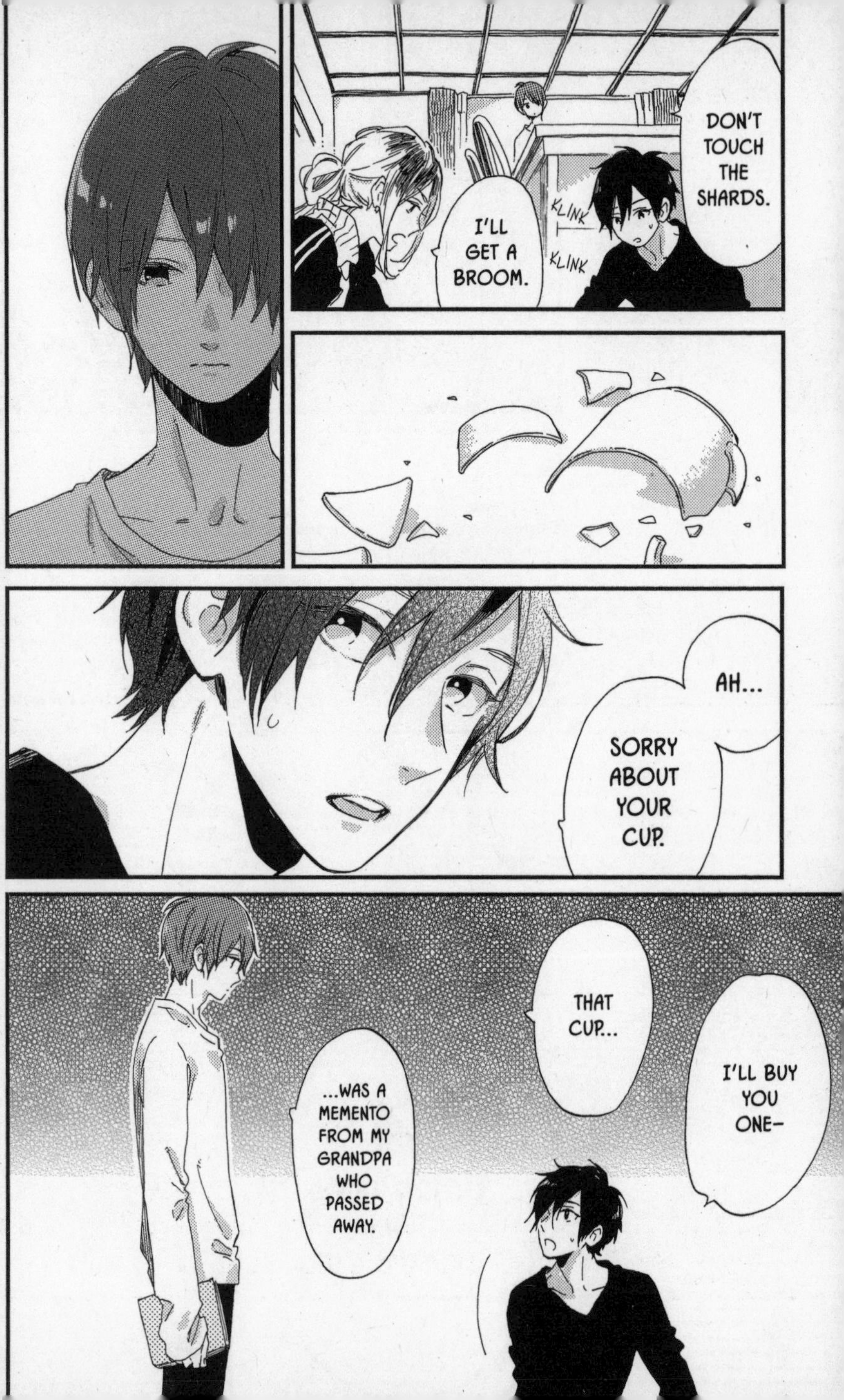
DON'T TOUCH THE SHARDS.
KLINK
KLINK
I'LL GET A BROOM.
AH...
SORRY ABOUT YOUR CUP.
I'LL BUY YOU ONE–
THAT CUP...
...WAS A MEMENTO FROM MY GRANDPA WHO PASSED AWAY.

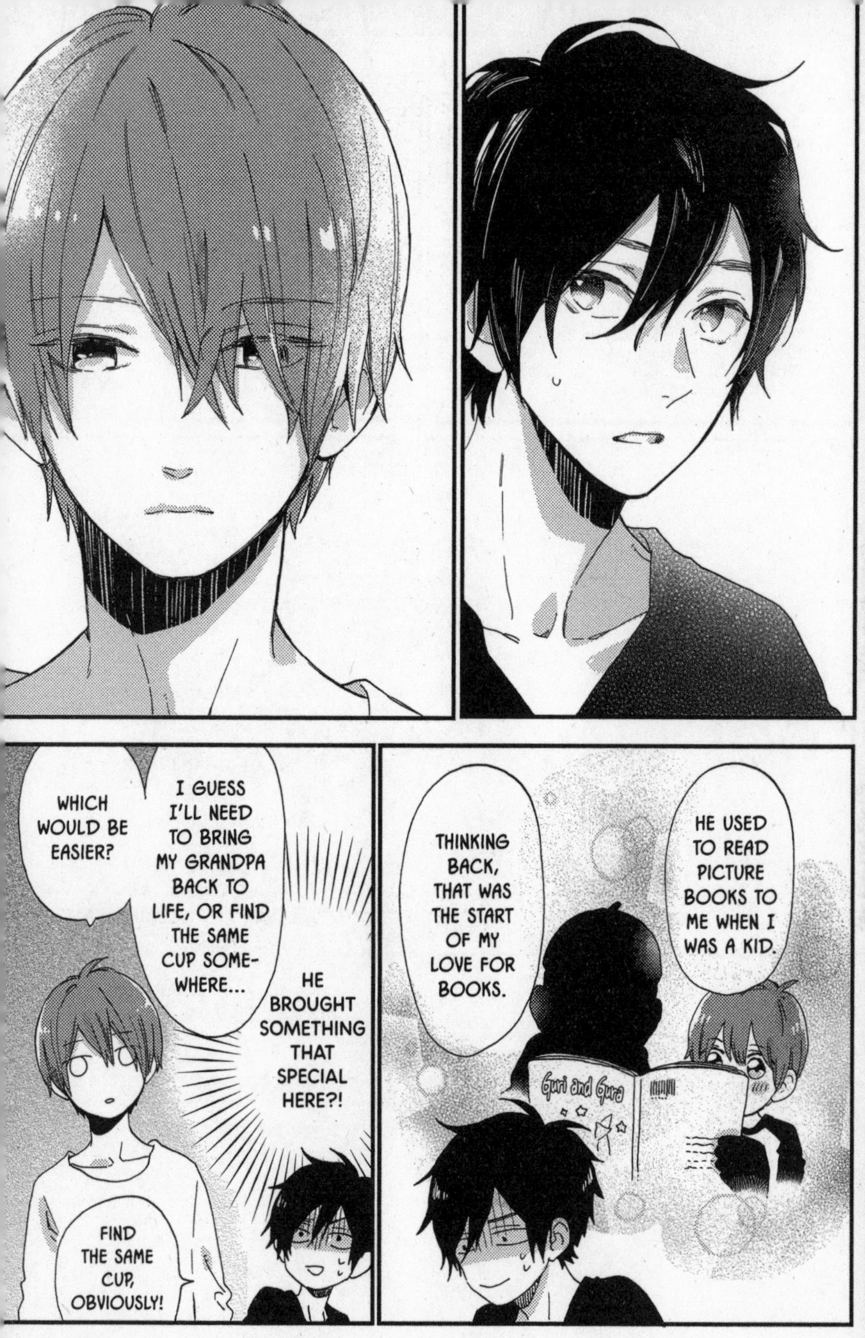
HE USED TO READ PICTURE BOOKS TO ME WHEN I WAS A KID.
THINKING BACK, THAT WAS THE START OF MY LOVE FOR BOOKS.
Guri and Gura
I GUESS I'LL NEED TO BRING MY GRANDPA BACK TO LIFE, OR FIND THE SAME CUP SOME-WHERE...
WHICH WOULD BE EASIER?
HE BROUGHT SOMETHING THAT SPECIAL HERE?!
FIND THE SAME CUP, OBVIOUSLY!

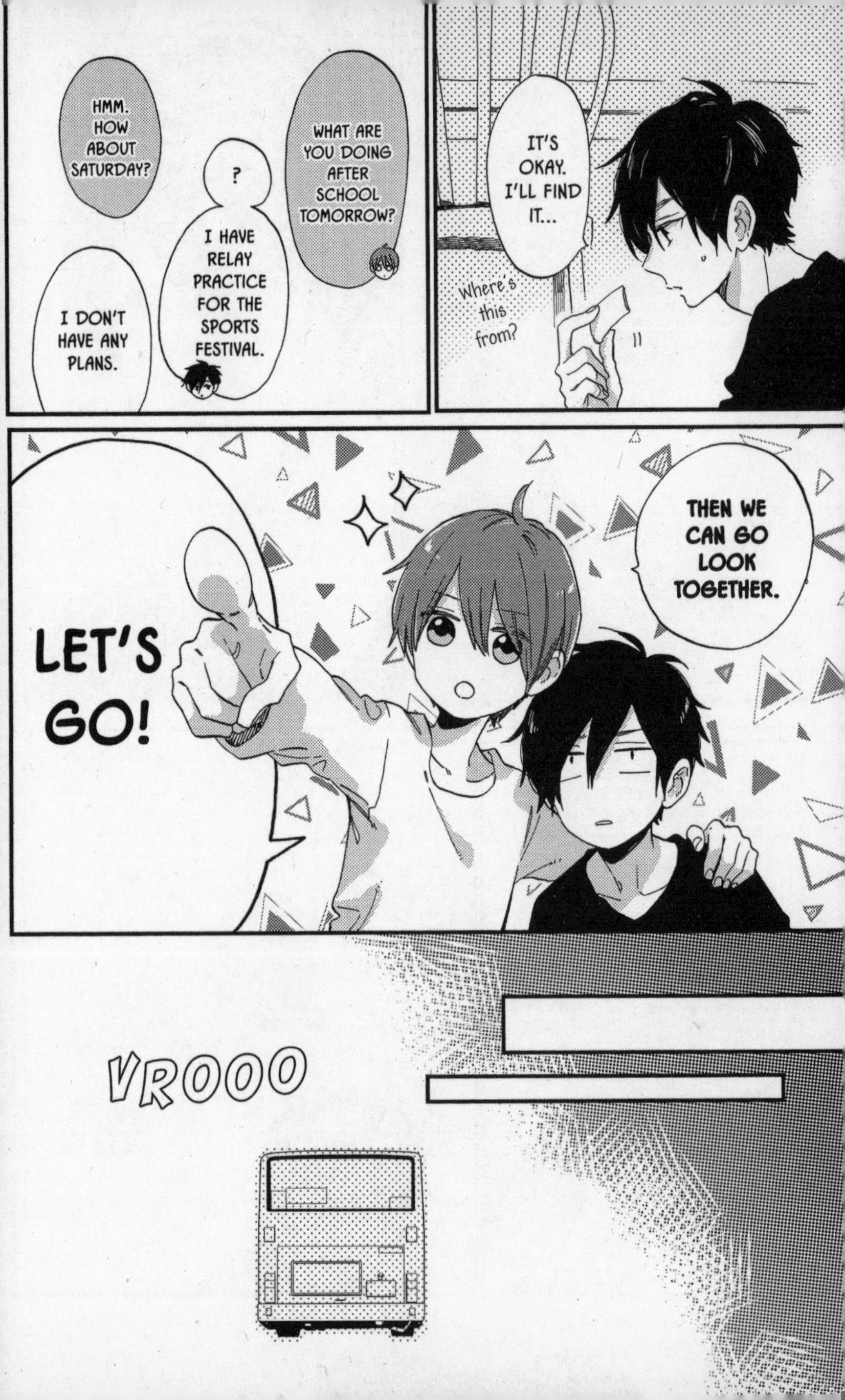
IT'S OKAY. I'LL FIND IT...
Where's this from?
WHAT ARE YOU DOING AFTER SCHOOL TOMORROW?
?
I HAVE RELAY PRACTICE FOR THE SPORTS FESTIVAL.
HMM. HOW ABOUT SATURDAY?
I DON'T HAVE ANY PLANS.
THEN WE CAN GO LOOK TOGETHER.
LET'S GO!
VROOO

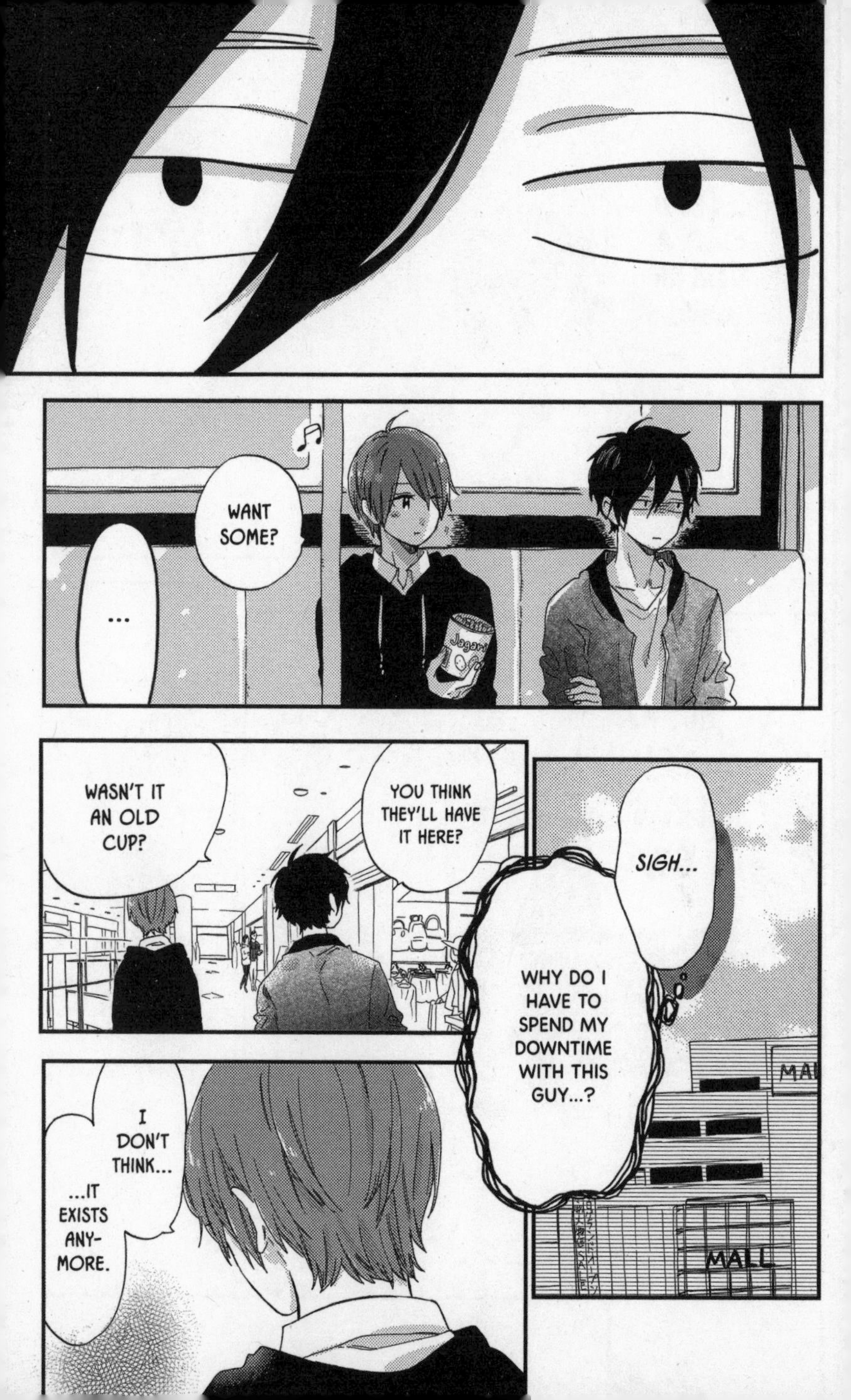
WANT SOME?
...
Jagari
SIGH...
WHY DO I HAVE TO SPEND MY DOWNTIME WITH THIS GUY...?
MALL
YOU THINK THEY'LL HAVE IT HERE?
WASN'T IT AN OLD CUP?
I DON'T THINK...
...IT EXISTS ANY-MORE.

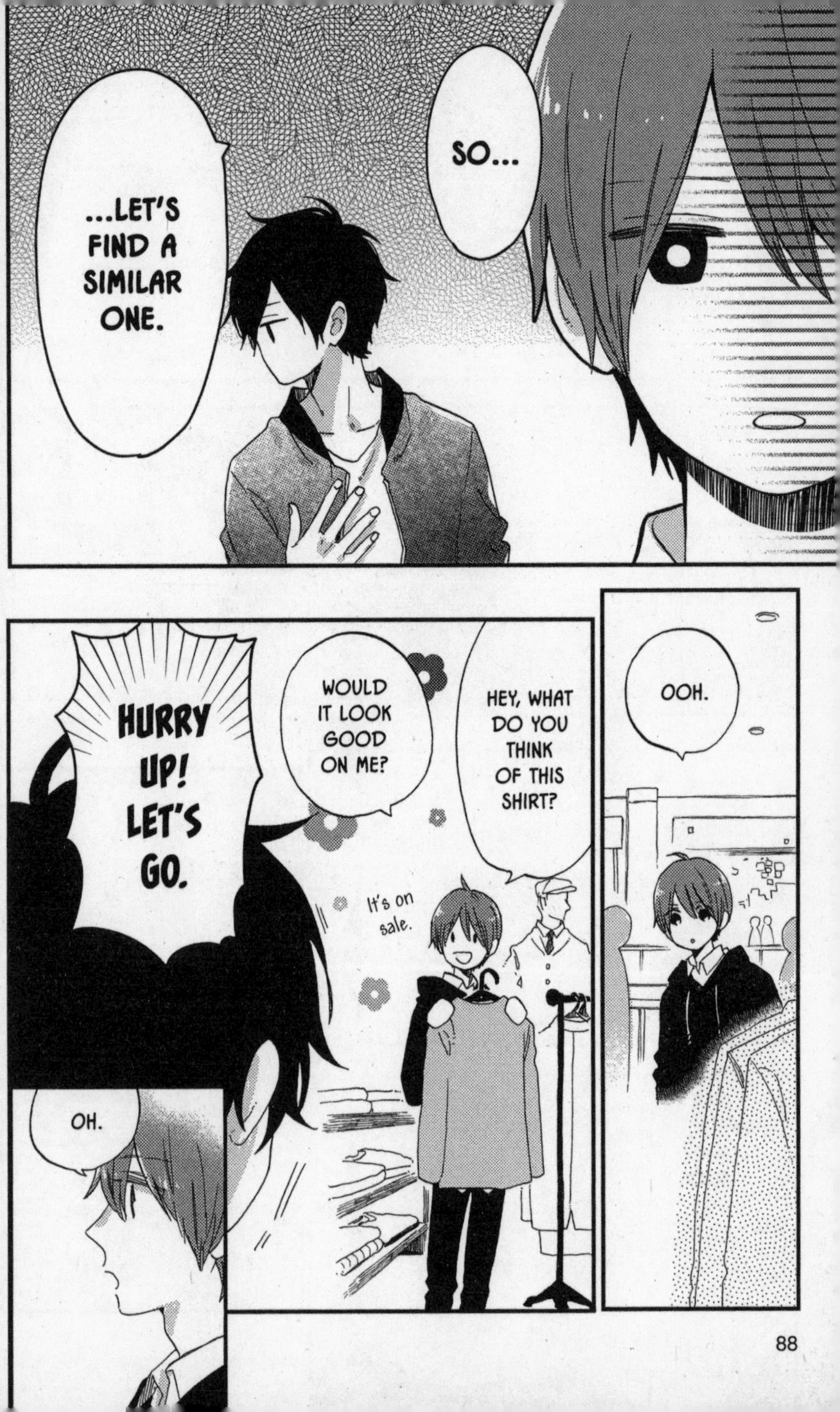
SO...
...LET'S FIND A SIMILAR ONE.
OOH.
HEY, WHAT DO YOU THINK OF THIS SHIRT?
WOULD IT LOOK GOOD ON ME?
It's on sale.
HURRY UP! LET'S GO.
OH.

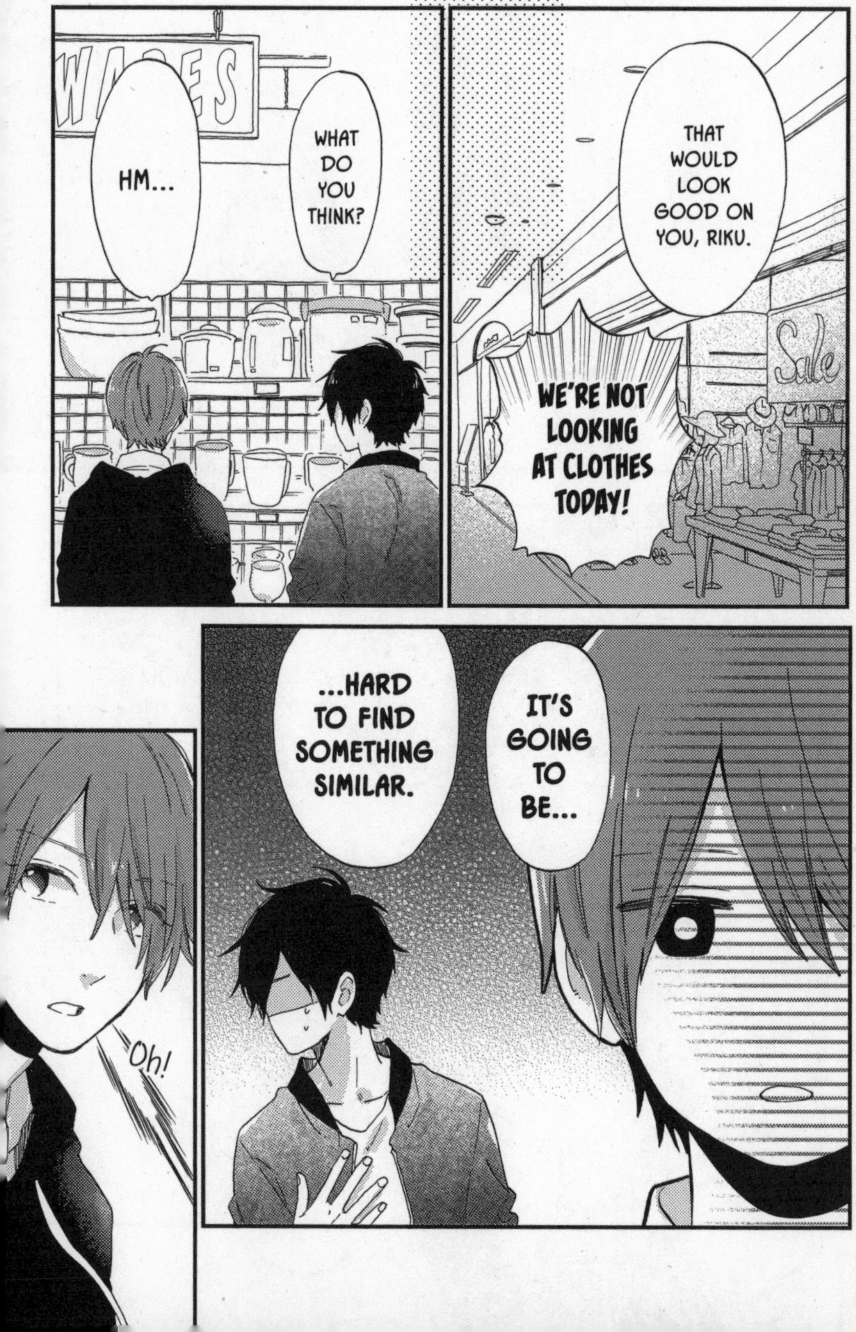
THAT WOULD LOOK GOOD ON YOU, RIKU.
Sale
WE'RE NOT LOOKING AT CLOTHES TODAY!
WHAT DO YOU THINK?
HM...
IT'S GOING TO BE...
...HARD TO FIND SOMETHING SIMILAR.
Oh!

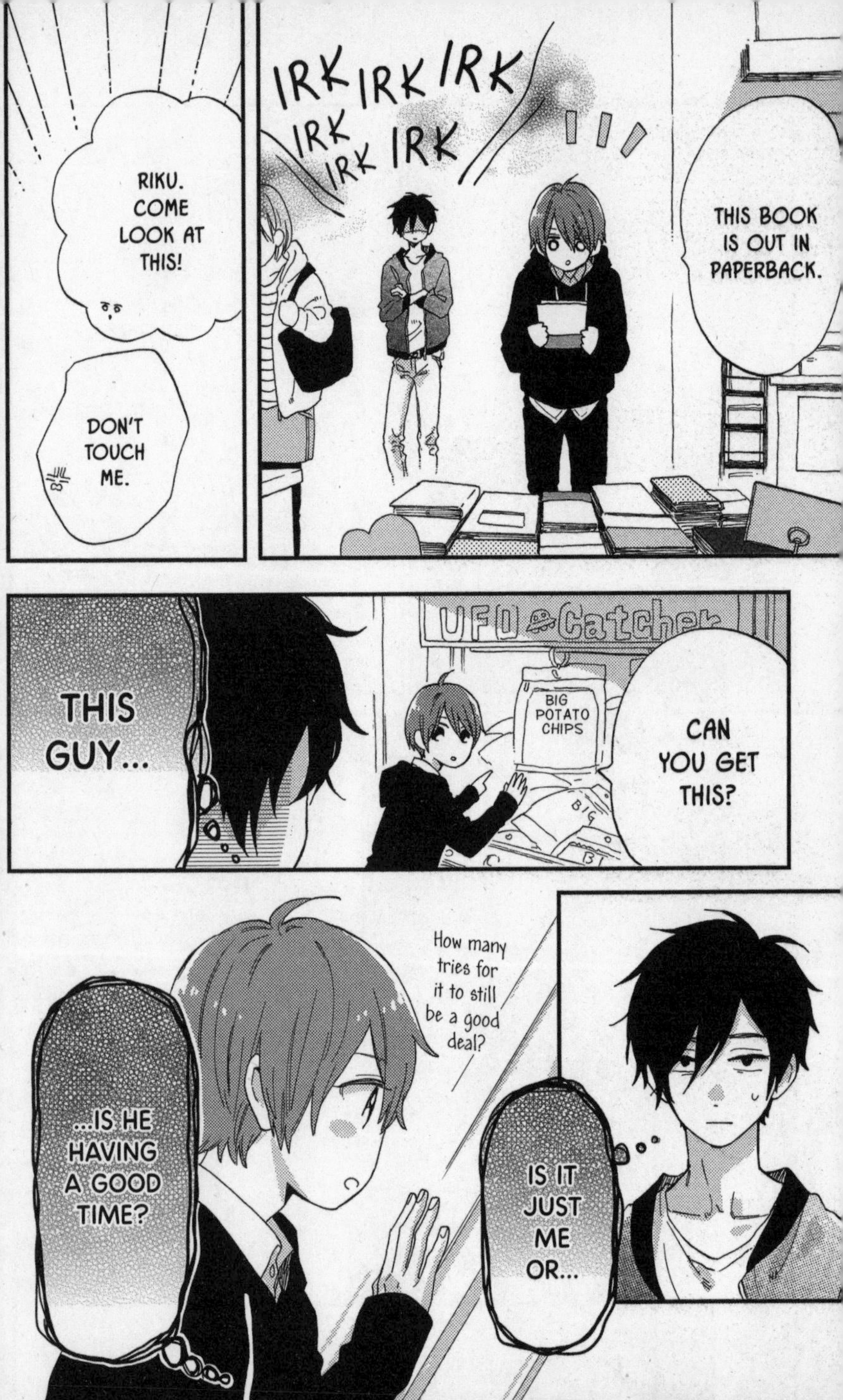
THIS BOOK IS OUT IN PAPERBACK.
IRK IRK IRK IRK IRK IRK
RIKU. COME LOOK AT THIS!
DON'T TOUCH ME.
UFO Catcher
CAN YOU GET THIS?
BIG POTATO CHIPS
THIS GUY...
IS IT JUST ME OR...
How many tries for it to still be a good deal?
...IS HE HAVING A GOOD TIME?

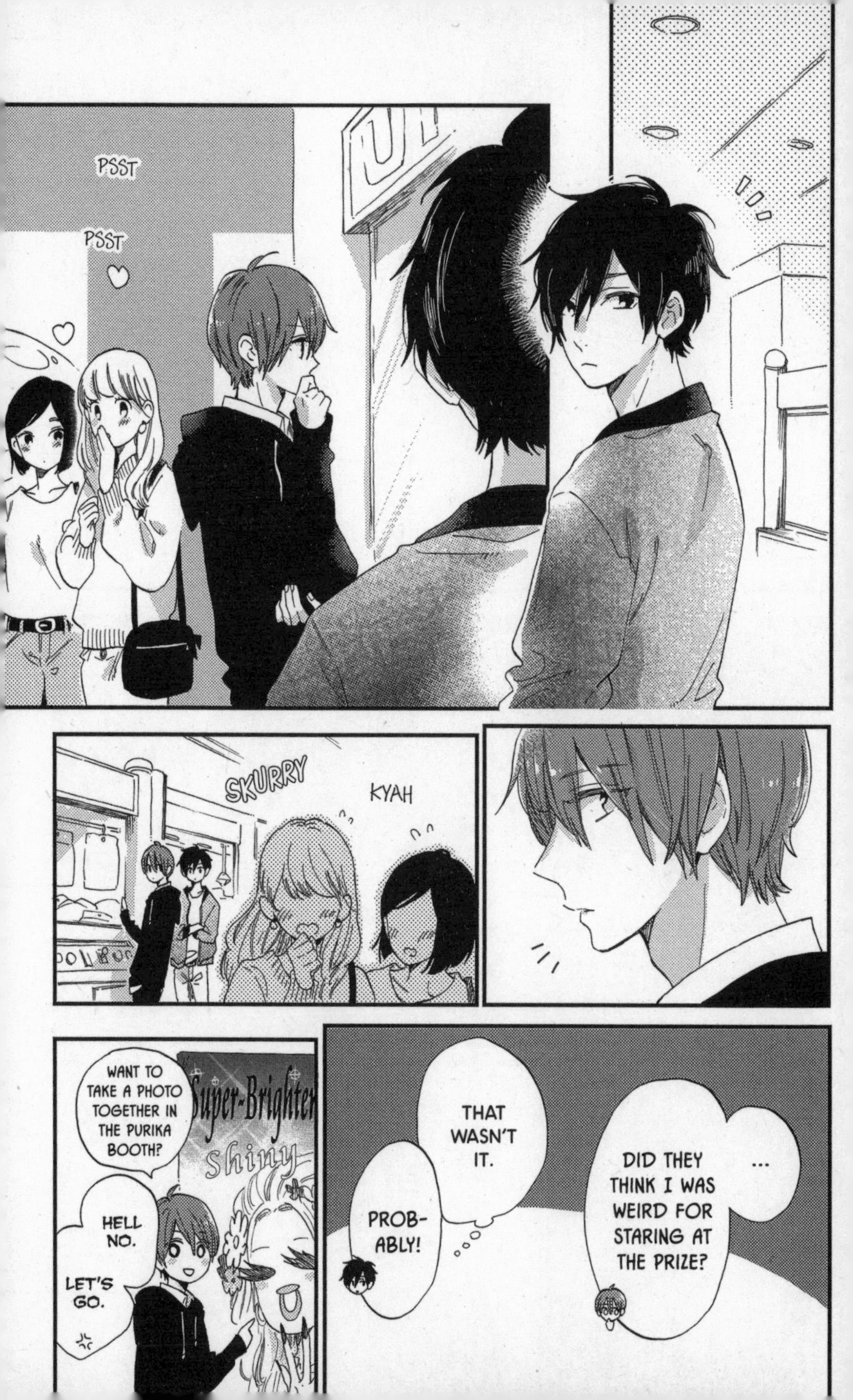
PSST
PSST
SKURRY
KYAH
...
DID THEY THINK I WAS WEIRD FOR STARING AT THE PRIZE?
THAT WASN'T IT.
PROB-ABLY!
WANT TO TAKE A PHOTO TOGETHER IN THE PURIKA BOOTH?
Super-Brighten
Shiny
HELL NO.
LET'S GO.

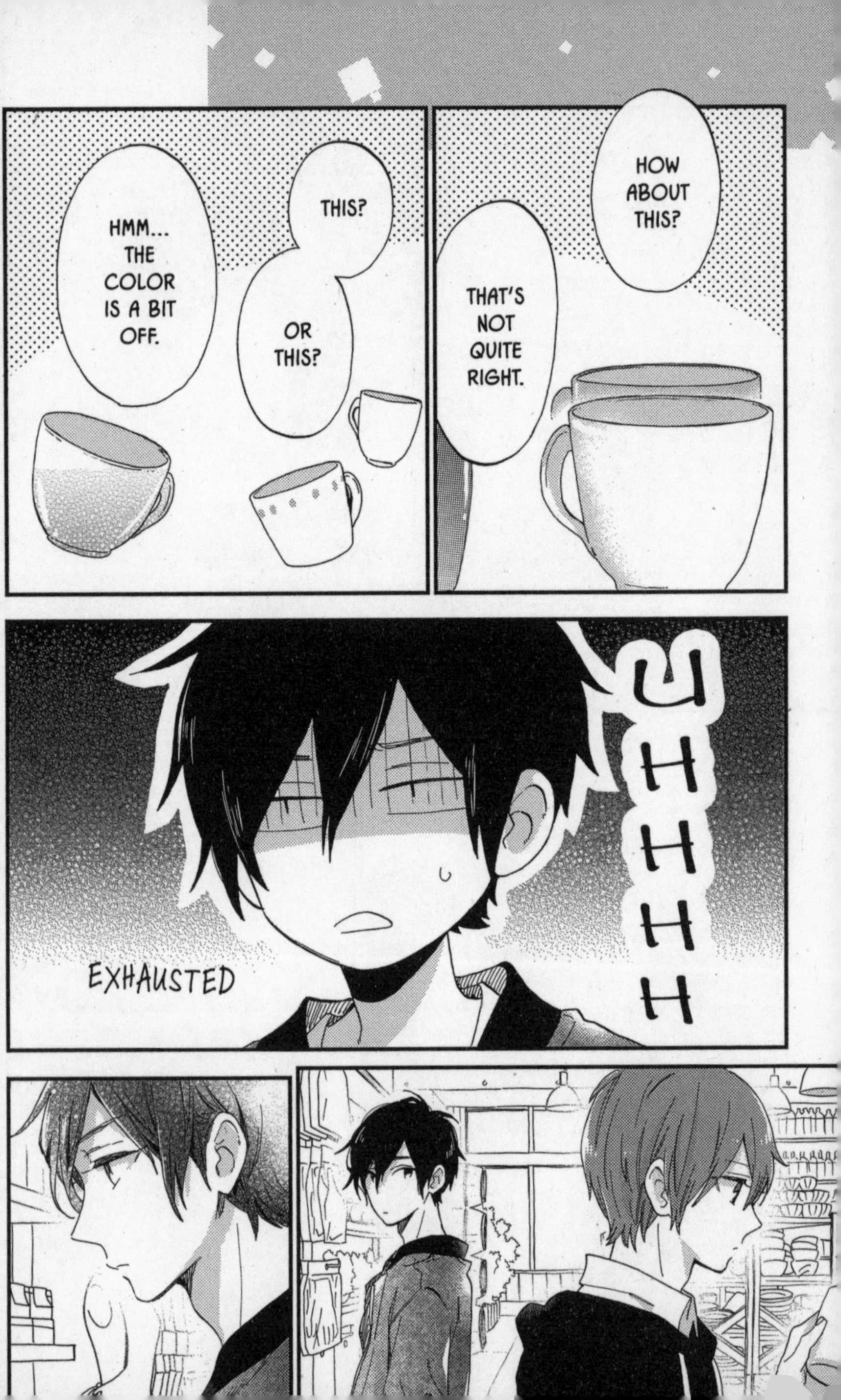
HOW ABOUT THIS?
THAT'S NOT QUITE RIGHT.
THIS?
OR THIS?
HMM... THE COLOR IS A BIT OFF.
UHHHHH
EXHAUSTED

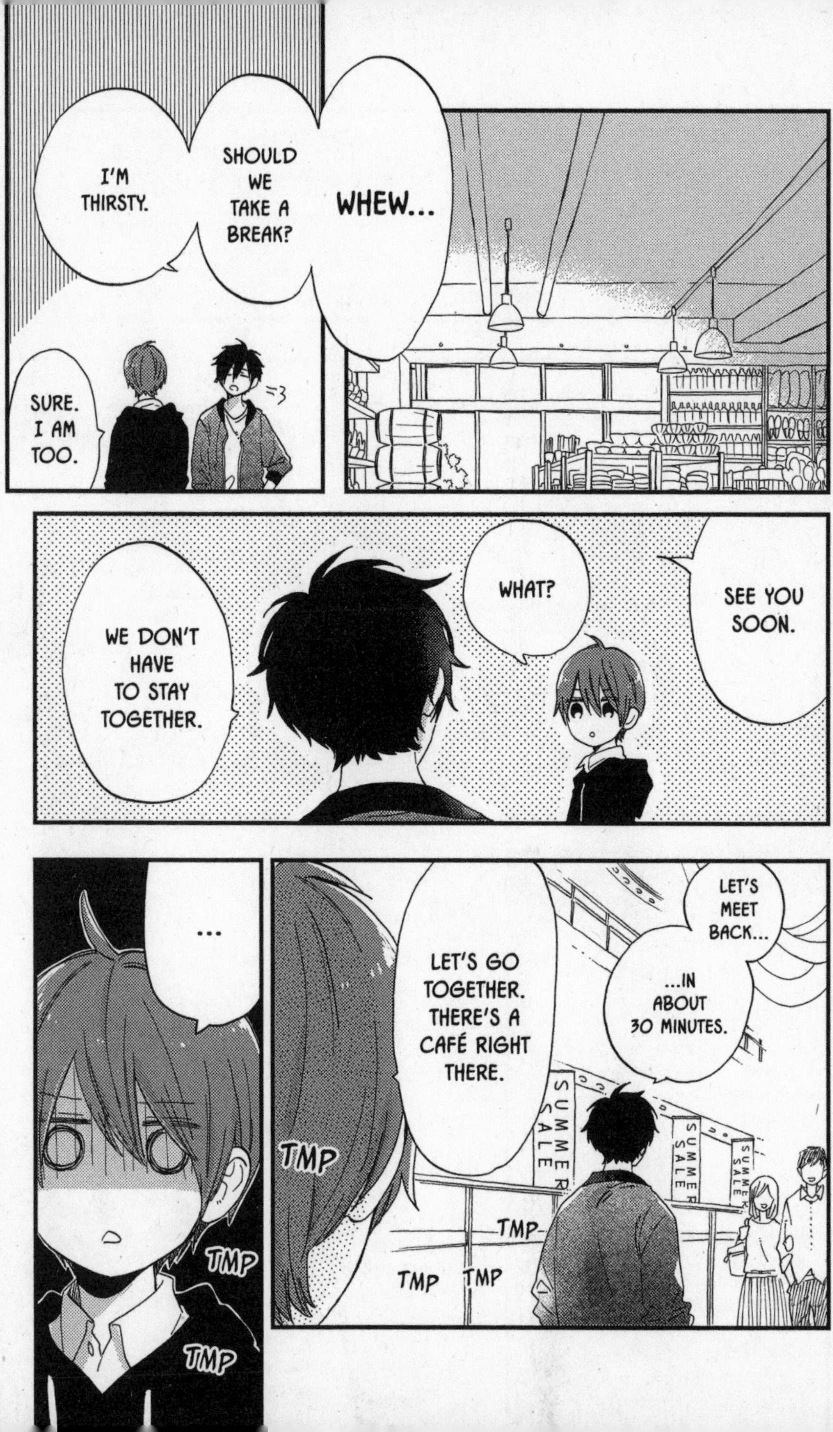
WHEW...
SHOULD WE TAKE A BREAK?
I'M THIRSTY.
SURE. I AM TOO.
SEE YOU SOON.
WHAT?
WE DON'T HAVE TO STAY TOGETHER.
LET'S MEET BACK...
...IN ABOUT 30 MINUTES.
LET'S GO TOGETHER. THERE'S A CAFÉ RIGHT THERE.
SUMMER SALE
SUMMER SALE
SUMMER SALE
TMP
TMP
TMP TMP
TMP
...
TMP
TMP

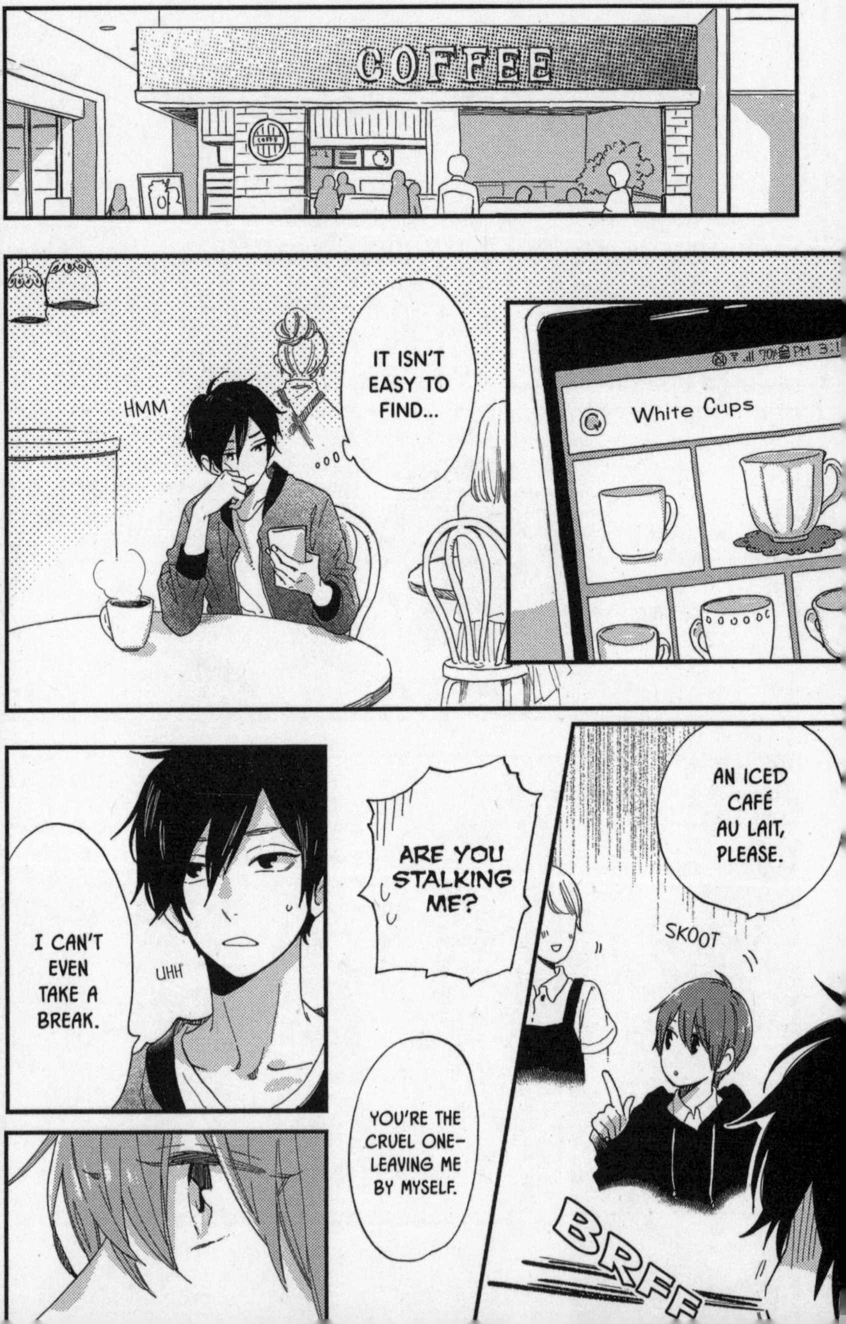
COFFEE
White Cups
HMM
IT ISN'T EASY TO FIND...
AN ICED CAFÉ AU LAIT, PLEASE.
SKOOT
BRFF
ARE YOU STALKING ME?
UHH
I CAN'T EVEN TAKE A BREAK.
YOU'RE THE CRUEL ONE—LEAVING ME BY MYSELF.

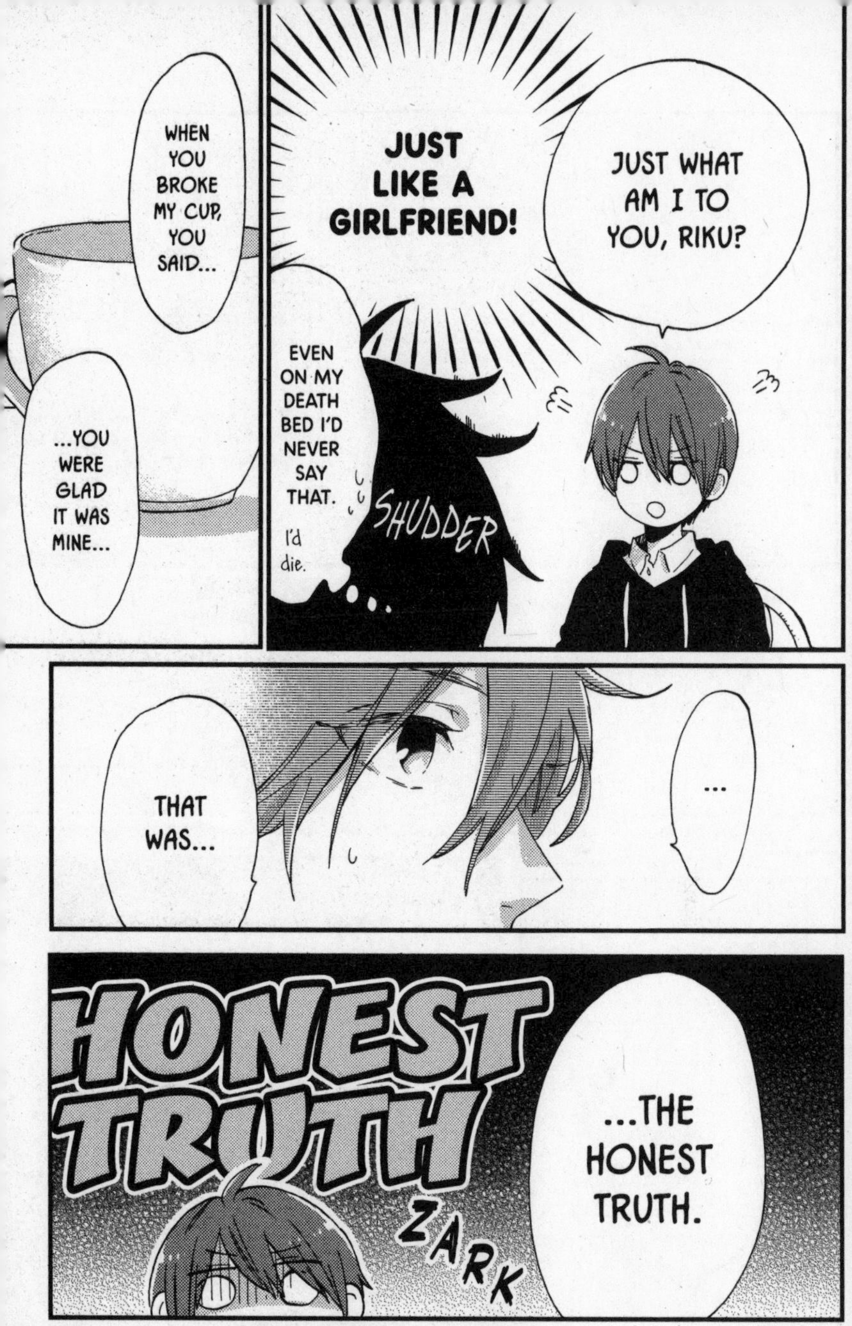
JUST WHAT AM I TO YOU, RIKU?
JUST LIKE A GIRLFRIEND!
EVEN ON MY DEATH BED I'D NEVER SAY THAT.
SHUDDER
I'd die.
WHEN YOU BROKE MY CUP, YOU SAID...
...YOU WERE GLAD IT WAS MINE...
...
THAT WAS...
...THE HONEST TRUTH.
HONEST TRUTH
ZARK

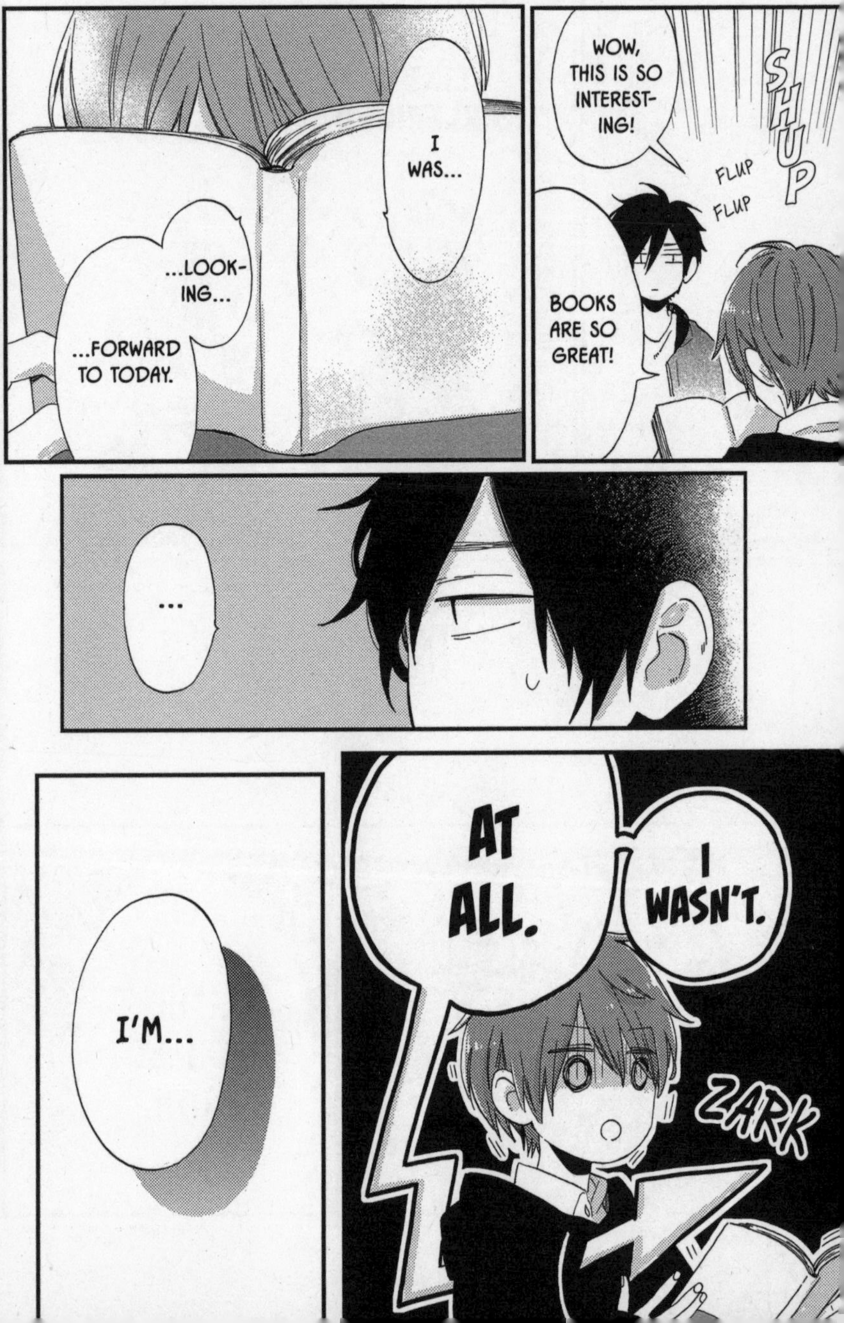
WOW, THIS IS SO INTEREST-ING!
SHUP
FLUP
FLUP
BOOKS ARE SO GREAT!
I WAS...
...LOOK-ING...
...FORWARD TO TODAY.
...
I WASN'T.
AT ALL.
ZARK
I'M...

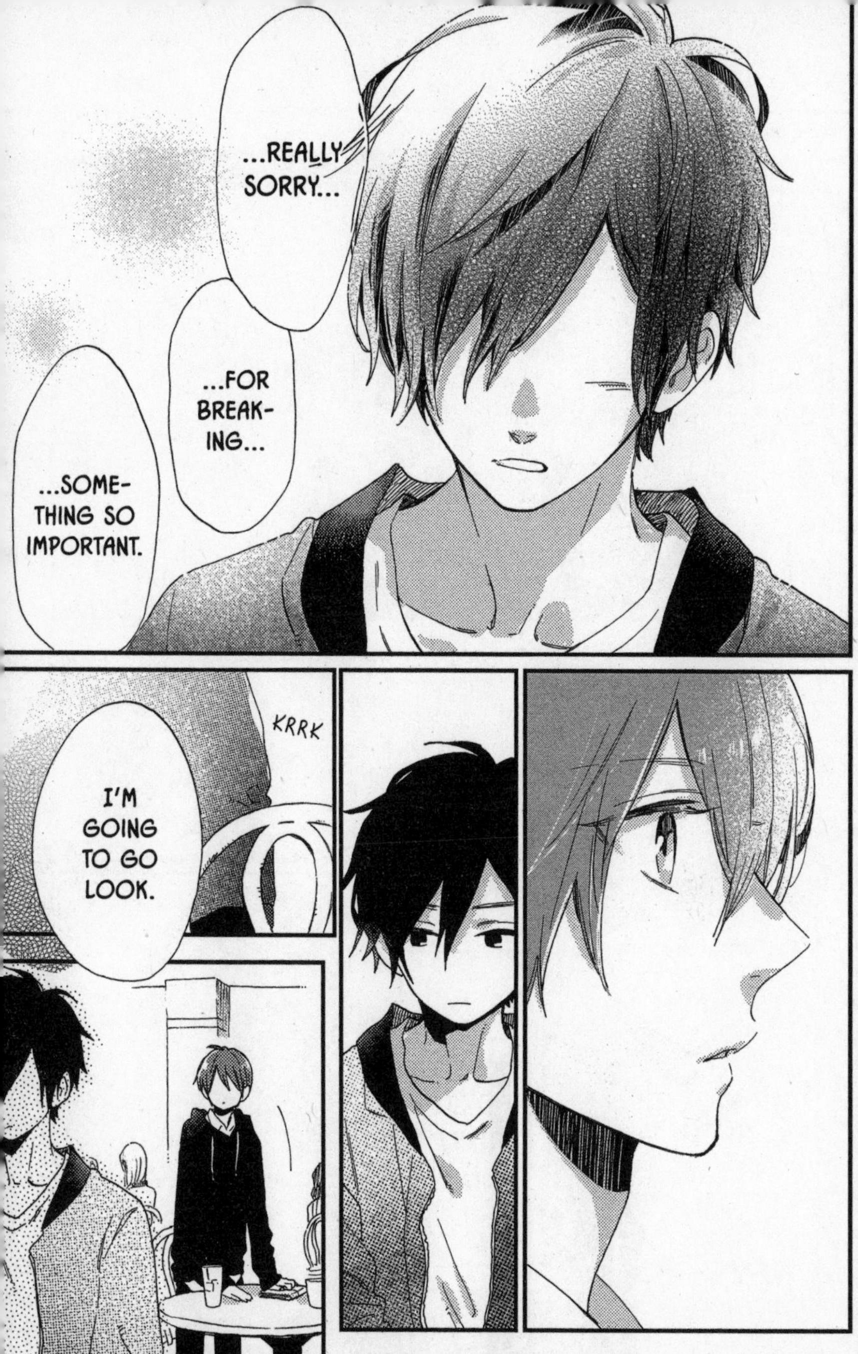
...REALLY SORRY...
...FOR BREAKING...
...SOMETHING SO IMPORTANT.
KRRK
I'M GOING TO GO LOOK.

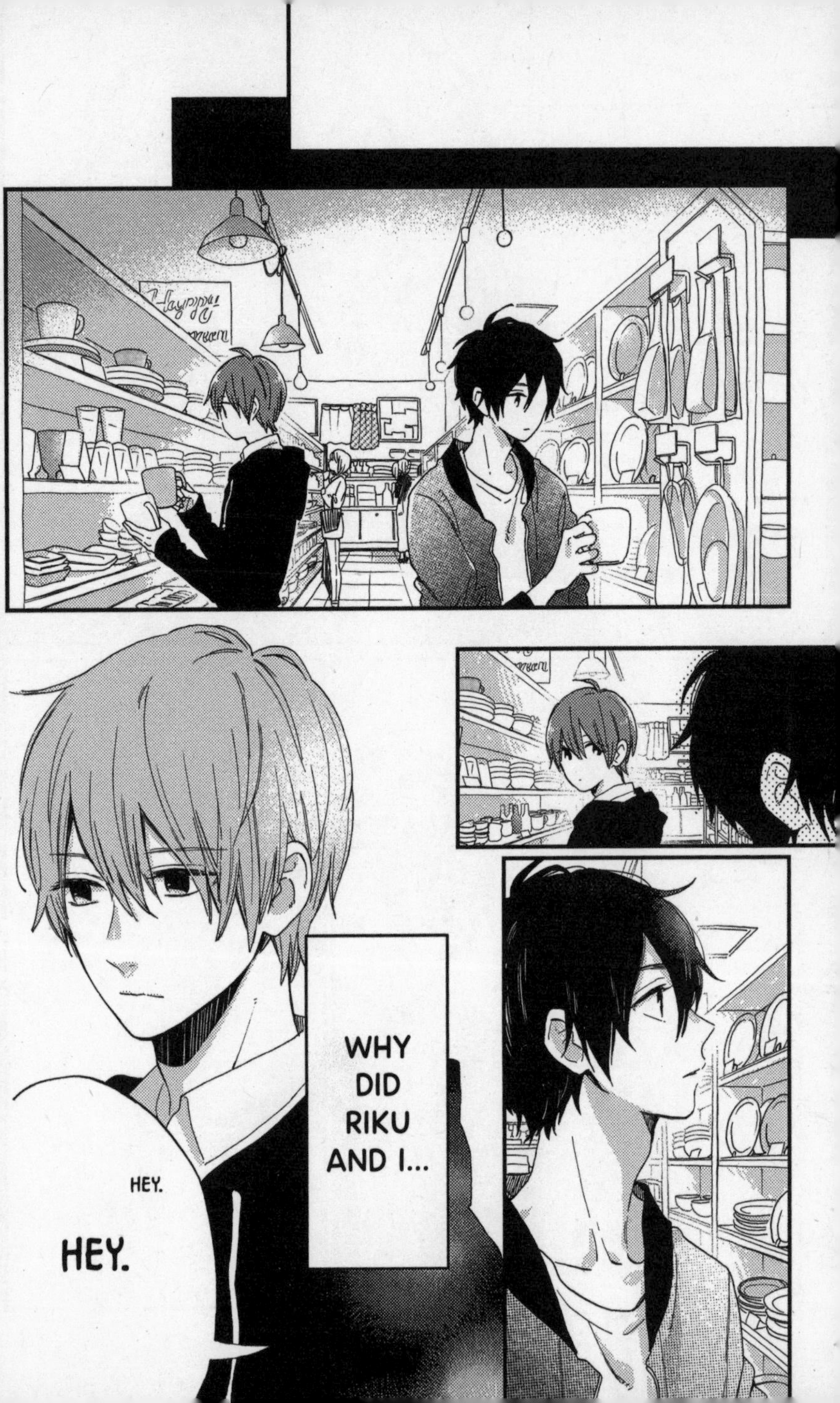
WHY DID RIKU AND I...
HEY.
HEY.

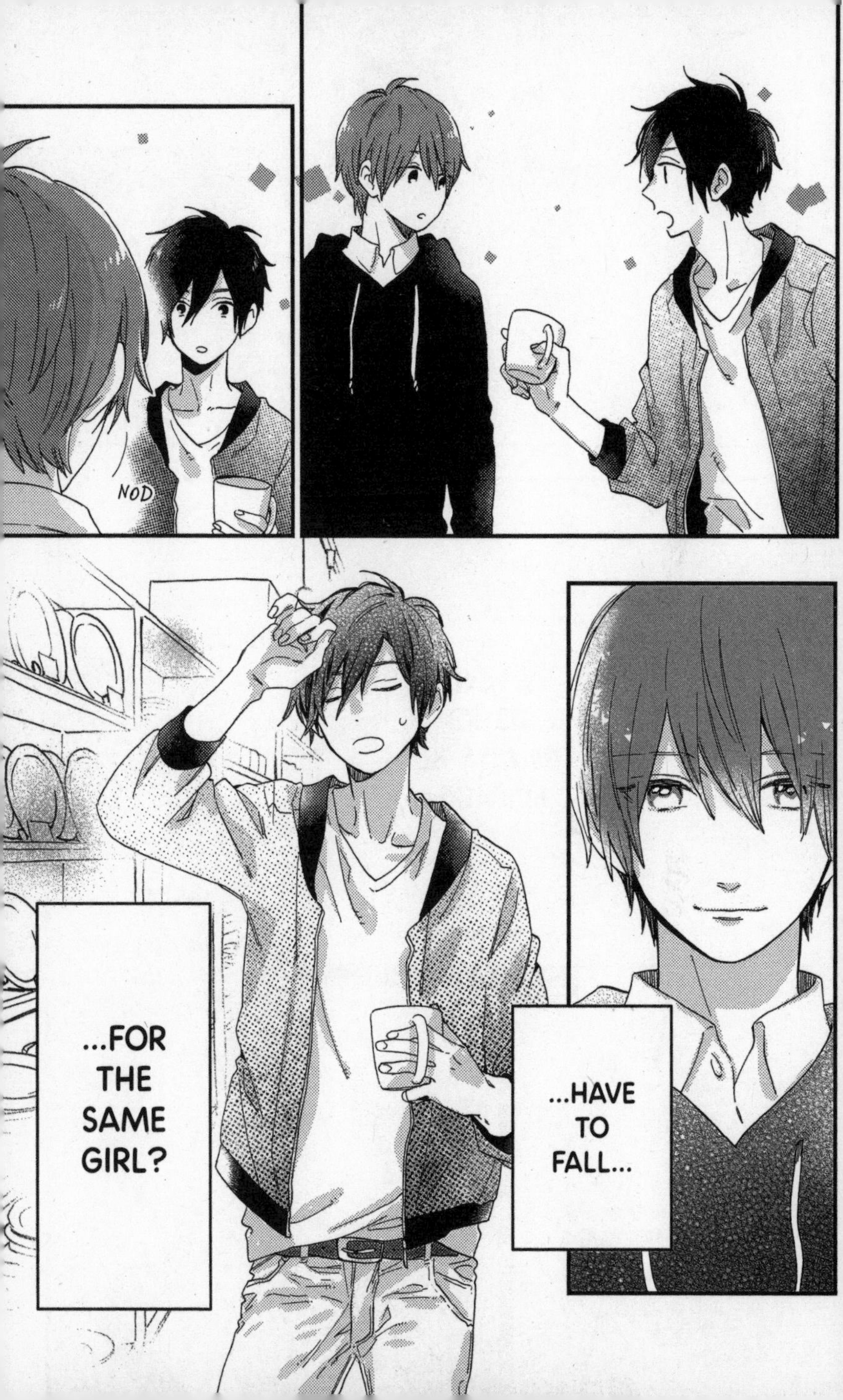
NOD
...HAVE TO FALL...
...FOR THE SAME GIRL?

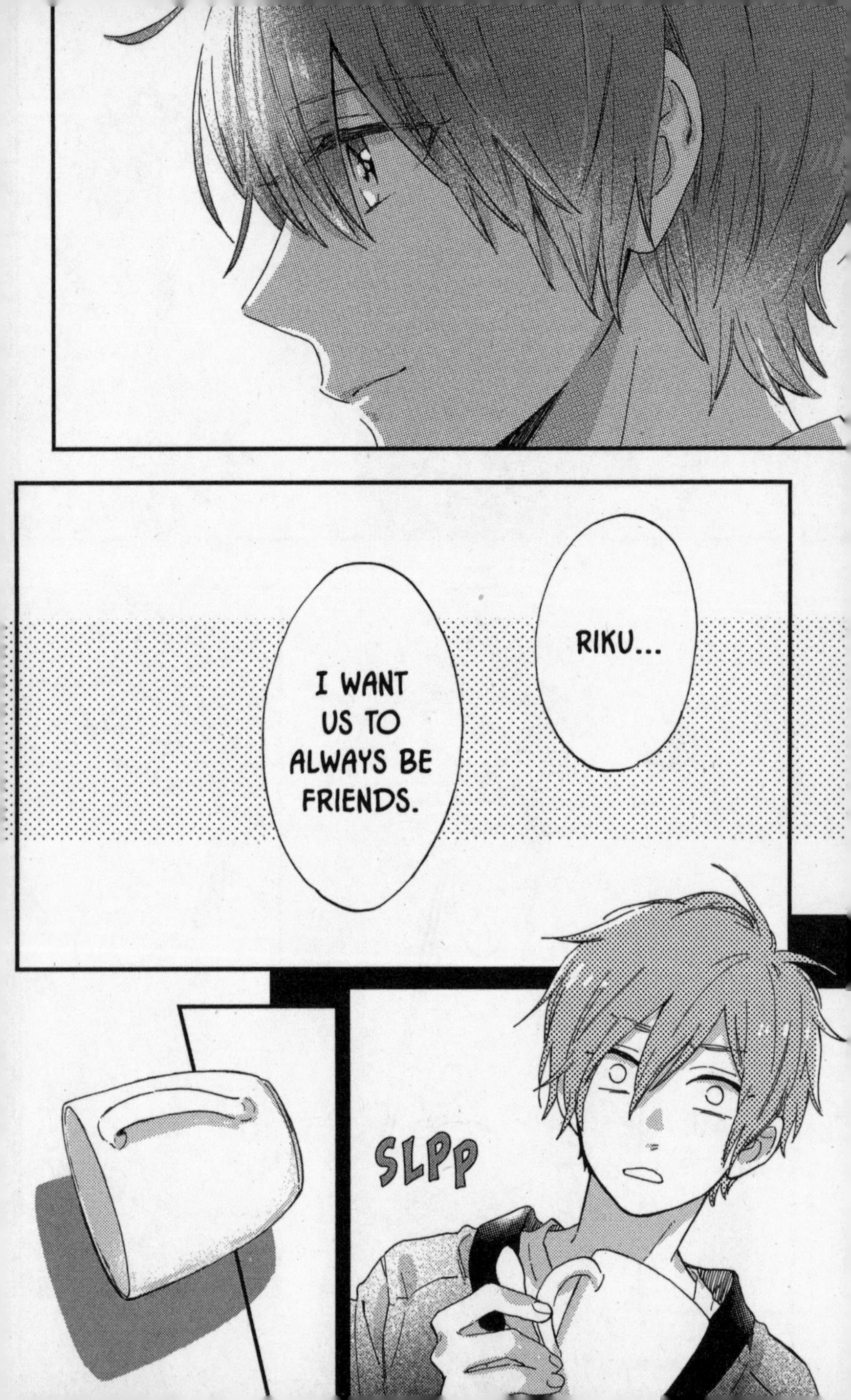
RIKU...
I WANT US TO ALWAYS BE FRIENDS.
SLPP

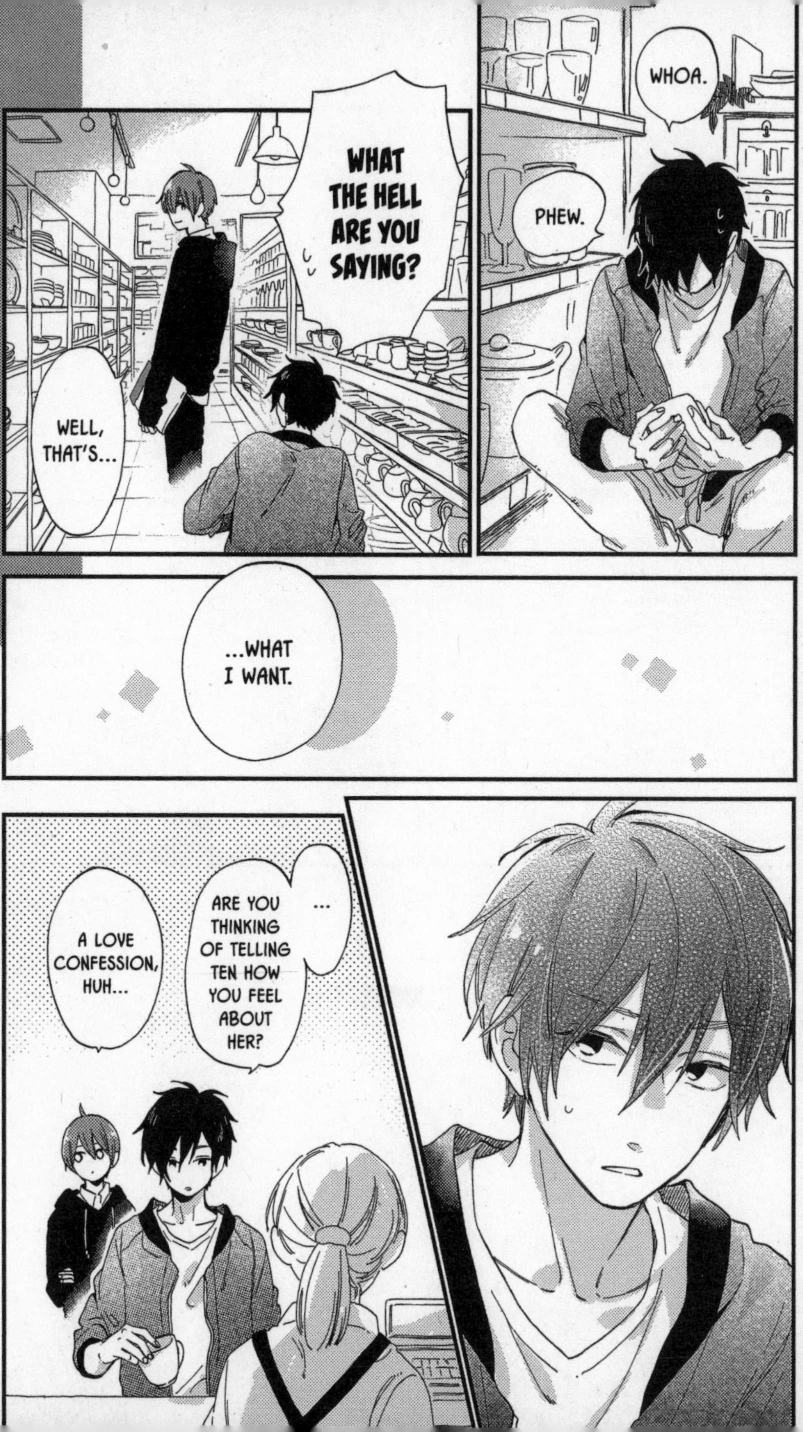
WHOA.
PHEW.
WHAT THE HELL ARE YOU SAYING?
WELL, THAT'S...
...WHAT I WANT.
...
ARE YOU THINKING OF TELLING TEN HOW YOU FEEL ABOUT HER?
A LOVE CONFESSION, HUH...

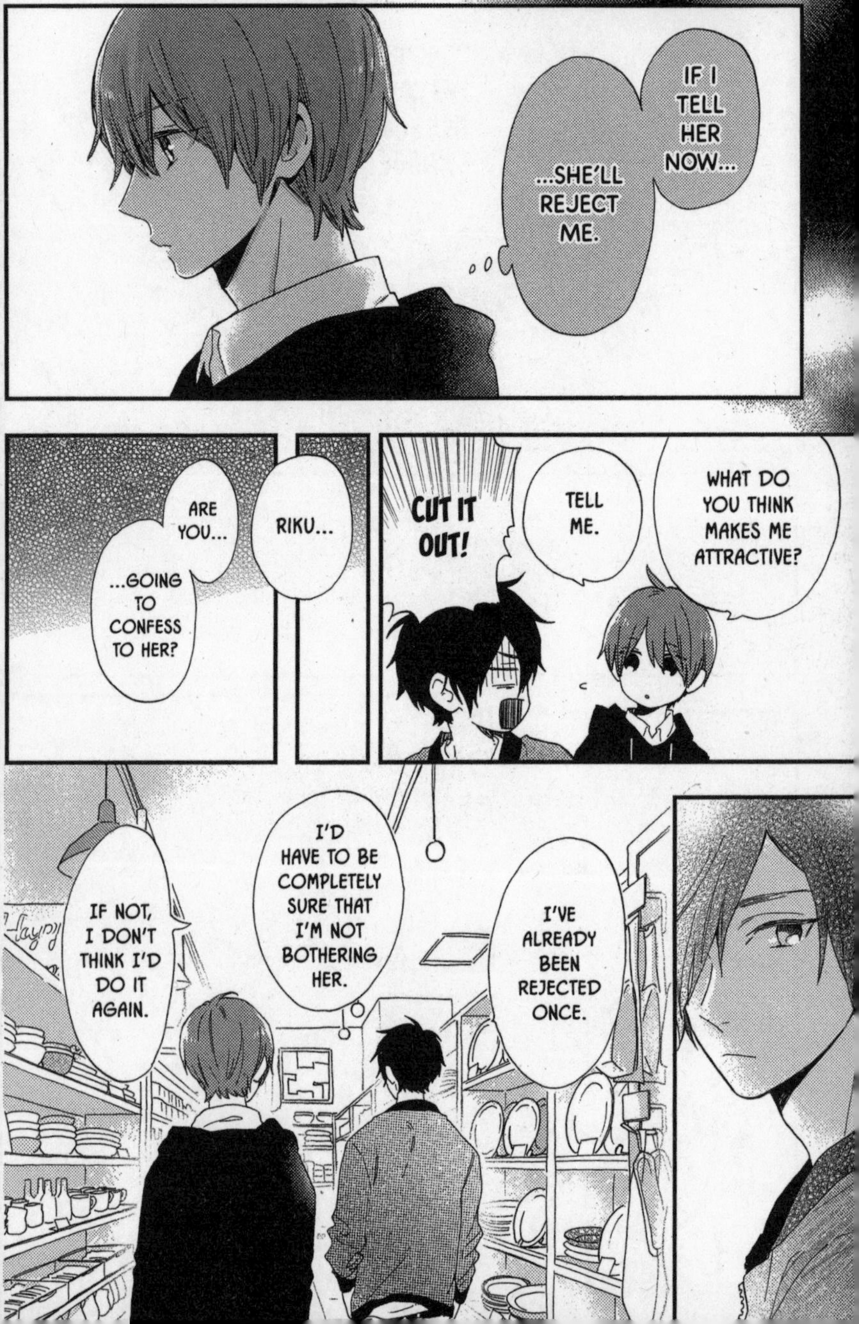
IF I TELL HER NOW...
...SHE'LL REJECT ME.
WHAT DO YOU THINK MAKES ME ATTRACTIVE?
TELL ME.
CUT IT OUT!
RIKU...
ARE YOU...
...GOING TO CONFESS TO HER?
I'VE ALREADY BEEN REJECTED ONCE.
I'D HAVE TO BE COMPLETELY SURE THAT I'M NOT BOTHERING HER.
IF NOT, I DON'T THINK I'D DO IT AGAIN.

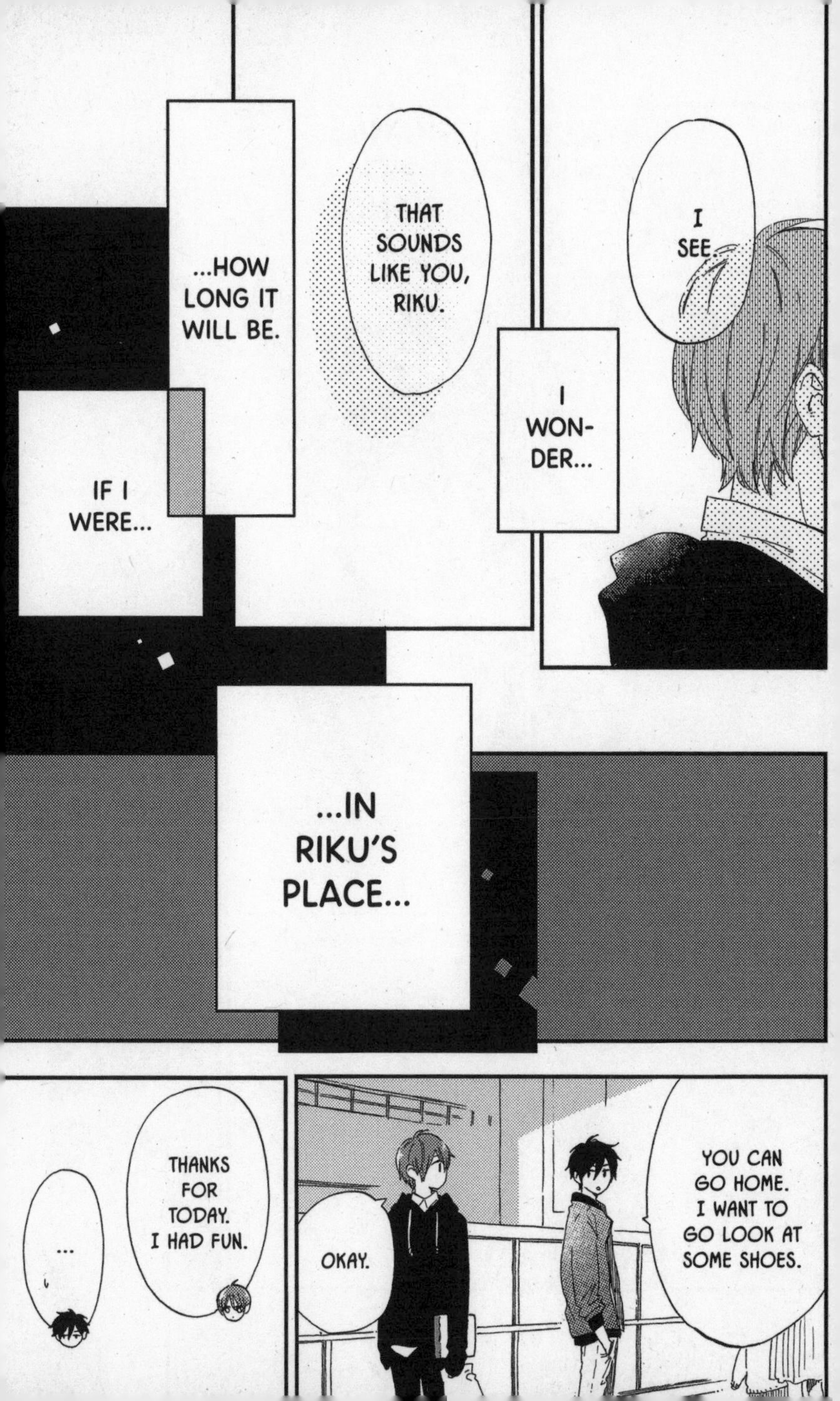
I SEE.
I WONDER...
THAT SOUNDS LIKE YOU, RIKU.
...HOW LONG IT WILL BE.
IF I WERE...
...IN RIKU'S PLACE...
YOU CAN GO HOME. I WANT TO GO LOOK AT SOME SHOES.
OKAY.
THANKS FOR TODAY. I HAD FUN.
...

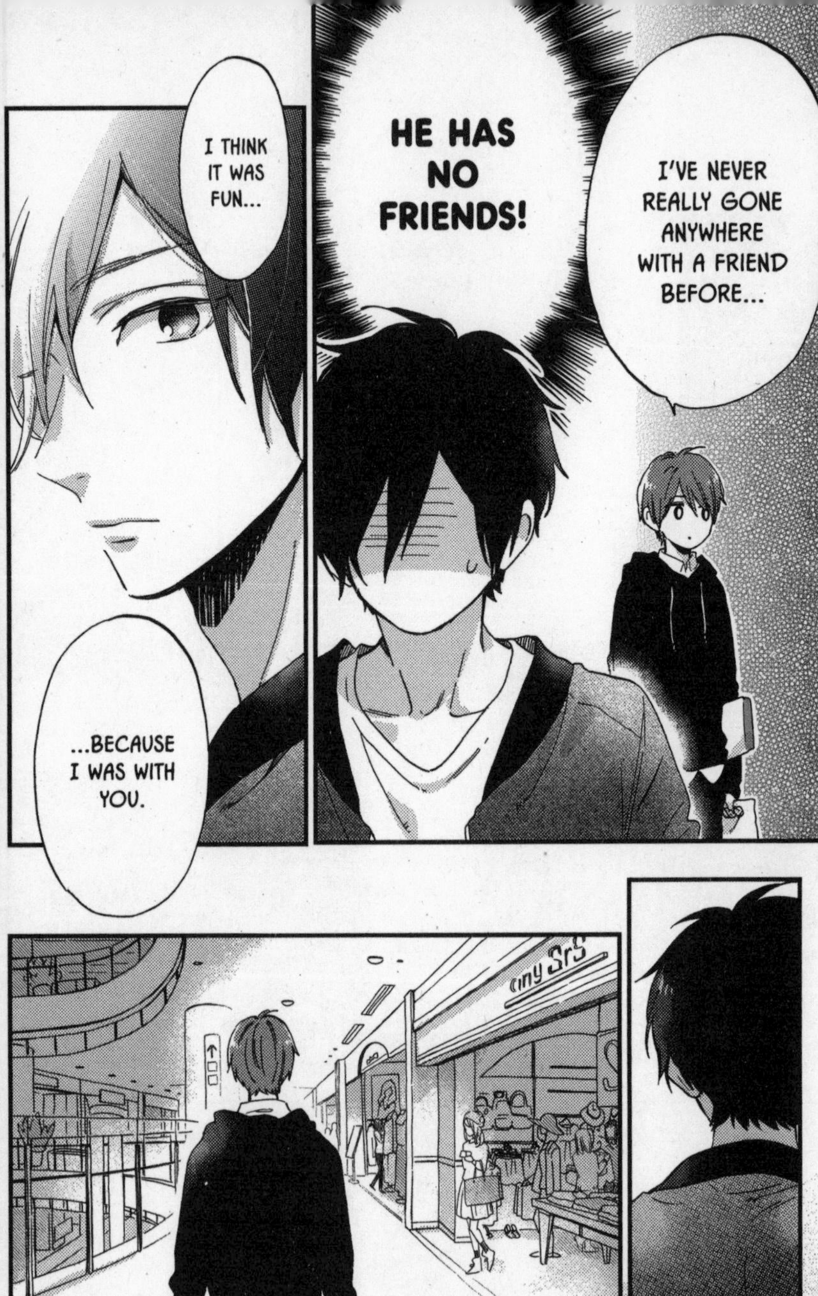
I'VE NEVER REALLY GONE ANYWHERE WITH A FRIEND BEFORE...
HE HAS NO FRIENDS!
I THINK IT WAS FUN...
...BECAUSE I WAS WITH YOU.

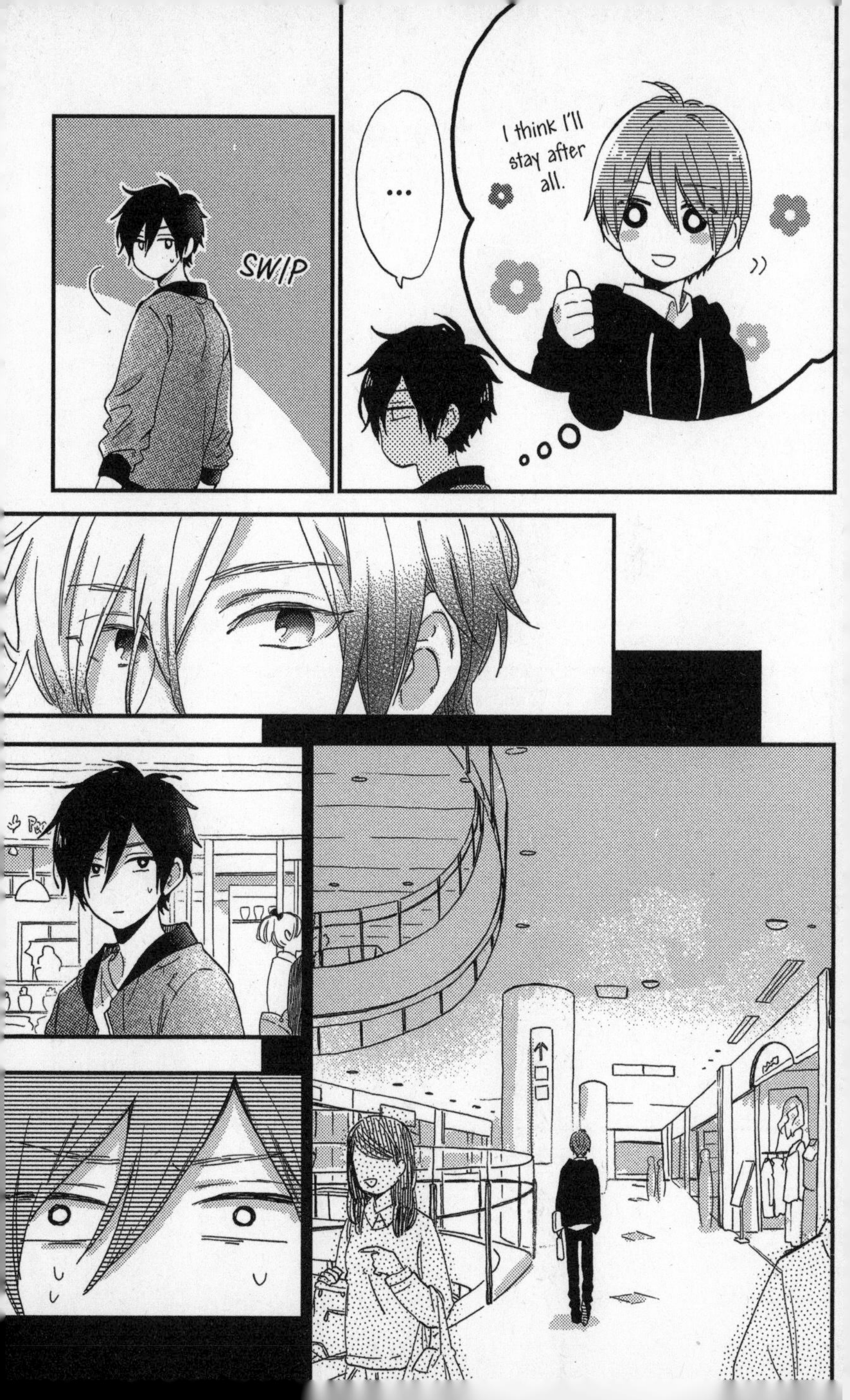
I think I'll stay after all.
...
SWIP

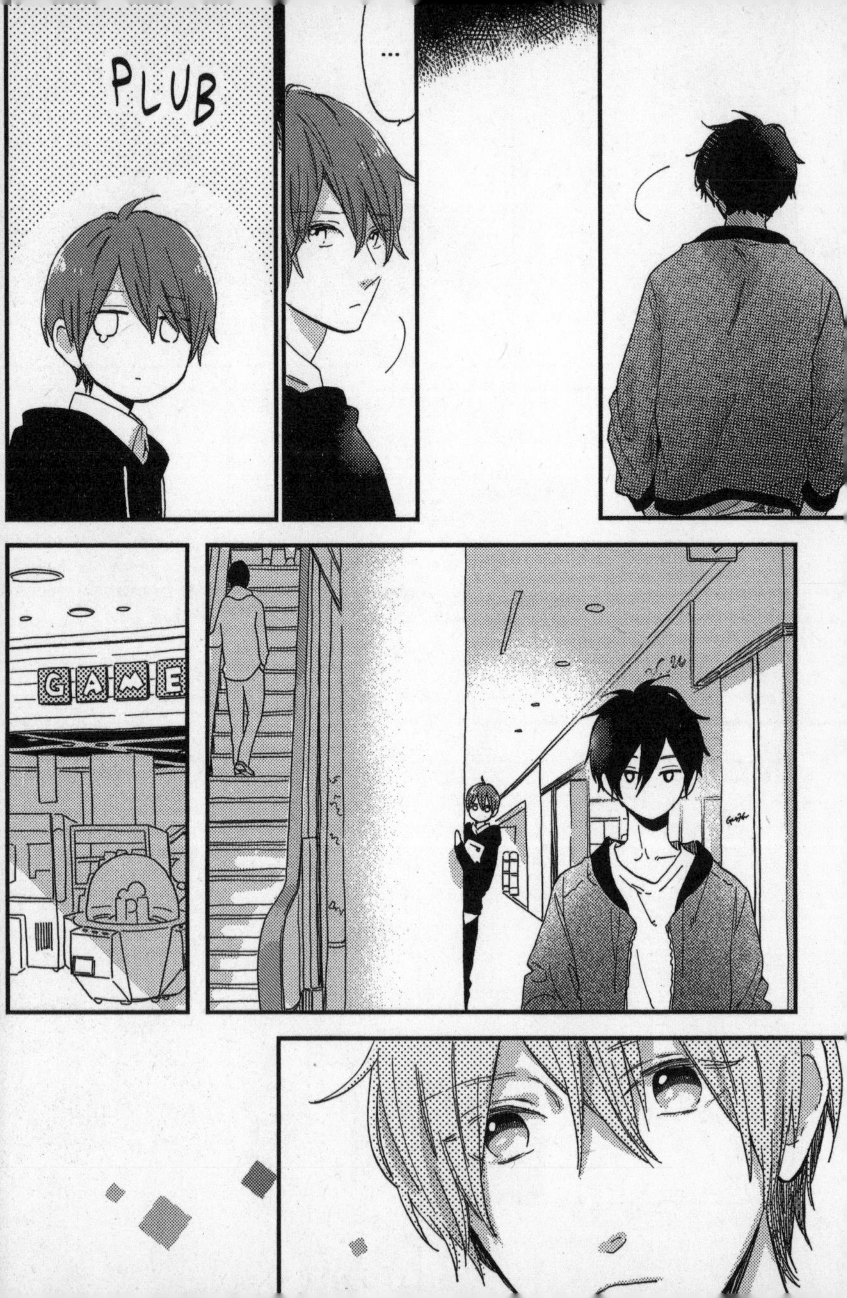
...
PLUB
GAME

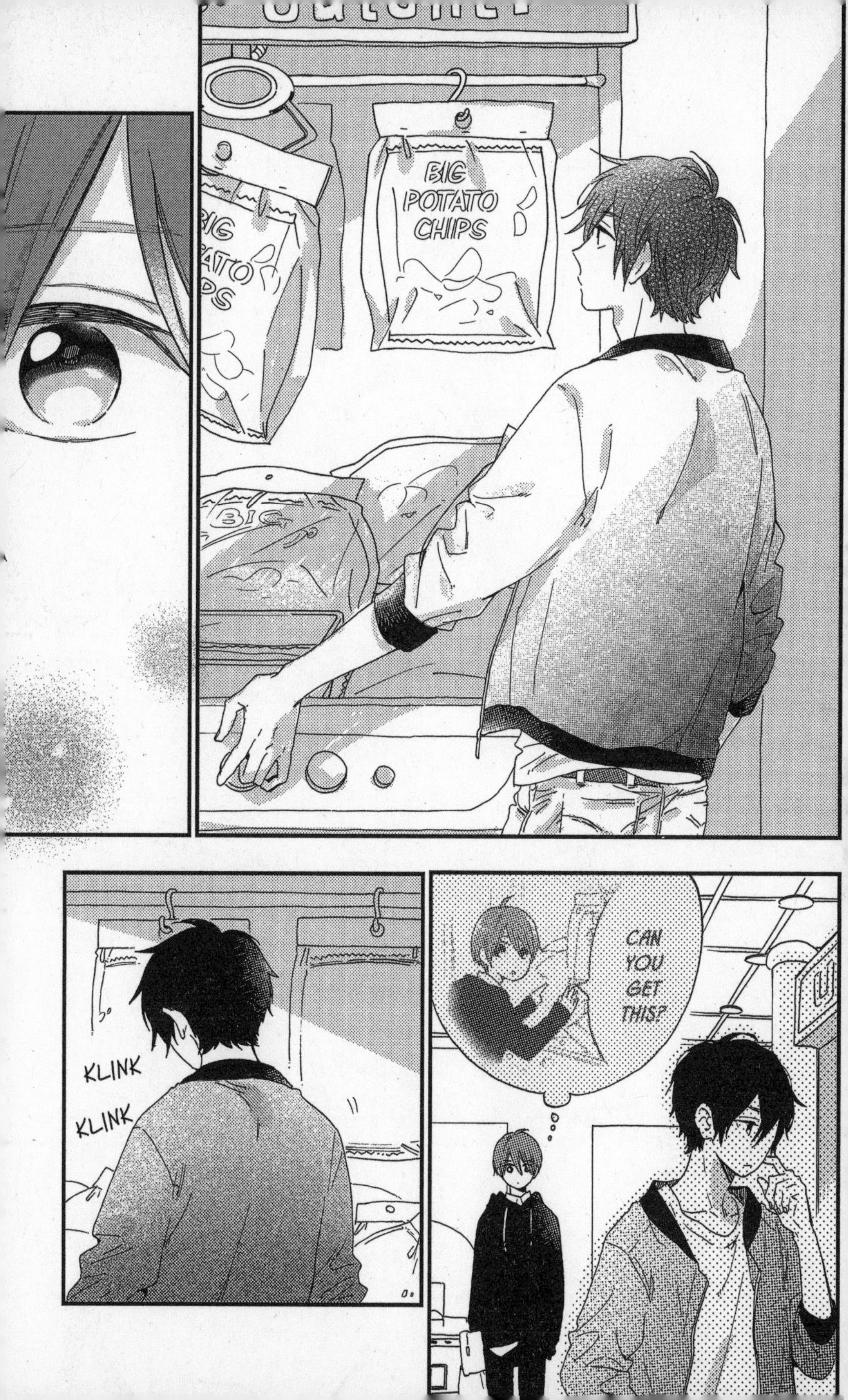
BIG POTATO CHIPS
CAN YOU GET THIS?
KLINK
KLINK

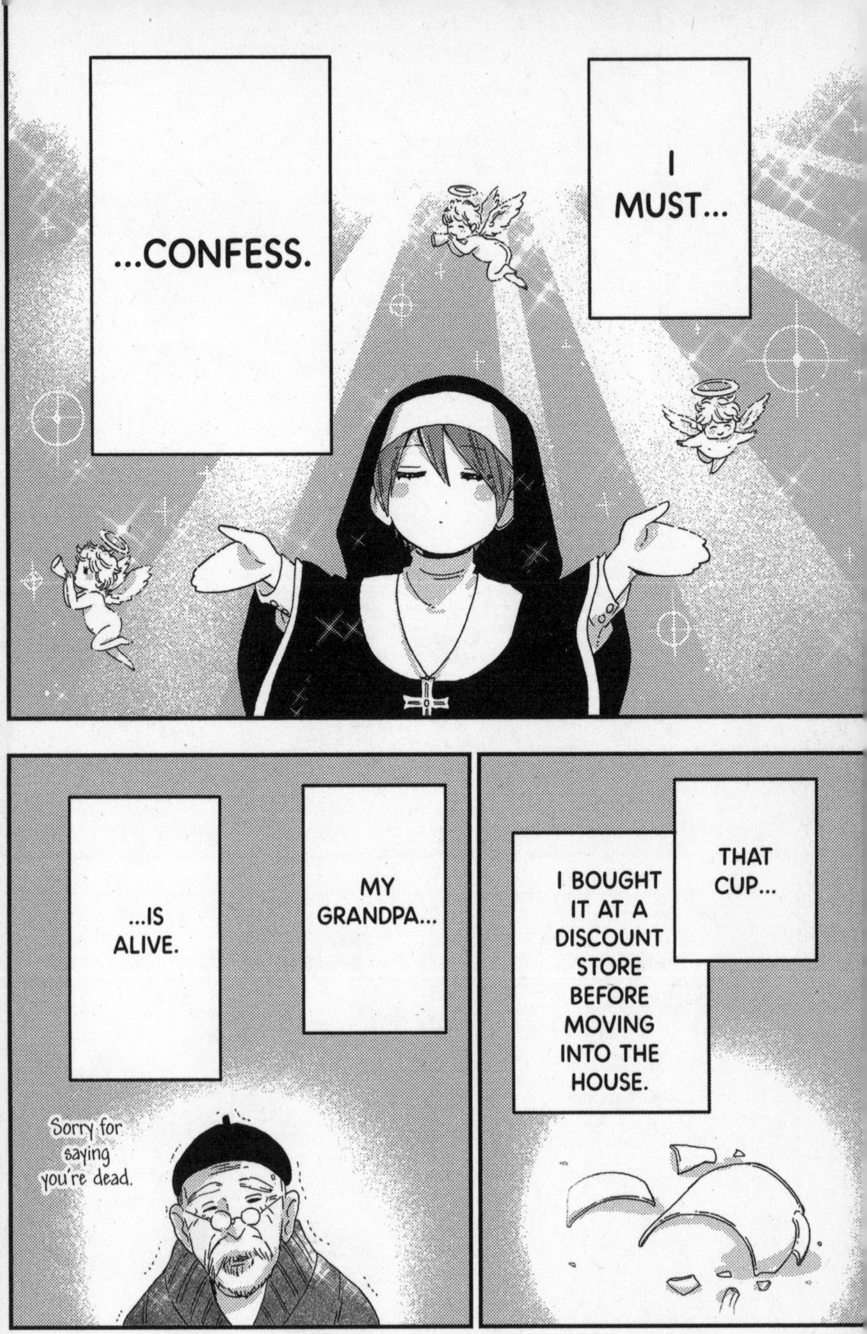
I MUST...
...CONFESS.
THAT CUP...
I BOUGHT IT AT A DISCOUNT STORE BEFORE MOVING INTO THE HOUSE.
MY GRANDPA...
...IS ALIVE.
Sorry for saying you're dead.

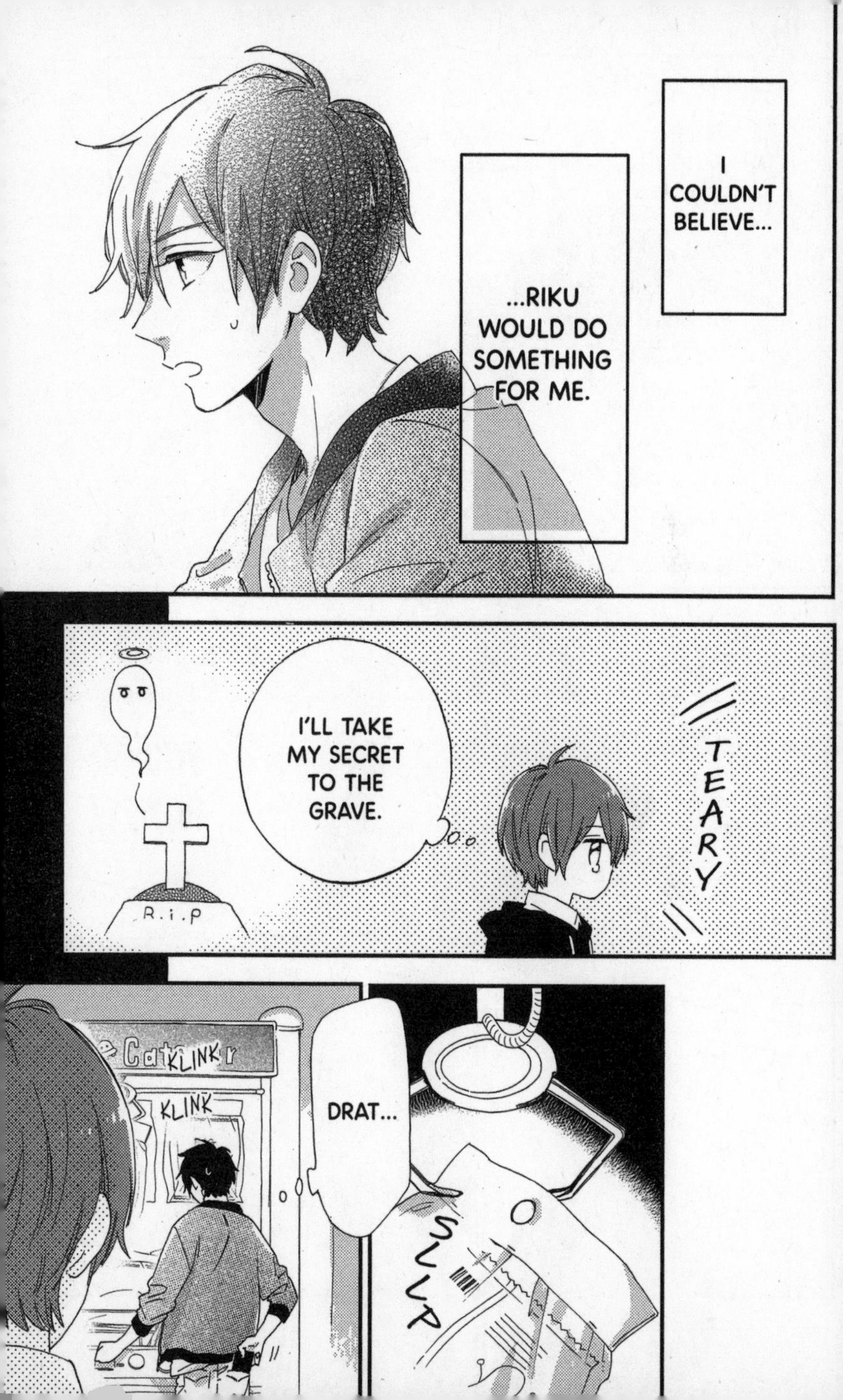
I COULDN'T BELIEVE...
...RIKU WOULD DO SOMETHING FOR ME.
TEARY
I'LL TAKE MY SECRET TO THE GRAVE.
R.I.P
DRAT...
SLURP
KLINK
KLINK

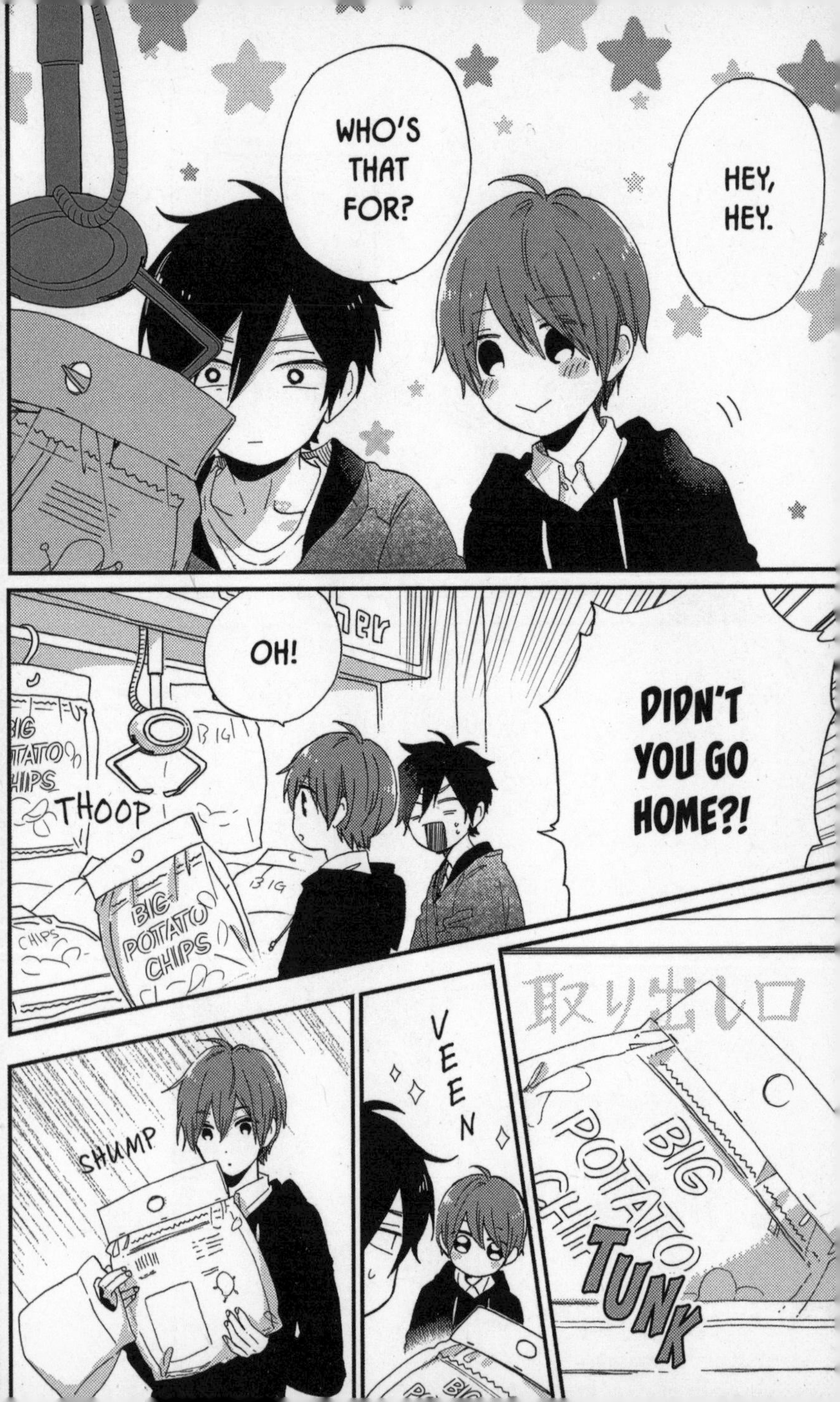
HEY, HEY.
WHO'S THAT FOR?
DIDN'T YOU GO HOME?!
OH!
THOOP
BIG POTATO CHIPS
取り出し口
BIG POTATO CHI
TUNK
VEEN
SHUMP

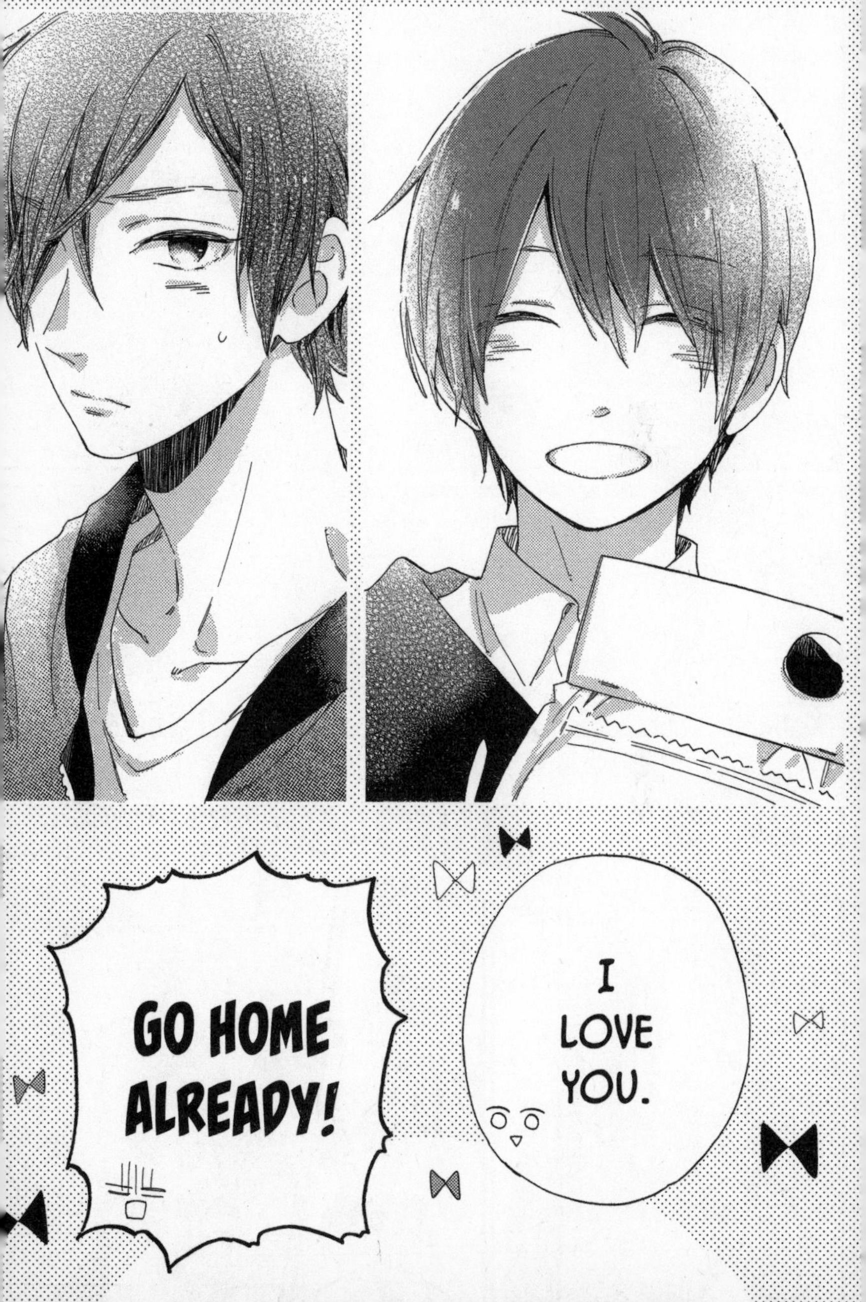
I LOVE YOU.
GO HOME ALREADY!

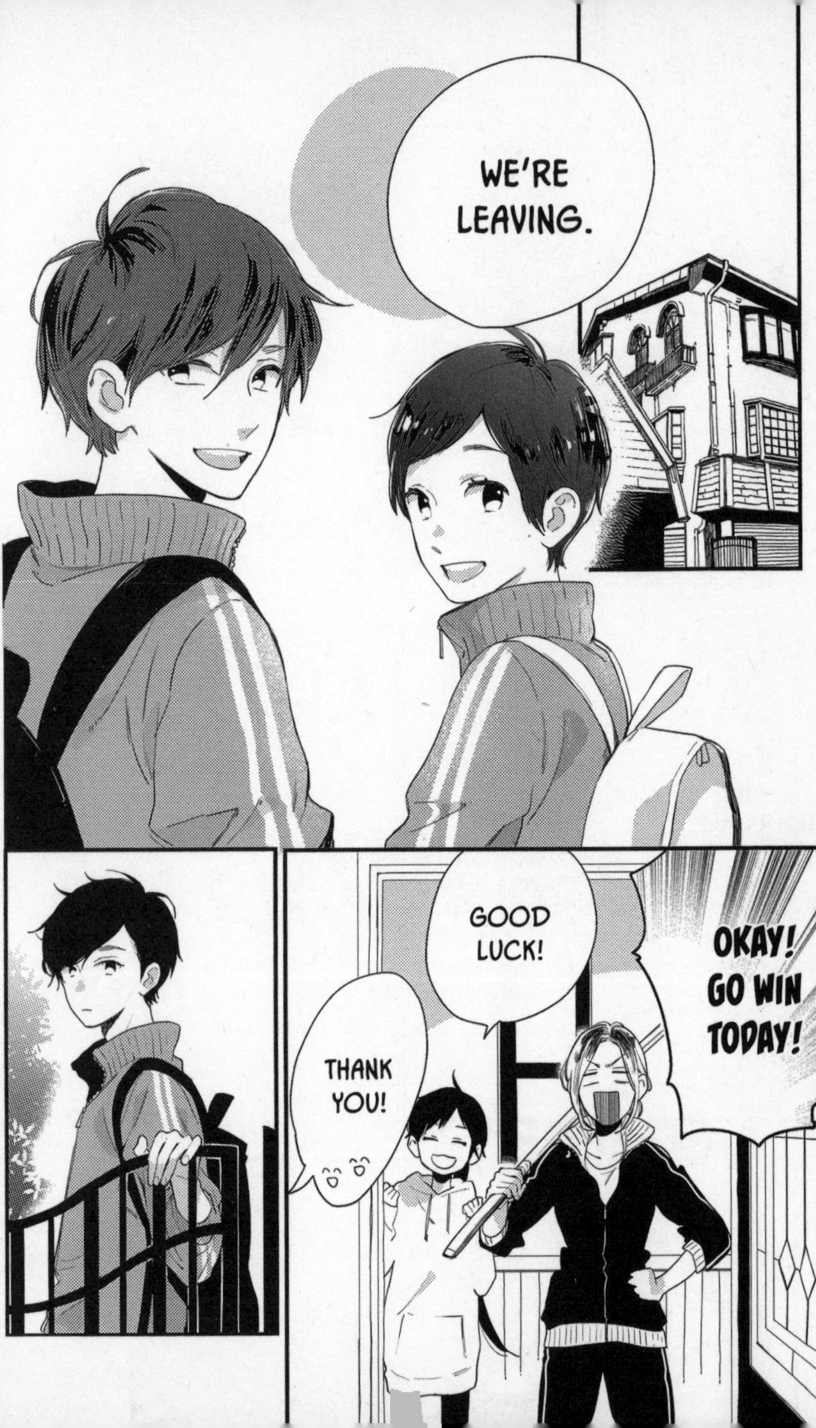
WE'RE LEAVING.
OKAY! GO WIN TODAY!
GOOD LUCK!
THANK YOU!

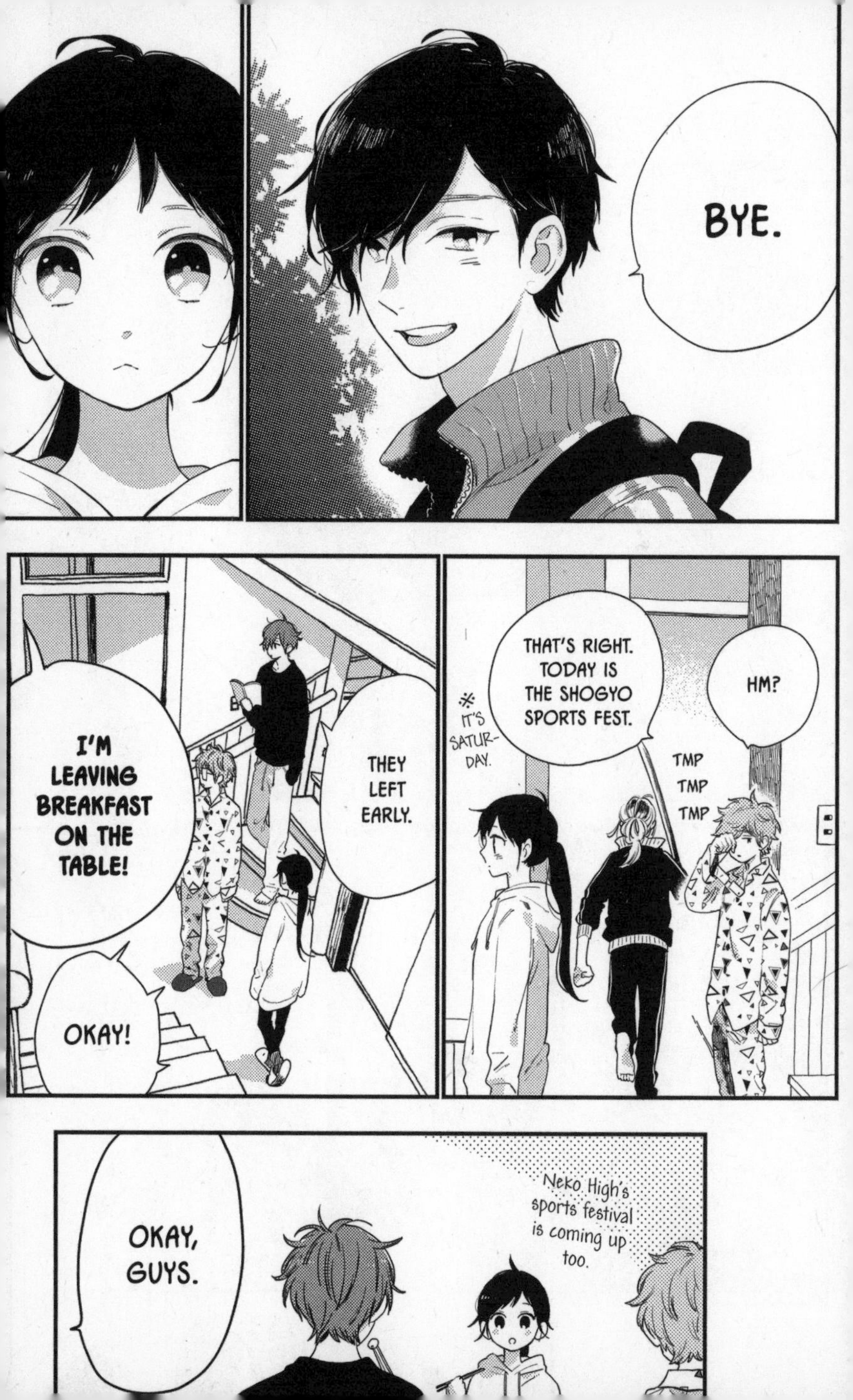
BYE.
HM?
TMP TMP TMP
THAT'S RIGHT. TODAY IS THE SHOGYO SPORTS FEST.
※IT'S SATURDAY.
THEY LEFT EARLY.
I'M LEAVING BREAKFAST ON THE TABLE!
OKAY!
Neko High's sports festival is coming up too.
OKAY, GUYS.

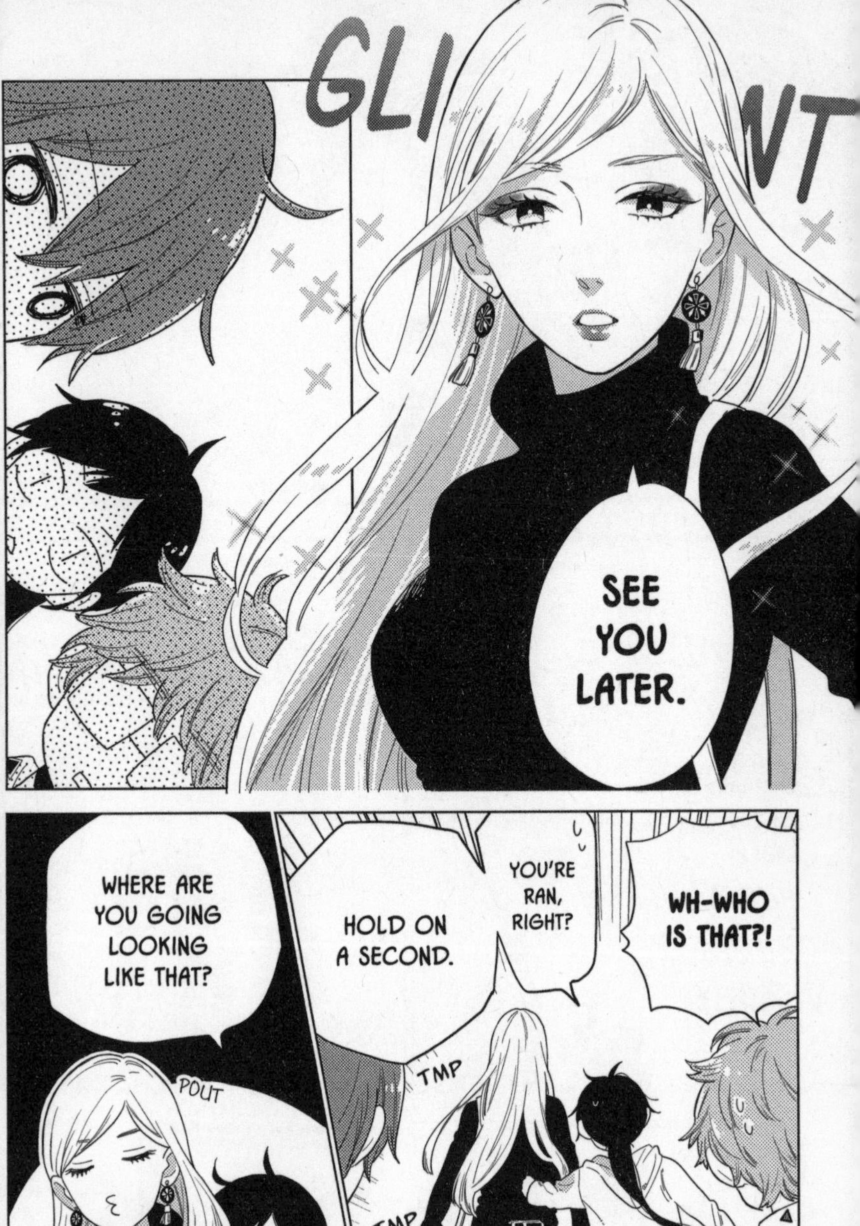
GLI NT
SEE YOU LATER.
WH-WHO IS THAT?!
YOU'RE RAN, RIGHT?
HOLD ON A SECOND.
TMP
TMP
WHERE ARE YOU GOING LOOKING LIKE THAT?
POUT

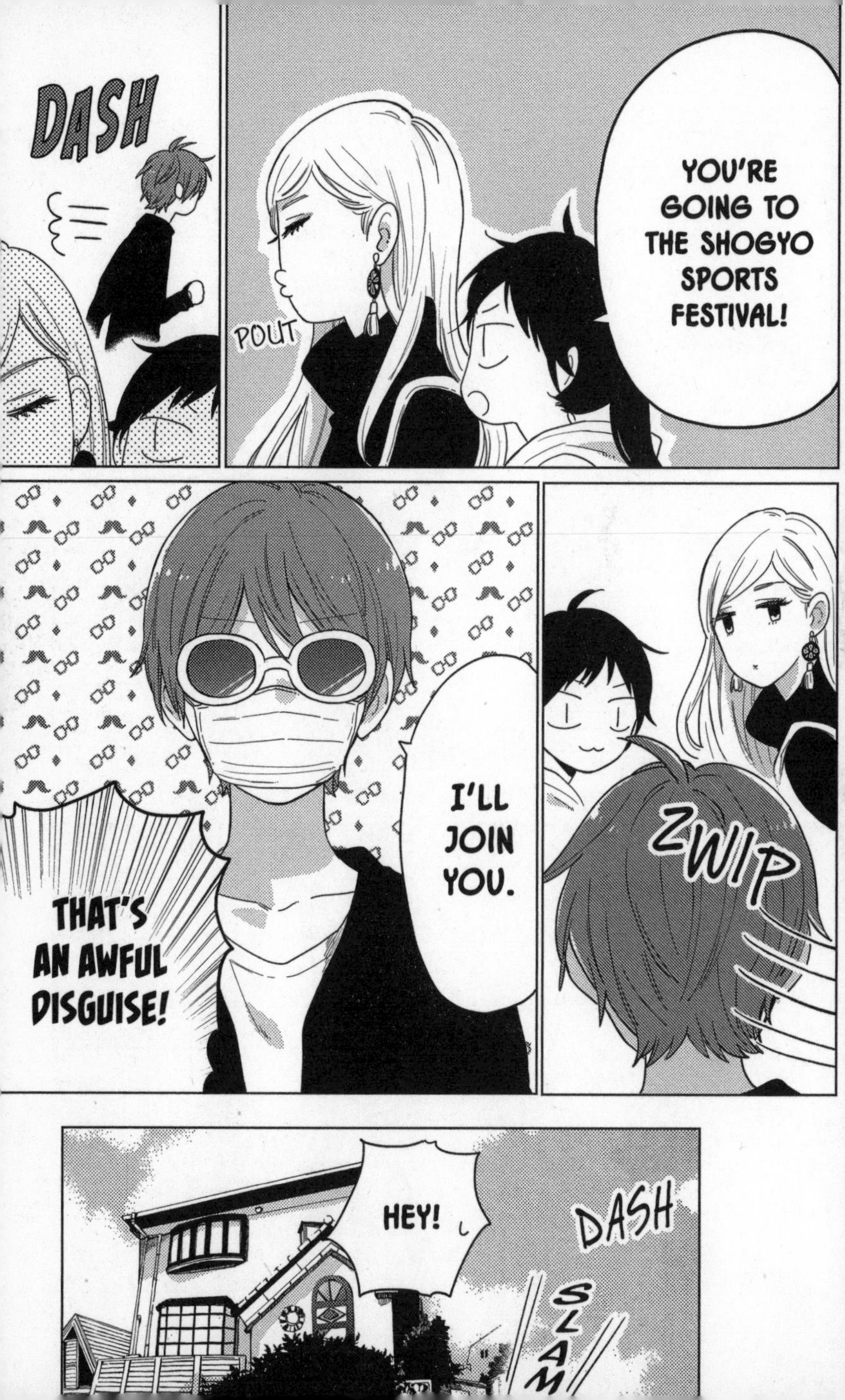
YOU'RE GOING TO THE SHOGYO SPORTS FESTIVAL!
POUT
DASH
ZWIP
I'LL JOIN YOU.
THAT'S AN AWFUL DISGUISE!
HEY!
DASH
SLAM

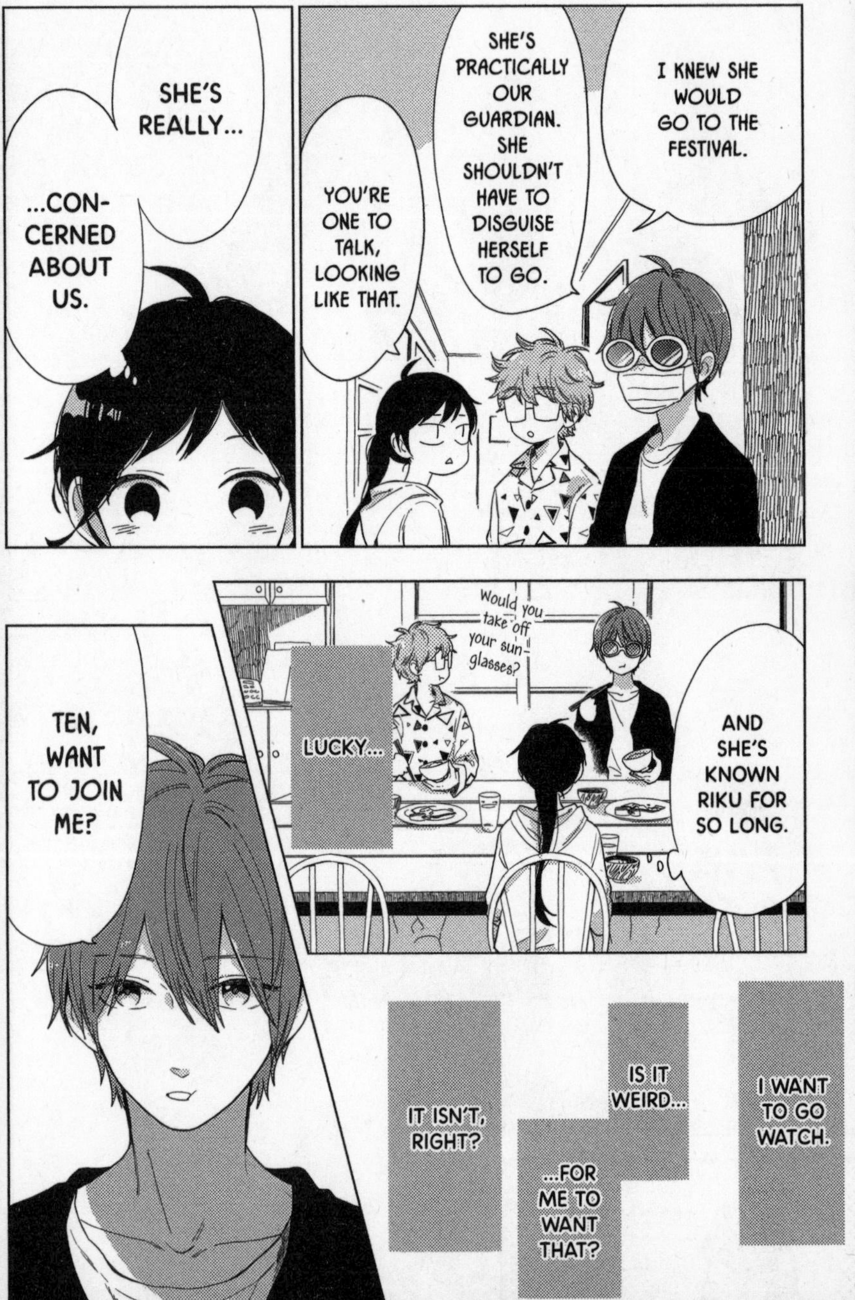
I KNEW SHE WOULD GO TO THE FESTIVAL.
SHE'S PRACTICALLY OUR GUARDIAN. SHE SHOULDN'T HAVE TO DISGUISE HERSELF TO GO.
YOU'RE ONE TO TALK, LOOKING LIKE THAT.
SHE'S REALLY...
...CON-CERNED ABOUT US.
AND SHE'S KNOWN RIKU FOR SO LONG.
Would you take off your sun-glasses?
LUCKY...
I WANT TO GO WATCH.
IS IT WEIRD...
...FOR ME TO WANT THAT?
IT ISN'T, RIGHT?
TEN, WANT TO JOIN ME?

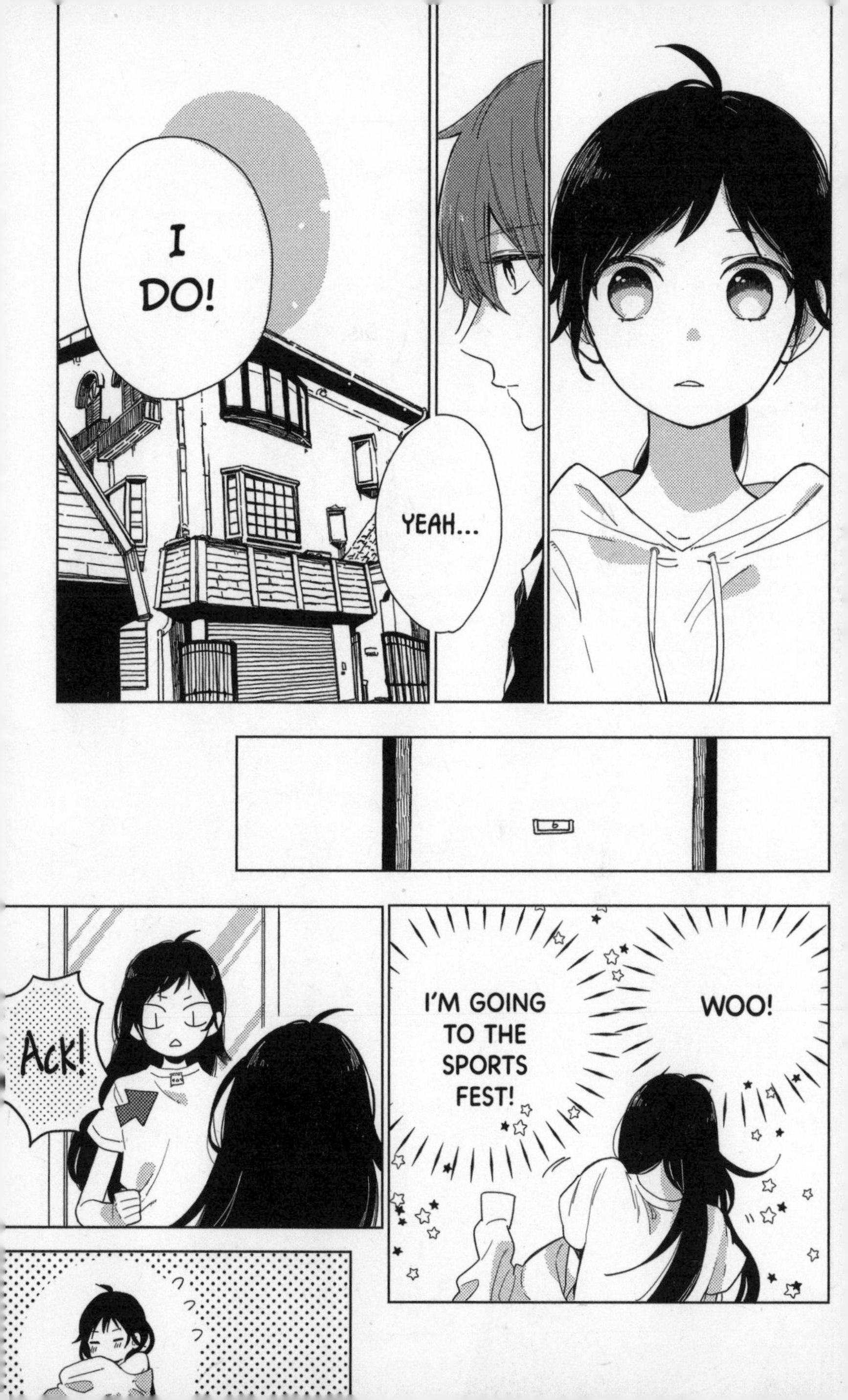
YEAH...
I DO!
WOO!
I'M GOING TO THE SPORTS FEST!
ACK!

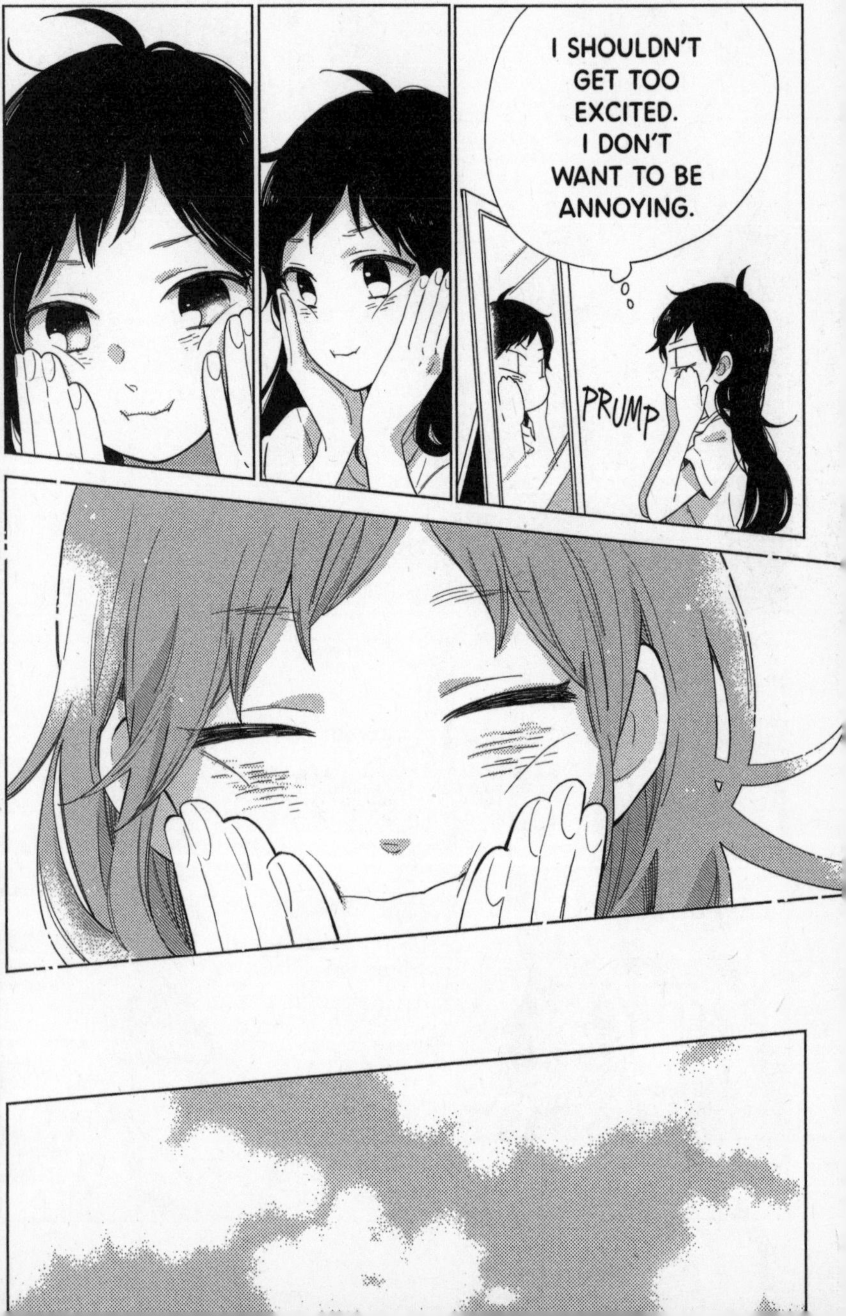
I SHOULDN'T GET TOO EXCITED. I DON'T WANT TO BE ANNOYING.
PRUMP

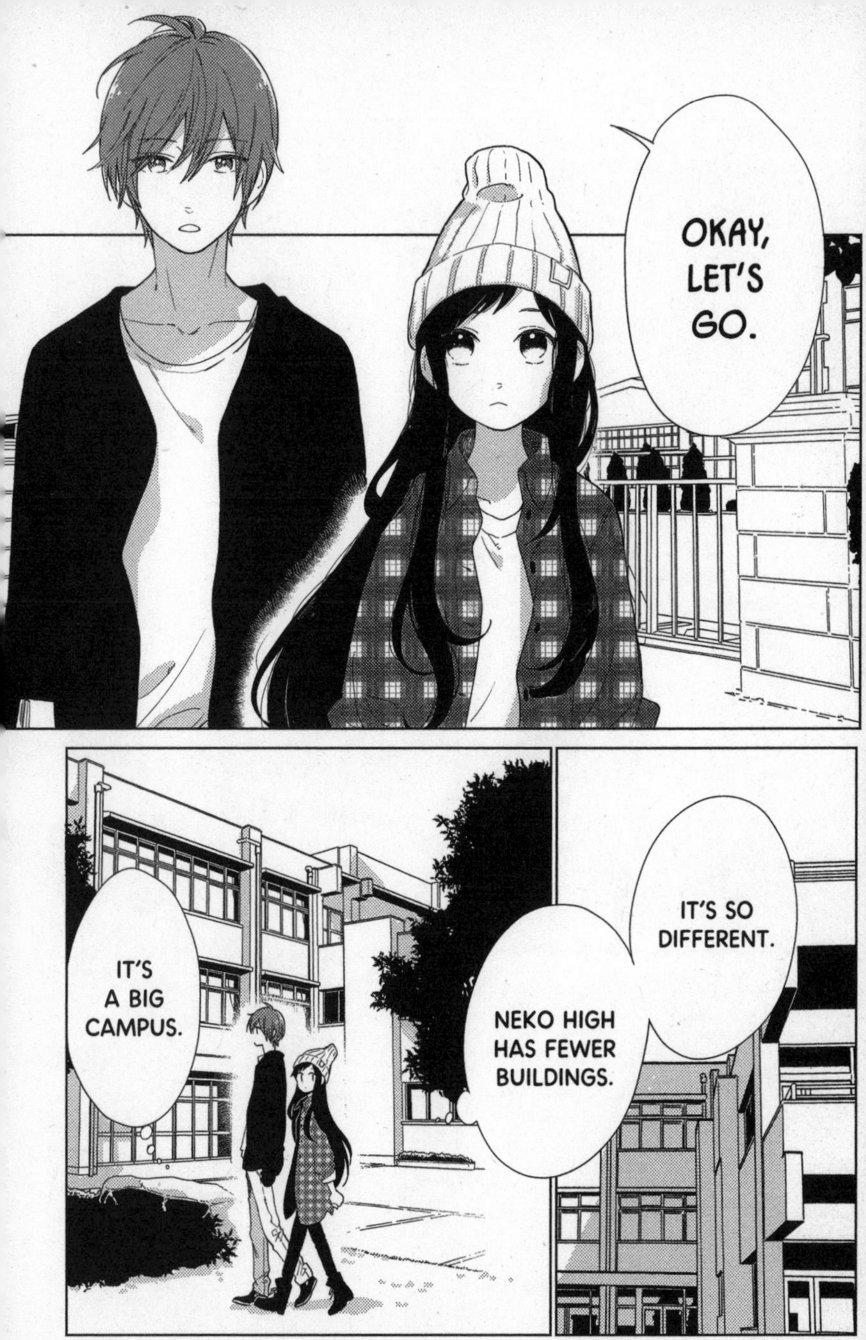
OKAY, LET'S GO.
IT'S SO DIFFERENT.
NEKO HIGH HAS FEWER BUILDINGS.
IT'S A BIG CAMPUS.

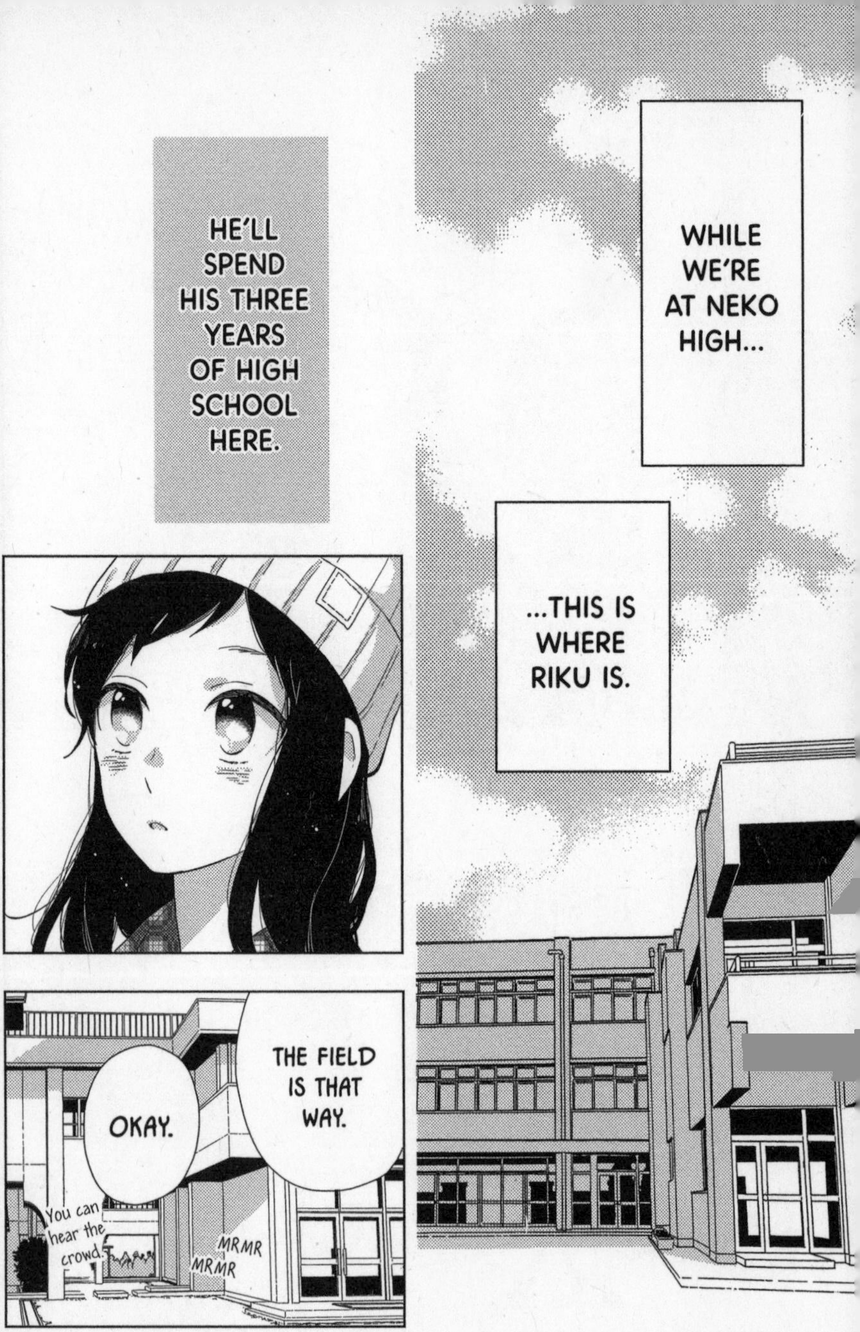
WHILE WE'RE AT NEKO HIGH...
...THIS IS WHERE RIKU IS.
HE'LL SPEND HIS THREE YEARS OF HIGH SCHOOL HERE.
THE FIELD IS THAT WAY.
OKAY.
You can hear the crowd.
MRMR
MRMR

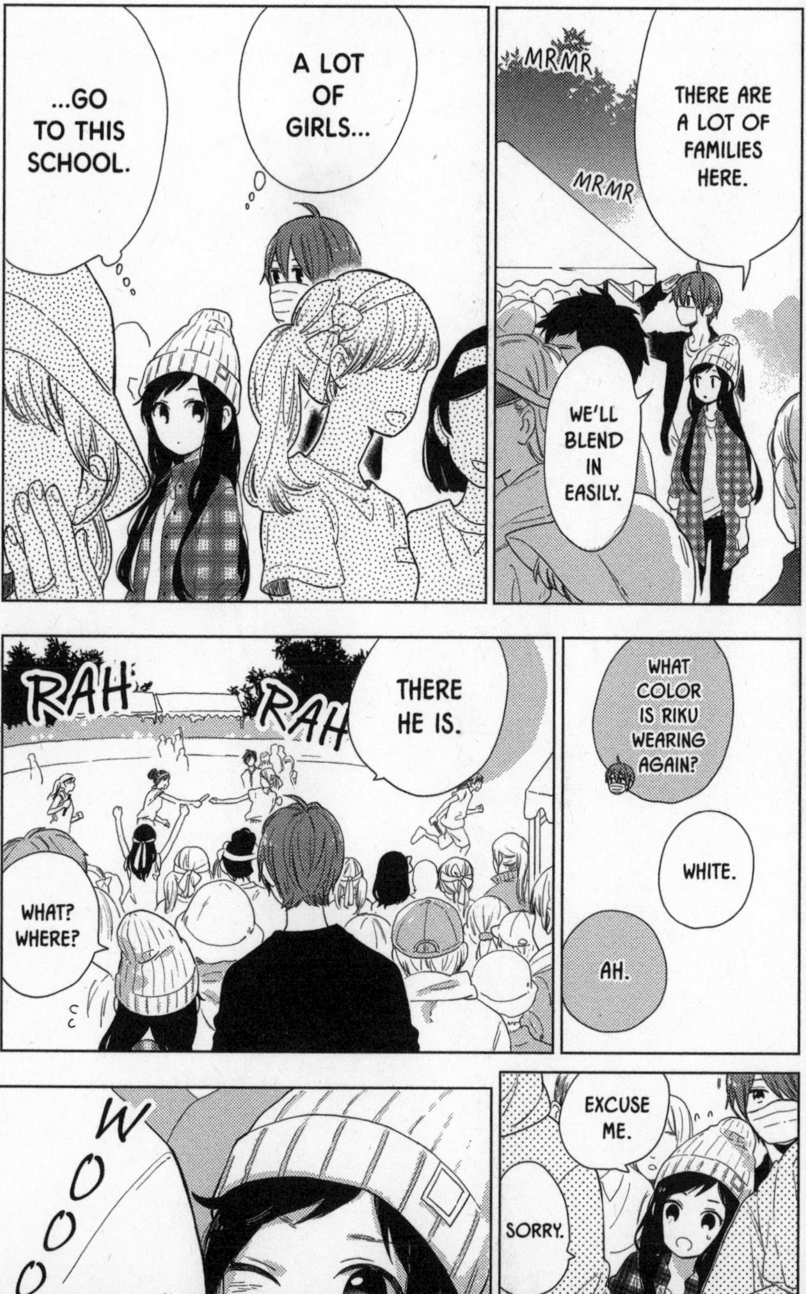
MRMR
THERE ARE A LOT OF FAMILIES HERE.
MRMR
WE'LL BLEND IN EASILY.
A LOT OF GIRLS...
...GO TO THIS SCHOOL.
WHAT COLOR IS RIKU WEARING AGAIN?
WHITE.
AH.
THERE HE IS.
RAH
RAH
WHAT? WHERE?
EXCUSE ME.
SORRY.
WOOOO

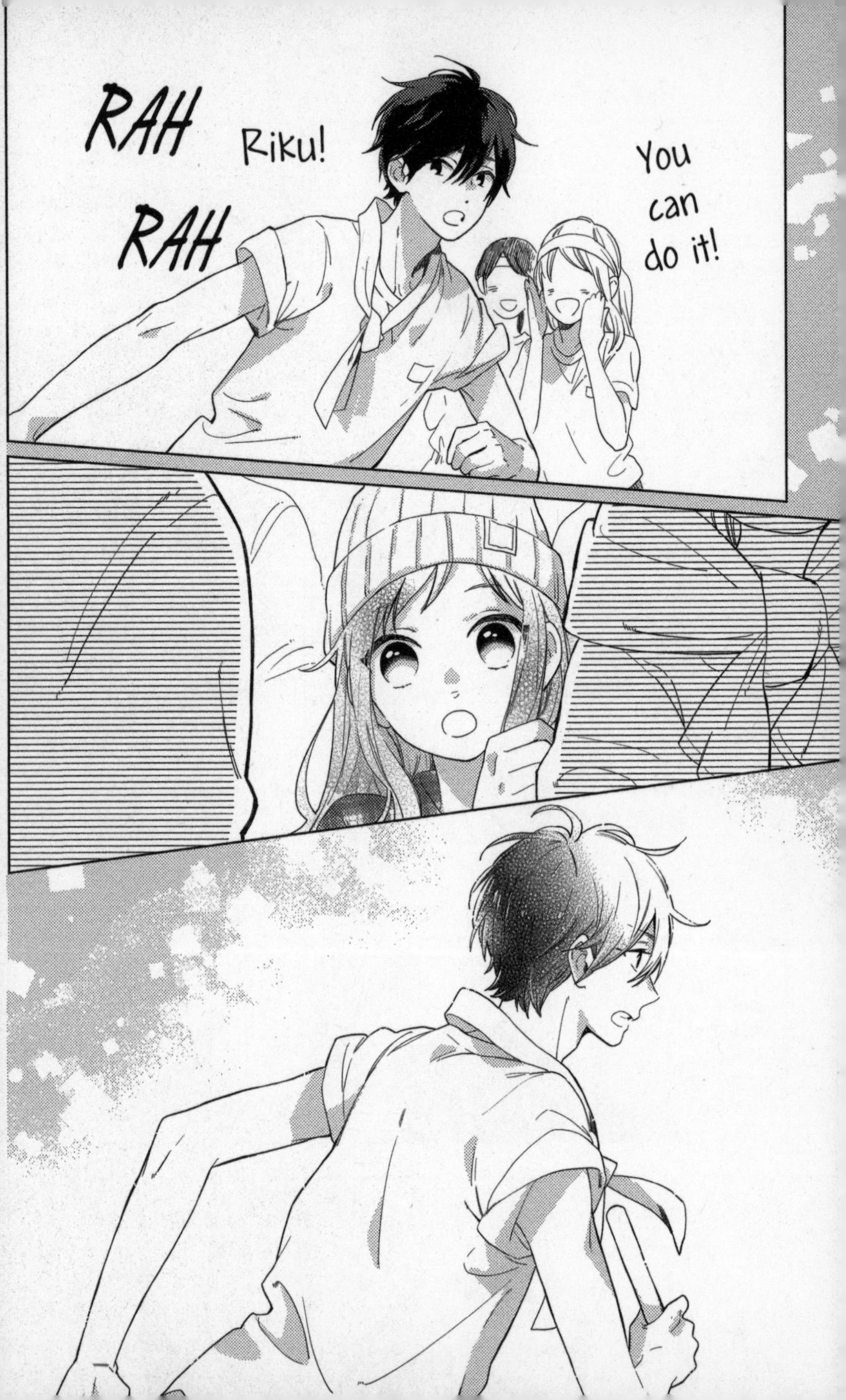
You can do it!
Riku!
RAH RAH

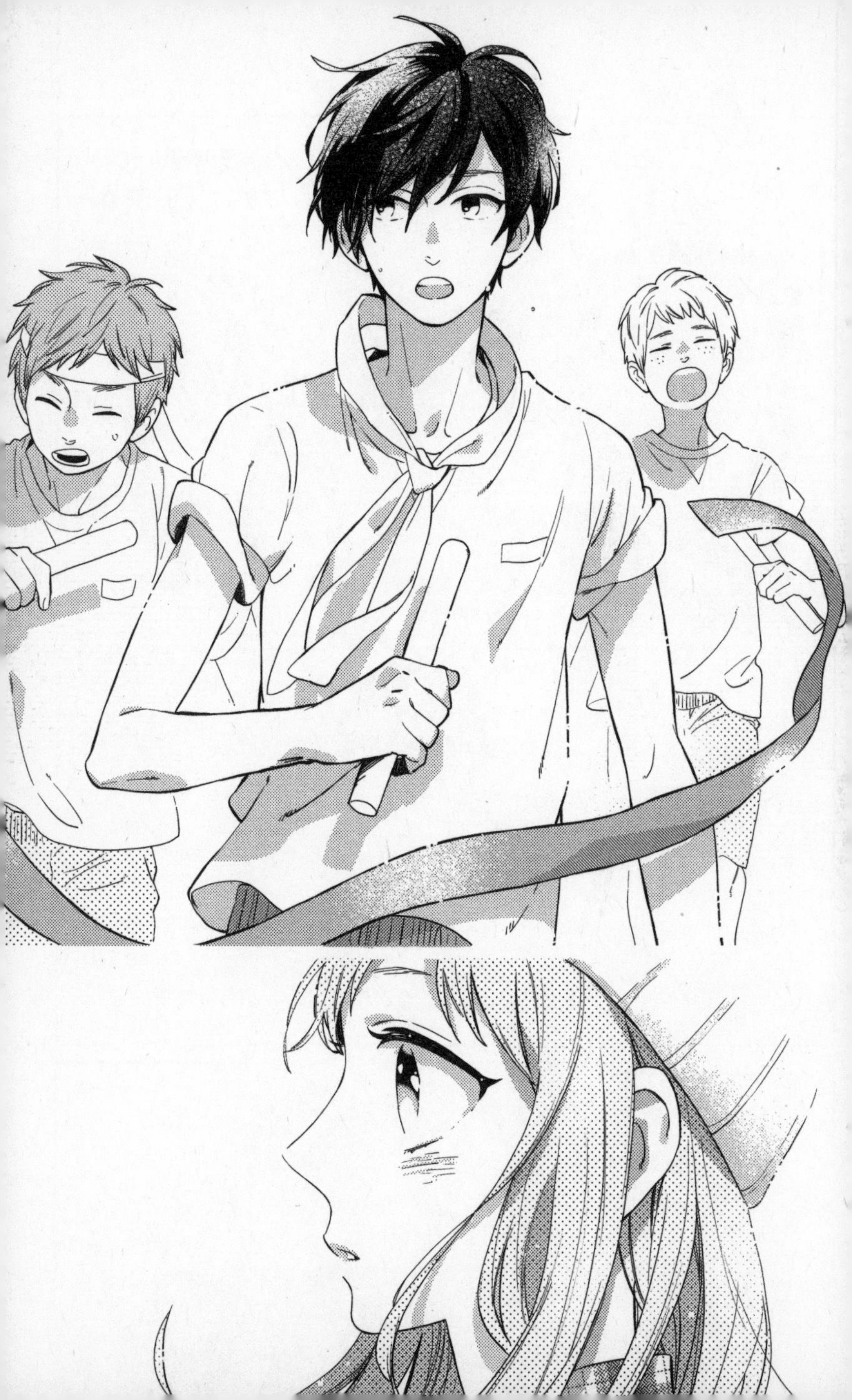

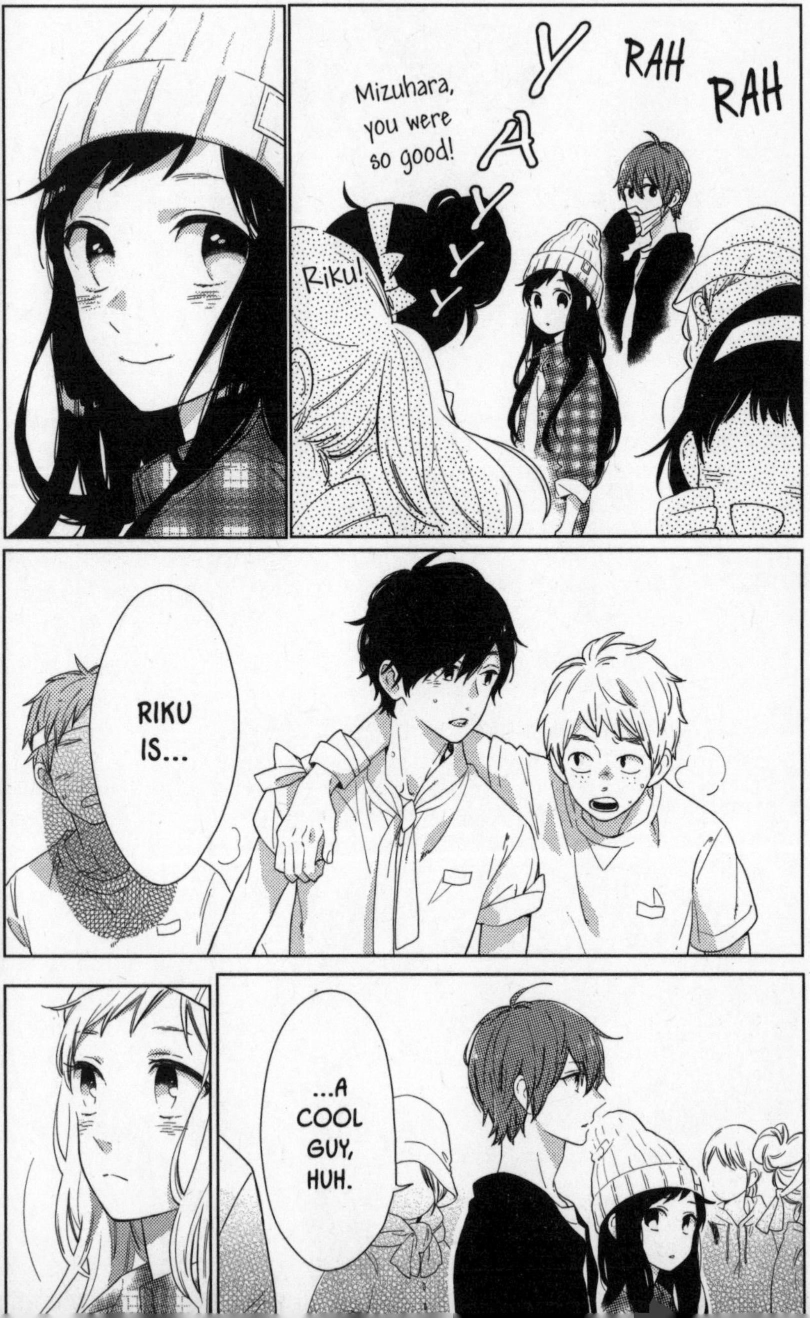
RAH
RAH
YAYYY
Mizuhara, you were so good!
Riku!
RIKU IS...
...A COOL GUY, HUH.

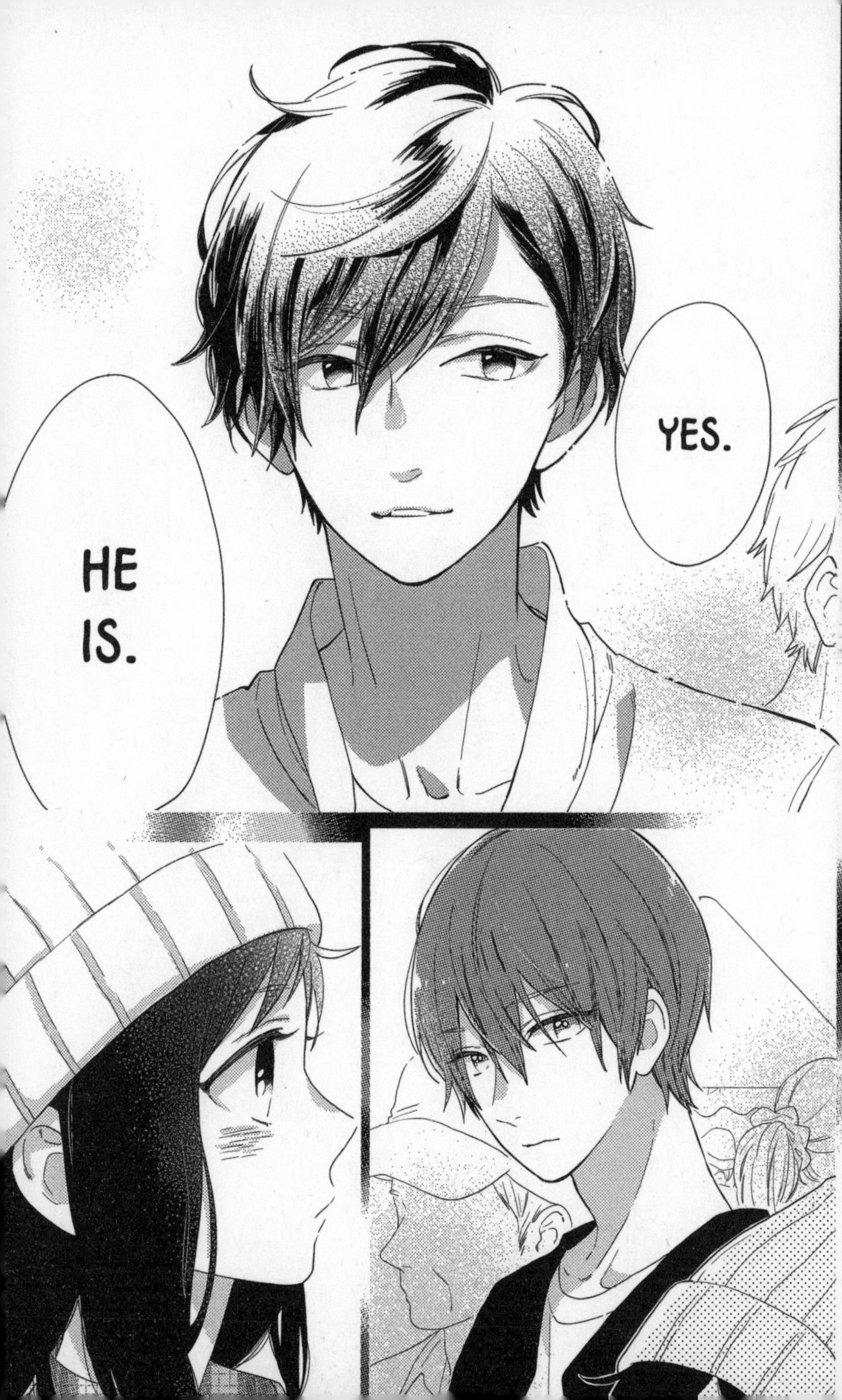
YES.
HE IS.

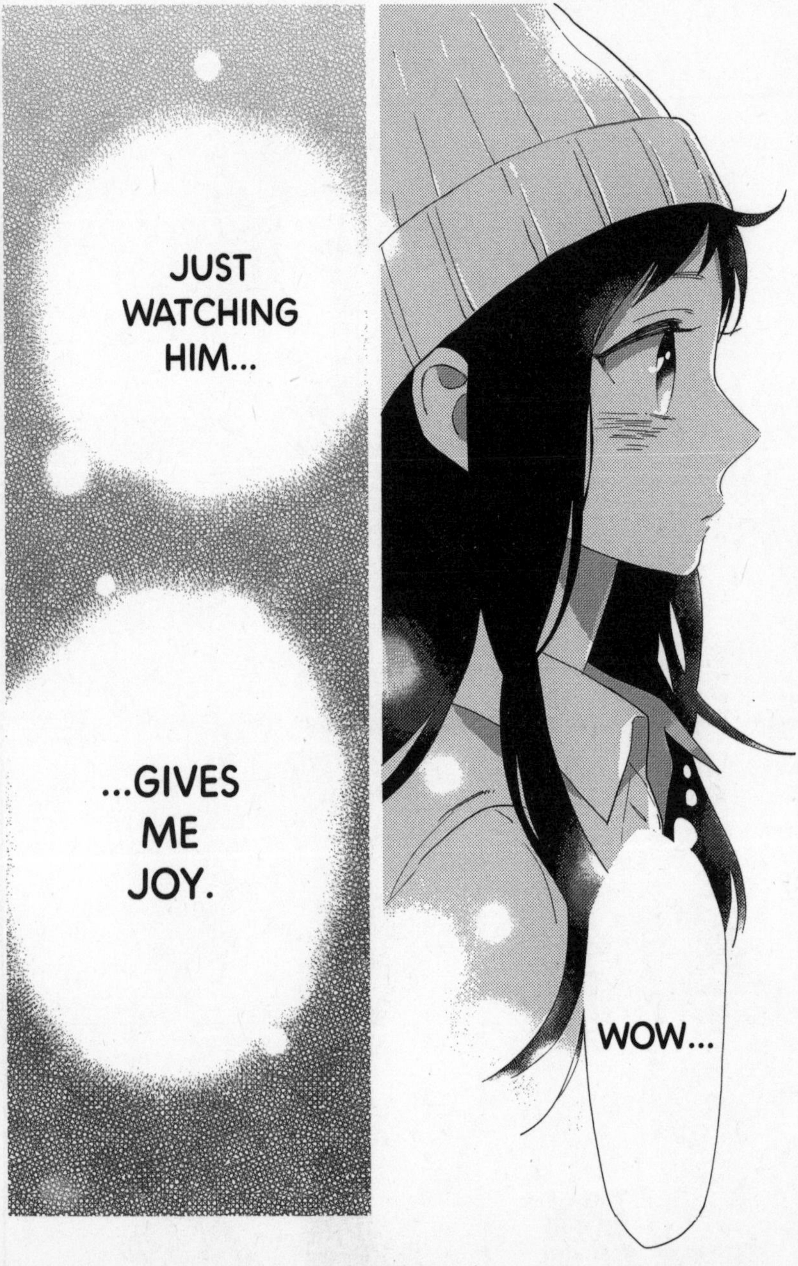
WOW...
JUST WATCHING HIM...
...GIVES ME JOY.

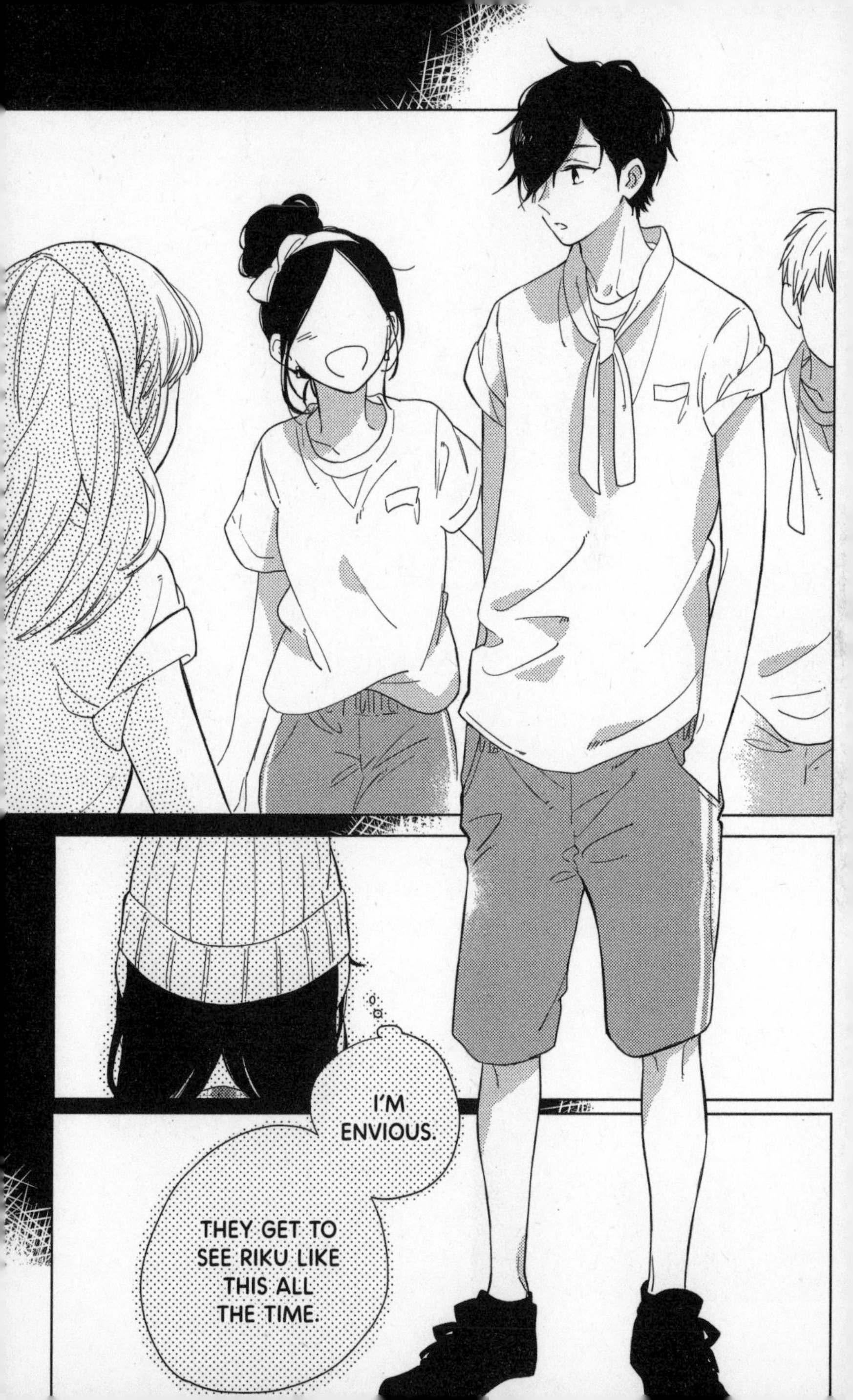
I'M ENVIOUS.
THEY GET TO SEE RIKU LIKE THIS ALL THE TIME.

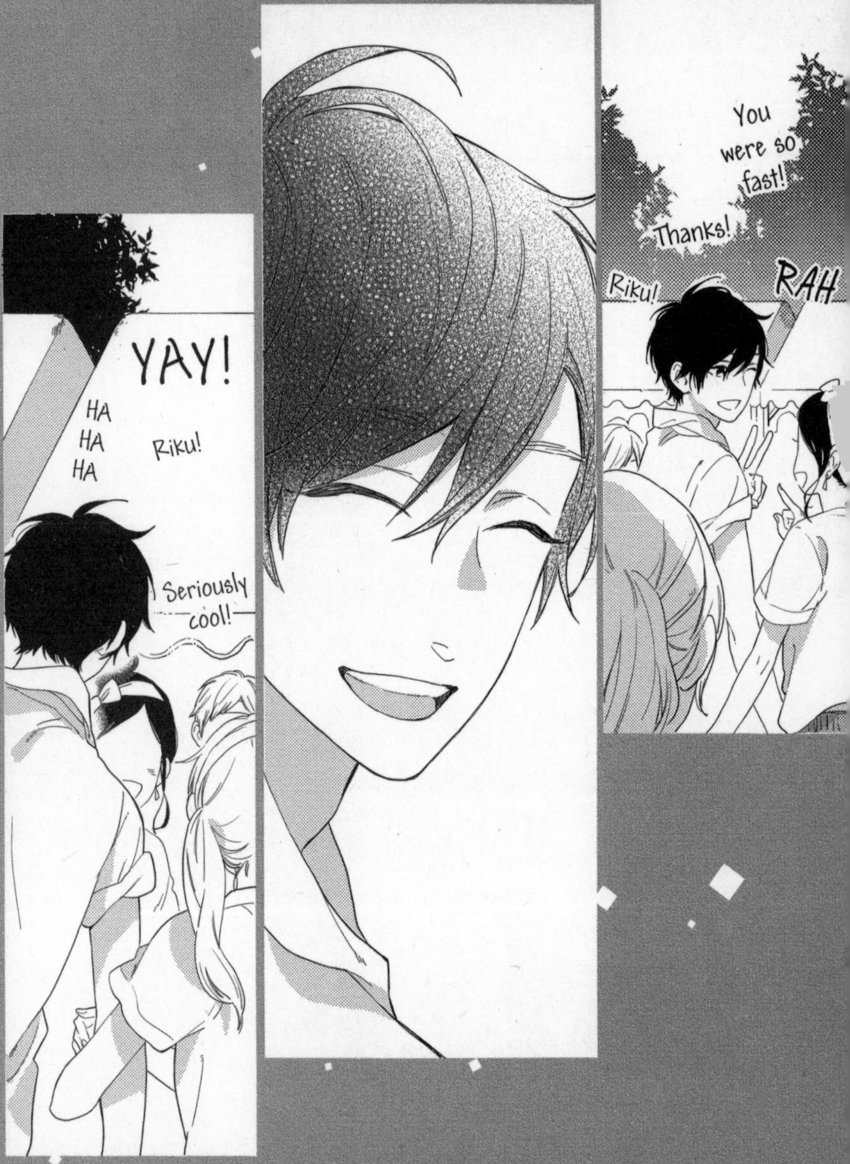

You were so fast!
Thanks!
RAH
Riku!
YAY!
Riku!
HA HA HA
Seriously cool!

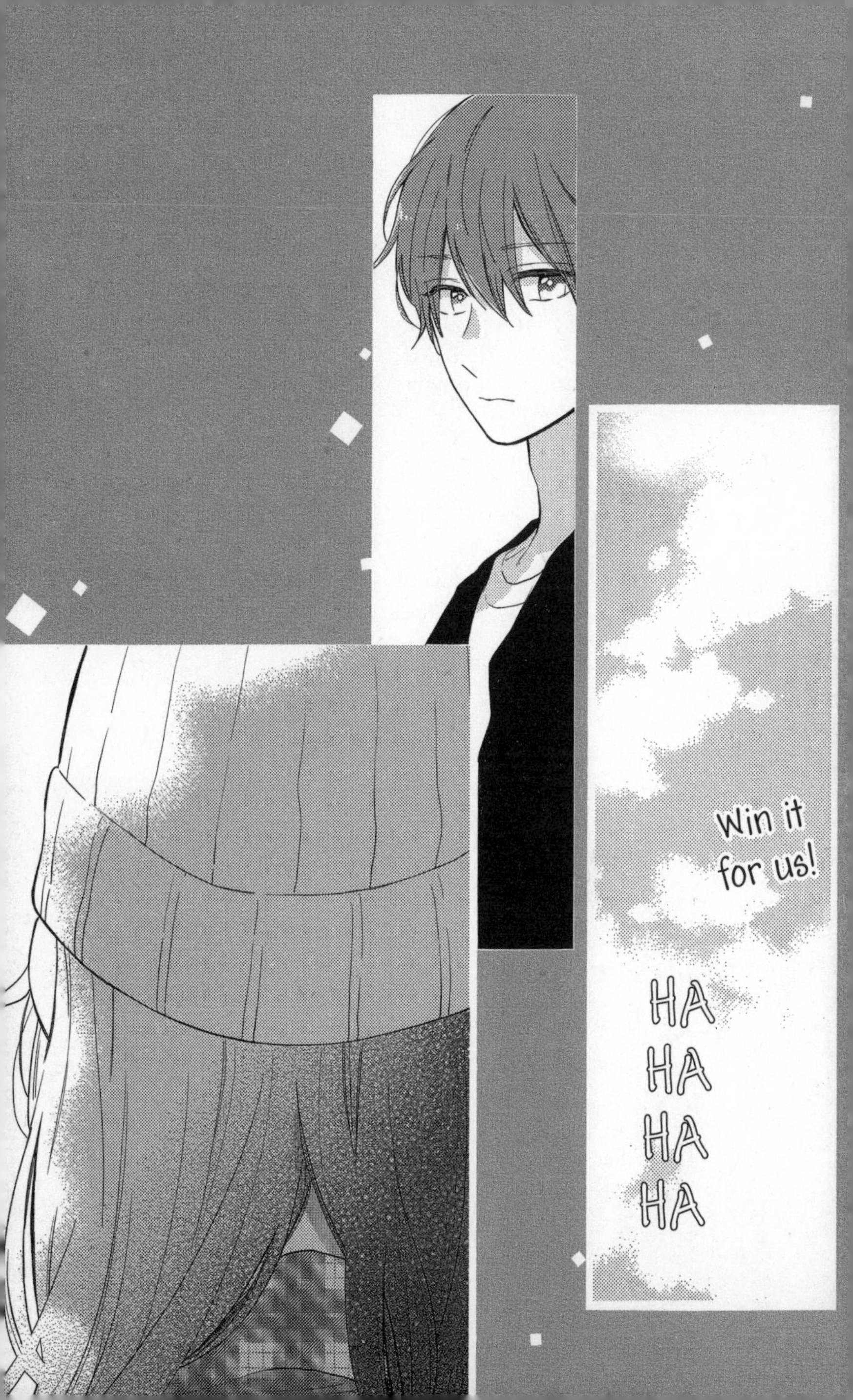
Win it for us!
HA HA HA HA

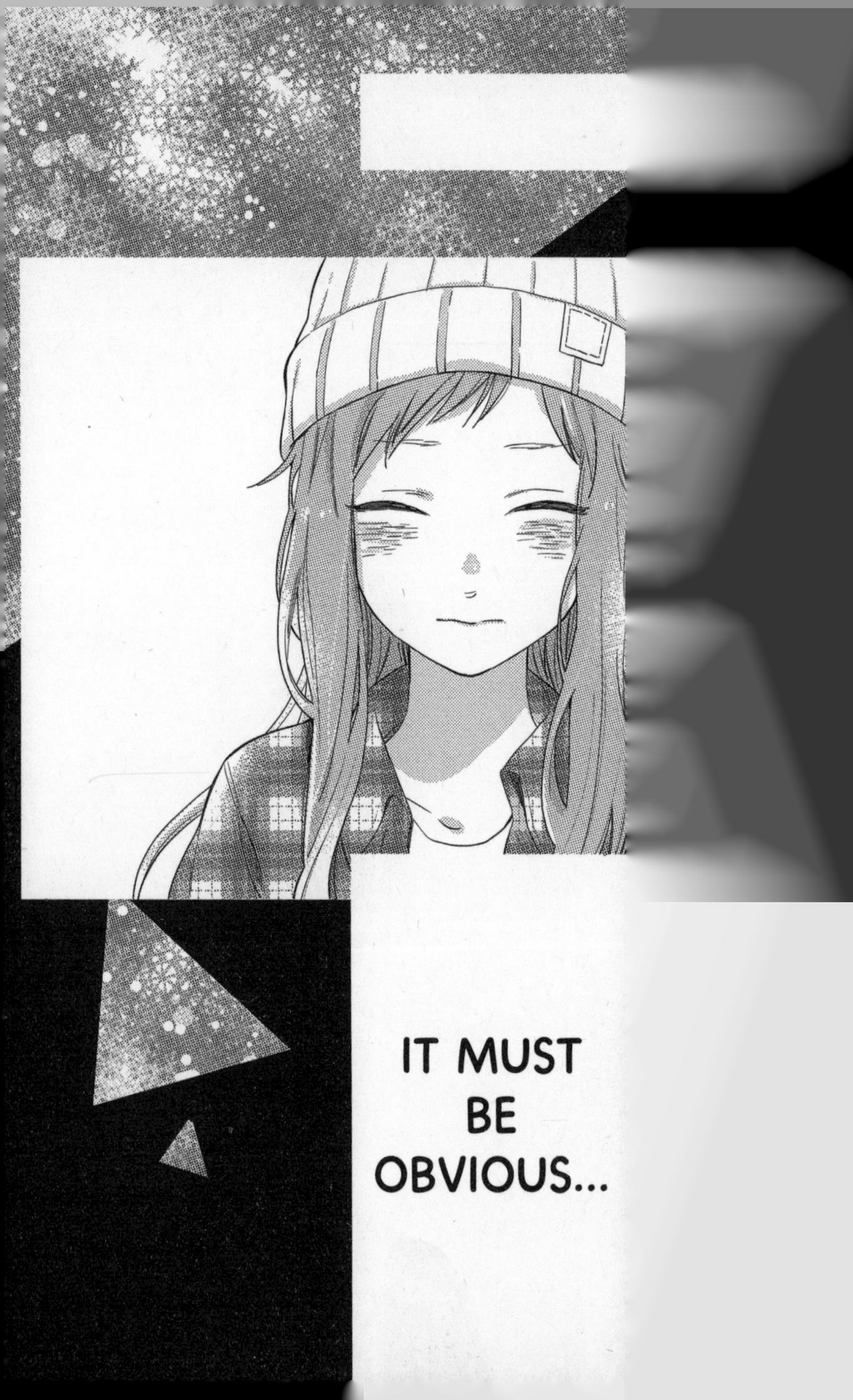
IT MUST
BE
OBVIOUS...

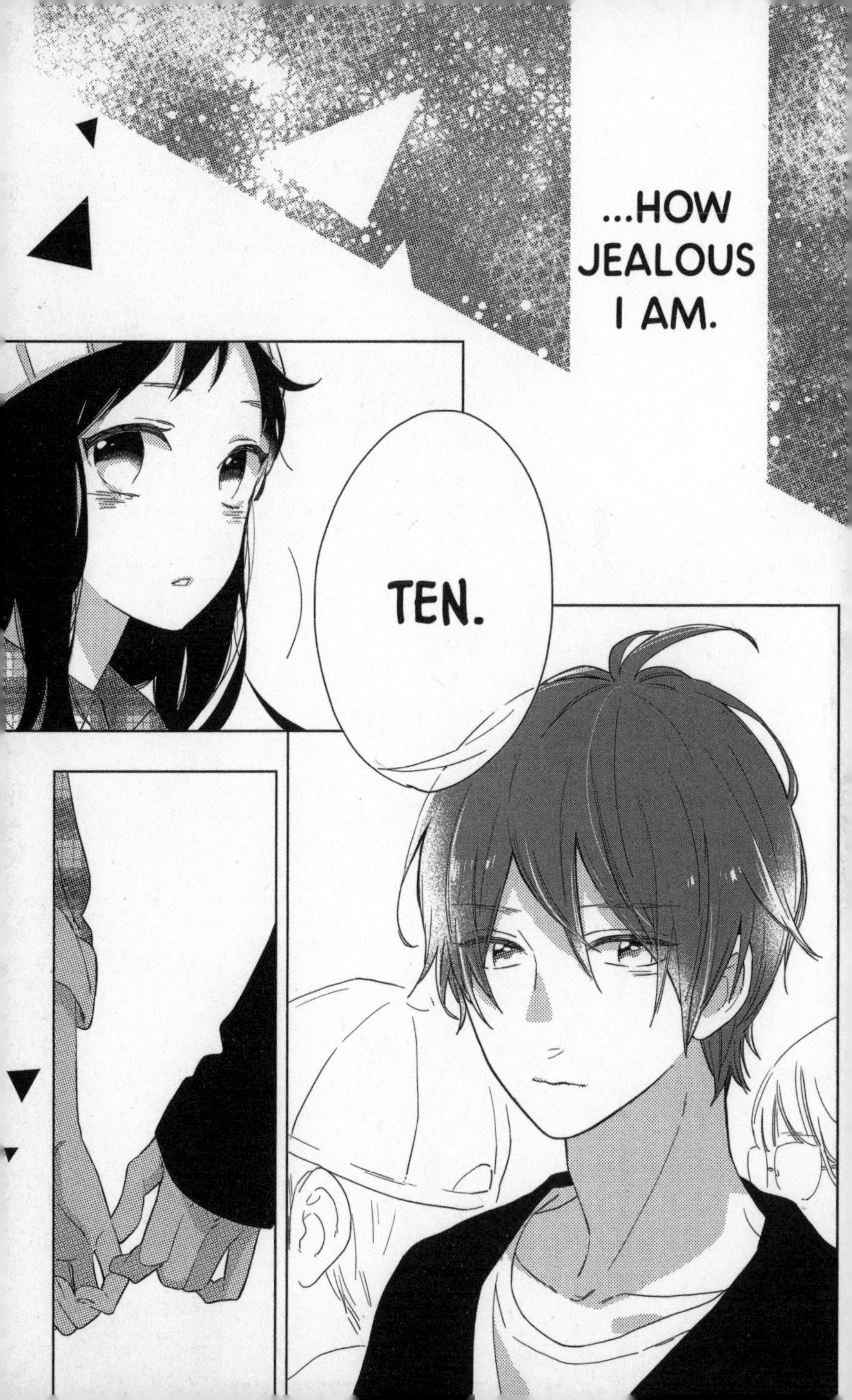
...HOW JEALOUS I AM.
TEN.

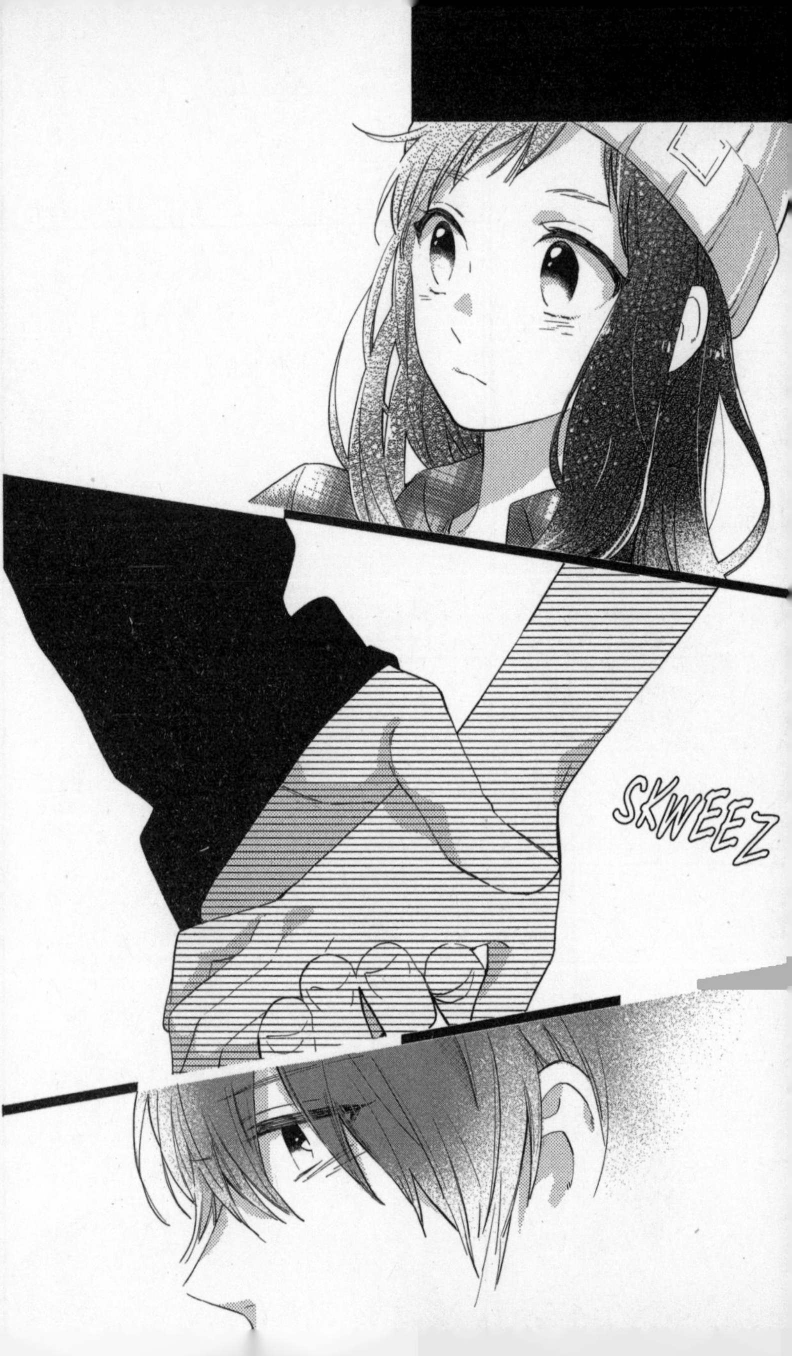
SKWEEZ

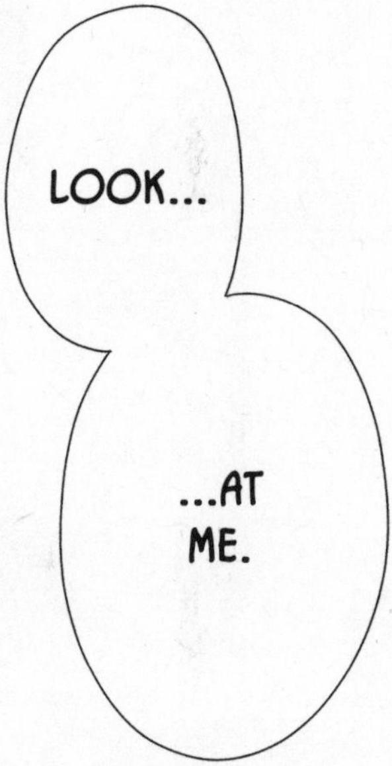
LOOK...
...AT ME.
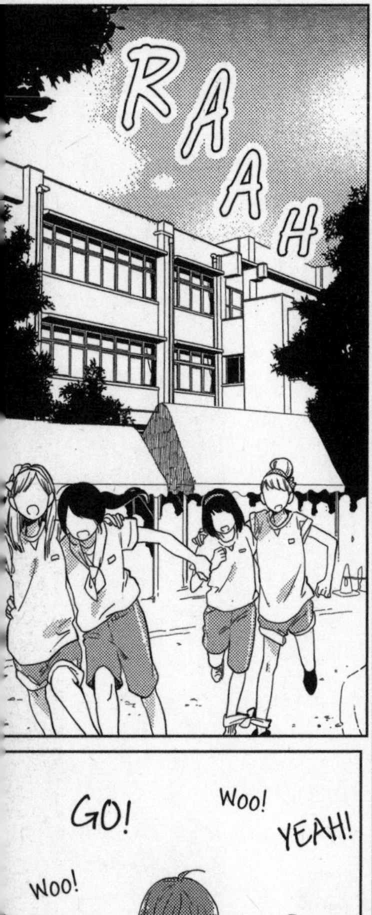
RAAH
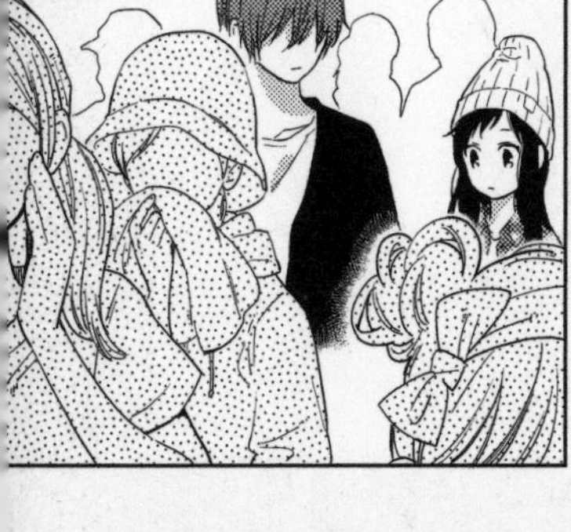
YEAH!
Woo!
GO!
Woo!

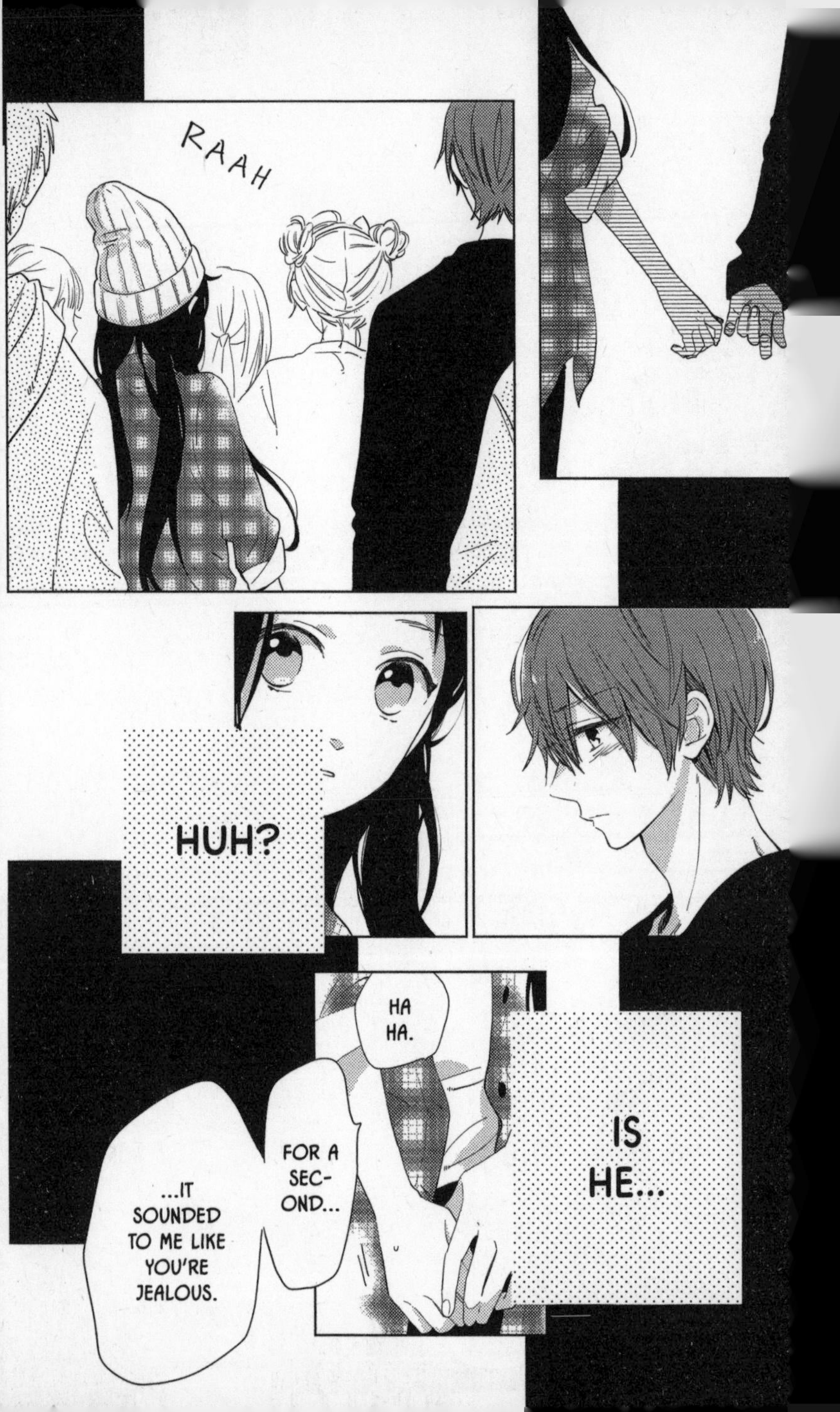
RAAH
HUH?
IS HE...
HA HA.
FOR A SEC- OND...
...IT SOUNDED TO ME LIKE YOU'RE JEALOUS.

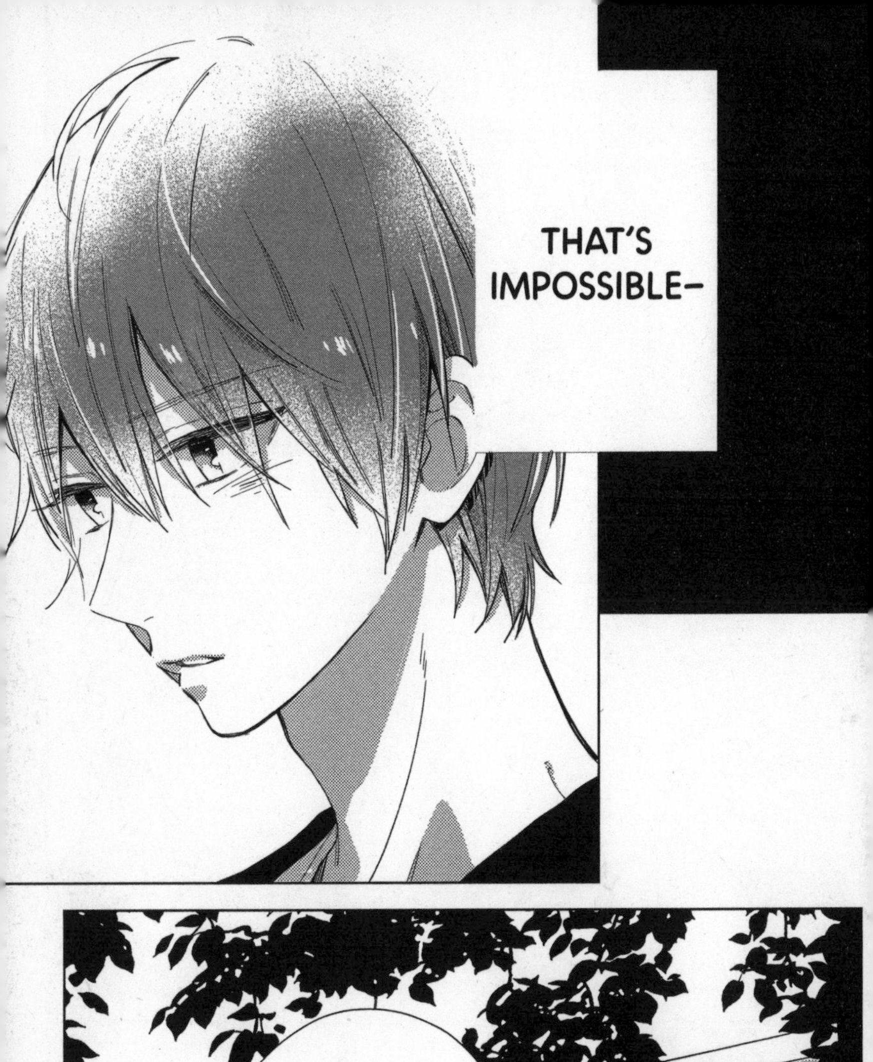
THAT'S IMPOSSIBLE–

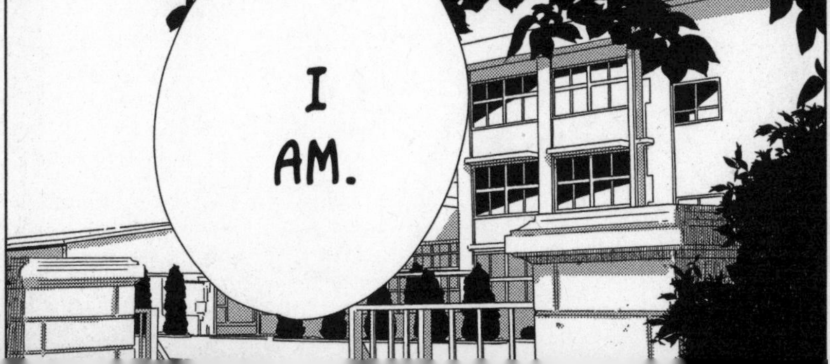
I AM.

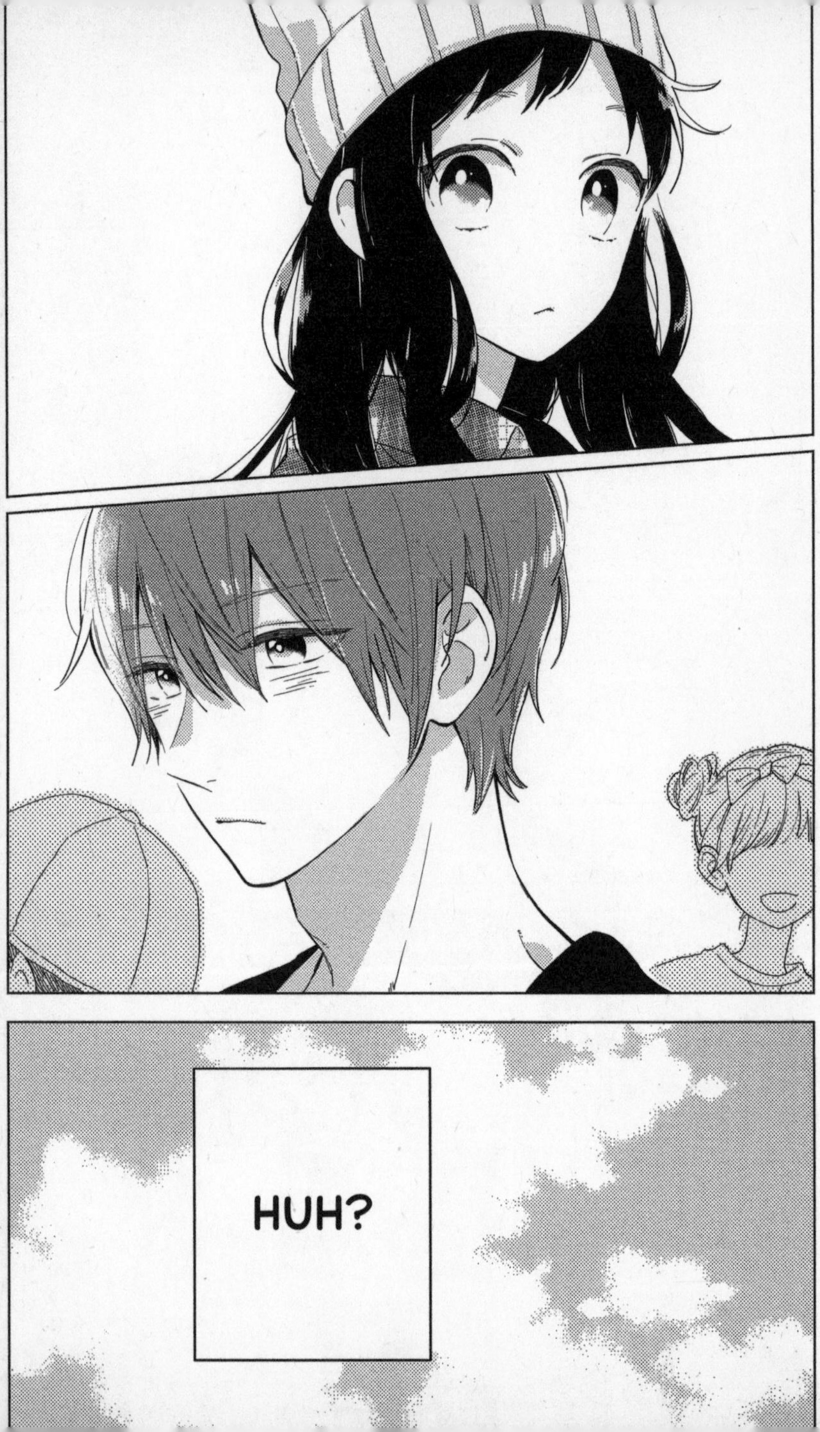
HUH?

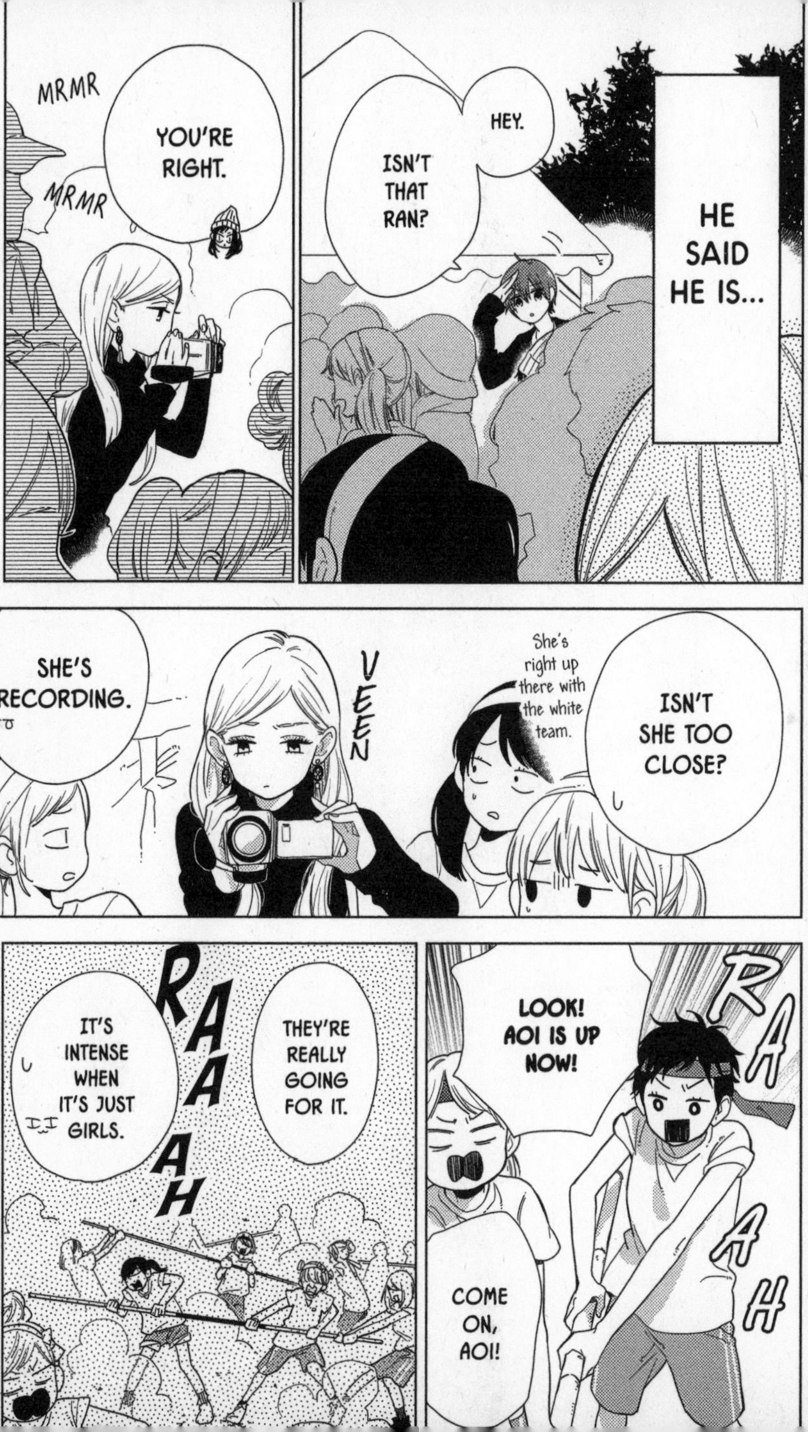
HE SAID HE IS...
HEY.
ISN'T THAT RAN?
YOU'RE RIGHT.
MRMR
MRMR
ISN'T SHE TOO CLOSE?
She's right up there with the white team.
VEEN
SHE'S RECORDING.
LOOK! AOI IS UP NOW!
RAAH
COME ON, AOI!
THEY'RE REALLY GOING FOR IT.
RAAAH
IT'S INTENSE WHEN IT'S JUST GIRLS.

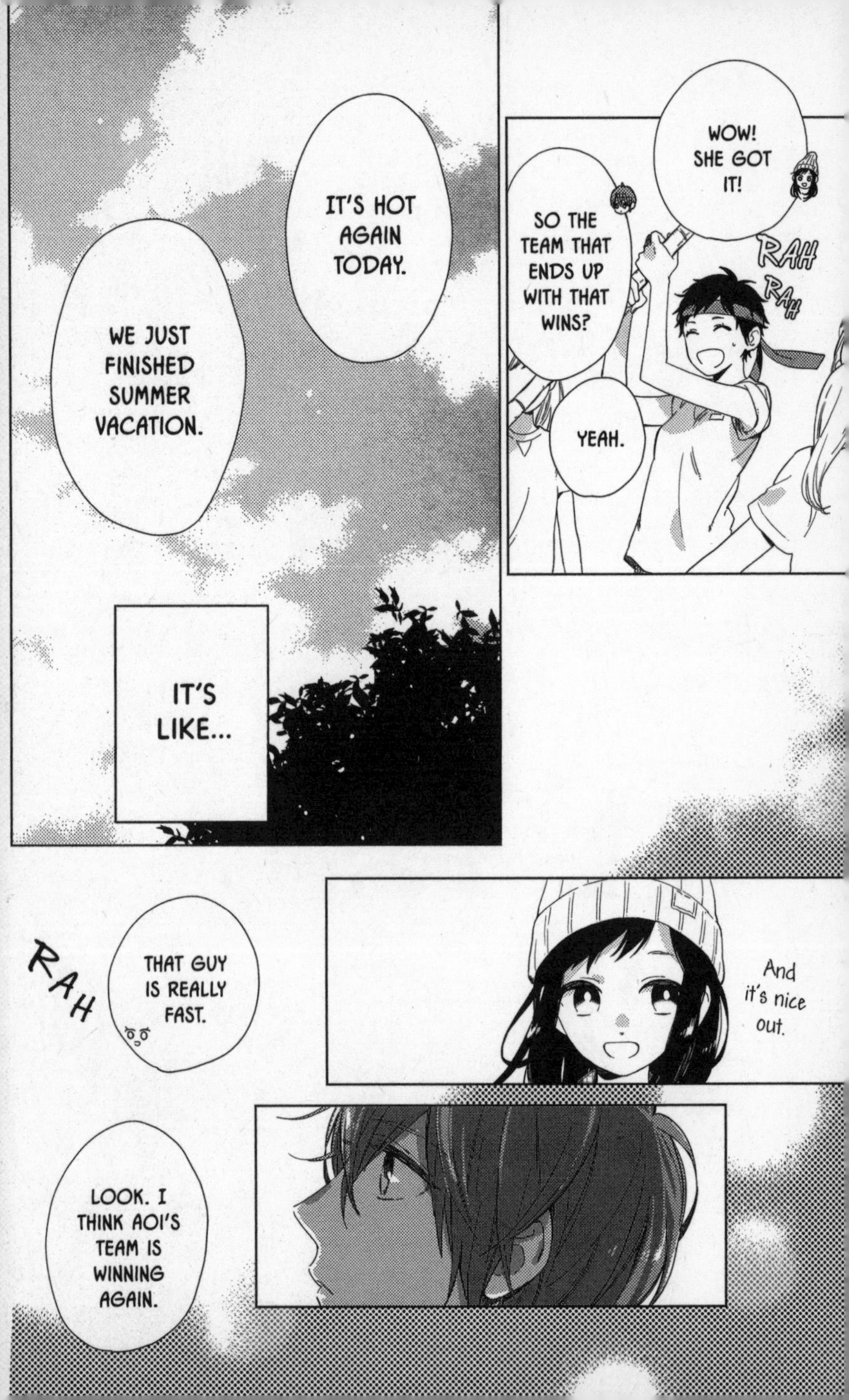
WOW! SHE GOT IT!
RAH
RAH
SO THE TEAM THAT ENDS UP WITH THAT WINS?
YEAH.
IT'S HOT AGAIN TODAY.
WE JUST FINISHED SUMMER VACATION.
IT'S LIKE...
And it's nice out.
THAT GUY IS REALLY FAST.
RAH
LOOK. I THINK AOI'S TEAM IS WINNING AGAIN.

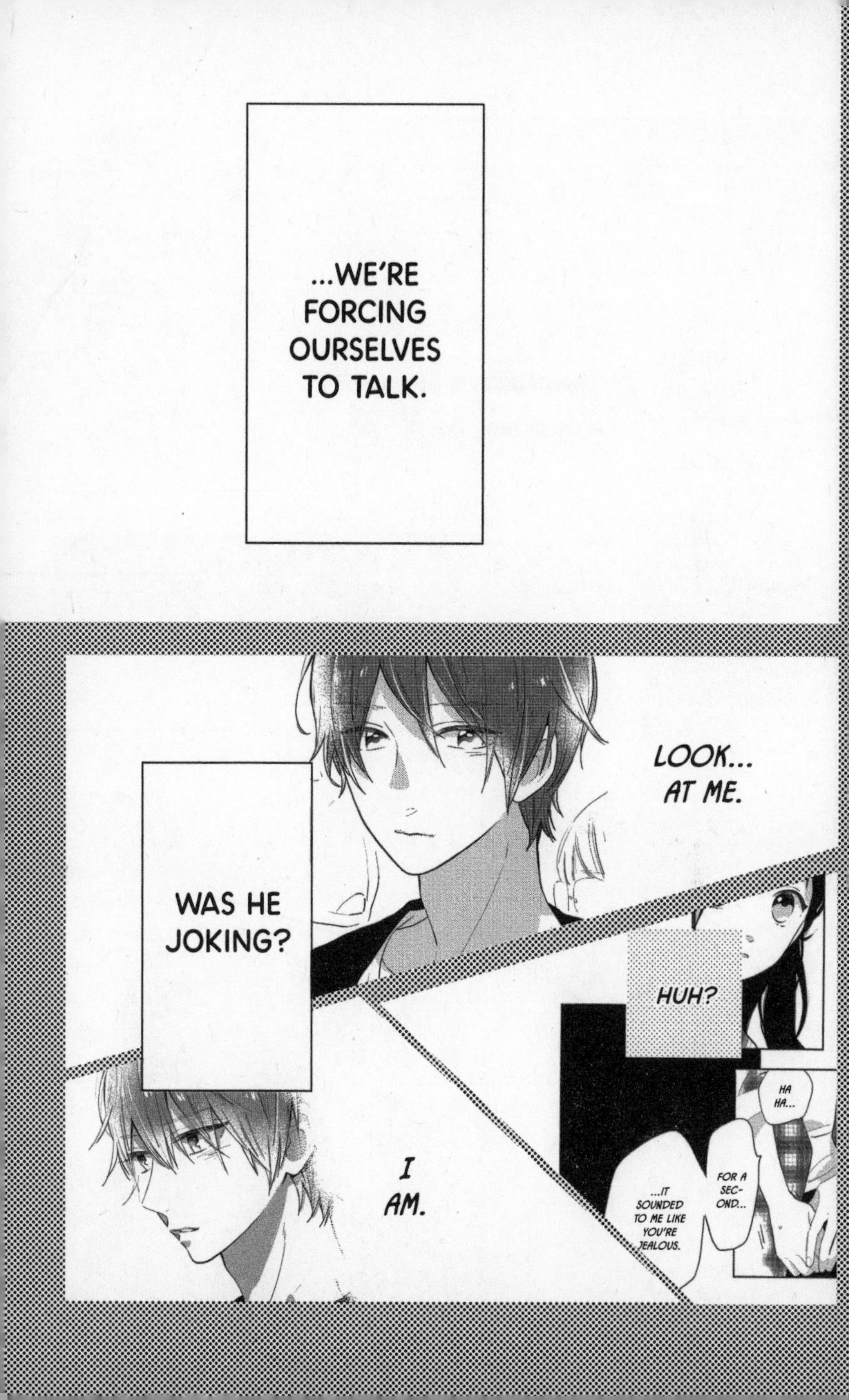
...WE'RE FORCING OURSELVES TO TALK.
LOOK... AT ME.
HUH?
HA HA...
FOR A SEC-OND...
...IT SOUNDED TO ME LIKE YOU'RE JEALOUS.
I AM.
WAS HE JOKING?

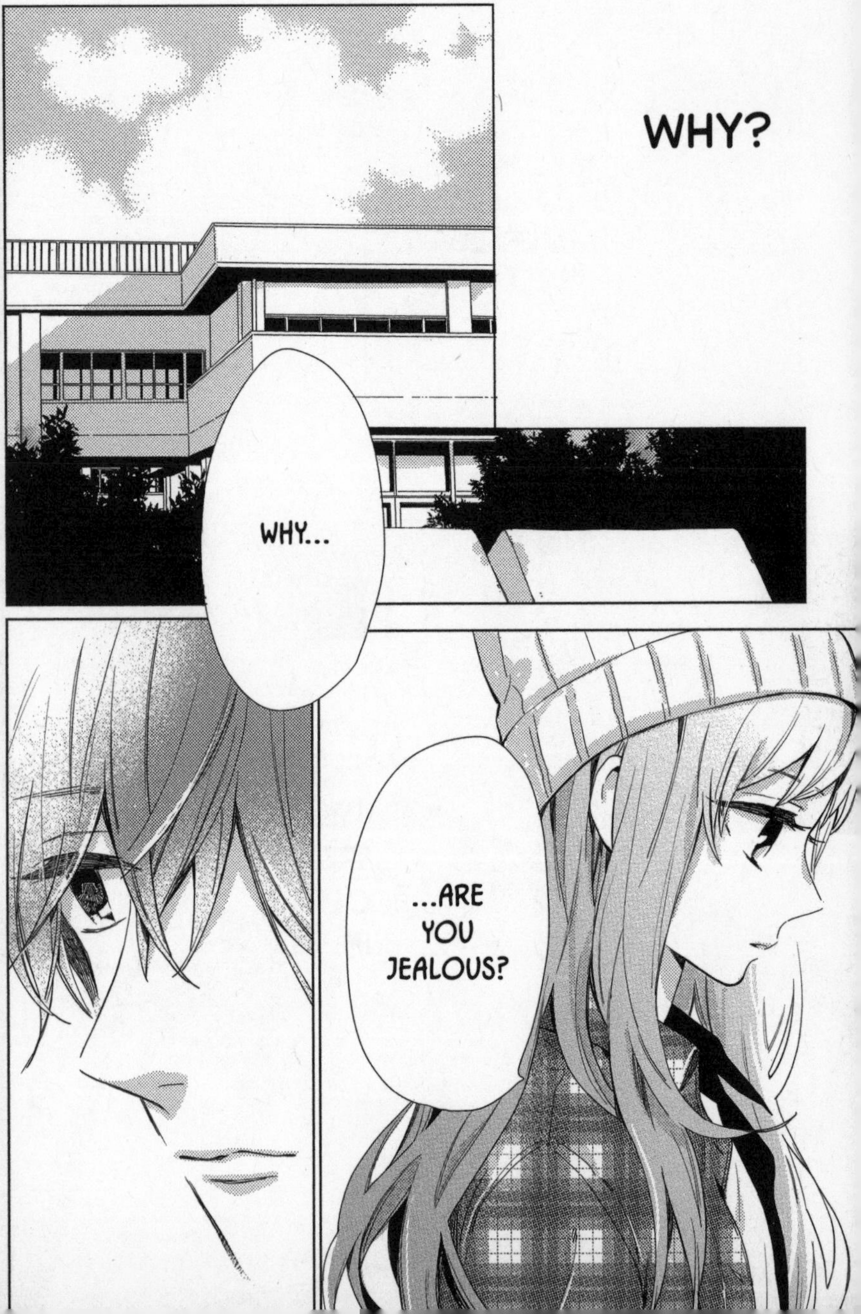
WHY?
WHY...
...ARE YOU JEALOUS?

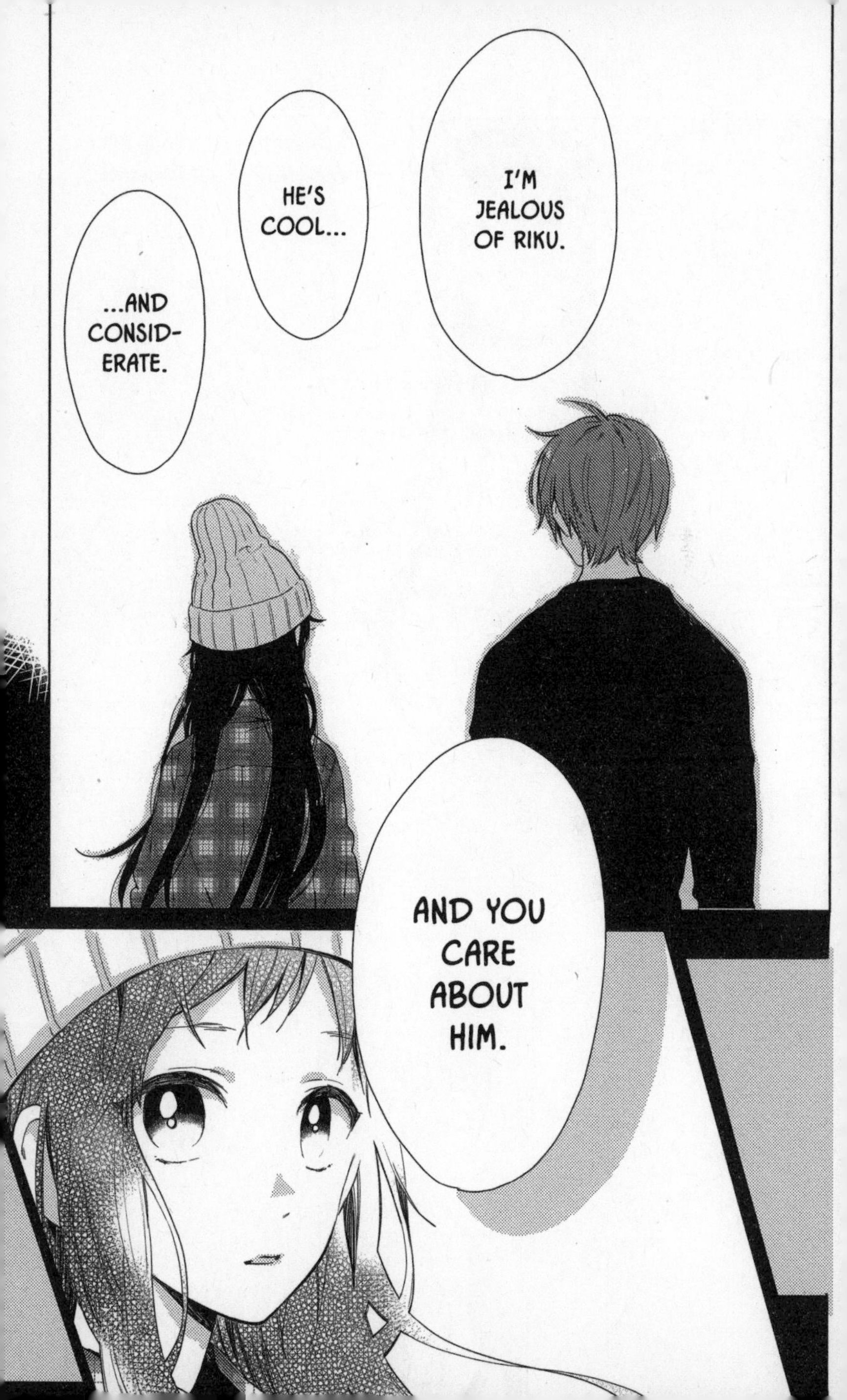
I'M JEALOUS OF RIKU.
HE'S COOL...
...AND CONSID-ERATE.
AND YOU CARE ABOUT HIM.

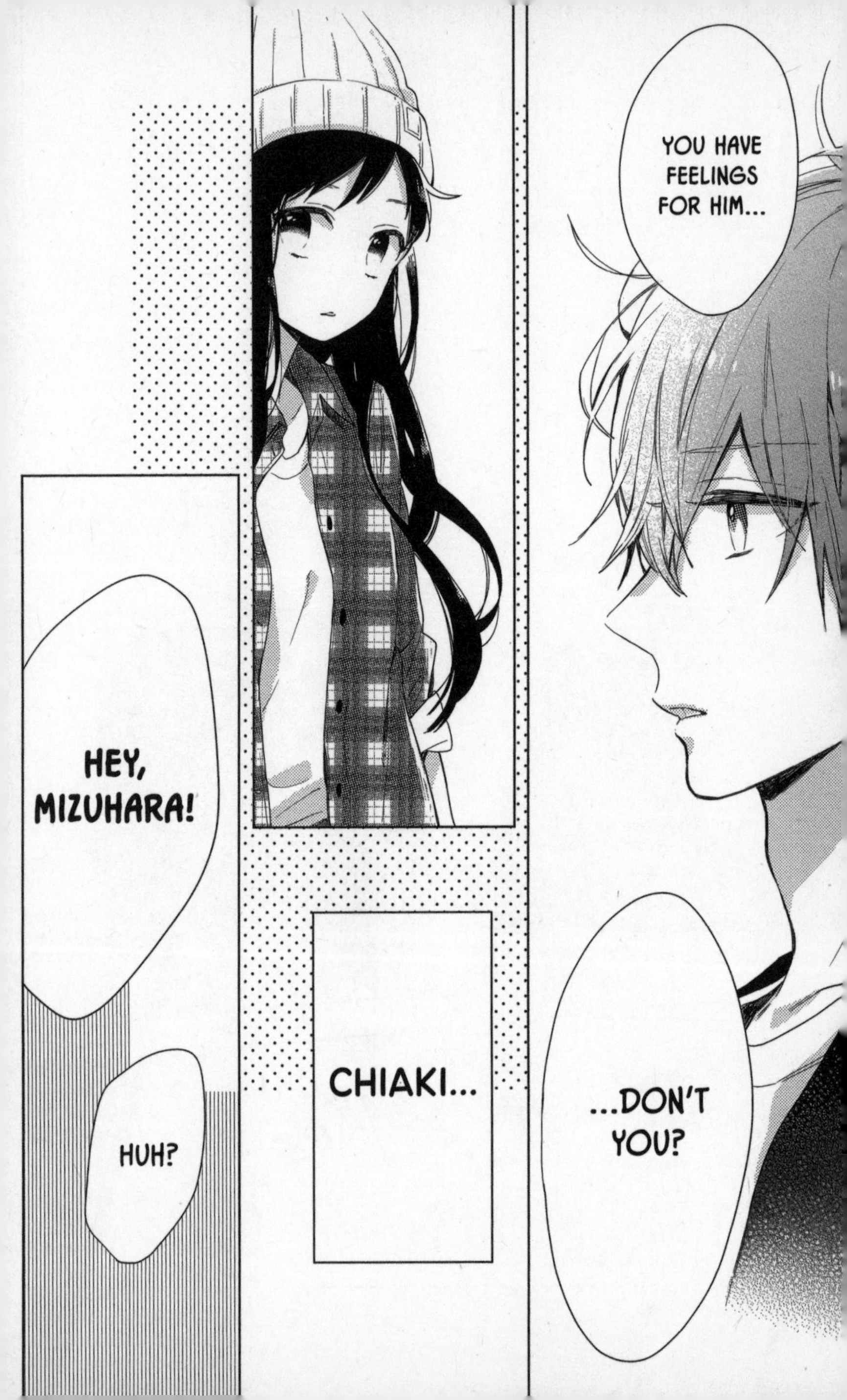
YOU HAVE FEELINGS FOR HIM...
...DON'T YOU?
CHIAKI...
HEY, MIZUHARA!
HUH?

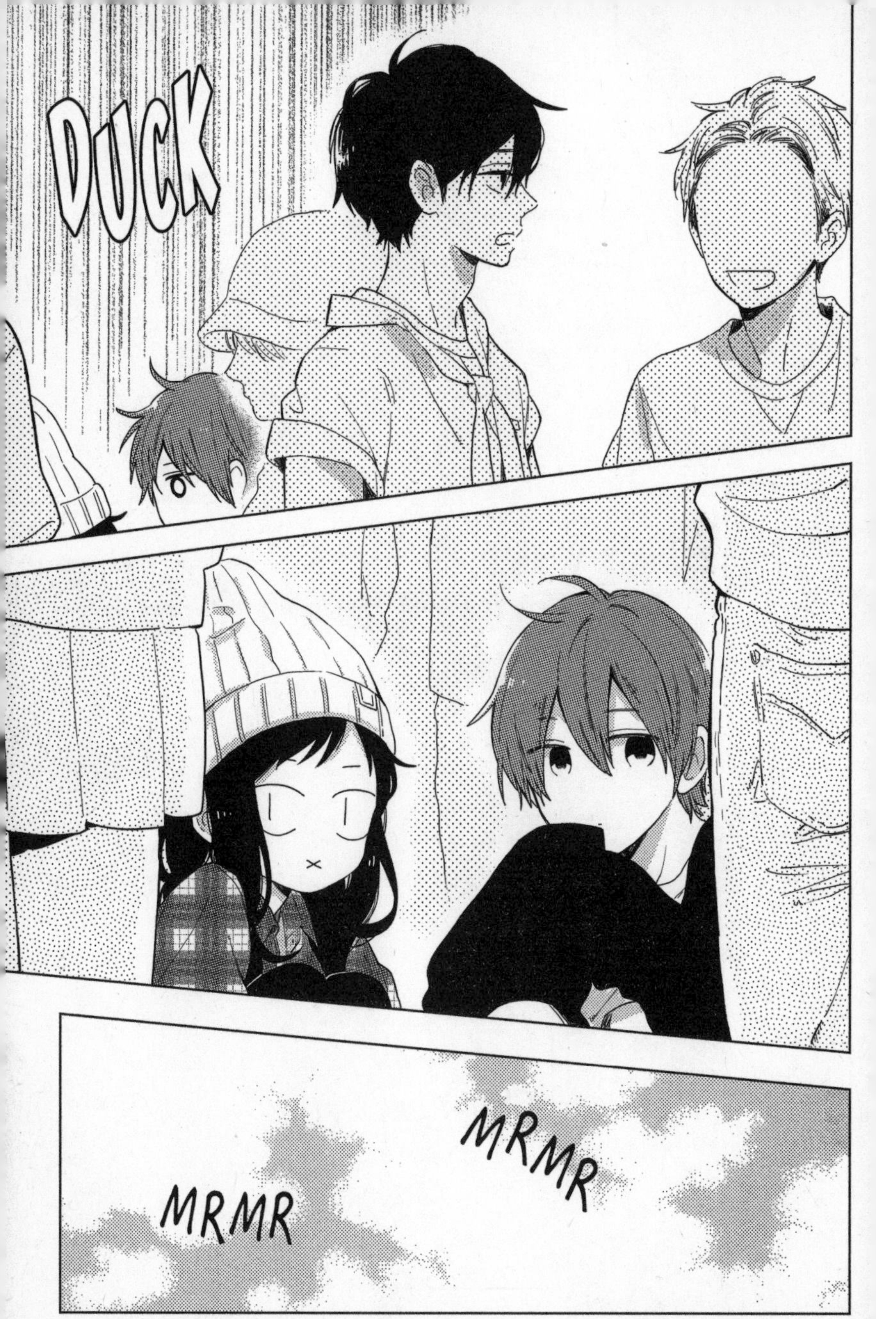
DUCK
MRMR
MRMR

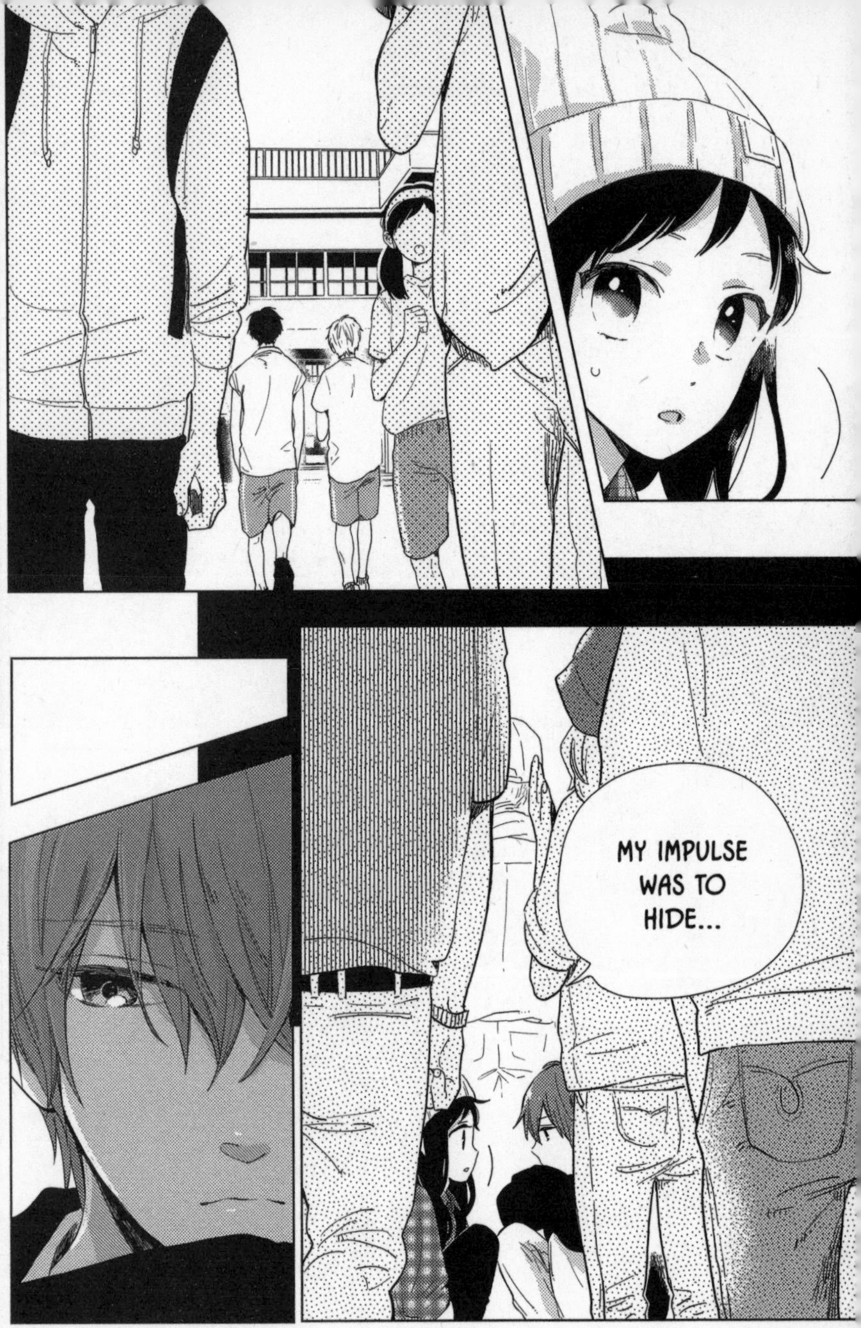
MY IMPULSE WAS TO HIDE...

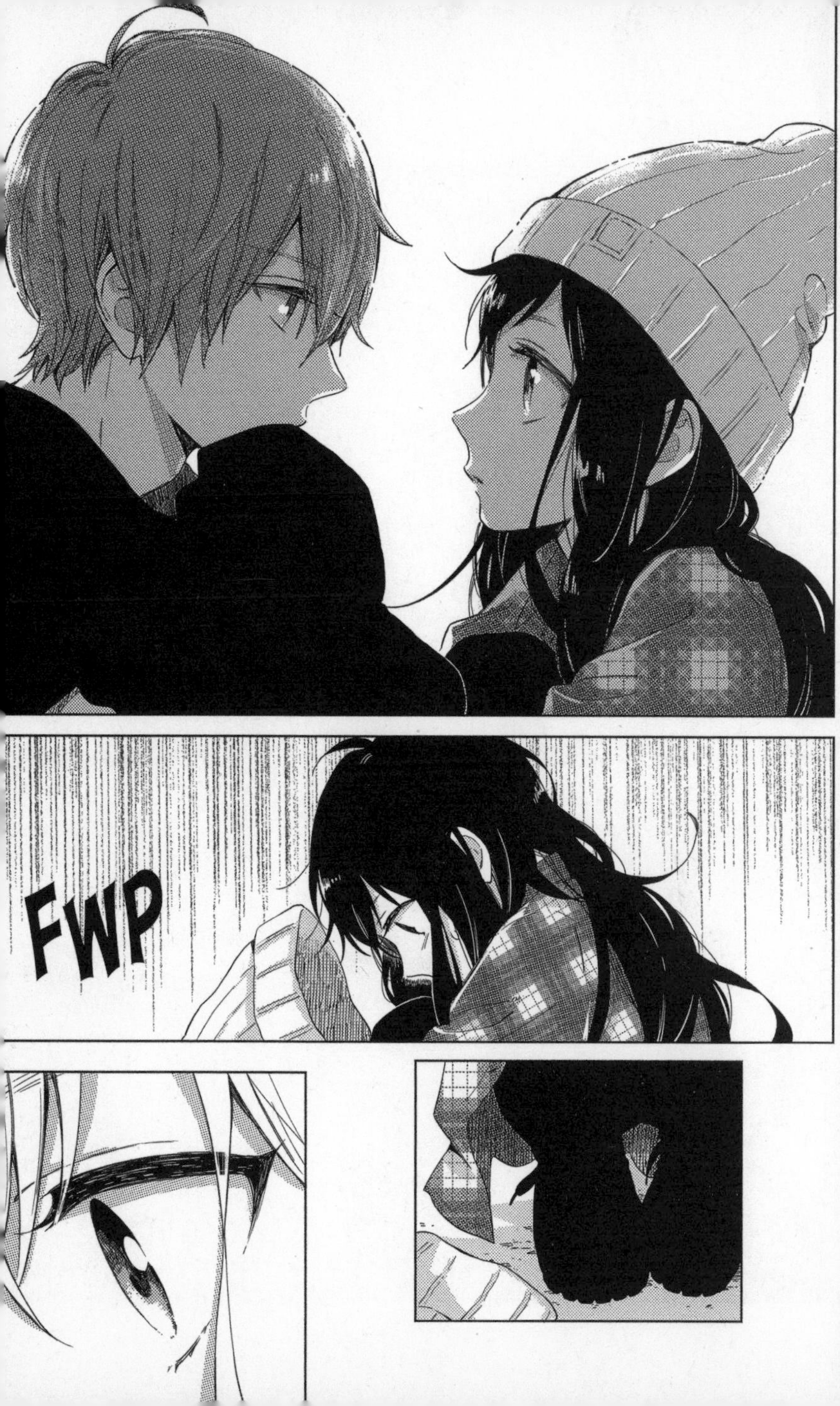
FWP

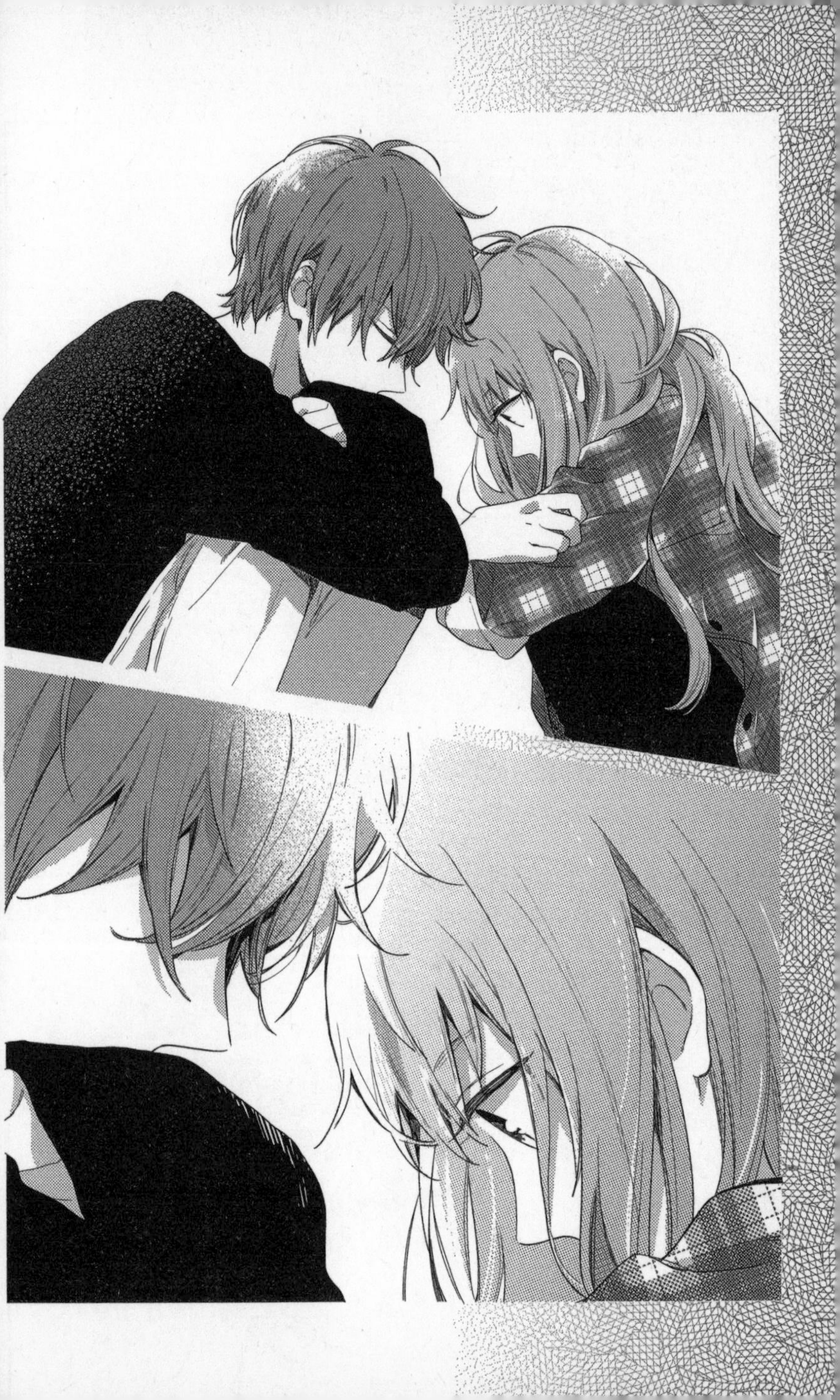

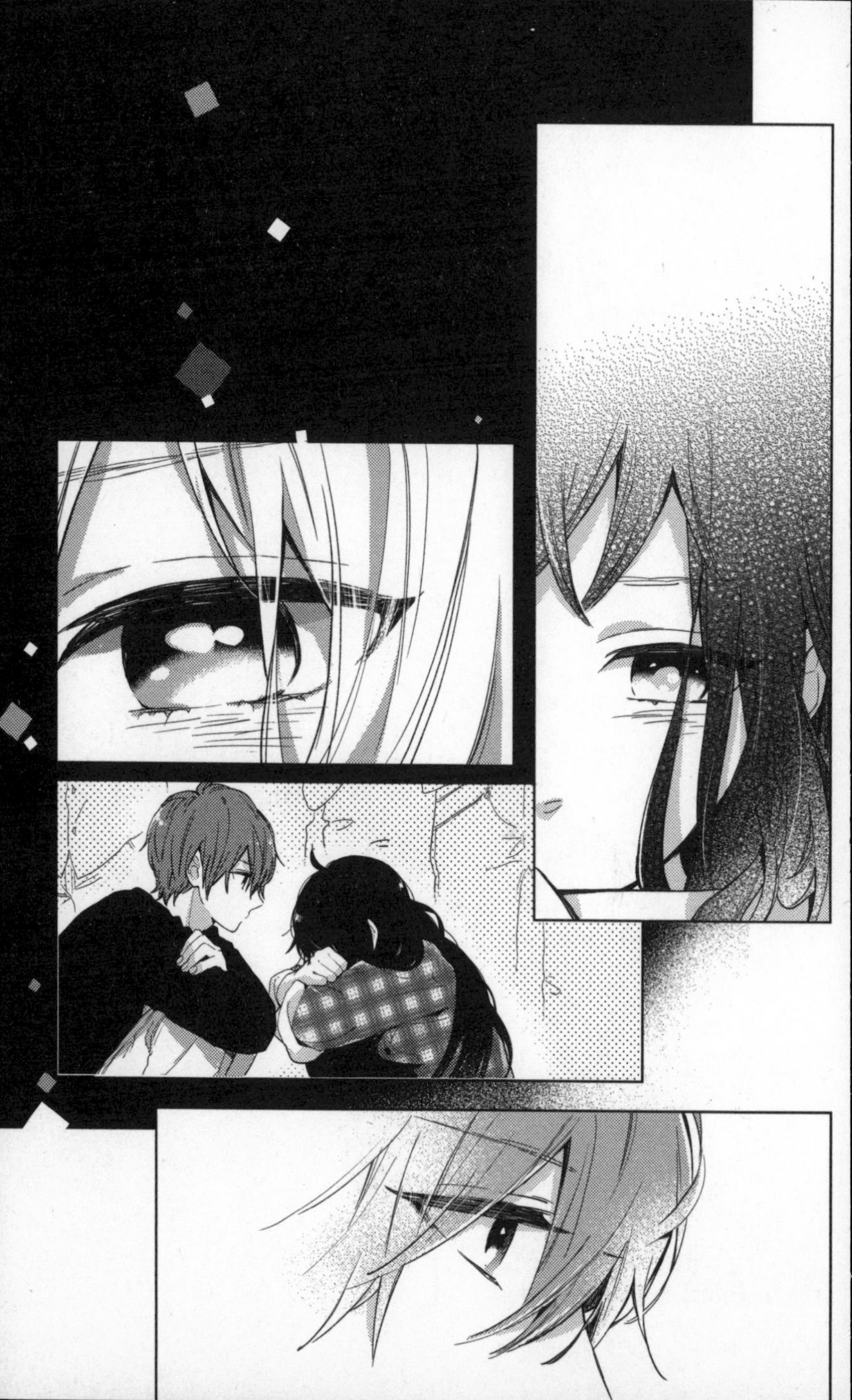

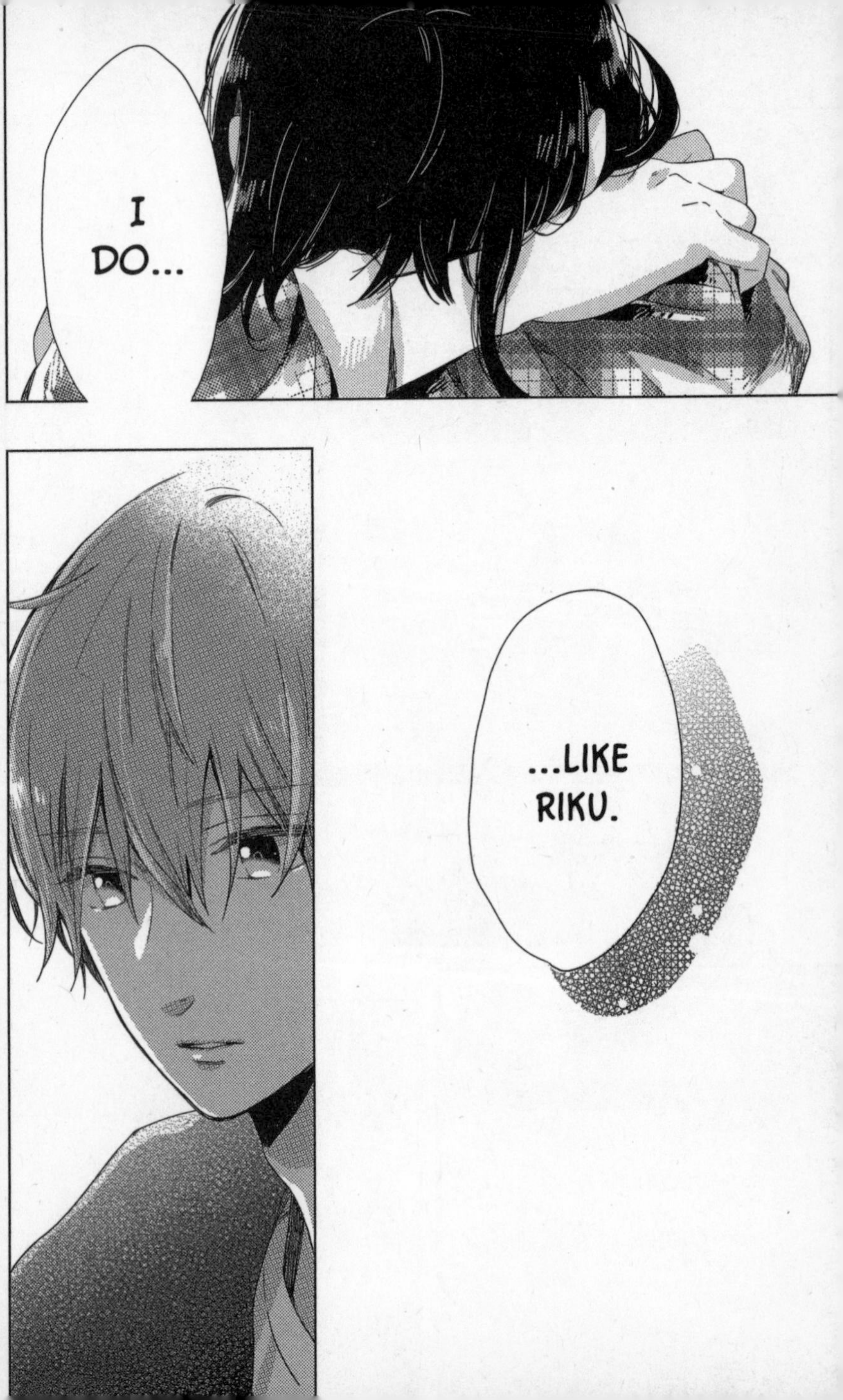
I DO...
...LIKE RIKU.

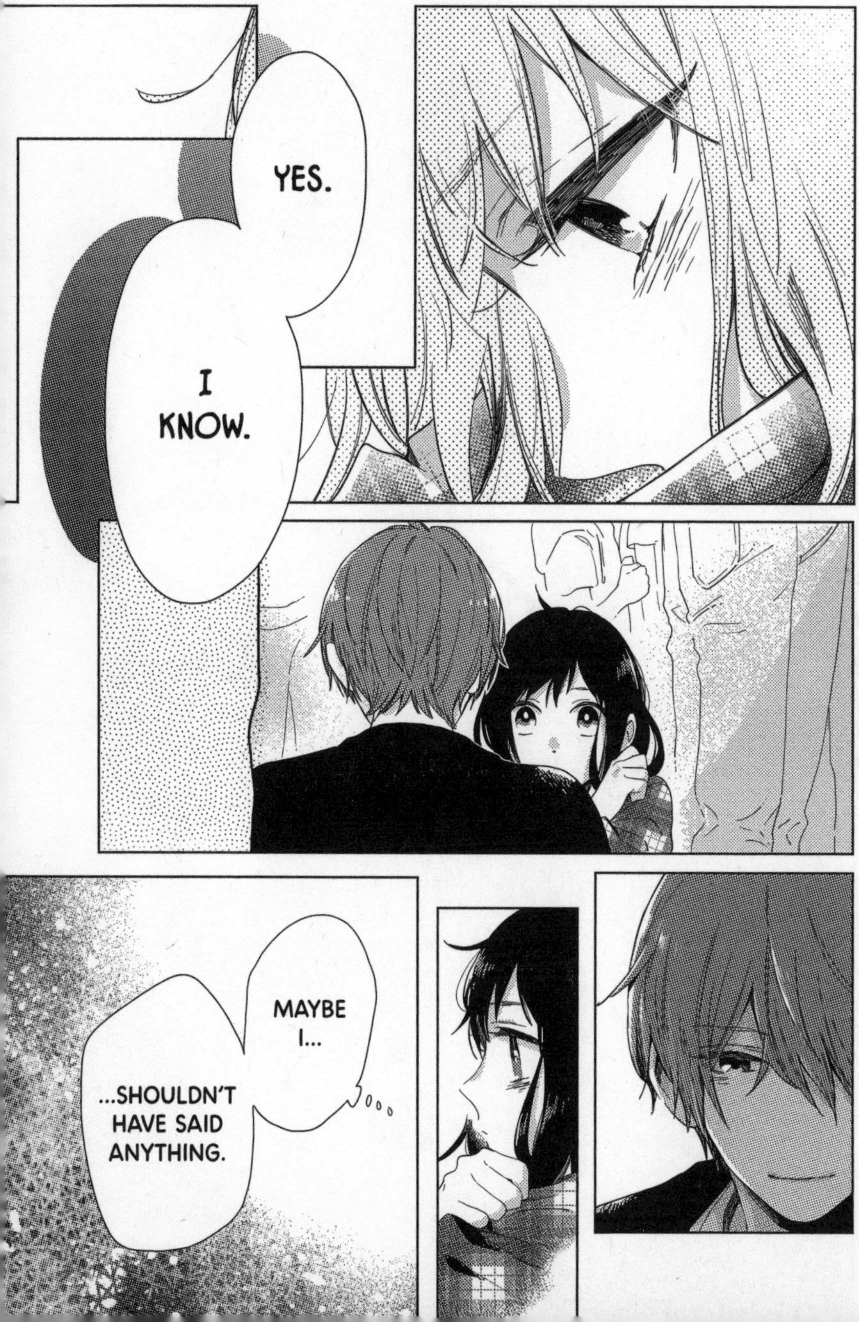
YES.
I KNOW.
MAYBE I...
...SHOULDN'T HAVE SAID ANYTHING.

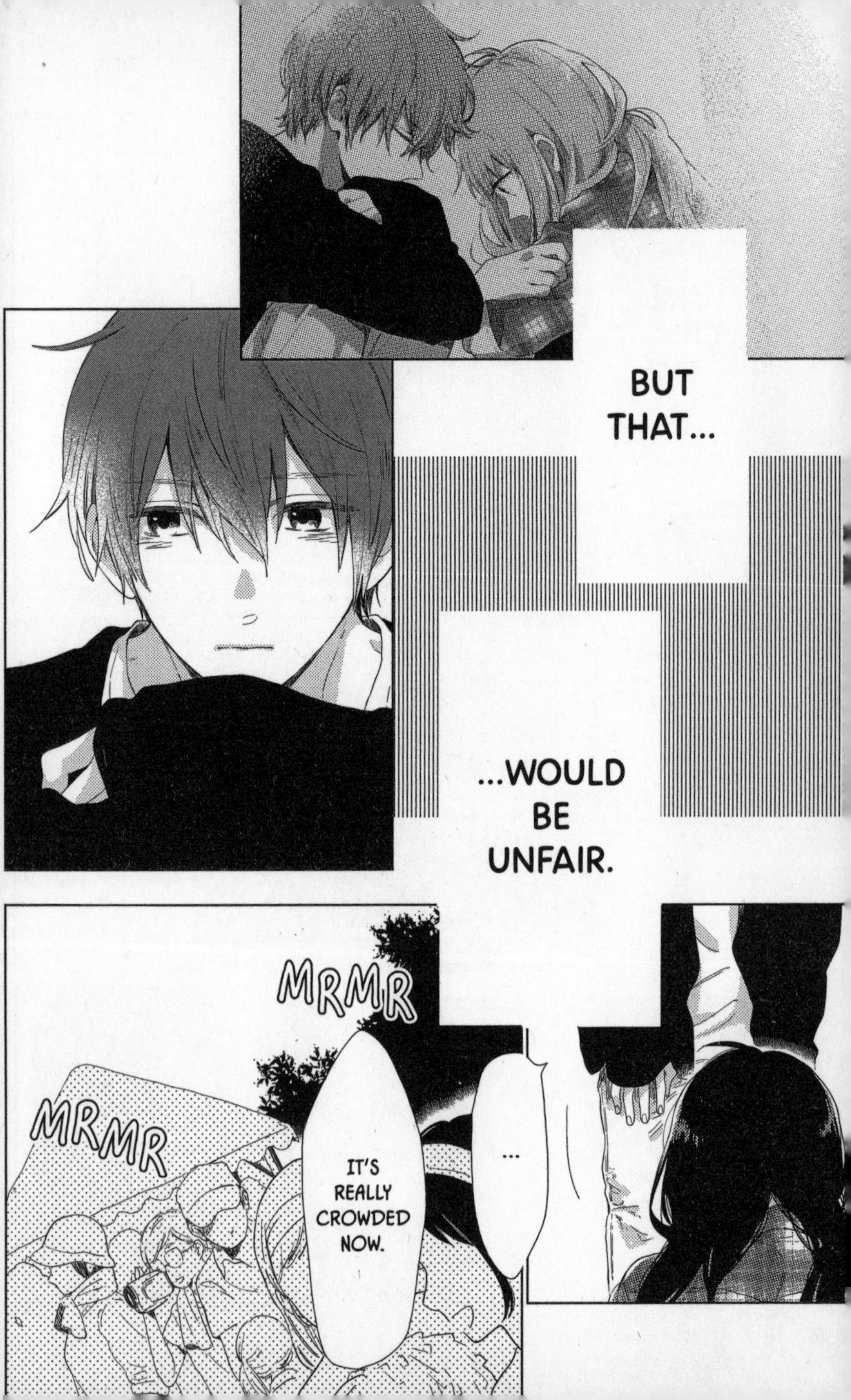
BUT THAT...
...WOULD BE UNFAIR.
...
MRMR
IT'S REALLY CROWDED NOW.
MRMR

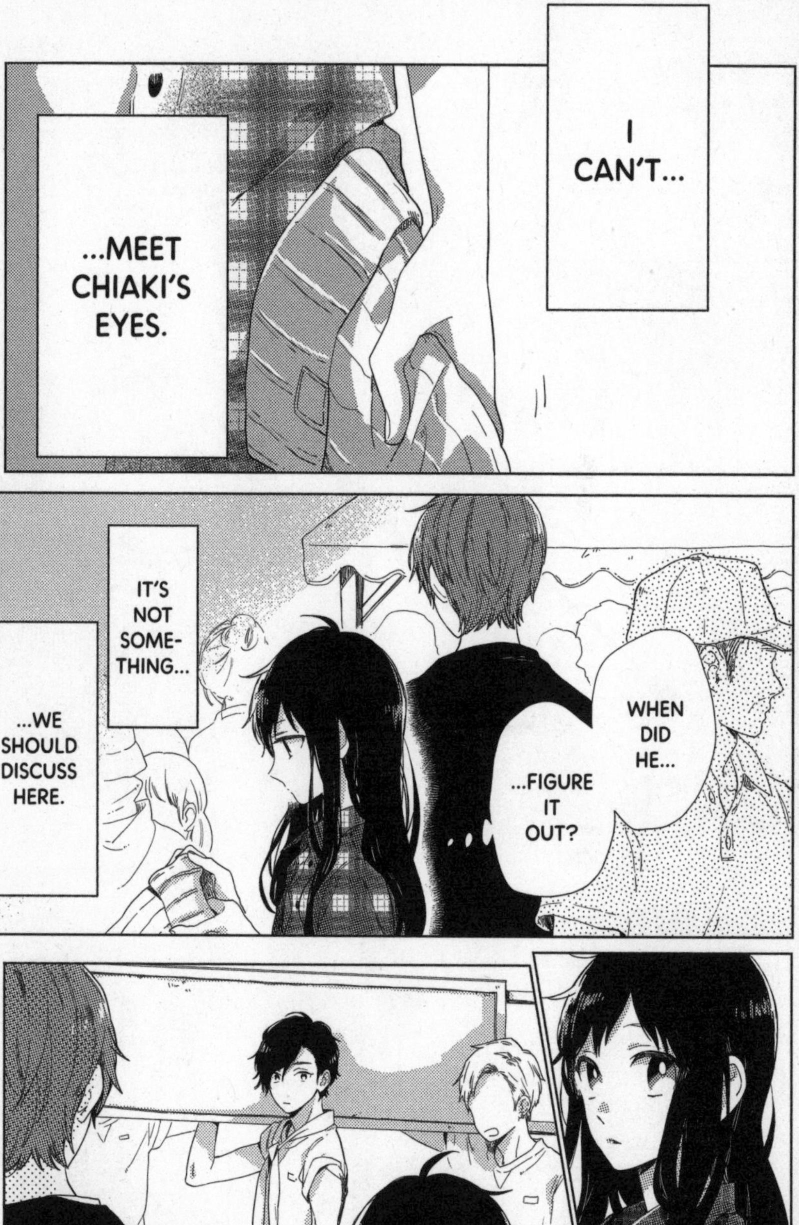
I CAN'T...
...MEET CHIAKI'S EYES.
WHEN DID HE...
...FIGURE IT OUT?
IT'S NOT SOME-THING...
...WE SHOULD DISCUSS HERE.

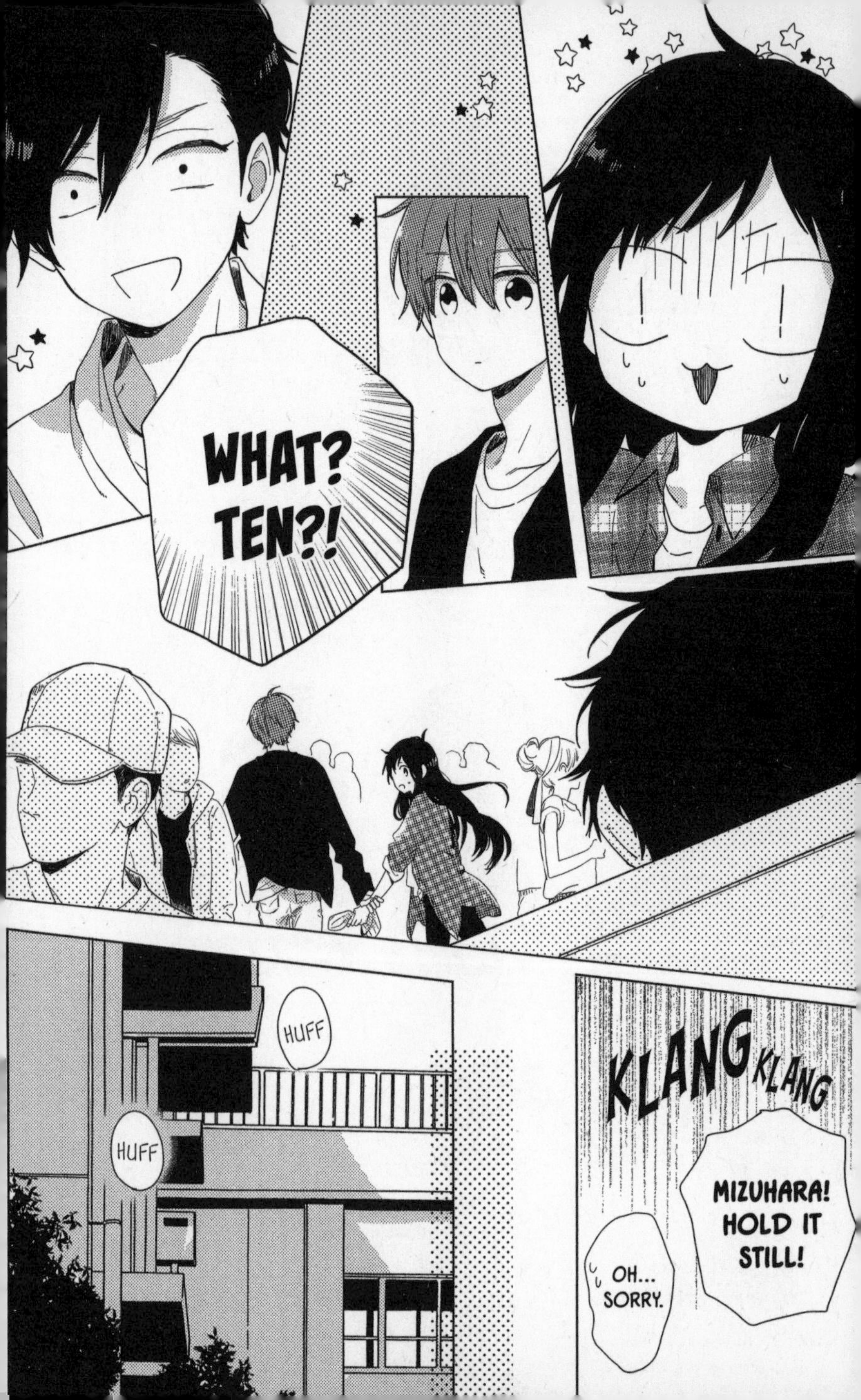
WHAT? TEN?!
KLANG KLANG
MIZUHARA! HOLD IT STILL!
OH... SORRY.
HUFF
HUFF

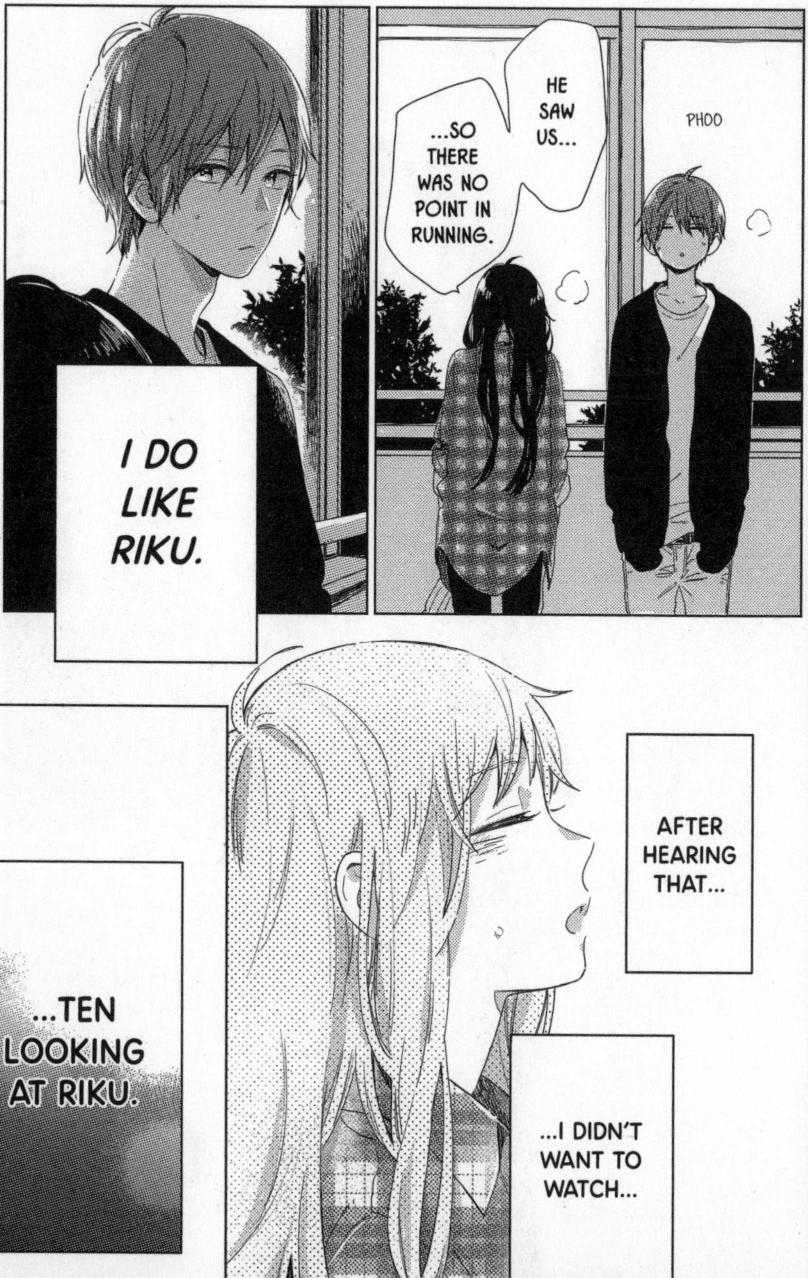
PHOO
HE SAW US...
...SO THERE WAS NO POINT IN RUNNING.
I DO LIKE RIKU.
AFTER HEARING THAT...
...I DIDN'T WANT TO WATCH...
...TEN LOOKING AT RIKU.

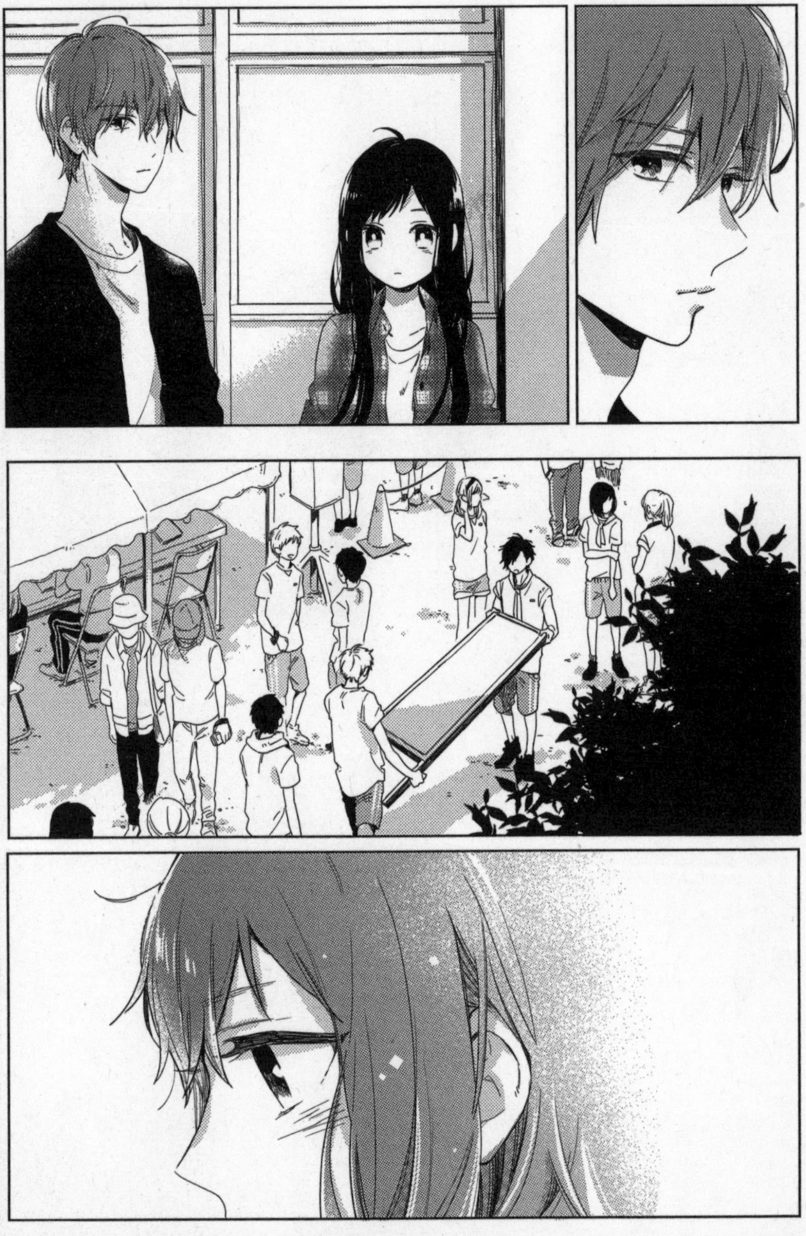

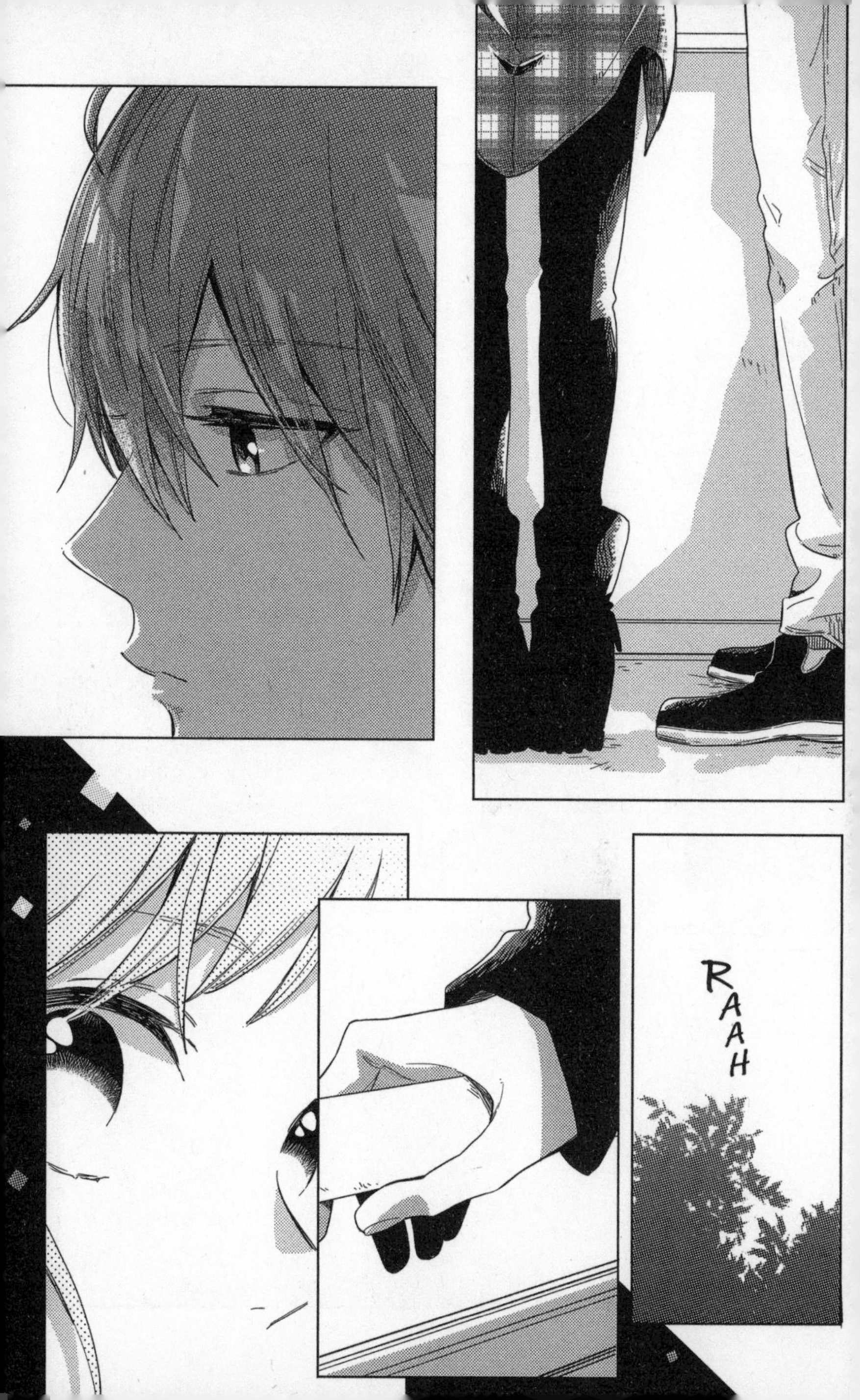
RAAH

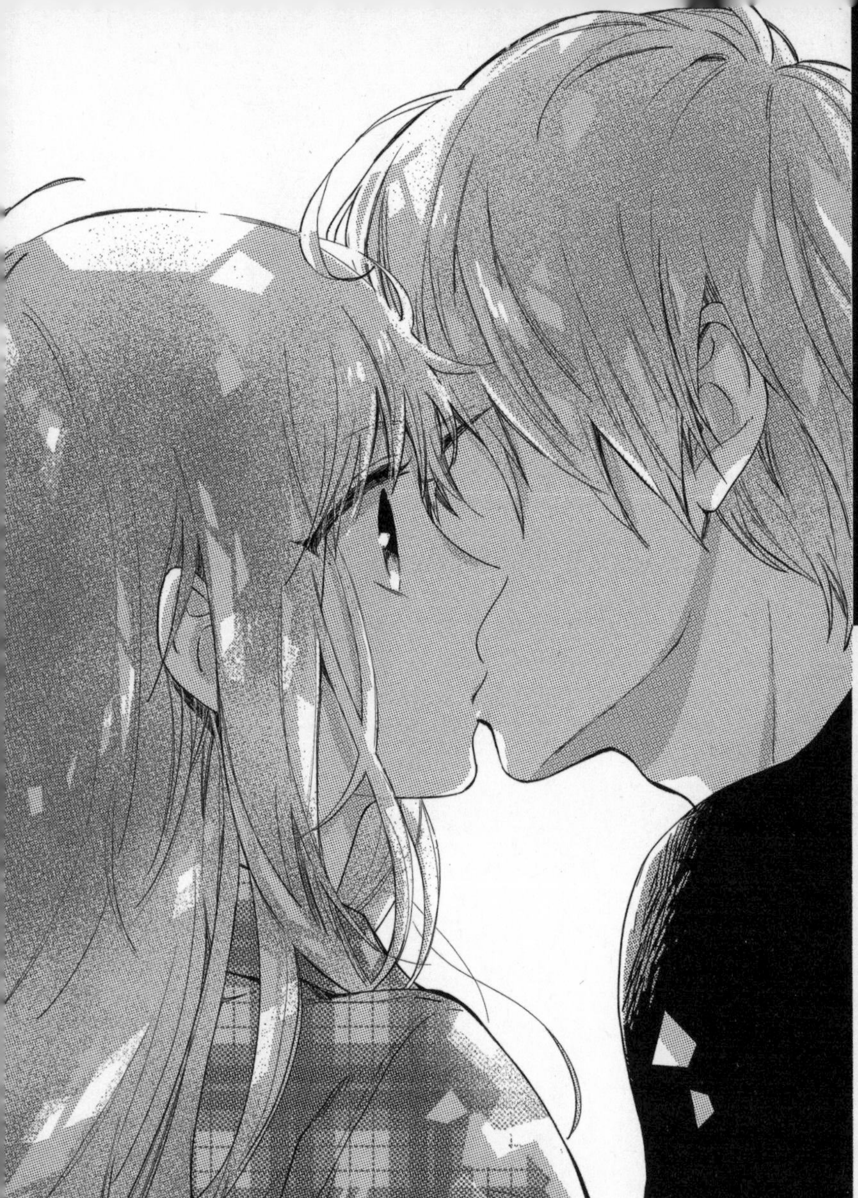

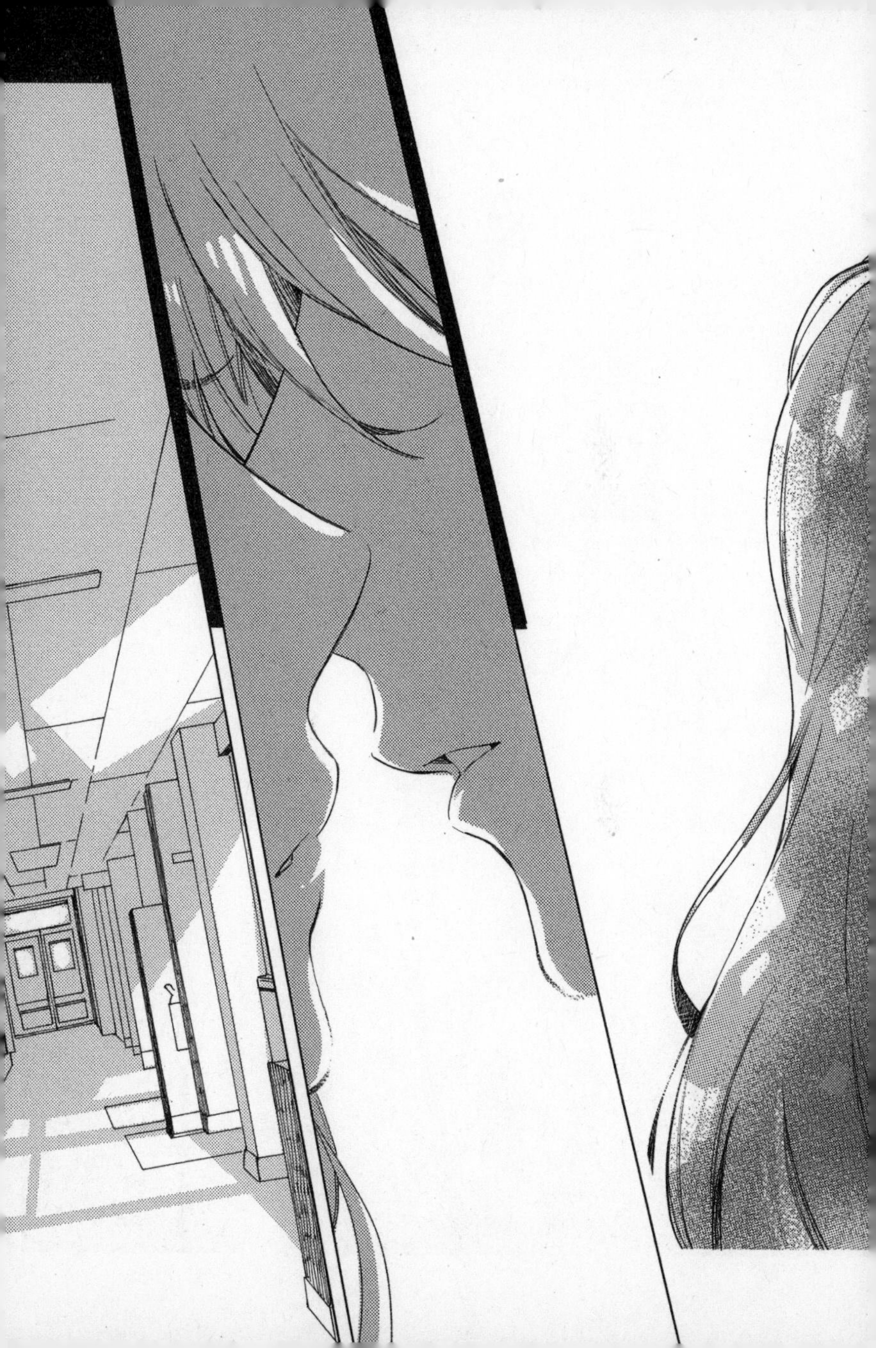

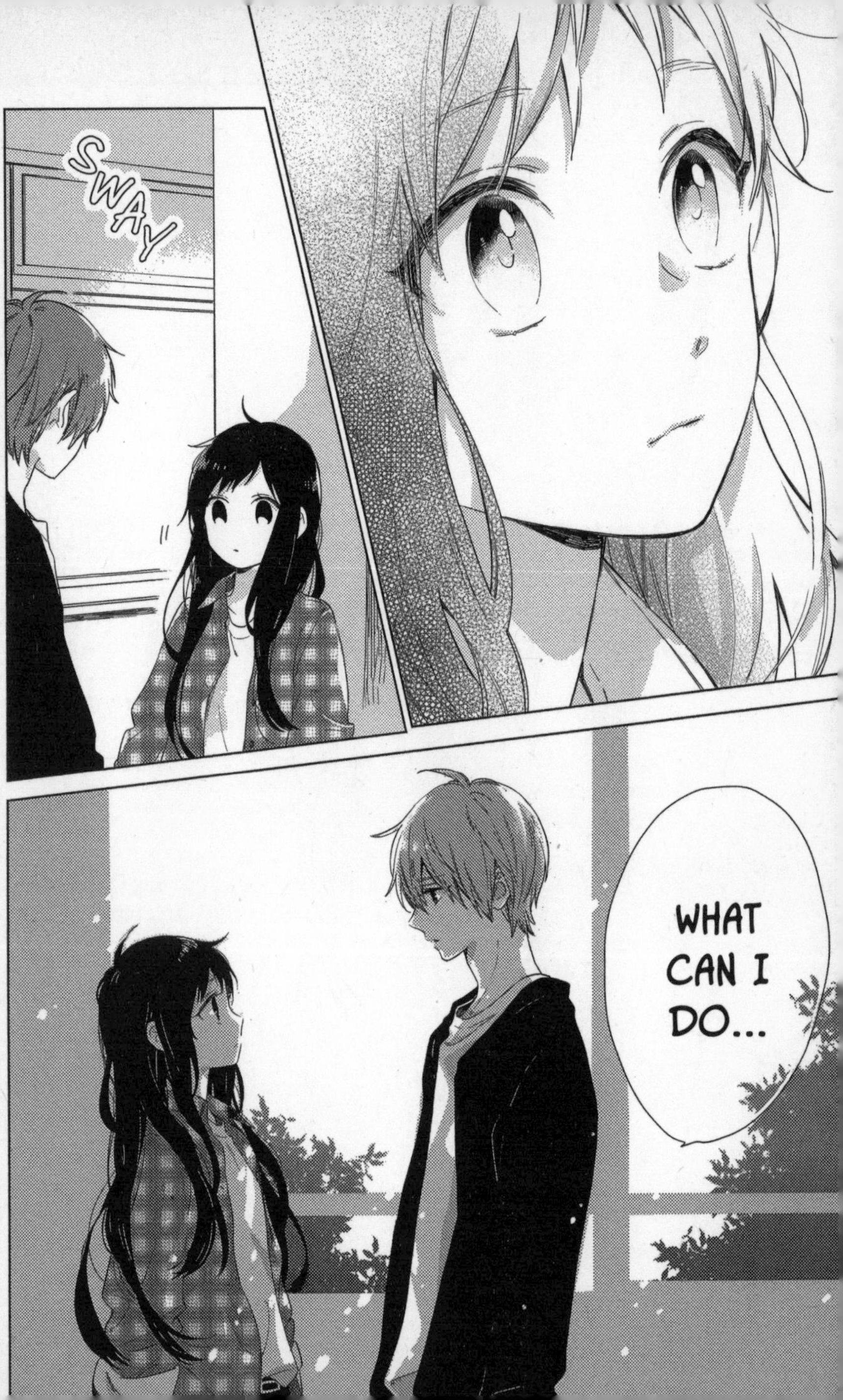
SWAY
WHAT CAN I DO...

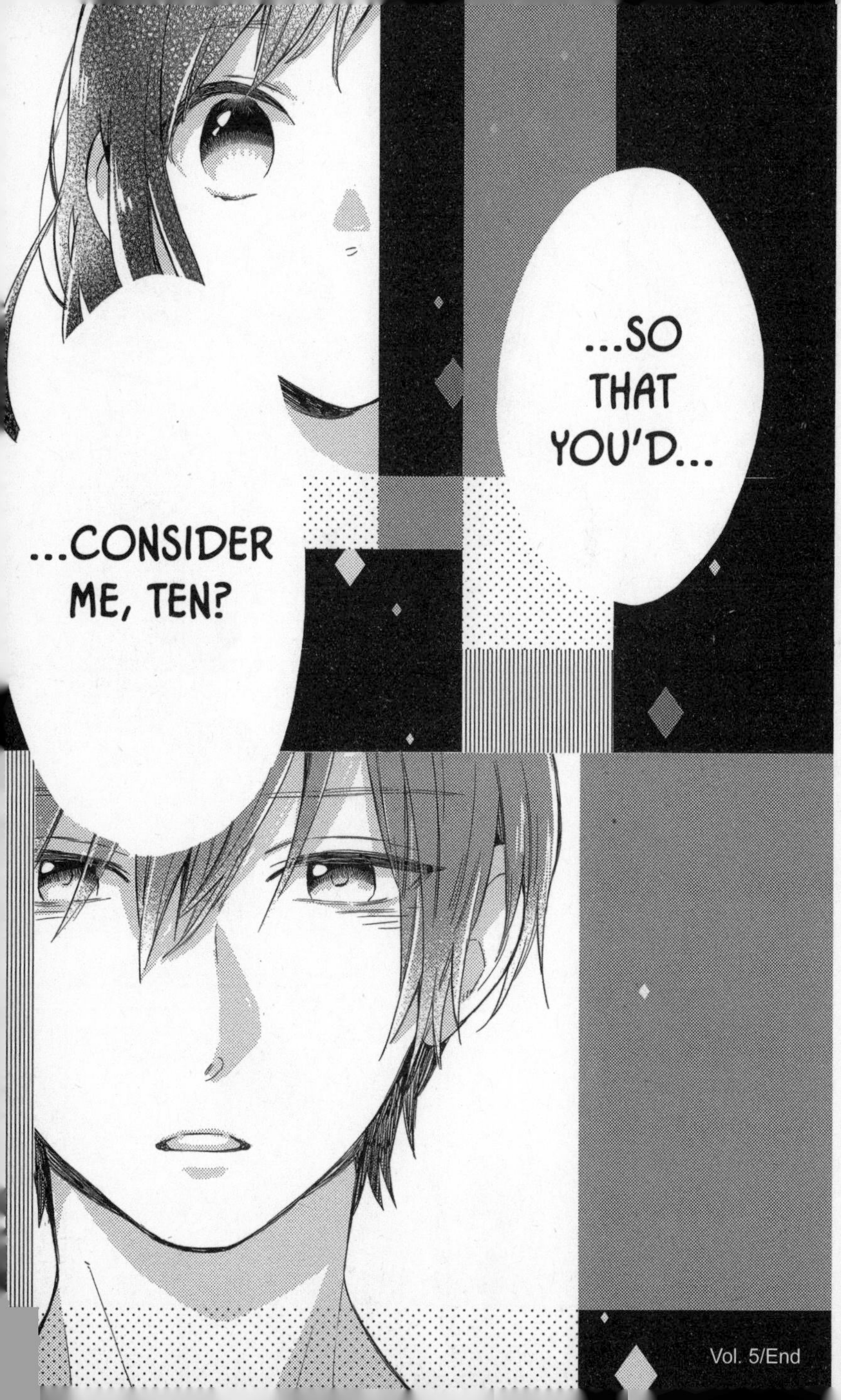
...SO THAT YOU'D...
...CONSIDER ME, TEN?
Vol. 5/End

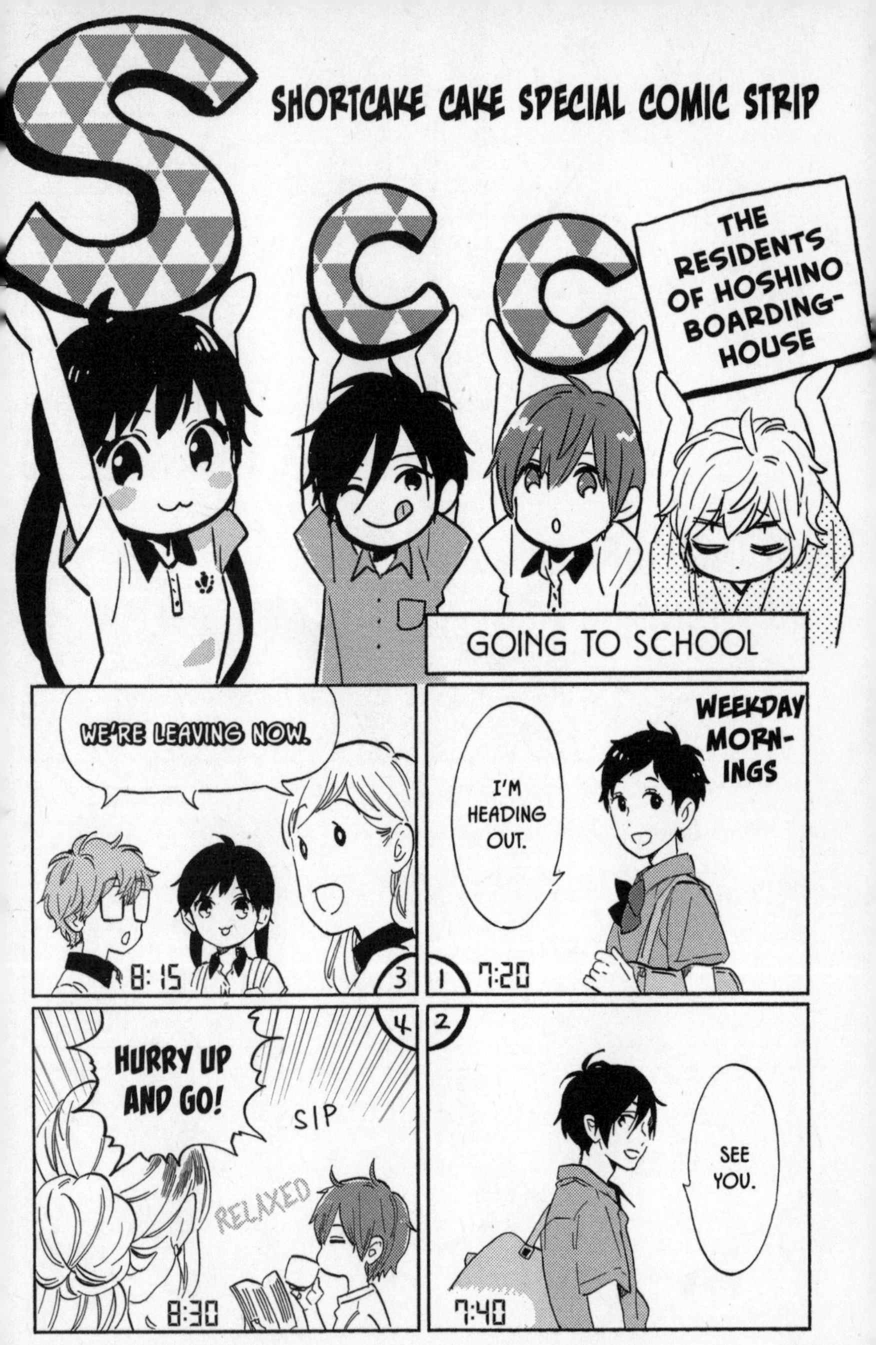
SHORTCAKE CAKE SPECIAL COMIC STRIP
SCC
THE RESIDENTS OF HOSHINO BOARDING-HOUSE
GOING TO SCHOOL
WEEKDAY MORNINGS
I'M HEADING OUT.
7:20
SEE YOU.
7:40
WE'RE LEAVING NOW.
8:15
HURRY UP AND GO!
SIP
RELAXED
8:30

WEEKEND MORNINGS

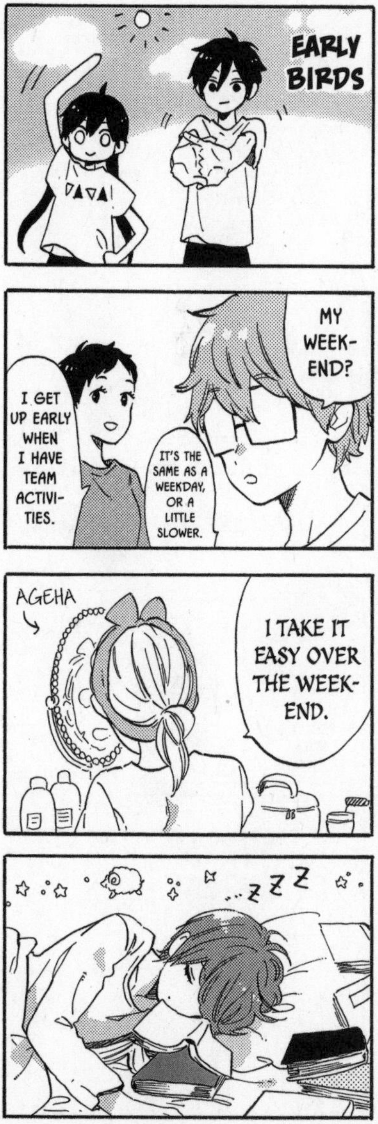
EARLY BIRDS
MY WEEK-END?
IT'S THE SAME AS A WEEKDAY, OR A LITTLE SLOWER.
I GET UP EARLY WHEN I HAVE TEAM ACTIVI-TIES.
I TAKE IT EASY OVER THE WEEK-END.
AGEHA
...Z Z Z

CHIAKI'S WEEKEND

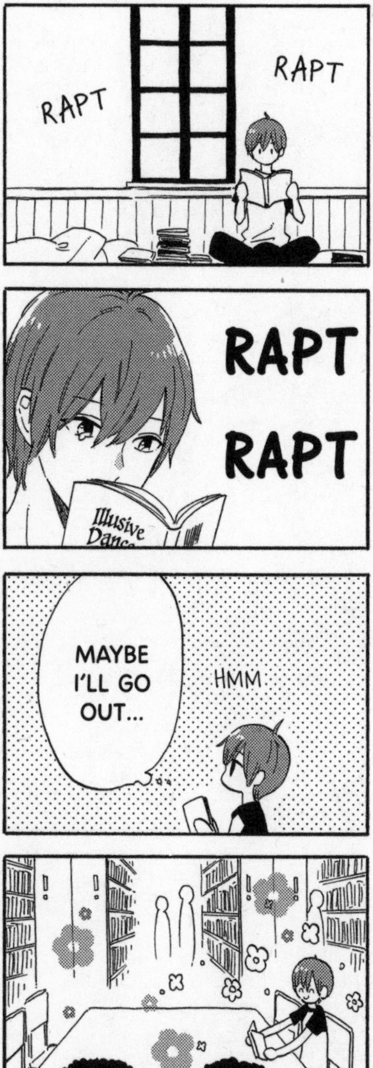
RAPT
RAPT
RAPT
RAPT
Illusive Dance
HMM
MAYBE I'LL GO OUT...

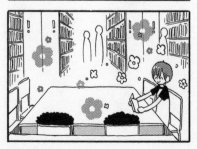

PAJAMAS

I USUALLY WEAR A HOODIE AND SWEATS TO BED.
YAWN
I WEAR REGULAR PAJAMAS OR A LONG TEE AND SWEATS.
FANCY
?!
JUST KIDDING!
I WEAR THE STUFF THEY SELL AT UNIQLO.
I DIDN'T NEED TO SEE THAT.
SWIP
SWIP

ALLOWANCE

I THINK I GOT ¥500 A WEEK WHEN I WAS IN ELEMENTARY SCHOOL.
I GOT GIFT CARDS FOR BOOKS.
FOR BOOKS?!
IS THAT WHAT YOU ASKED FOR?
HMPH
Chi
THAT'S SO LIKE YOU, CHIAKI.
!
I GET TO BUY ANYTHING I WANT...
...WITH MY CREDIT CARD!
THAT MAKES ME ANGRY, BUT I'M ALSO IMPRESSED.
↑ REI, SON OF THE HOSHINO BOARDINGHOUSE LANDLORD
SHIRAOKA!
NONE OF THE STORES IN THIS NEIGHBORHOOD TAKE CARDS!
THAT'S WHY YOUR PARENTS GAVE IT TO YOU, MASTER REI.

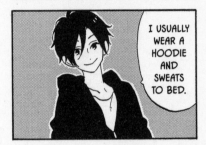

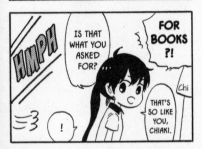

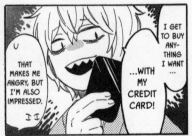

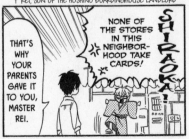

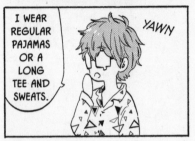

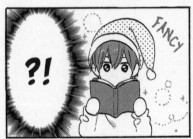

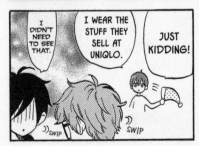

WHY WE LOVE NEKOCHIYA

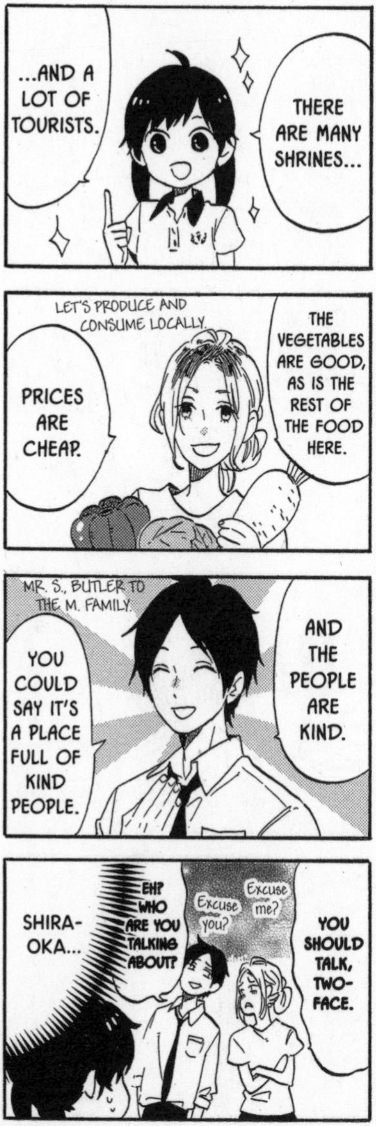
THERE ARE MANY SHRINES...
...AND A LOT OF TOURISTS.
THE VEGETABLES ARE GOOD, AS IS THE REST OF THE FOOD HERE.
LET'S PRODUCE AND CONSUME LOCALLY.
PRICES ARE CHEAP.
AND THE PEOPLE ARE KIND.
MR. S., BUTLER TO THE M. FAMILY.
YOU COULD SAY IT'S A PLACE FULL OF KIND PEOPLE.
YOU SHOULD TALK, TWO-FACE.
Excuse me?
Excuse you?
EH? WHO ARE YOU TALKING ABOUT?
SHIRA-OKA...

AOI AND AGEHA

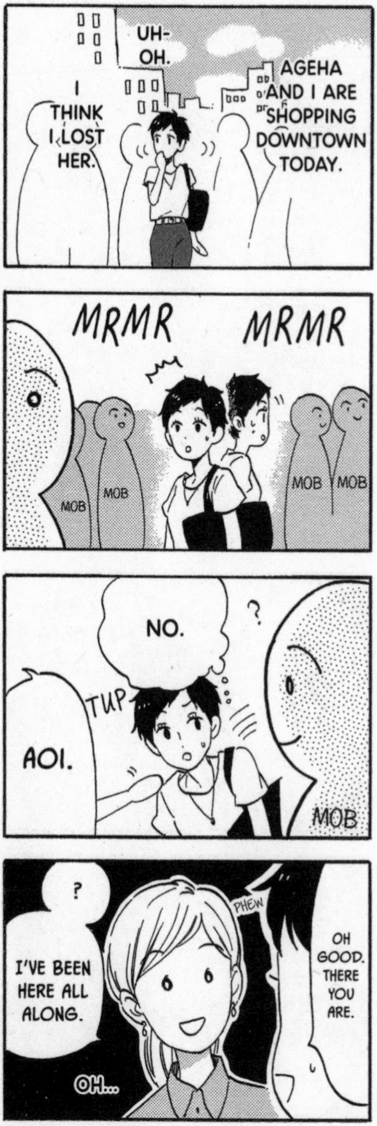
AGEHA AND I ARE SHOPPING DOWNTOWN TODAY.
UH-OH.
I THINK I LOST HER.
MRMR
MRMR
MOB
MOB
MOB
MOB
?
NO.
TUP
AOI.
MOB
OH GOOD. THERE YOU ARE.
PHEW
?
I'VE BEEN HERE ALL ALONG.
OH...

RIKU

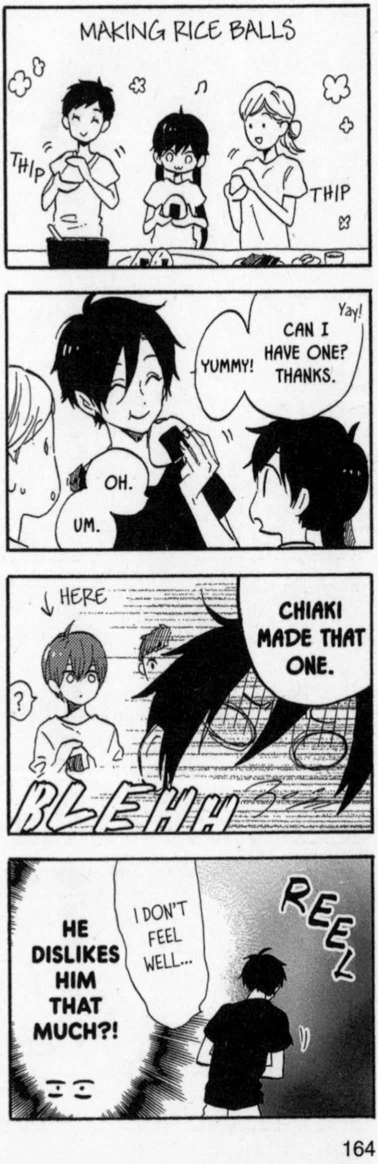
MAKING RICE BALLS
THIP
THIP
Yay!
CAN I HAVE ONE? THANKS.
YUMMY!
OH.
UM.
CHIAKI MADE THAT ONE.
HERE
?
BLEHH
REEL
I DON'T FEEL WELL...
HE DISLIKES HIM THAT MUCH?!

RUSSIAN ROULETTE

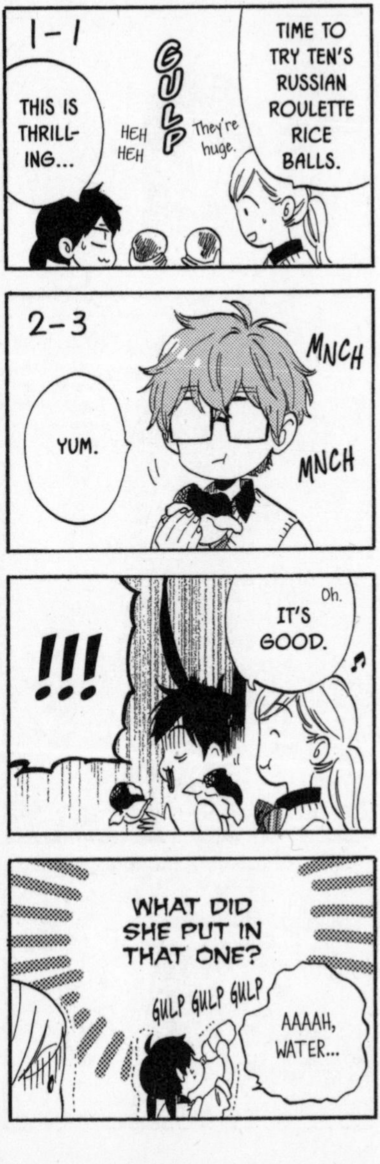
TIME TO TRY TEN'S RUSSIAN ROULETTE RICE BALLS.
They're huge.
GULP
1-1
HEH HEH
THIS IS THRILL-ING...
MNCH
2-3
MNCH
YUM.
Oh.
IT'S GOOD.
!!!
WHAT DID SHE PUT IN THAT ONE?
AAAAH, WATER...
GULP GULP GULP

PREFERENCE

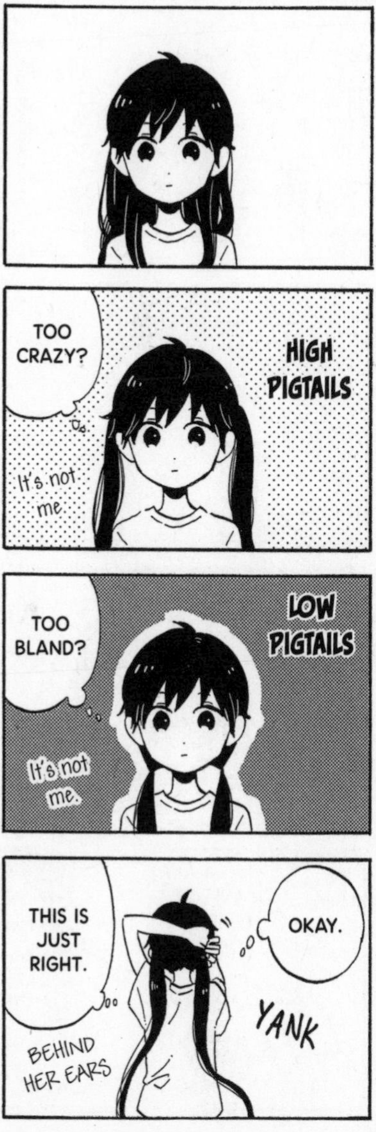
HIGH PIGTAILS
TOO CRAZY?
It's not me.
LOW PIGTAILS
TOO BLAND?
It's not me.
OKAY.
YANK
THIS IS JUST RIGHT.
BEHIND HER EARS

TEN (TODDLER)

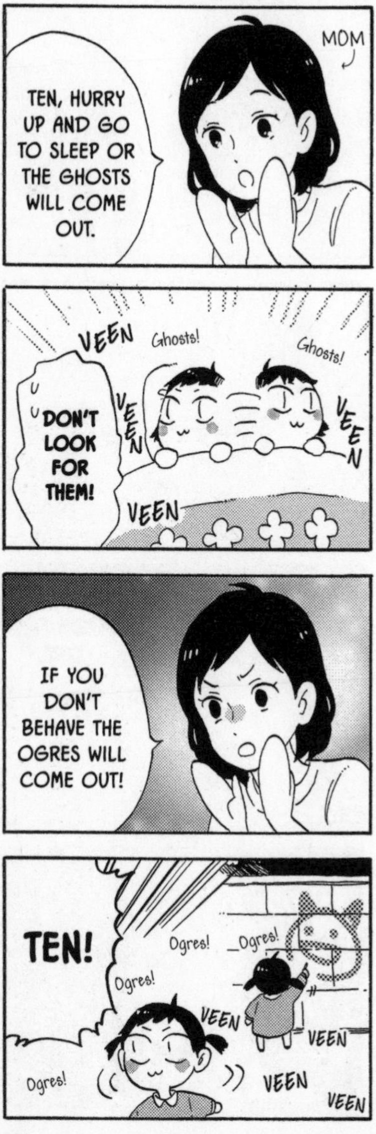
MOM
TEN, HURRY UP AND GO TO SLEEP OR THE GHOSTS WILL COME OUT.
Ghosts!
VEEN
Ghosts!
VEEN
VEEN
DON'T LOOK FOR THEM!
VEEN
IF YOU DON'T BEHAVE THE OGRES WILL COME OUT!
Ogres!
Ogres!
VEEN
VEEN
VEEN
VEEN
TEN!
Ogres!
Ogres!

ON THE STREET

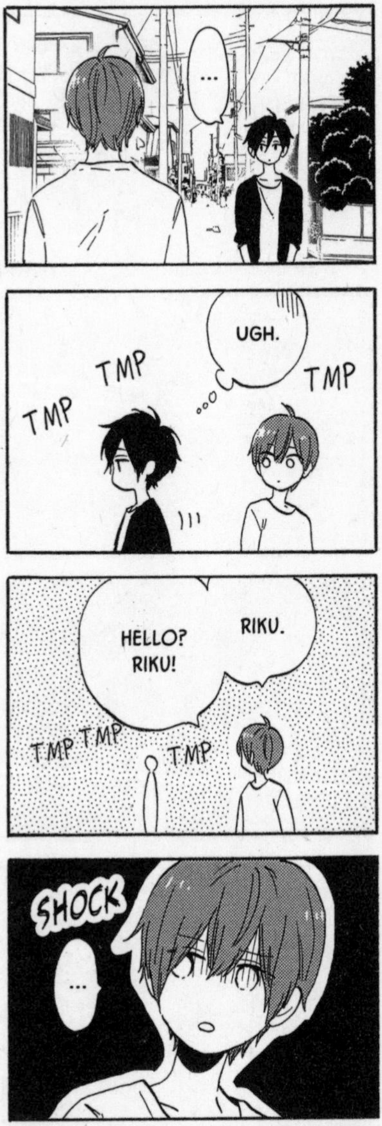
...
UGH.
TMP
TMP
TMP
RIKU.
HELLO? RIKU!
TMP TMP
TMP
SHOCK
...

ON THE STREET (2)

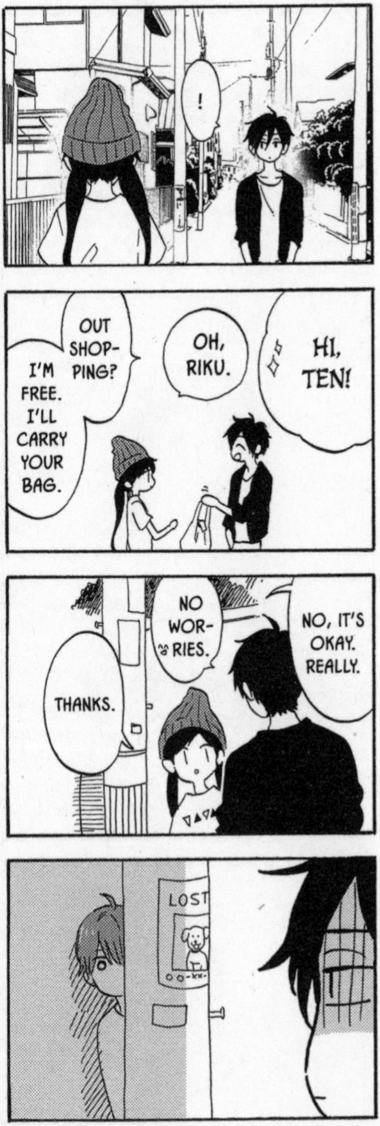
!
HI, TEN!
OH, RIKU.
OUT SHOP-PING?
I'M FREE. I'LL CARRY YOUR BAG.
NO, IT'S OKAY. REALLY.
NO WOR-RIES.
THANKS.
LOST

CHIAKI AND EITA

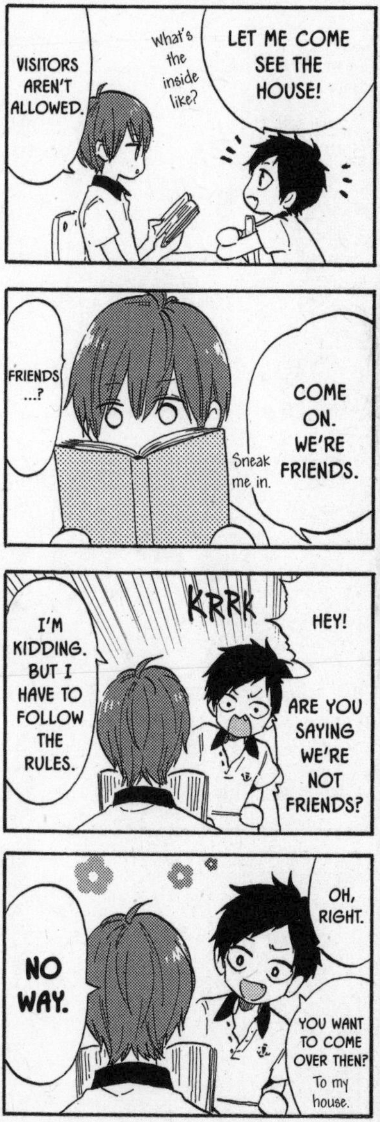
LET ME COME SEE THE HOUSE!
What's the inside like?
VISITORS AREN'T ALLOWED.
COME ON. WE'RE FRIENDS.
Sneak me in.
FRIENDS ...?
KRRK
HEY!
ARE YOU SAYING WE'RE NOT FRIENDS?
I'M KIDDING. BUT I HAVE TO FOLLOW THE RULES.
OH, RIGHT.
YOU WANT TO COME OVER THEN?
To my house.
NO WAY.

CHIAKI AND EITA (2)

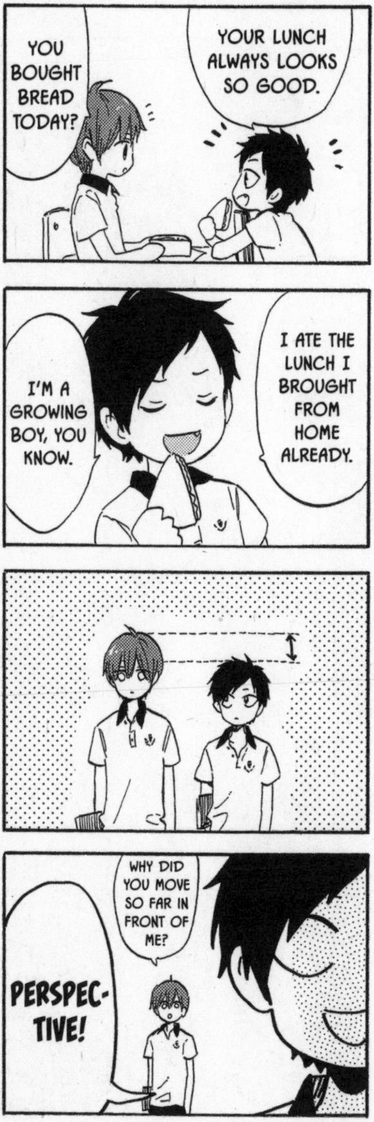
YOUR LUNCH ALWAYS LOOKS SO GOOD.
YOU BOUGHT BREAD TODAY?
I ATE THE LUNCH I BROUGHT FROM HOME ALREADY.
I'M A GROWING BOY, YOU KNOW.
WHY DID YOU MOVE SO FAR IN FRONT OF ME?
PERSPEC-TIVE!

WHY I GATHERED EVERYONE HERE

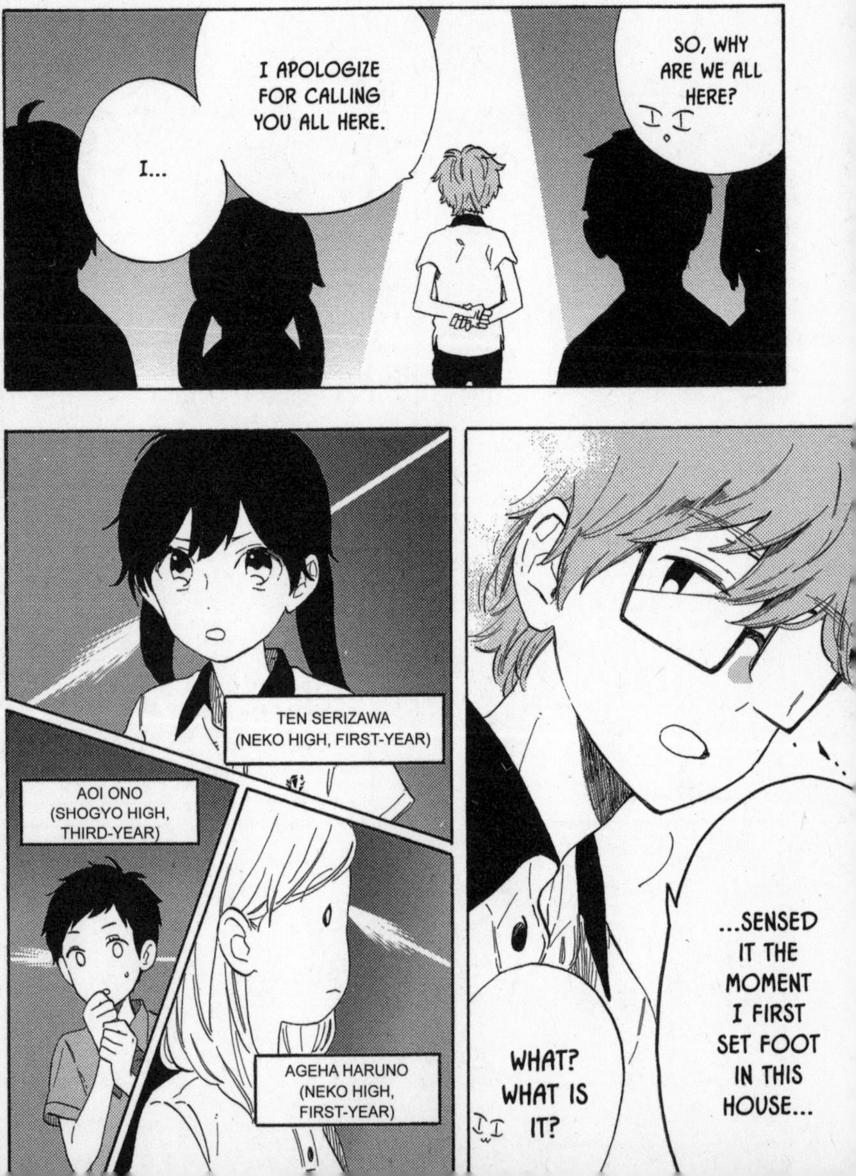
SO, WHY ARE WE ALL HERE?
I APOLOGIZE FOR CALLING YOU ALL HERE.
I...
...SENSED IT THE MOMENT I FIRST SET FOOT IN THIS HOUSE...
WHAT? WHAT IS IT?
TEN SERIZAWA (NEKO HIGH, FIRST-YEAR)
AOI ONO (SHOGYO HIGH, THIRD-YEAR)
AGEHA HARUNO (NEKO HIGH, FIRST-YEAR)

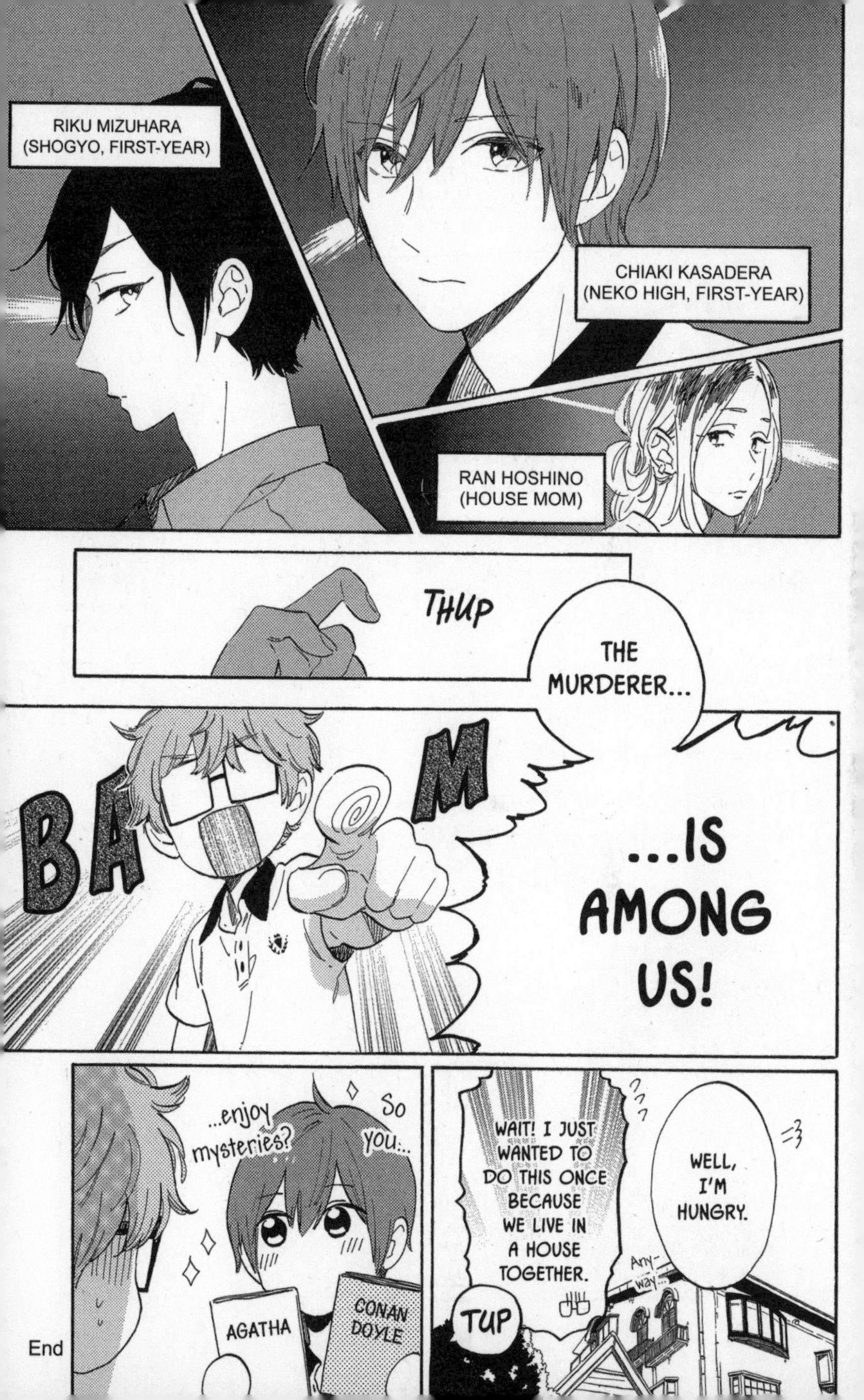
CHIAKI KASADERA
(NEKO HIGH, FIRST-YEAR)
RAN HOSHINO
(HOUSE MOM)
RIKU MIZUHARA
(SHOGYO, FIRST-YEAR)
THUP
THE MURDERER...
BAM
...IS AMONG US!
WELL, I'M HUNGRY.
WAIT! I JUST WANTED TO DO THIS ONCE BECAUSE WE LIVE IN A HOUSE TOGETHER.
Any-way...
TUP
So you:...
...enjoy mysteries?
CONAN DOYLE
AGATHA

End

▽▲Series Details▽▲▽▲

Fans who draw or cosplay this series have asked about the characters' official hair colors, so I'll share them here. ☺

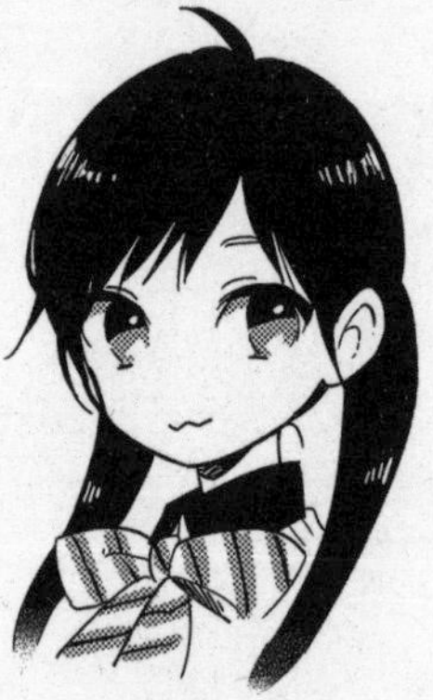

TEN

I imagine her hair to be between blue and blueish purple. When I work in color, I often do so with this color in mind, but in reality, her hair is just black! Maybe a slightly blueish black or navy?

CHIAKI

I imagine his hair is pink to reddish purple. In reality, his hair is brown with a reddish tint.

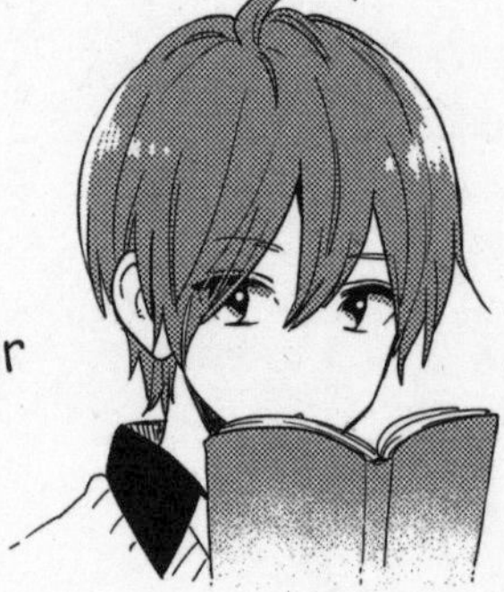

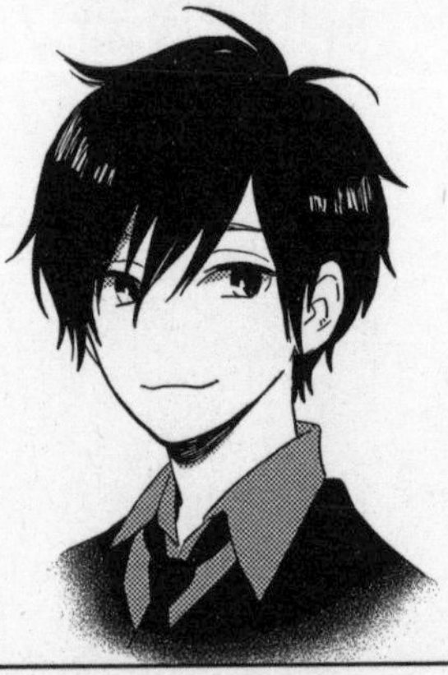

RIKU

I imagine his hair is green to deep green. It's actually black, but a bit ashy colored.

More on the other characters next time!

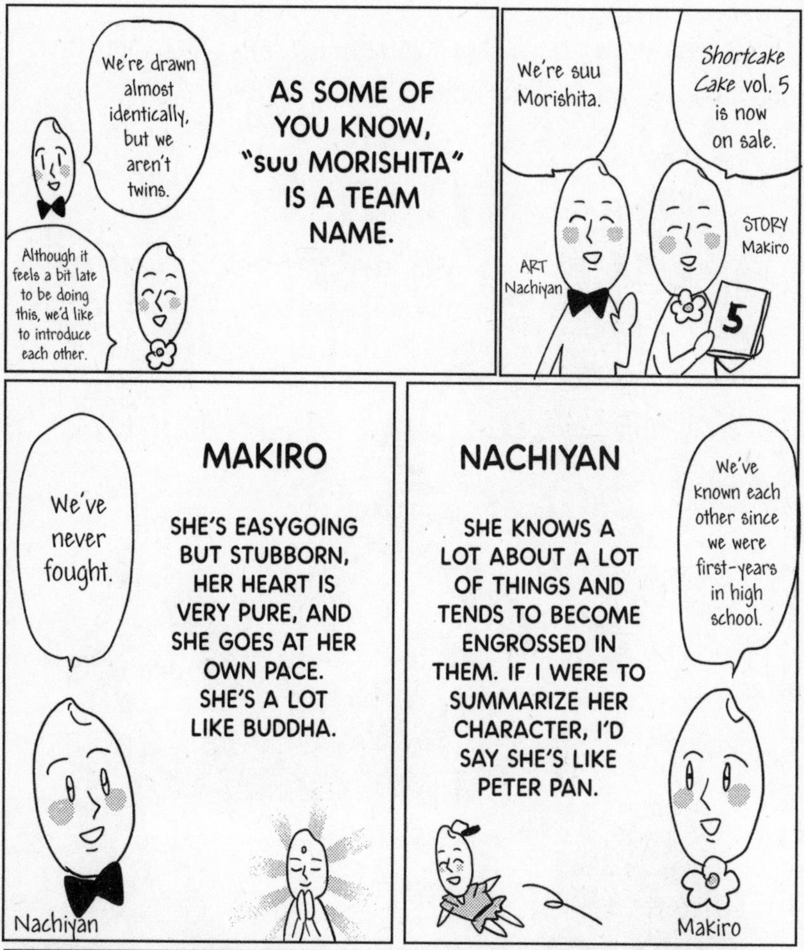
Shortcake Cake vol. 5 is now on sale.
We're suu Morishita.
STORY Makiro
ART Nachiyan
5
AS SOME OF YOU KNOW, "suu MORISHITA" IS A TEAM NAME.
We're drawn almost identically, but we aren't twins.
Although it feels a bit late to be doing this, we'd like to introduce each other.
NACHIYAN
We've known each other since we were first-years in high school.
SHE KNOWS A LOT ABOUT A LOT OF THINGS AND TENDS TO BECOME ENGROSSED IN THEM. IF I WERE TO SUMMARIZE HER CHARACTER, I'D SAY SHE'S LIKE PETER PAN.
Makiro
MAKIRO
We've never fought.
SHE'S EASYGOING BUT STUBBORN, HER HEART IS VERY PURE, AND SHE GOES AT HER OWN PACE. SHE'S A LOT LIKE BUDDHA.
Nachiyan

Special Thanks

- Tanyaka
- The Margaret editorial team
- Our designer, Yasuhisa Kawatani
- Our assistant, Nao Hamaguchi
- Our assistant's helper, Kame-chimu

And all our readers ♡

Instagram: morishita.suu

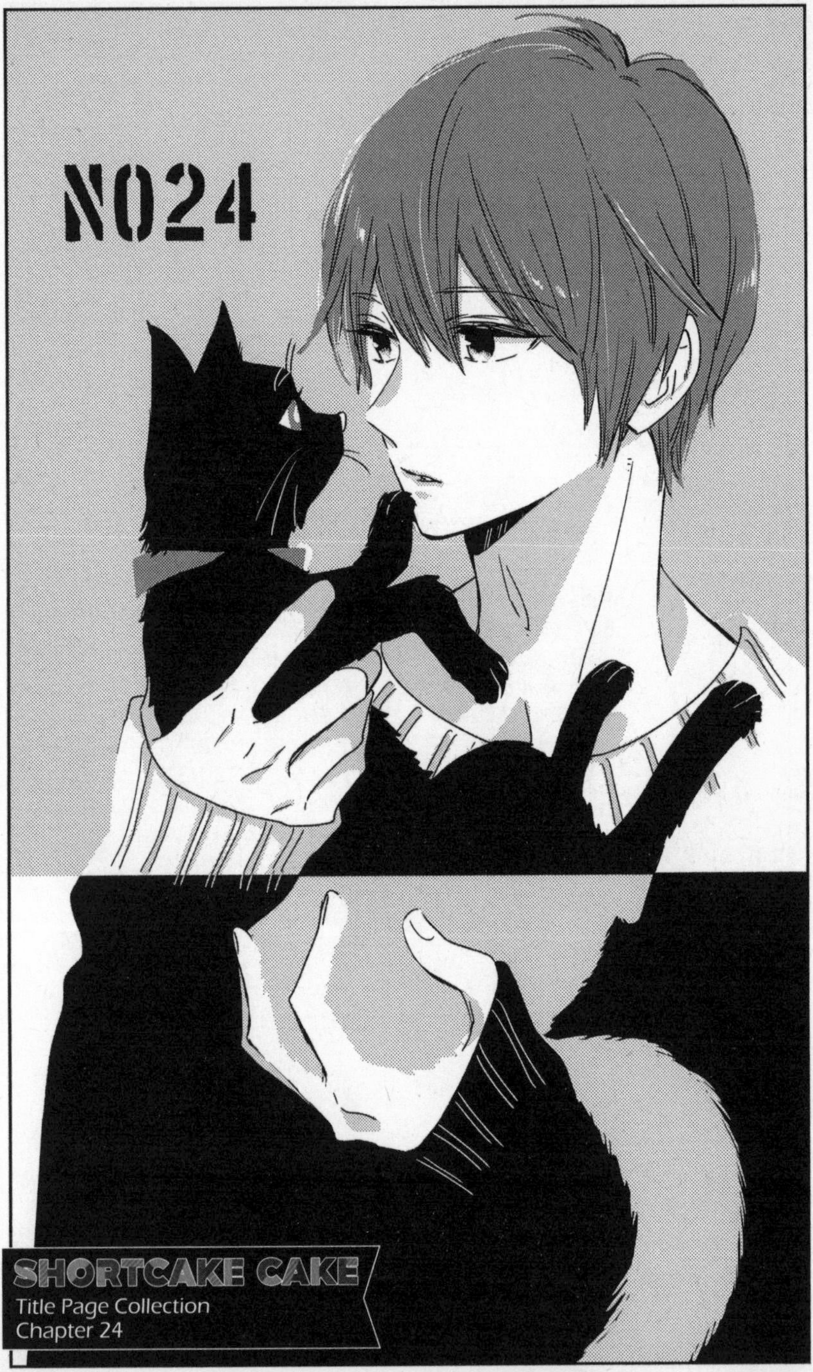
NO24
SHORTCAKE CAKE
Title Page Collection
Chapter 24

SHORTCAKE CAKE

Title Page Collection

Issue 1 Magazine Cover

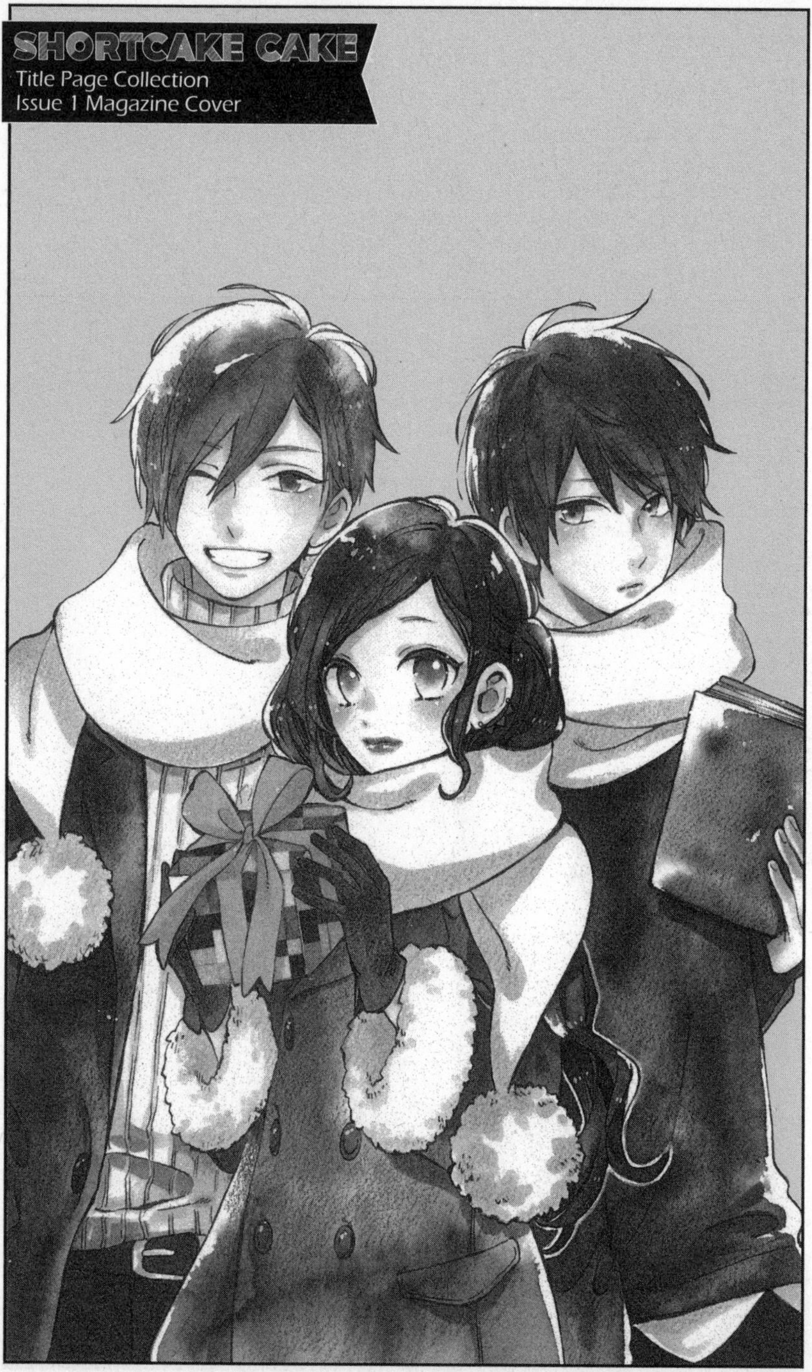

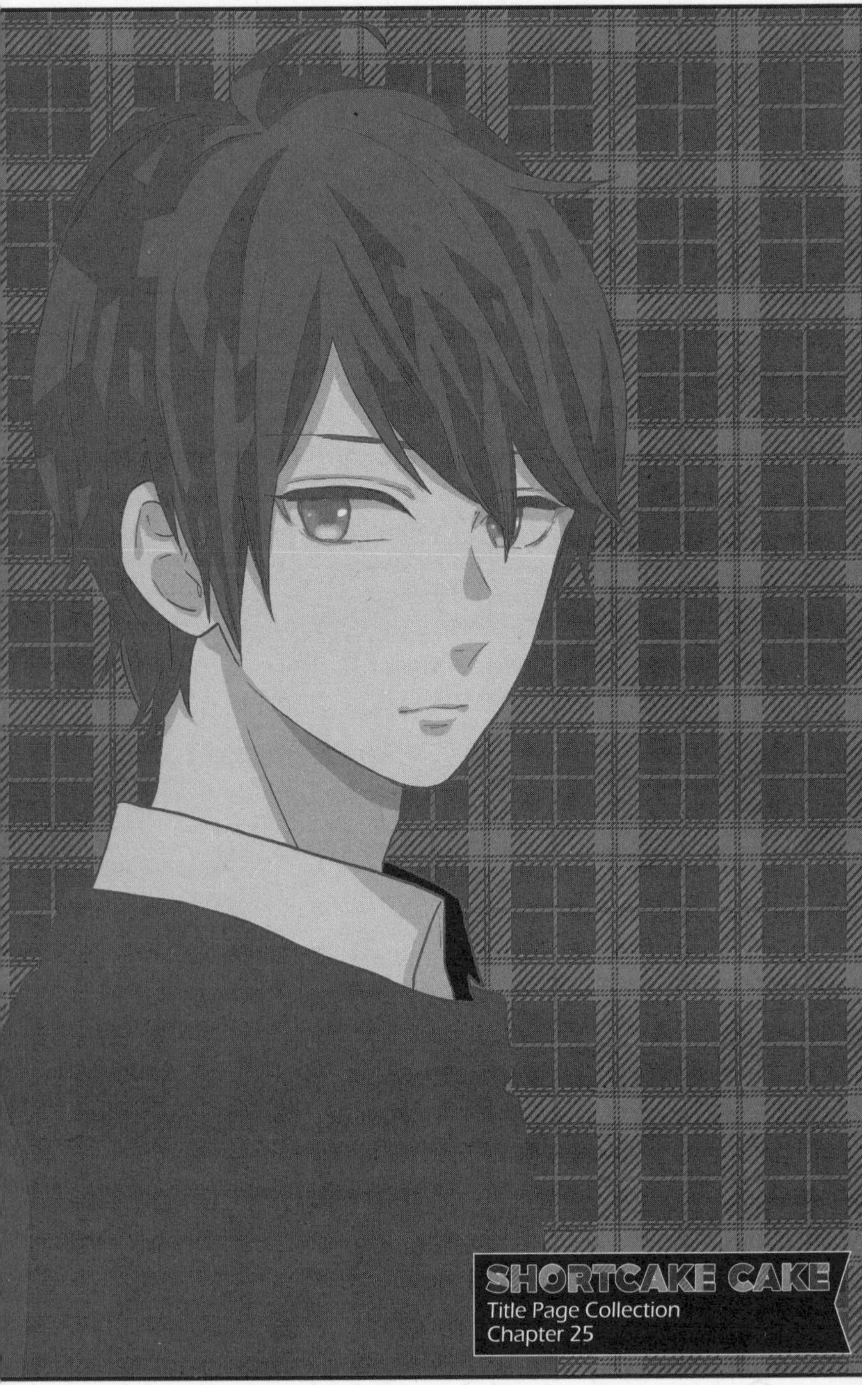
SHORTCAKE CAKE
Title Page Collection
Chapter 25

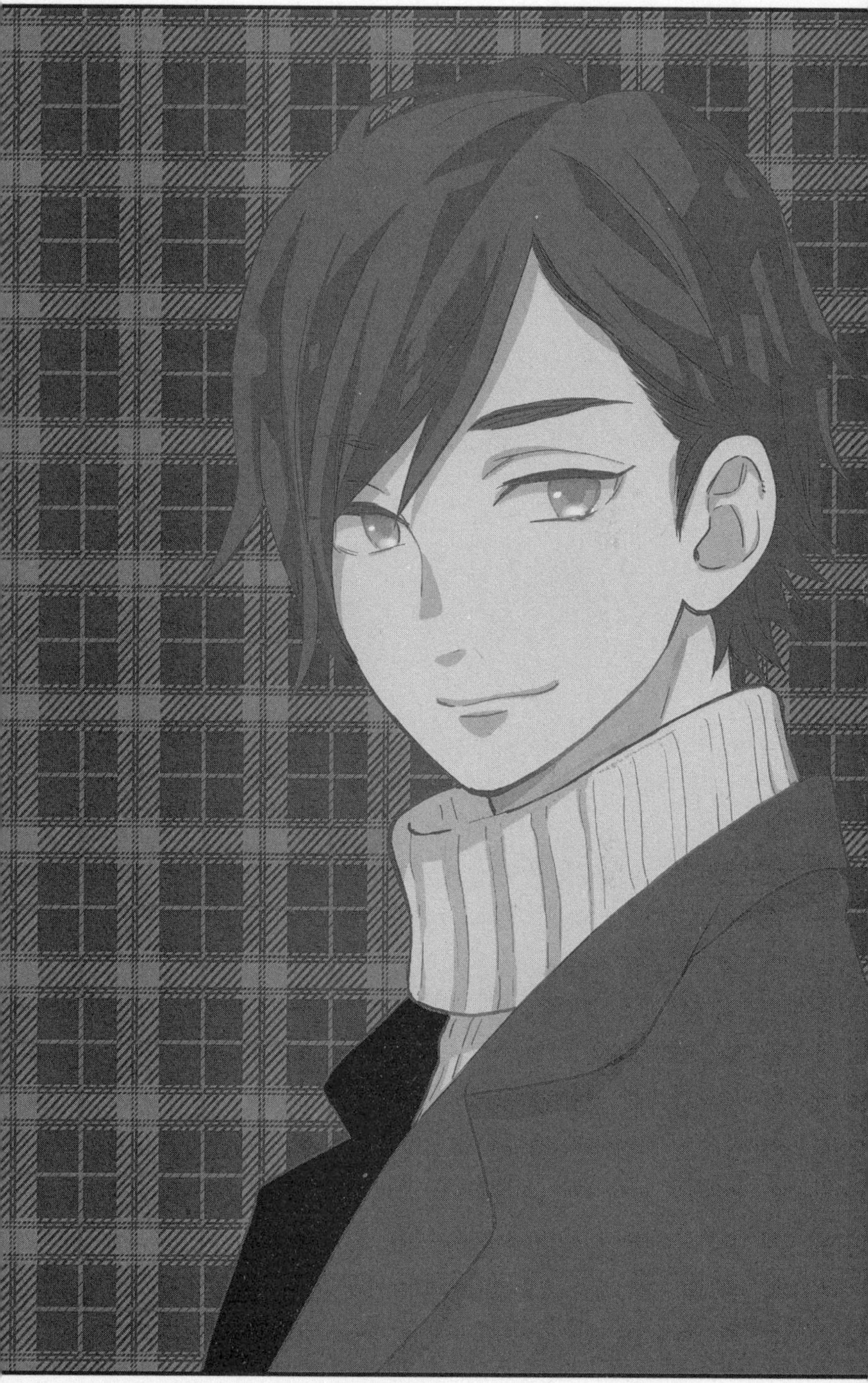

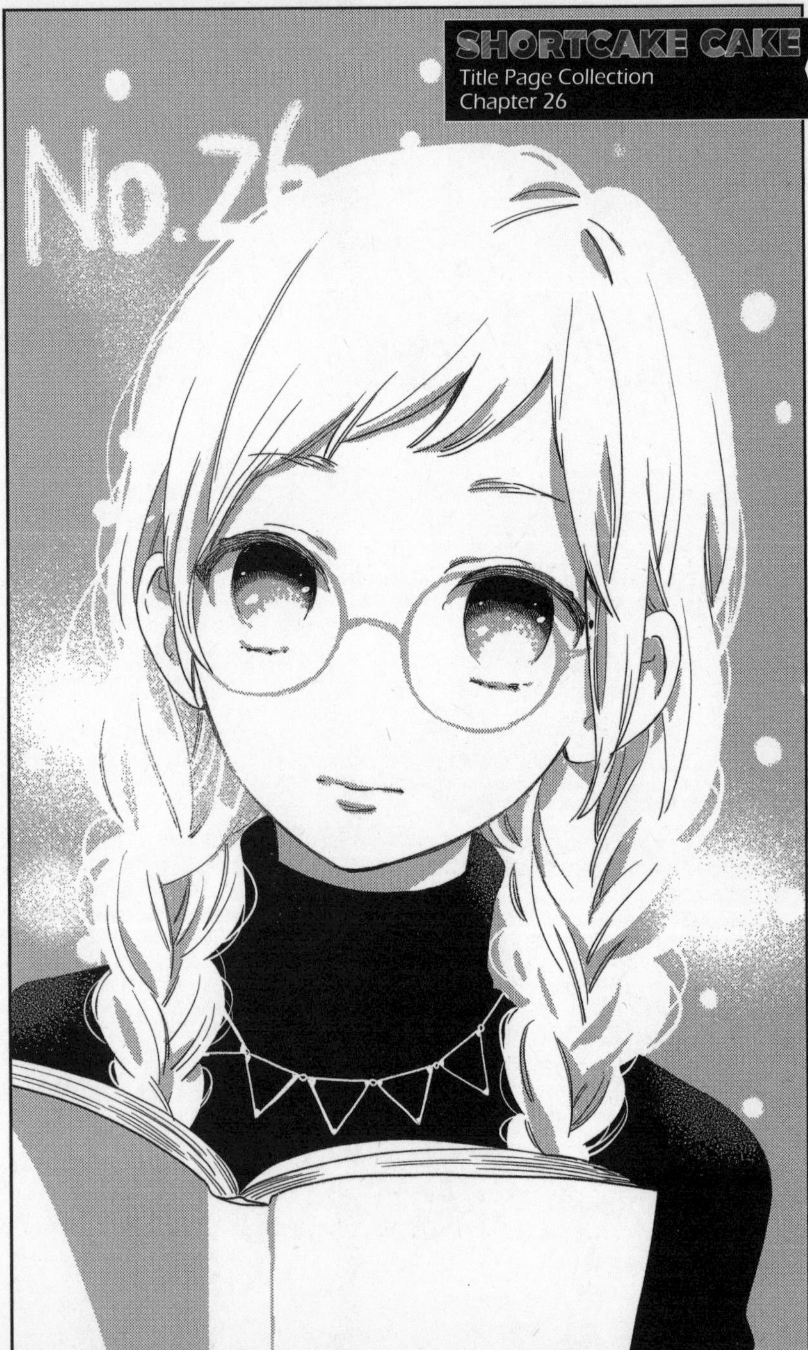
SHORTCAKE CAKE
Title Page Collection
Chapter 26
No.26

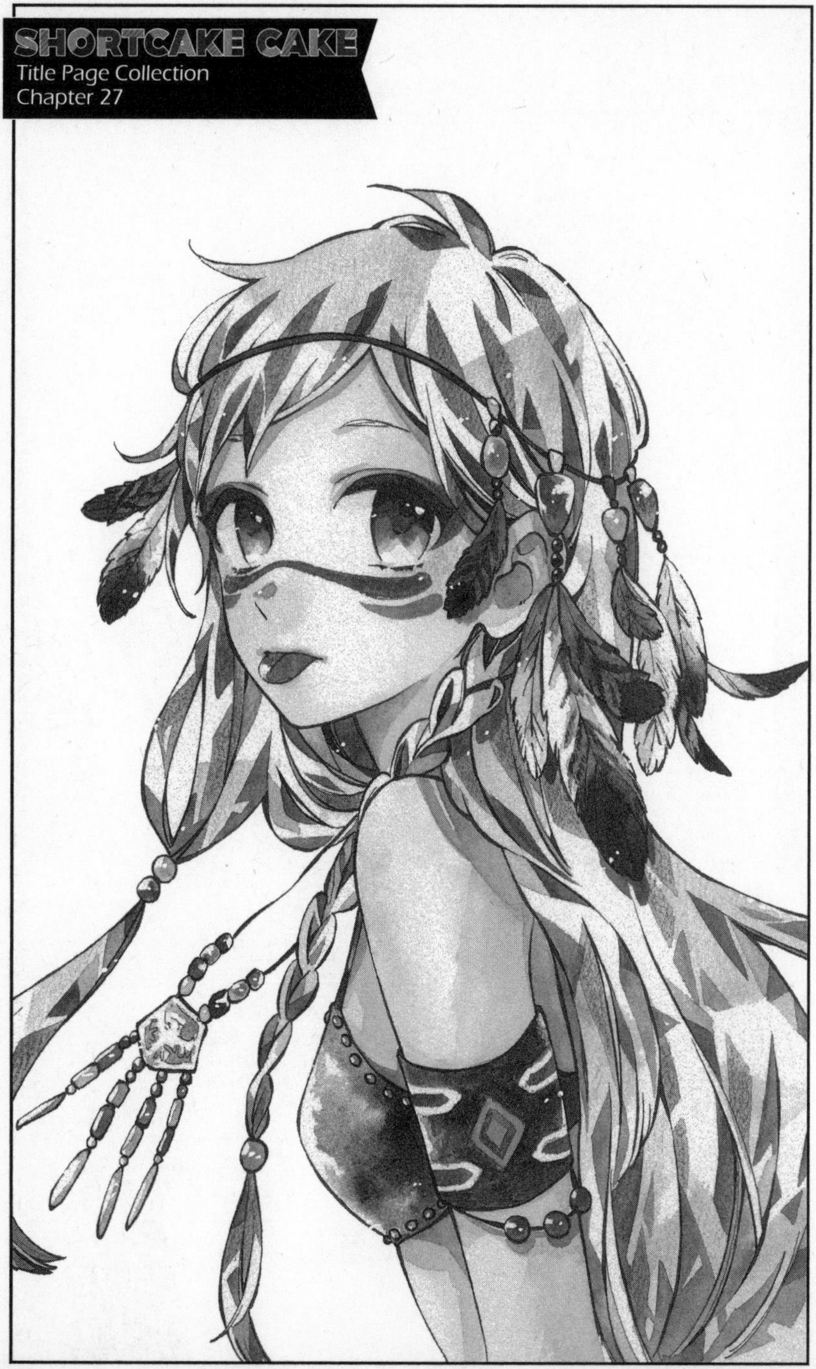
SHORTCAKE CAKE
Title Page Collection
Chapter 27

SHORTCAKE CAKE
Title Page Collection
Chapter 28

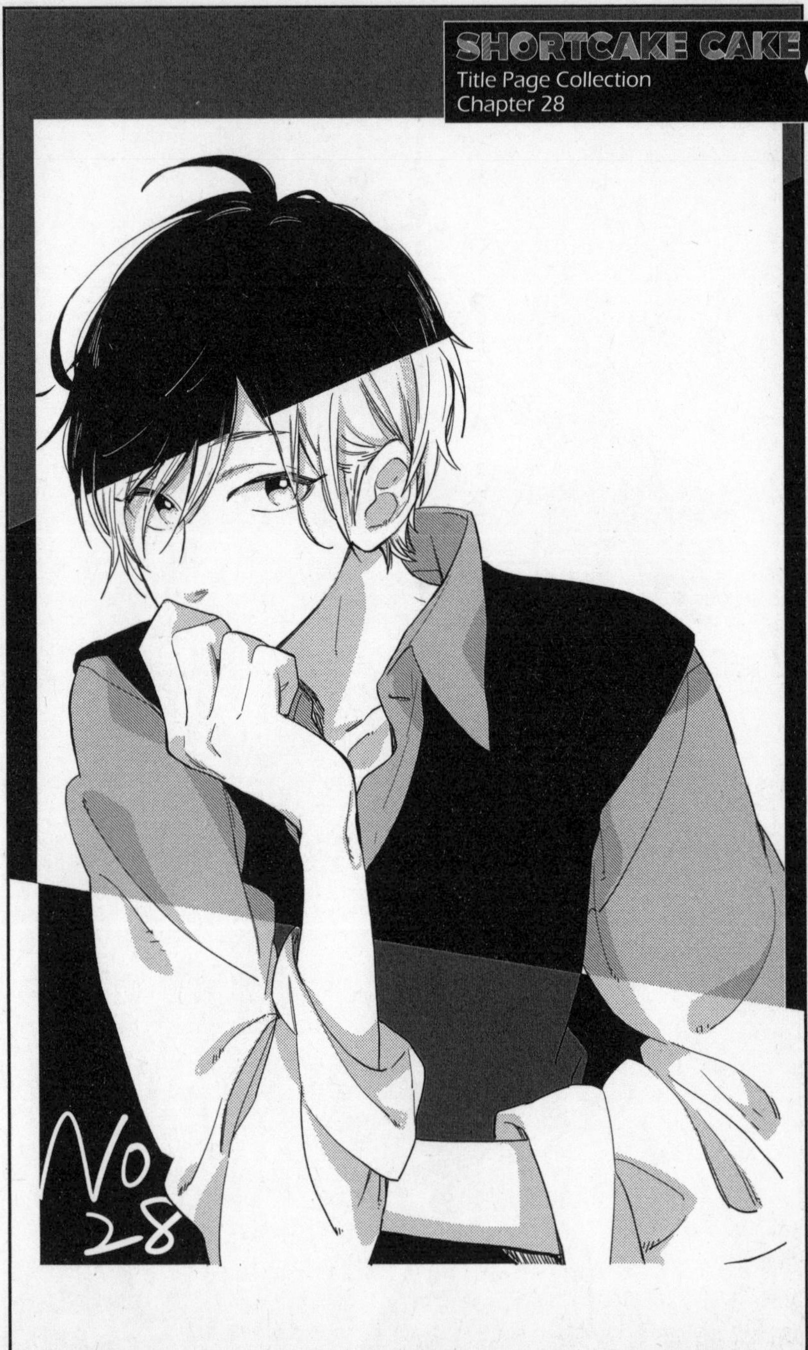
No 28

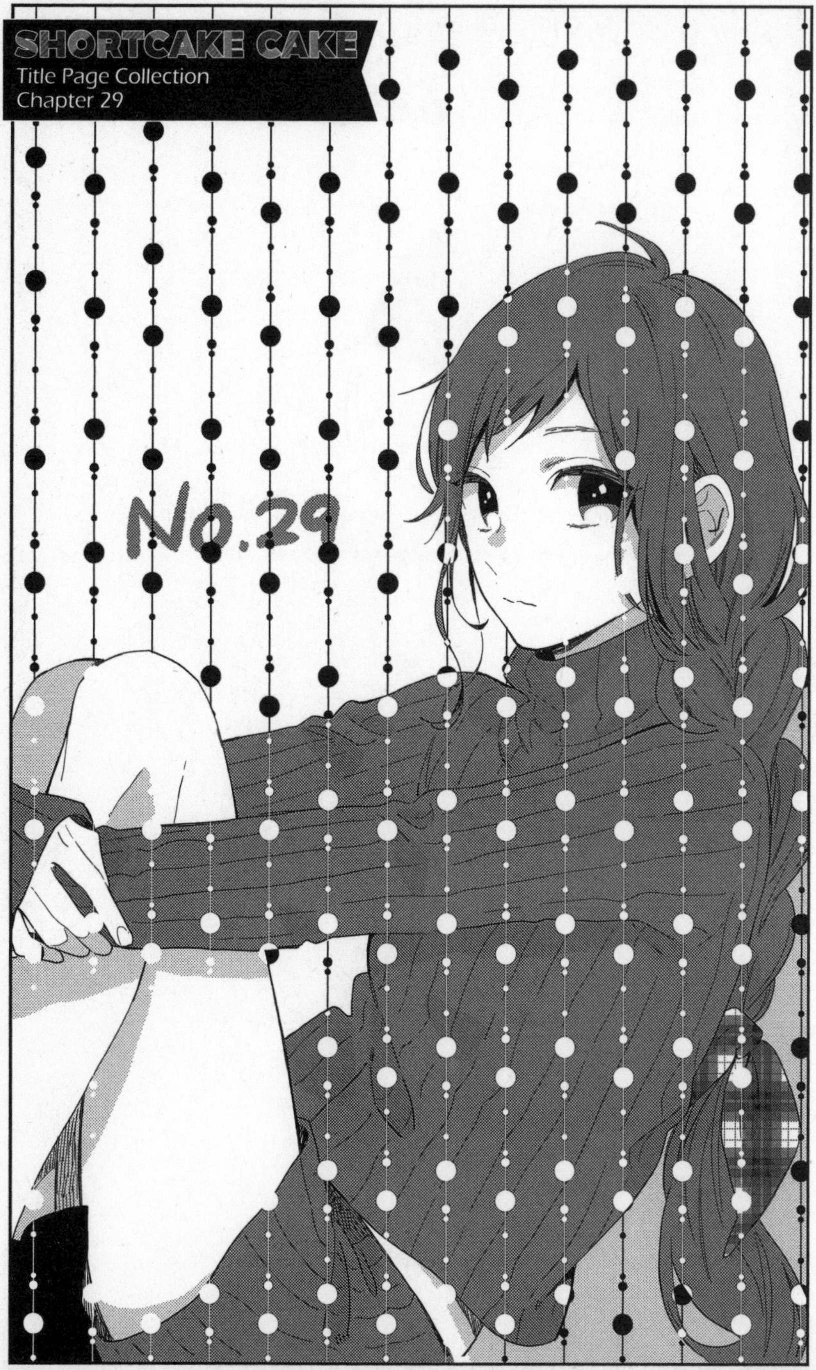
SHORTCAKE CAKE
Title Page Collection
Chapter 29
No.29

I tried something different with the cover illustration.
I would love to know what you think of it.

—suu Morishita

suu Morishita is a creator duo.
The story is by Makiro, and the art is by
Nachiyan. In 2010 they debuted with the
one-shot "Anote Konote." Their works include
Hibi Chouchou and *Shortcake Cake*.

VOLUME 5
SHOJO BEAT EDITION

STORY + ART BY **suu Morishita**

TRANSLATION **Emi Louie-Nishikawa**
TOUCH-UP ART + LETTERING **Inori Fukuda Trant**
DESIGN **Shawn Carrico**
EDITOR **Nancy Thistlethwaite**

SHORTCAKE CAKE © 2015 by Suu Morishita
All rights reserved.
First published in Japan in 2015 by SHUEISHA Inc., Tokyo.
English translation rights arranged by SHUEISHA Inc.

The stories, characters and incidents mentioned
in this publication are entirely fictional.

Printed in the U.S.A.

Published by VIZ Media, LLC
P.O. Box 77010
San Francisco, CA 94107

10 9 8 7 6 5 4 3 2 1
First printing, August 2019

PARENTAL ADVISORY
SHORTCAKE CAKE is rated T for Teen
and is recommended for ages 13 and up.

viz.com   shojobeat.com

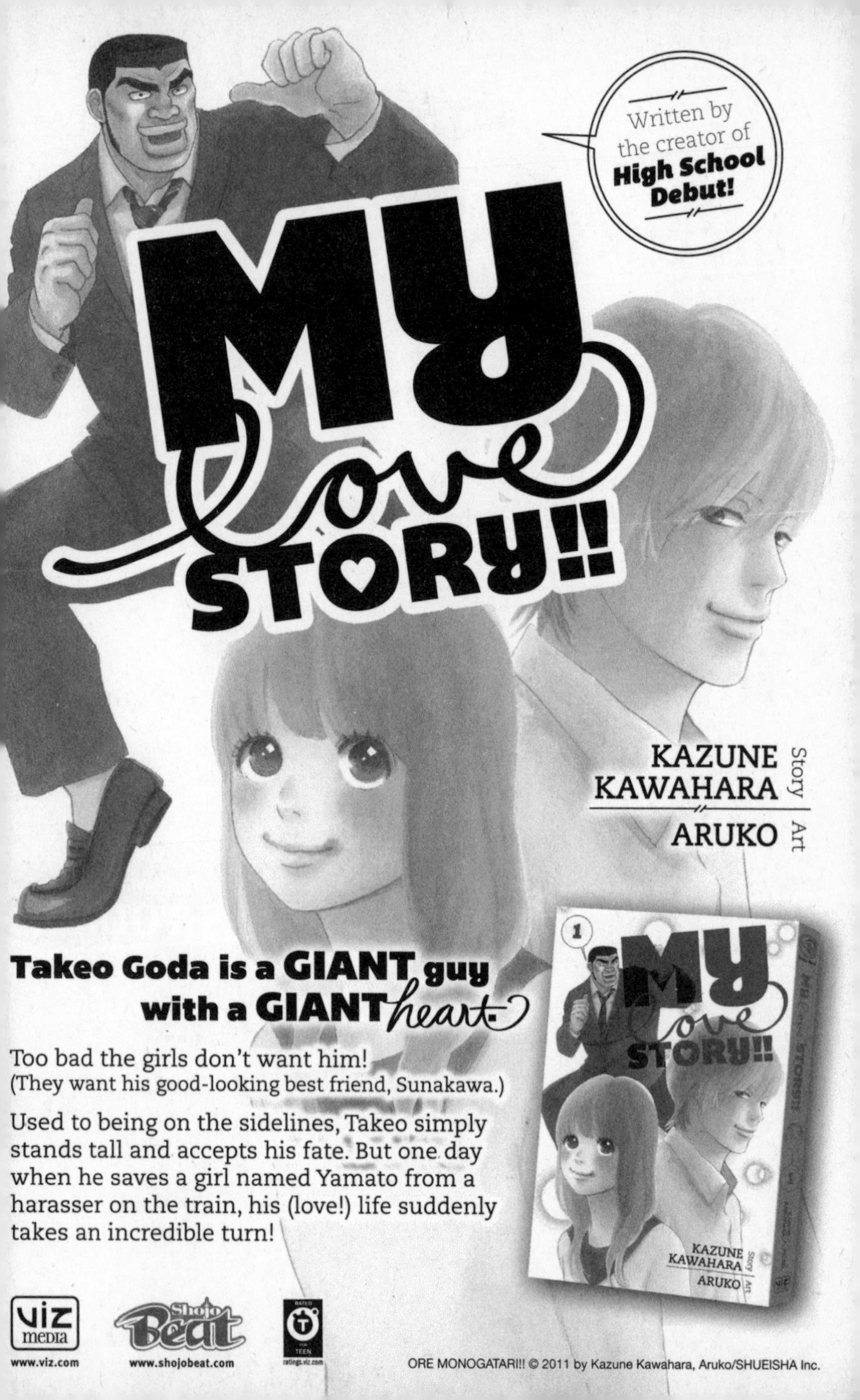
Written by the creator of High School Debut!
MY love STORY!!
KAZUNE KAWAHARA Story
ARUKO Art
Takeo Goda is a GIANT guy with a GIANT heart.
Too bad the girls don't want him! (They want his good-looking best friend, Sunakawa.)
Used to being on the sidelines, Takeo simply stands tall and accepts his fate. But one day when he saves a girl named Yamato from a harasser on the train, his (love!) life suddenly takes an incredible turn!
viz media
www.viz.com
Shojo Beat
www.shojobeat.com
RATED T TEEN
ratings.viz.com
ORE MONOGATARI!! © 2011 by Kazune Kawahara, Aruko/SHUEISHA Inc.

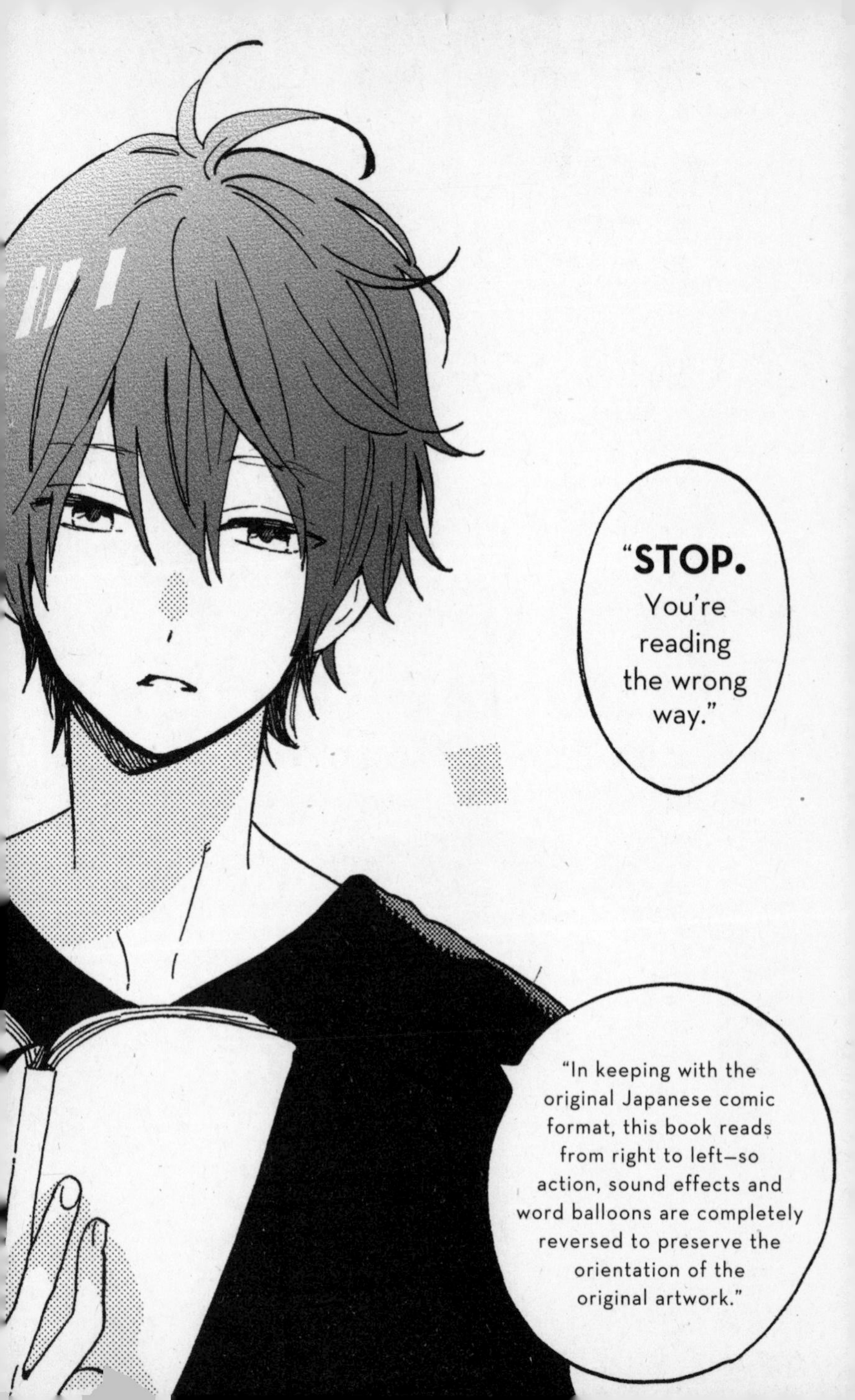
"STOP. You're reading the wrong way."
"In keeping with the original Japanese comic format, this book reads from right to left—so action, sound effects and word balloons are completely reversed to preserve the orientation of the original artwork."